The Great Powers and the European States System 1814–1914

The Great Powers and the European States System 1814–1914

SECOND EDITION

F.R. Bridge and Roger Bullen

PEARSON

Longman

Harlow, England • London • New York • Boston • San Francisco • Toronto
Sydney • Tokyo • Singapore • Hong Kong • Seoul • Taipei • New Delhi
Cape Town • Madrid • Mexico City • Amsterdam • Munich • Paris • Milan

PEARSON EDUCATION LIMITED

Edinburgh Gate
Harlow CM20 2JE
United Kingdom
Tel: +44 (0)1279 623623
Fax: +44 (0)1279 431059
Website: www.pearsoned.co.uk

First edition published in Great Britain in 1980
This second edition published 2005

© Pearson Education Limited 1980, 2005

The rights of F.R. Bridge and Roger Bullen to be identified as authors
of this work have been asserted in accordance with the Copyright,
Designs and Patents Act 1988.

ISBN 978 0 582 78458 1

British Library Cataloguing in Publication Data
A CIP catalogue record for this book can be obtained from the British Library

Library of Congress Cataloging in Publication Data
Bridge, F.R.
    The great powers and the European states system 1814–1914 / F.R. Bridge and
Roger Bullen. — 2nd ed.
       p. cm.
    Includes bibliographical references and index.
    ISBN 0–582–78458–1
    1. Europe—Foreign relations—1815–1871.   2. Europe—Foreign relations—
1871–1918.   3. Europe—Politics and government—1815–1871.   4. Europe—
Politics and government—1871–1918.   I. Bullen, R.J.   II. Title.

D363.B75 2004
327.1′7′094—dc22
                                                                           2004044524

10 9 8 7 6 5
10 09

Set by 35 in 10/13.5pt Sabon
Printed in Malaysia (CTP–VVP)

The Publisher's policy is to use paper manufactured from sustainable forests.

In memory of Alison

Contents

Maps

Acknowledgements

The popular success, since its appearance over twenty years ago, of the original 'Bridge and Bullen' suggests that it would be worthwhile to produce an updated, and above all, substantially expanded edition for the benefit of students and general readers who may have found the original somewhat jejune and allusive. In doing so, I have decided to retain in their original form the general observations contained in the Introduction, which was a joint effort by my late friend and colleague and me; and, in much of Chapter 4 and the first section of Chapter 5, Roger's original account of his own research period, which even after twenty years is still far superior to anything I could have written myself. The rest, I have entirely rewritten, and wish here to thank, for their invaluable questions and suggestions over the years, those students – and particularly Dr Peter Edwards – who attended my tutorials on 'International History 1814–1918' and 'The Great Powers and the Balkans 1908–14', at the University of Leeds. For a number of (short) quotations, I am indebted to the officials of the Public Record Office, London; the Haus-, Hof-, und Staatsarchiv, Vienna; the Bayrisches Staatsarchiv, Munich, and the Archives of the Ministère des Affaires Étrangères, Paris for permission to use the archives within their care.

F.R. Bridge
Leeds
August 2003

CHAPTER 1

Introduction: The character of international relations, 1814–1914

In the century between the Congress of Vienna and the outbreak of the First World War international relations in Europe were largely dominated by five great powers: Austria (after 1867 Austria-Hungary), France, Great Britain, Prussia (after 1871 Germany) and Russia. There was always a clear distinction between what contemporaries called 'first-rate powers' and 'secondary states', and there was rarely any doubt into which category any state should be placed. The great powers jealously guarded their status and were at all times disinclined to admit new members into their ranks. After her unification in the 1860s Italy liked to be regarded as a great power, but it was only in the capacity of an ally of the Central Powers after 1882, and as a member of the Concert dealing with the affairs of the Ottoman Empire that she could claim anything like equality with the other five. The dominance of the five or six powers over such a long period gave an underlying stability to international relations, a stability not found in either the eighteenth or the twentieth centuries. During the former both Spain and Sweden clung tenaciously to great-power status long after they had ceased to possess its attributes, and both Prussia and Russia effectively transformed themselves from second-class states into great powers. In the twentieth century great powers have fought to destroy each other, and the status of a European great power has ceased to have the same importance as it had before the First World War. The nineteenth century witnessed no such dramatic changes. In the upheavals of 1848–49 Austria came close to the brink of disintegration, but Russia rallied to her defence and preserved the five-power system. The four great-power wars of the mid-century were not fought *à l'outrance*:

the belligerents were concerned essentially with limited and localized objectives. Despite two defeats, in 1859 and 1866, Austria continued to be treated as a great power, and so did France after her military collapse in 1871. For the most part the great powers respected each other's status: they were accustomed to a great-power system, and strove to maintain it. There was a constant and conscious fear that its demise would bring untold disasters to them all. This was perhaps the most permanent consequence of Napoleon's bid for the mastery of Europe.

Throughout the nineteenth century the European great powers claimed for themselves special rights and responsibilities which they were unwilling to accord to other states. They usually consulted each other, although not the small states, on major issues. They regarded themselves as the guardians of the Peace of Europe, and they assumed responsibility for the maintenance of order within their neighbouring states. It was the strongest second-class states which resented the existence of this 'exclusive club' of great powers. Their resentment was particularly evident at the Congress of Vienna when the four victorious powers treated states such as Sweden, Spain and Holland as inferior supplicants rather than as equal allies. The very fact that at the congress the previously vexed question of the precedence of diplomatic envoys was settled by the simple rule of 'length of service' attests to the new confidence of the great powers in their status: they no longer thought it necessary to prove their importance by squabbles over precedence at ceremonial occasions. In the years after 1815 German states such as Bavaria, Saxony and Hanover often found Austro-Prussian domination of the Germanic Confederation irksome. Indeed, during the revolutionary years 1848–49 they even tried to shake it off; but they failed largely because neither the Austrians nor the Prussians were prepared to tolerate such pretensions. For the most part, however, all the small states of Europe accepted the pre-eminence of the great powers and were content to place themselves under the protection of one or more of them. Moreover, just as the great powers claimed special rights for themselves, so the small states claimed that the great had special responsibilities for their well-being: they expected protection from external aggression and military assistance to suppress revolution. In some cases the great powers were expected to provide, either directly or indirectly, financial assistance to stave off public bankruptcy in small states. Many of the weaker states of Europe thus willingly cast themselves in the role of client states, and came to regard it as advantageous to be dependent on their great-power patrons.

Occasionally one or more great powers would find it necessary to 'discipline' a recalcitrant small state. In 1832 the British and the French had to take military action to force the Dutch government to accept the decisions of the London Conference on the delimitation of the border after the separation of Belgium from Holland. In 1864 the Austrians and the Prussians were able to claim that their invasion of the two duchies of Schleswig and Holstein was intended to force the Danes to comply with the provisions of the Treaty of London of 1852. This was a stand which they knew the other powers would find it difficult to oppose. Similarly, in the later nineteenth century, Austria-Hungary and Russia – equally claiming to act in defence of the territorial settlement established by the Concert at the Congress of Berlin – frequently threatened military intervention of a punitive or restraining nature against small states in the Balkans. In return for the protection they afforded the small states, the great powers expected a degree of obedience from them. It was not always forthcoming; for Portuguese governments it was almost a matter of principle to defy British governments which, on three separate occasions between 1826 and 1847 had to intervene to protect the Portuguese monarchy against rebel factions. In eastern Europe the close involvement of several rival powers, and the growing tension in the second half of the century, made drastic intervention of this kind an increasingly dangerous proposition; but Russia was certainly considering the use of force to maintain a puppet regime in Bulgaria in 1886–87; and armed intervention to re-establish an Austrophile regime in Serbia was discussed often enough in Vienna even in the twentieth century.

The only state which did not know its place in the hierarchy of power was the Ottoman Empire. Although it had extensive possessions in the Balkans and although the Treaty of Paris of 1856 formally admitted it to the Concert of Europe, it was never regarded as a European state. There was a general assumption that only Christian states could properly be regarded as members of the European community of nations. In 1897, for example, even Turkey's friends in the Concert agreed that Christian territory once freed from Ottoman rule, could never be returned; and Turkey was not allowed to profit from her victory in her war with Greece. Ottoman governments oscillated between the most abject dependence on the great powers and defiance of them. In its relations with the European powers, the Ottoman empire faced two almost insuperable problems: it could not please all the powers all the time, and it did not always know which one to fear most. It was these problems that were at the root of the Near Eastern conflict which eventually degenerated into the Crimean War and which continued to preoccupy the diplomatists of Europe until 1918.

From the Treaty of Chaumont (1814) onwards, the dominance enjoyed by the great powers was given increasingly formal recognition. The

Quadruple Alliance of November 1815 was specifically limited to the four great powers of the anti-French coalition. This was one reason why it was so much more important than the rival Russian-inspired Holy Alliance, which was signed by a motley collection of great and minor states. In 1818 France was formally rehabilitated as a great power, after defeat and occupation, by the creation of a new five-power concert. The clear notion behind both the Quadruple Alliance and the Concert was that there should be some formal and recognized procedure by which the great powers could maintain peace and the territorial *status quo*, which contemporary statesmen called 'the public law of Europe', and it usually took the form of conference diplomacy. Between 1822 and 1913 there were twenty-six conferences attended by representatives of all the great powers – the last of which, in London, lasted nearly eight months; and many more at which two or more great powers reached agreement. One of the principal assumptions of 'concert diplomacy', was that changes in the territorial order required the consent of the great powers. This doctrine was forcibly stated by Palmerston in 1846 when he wrote that it was impossible for any state to attempt to change the territorial order 'in a manner inconsistent with the Treaty of Vienna without the concurrence of the other powers who were party to that Treaty'. In the fifteen years from the Crimean War to the treaty of Frankfort this view of the purpose of the Concert was all but abandoned and peace treaties between belligerent great powers replaced the Concert as the principal means of territorial revision. But the London Protocol of 1871 formally restated the principle that treaties could not be altered without the consent of all the signatory powers – an important issue in the crisis over the annexation of Bosnia nearly forty years later.

In practical terms the Concert of Europe could successfully allocate territory from one small or weak state to another. It could also provide the framework for the settlement of crises in which the powers were anxious to reach agreement. But it could not satisfy the territorial ambitions of great powers when these were in conflict with each other. Not one of the many suggestions for five-power discussion of territorial revision made between 1856 and 1871 was ever taken up and after 1871 the status of Alsace-Lorraine was an issue over which France and Germany differed so profoundly as to doom to failure any attempts at a compromise solution, let alone any general entente between the two powers. Equally, although in 1897 Russia and Austria-Hungary reached an agreement to co-exist in the Near East this was only possible on the basis of both powers renouncing any selfish territorial ambitions there. Much the same can be said of Austro-Italian agreements about the future of the Adriatic territories of the Ottoman Empire. In peacetime, powers were reluctant openly to avow their expansionist objectives; only victory on the battlefield would give both force and righteousness to their demands. The successful operation of the Concert depended in fact upon a self-denying ordinance from each of the great powers. When two or more powers sought either treaty revision or territorial expansion and were prepared to bargain with each other on this basis, the Concert could not control them. This did not mean that it ceased to exist, merely that it failed to operate in particular circumstances. It was quite frequently revived if the great powers were confronted by new issues on which they were disposed to compromise.

Almost immediately after the defeat of Napoleon, informed observers of international relations began to distinguish between two categories of European great power. There were firstly those with exclusively European territory and interests, for example Austria and Prussia. Then there were those, such as Great Britain and Russia, with extensive possessions, influence and interests outside Europe. The former owed her world power to her vast commercial interests in every continent, to her Indian empire and her overwhelming sea-power. Russia enjoyed the same status because of the vast and unknown size of her Asiatic possessions. It was, moreover, the growth of the French empire in North Africa after the occupation of Algiers in 1830 that placed France in the ranks of the world powers. In the 1870s the French reacted to their second defeat with a renewed emphasis on colonial expansion. Thus, as in the 1820s and 1830s, many Frenchmen believed that their empire overseas would help provide France with the strength she needed to recover lost status and territory in Europe. By the late nineteenth century it was clear that the fears entertained by many continental diplomats earlier in the century that England and Russia would divide the world between them had proved unfounded. Nevertheless the worldwide rivalry of these two powers was certainly a constant element shaping their European alignments. The welcome if somewhat uneasy end of this struggle in the early twentieth century was an important factor in the British decision to stand by Russia in 1914.

The distinction between the purely European powers and the world powers was perhaps rather less significant before 1870. In the early nineteenth century Europe itself offered ample commercial opportunities for expanding economies. Moreover, there was very little reliance on raw materials produced outside Europe, and from the 1840s onwards railway building absorbed most surplus capital. In the period before 1870

England was the only great power to have an export economy geared to worldwide trade. Moreover, as far as the four continental powers were concerned, the dominant problems of international relations were European. Until the 1850s the European ruling élite was determined to ensure its own survival and to contain or destroy the challenges it faced from liberalism and nationalism. In the late 1850s and the 1860s their preoccupations were different but still European: the great powers concentrated on territorial expansion in Europe itself. Until 1870 the French certainly attached more importance to Italy and the Rhineland than they did to expansion in North Africa; as late as the 1860s the Russians were more concerned about retaining the congress kingdom of Poland than expanding their possessions in central Asia.

The only non-European issues which significantly affected the relations of the great powers in the first half of the nineteenth century arose as a result of the collapse of the authority of the Ottoman Empire in its outlying provinces in central Asia and in North Africa. In central Asia the British feared that the Russians would fill the vacuum left by the Turks and eventually push southwards to threaten the British empire in India; in North Africa the British likewise believed that the French were intent upon expansion from Algiers to Egypt – all of which apprehensions marked British policy until the twentieth century. The effect of these British anxieties, however, was not to create new patterns of rivalry but to confirm and extend rivalries which already existed and which were European in origin. Neither the Prussian nor the Austrian government shared the alarm of the British over the extra-European expansion of France and Russia. In the Atlantic the French never really attempted to exploit Anglo-American rivalry nor the British dread of American expansion into Canada. Although British governments sometimes feared that they might, French governments in fact never managed to establish close relations with the United States. For most of the century after the end of the War of 1812 the Americans were rather more suspicious of the imperial ambitions of the French in Central and South America than they were of the British. By the turn of the century the British had decided that a war against the United States was the one war they must never fight. Atlantic rivalry, which had played such an important part in Anglo-French relations in the late eighteenth century, was a negligible factor after 1815.

With the defeat of the Second Empire territorial gains on the Rhine ceased to be a practical proposition for the French; and Russia, having no longer to fear Napoleon III or a Crimean Coalition, at last gained security in both Poland and the Near East. These were but two of the factors leading the great powers to concentrate more of their attention on expansion outside Europe. The 1870s saw the spread of both a worldwide depression and of fears on the part of some governments – particularly those of Great Britain and Germany – that large annexations of territory by commercial rivals might be accompanied by the closure of markets hitherto open to them under the system of 'informal empire'. The 1880s and 1890s were marked by a spate of 'imperialist' activity – the partition of Africa and the intervention of the European Powers in China – all of which, however, was accomplished without serious danger of war, due largely to Great Britain's and Germany's willingness to co-operate in defence of the 'open door' to trade. It is true that relations between Great Britain on the one hand and France and Russia on the other took a turn for the worse: indeed, to a very large extent Great Britain was the real target of the Franco-Russian alliance of the 1890s. But the extra-European activities of the great powers had not fundamentally altered their priorities. Even those powers that were only semi-European never lost sight of their essentially European interests: the need to seek security in Europe by preventing any power or group of powers from establishing a Napoleonic domination of the continent. This continued to be the fundamental aim of their diplomacy.

In the last resort, great-power status was a reflection of economic, military and naval strength. The great powers were the largest, richest and most populous states. The ability to wage war on a massive scale was the ultimate test of great-power status. This was the simple and brutal reality underlying the complex edifice of international relations. In the French Revolutionary and Napoleonic Wars each of the five great powers had put its status to the test. The fact that Austria and Prussia narrowly escaped destruction at the hands of the French, combined with the belief that they had been saved by the financial resources of the British and the military strength of the Russians, cast a long shadow over great-power relations until the Crimean War. It established the hierarchy of power which existed within the ranks of the great powers. In the years after the Congress of Vienna British financial and naval strength, and the military power at the disposal of the Russian emperor, were the decisive underlying factors in European diplomacy. It was these resources that the French knew they would have to match before they could contemplate an all-out attack on the Vienna settlement. The fact that it had taken the combined efforts of four powers to defeat France had given her a unique status within the new order, as the power least satisfied with the arrangements made in 1815, and the power with the greatest potential for disruption. In the decades after 1871 France was, of course, still a highly dissatisfied power. But in view of her continuing diplomatic isolation and of the steady growth of German demographic, industrial and military preponderance, she was in no position to challenge the 1871 settlement. Even so, this settlement lacked the moral validity of the treaties of 1815. After 1871 peace was maintained, not by the moral consensus of a conservative coalition comprising at least three and sometimes four great powers, but simply by the brutal fact of German military superiority over France, and it would last only so long as that superiority was maintained.

In the first half of the nineteenth century none of the great powers made regular and precise estimates of each other's military and naval strength. For the most part they had very hazy notions of the military and naval resources at each other's disposal. There was, moreover, hardly any detailed forward planning by military leaders for future wars. None of the political leaders who took the decisions to go to war in the years from 1854 to 1870 attached decisive importance to the opinions of their military advisers. In the early nineteenth century the task of the military was to win wars after they had been declared. Before 1848 it was generally assumed that the next war would be a repetition of the last, a four-power coalition against France fought, like the campaigns of 1813 and 1814, in the west. In fact this war never materialized. When the great powers did fight in Europe in the late 1850s and 1860s it was with new weapons, a new technology, a new speed and smaller armies. Contemporary opinion was by no means certain in advance of the outcome of these wars; in 1866 and 1870 many military experts were convinced that the belligerents were evenly matched and that the wars would be long and inconclusive.

The speedy and catastrophic defeats of Austria and France seemed to portend a revolution in the role of the military in the formation of state policy. Prussia's victories had clearly demonstrated the importance of the efficient organization of manpower resources, their armament, and their speedy and effective deployment on the battlefield. After the wars of 1866 and 1870, efficiency and speed seemed more important than ever; and in succeeding years all the continental powers made frantic efforts to improve their war-making capacity. Conscription became the rule; general staffs were created to devise war plans and supervise other reforms on the Prussian model. The concentration on the building of strategic railways testified to the importance generally accorded to speed of mobilization. After 1871 military planning came into its own, and elaborate schemes were drawn up to cater for even the most improbable contingencies. The significance of this change should not be exaggerated. State policy still remained in the hands of monarchs and statesmen. Bismarck steadily and successfully set his face against a veritable stream of advice from Prussian and Austrian military planners in favour of a preventive war against Russia in the late 1880s; and in 1911 the emperor of Austria dismissed his chief of staff for persistently advocating war with Italy against the wishes of his foreign minister. But on occasions, when political and military leaders took the same view, the military could become more than the mere servants of the civilian authorities, and the emphasis placed by the military on the importance of detailed contingency plans could influence the course of events. The Franco-Russian military convention of 1892 formed the basis of the alliance of 1894 and blind faith in military advice as illustrated by the German government's decision to treat Russian mobilization as a *casus belli* had even more momentous consequences in July 1914.

In the exercise of their dominance over the European state system the great powers showed remarkable restraint, particularly in the decades from 1815 to 1856. They rarely acted arbitrarily or capriciously. It was not until the 1850s that any of the four victorious allies actually provoked a major diplomatic crisis. Most of the important problems of the pre-Crimean period were either provoked by small states or by dissident elements within small states. The great powers merely reacted to these crises, and attempted to prevent them from disturbing the peace of Europe. Nor was there any inclination among the four powers to exploit a local crisis produced by or within small states to embark upon an ambitious and forward policy which seriously and adversely affected the interests of other powers. The French were the exception to this rule: in Spain in 1823, in Belgium in 1830, and in Italy in 1848 they were intent upon securing important advantages for themselves. Until 1856, however, France was the only revisionist great power; her conduct was necessarily different from that of her satiated rivals. Moreover, French governments themselves provoked two major crises: in 1840 Thiers transformed a local Near Eastern conflict into a question of peace and war on the Rhine; and in 1852 Napoleon III successfully broke what he regarded as the deadlock of peace between the powers by an adventurous policy in the Near East. From 1856 to 1870, the other great powers also provoked crises, embarked upon wars of aggression, and exploited problems arising in small states in order to secure both political and territorial advantages for themselves.

Even so, the late 1850s and the 1860s proved to be an untypical interlude, an aberration. The decades after 1871 resemble those after 1815, with crises again being provoked by small states on the periphery of the continent while compromise and restraint characterized the diplomacy of the great powers. The latter had been unpleasantly reminded, by the bloodshed of the Commune in Paris, that the revolutionary hydra was not yet dead; and they were increasingly aware, as they became enmeshed in complex alliance obligations, of the potential extent of any conflict that was allowed to develop in Europe. It was only in the years after 1900 that some continental statesmen began to argue that the risks of war could be minimized and that war could solve problems which were otherwise insoluble. There was, moreover, amongst many German leaders a growing conviction that the cautious diplomacy of the post-1871 period had paid few dividends.

The Vienna states system, like the international orders which preceded and followed it, ultimately rested on the sanction of force. Yet the attitudes of the powers towards the use of force varied with circumstances. In general terms, for most of the nineteenth century, liberal opinion in England and France strongly condemned war as a crime against civilization; whereas in the military monarchies of central and eastern Europe war was always regarded as a noble activity, especially if it was for the defence of the sacred institution of monarchy against revolution. In particular instances, for example in the 1850s and 1860s, intellectuals in western and central Europe were prepared to justify war as an essential activity in the onward march of progress. But, on the whole, as far as the statesmen and diplomats of the nineteenth century were concerned, the use of force, both within the state and between states, was a necessary evil and the organization of war was an essential task of government. It was the only activity to which they gave their undivided attention and over which they sought exclusive control. The great powers issued threats of force with some frequency to each other and to small states. They were usually intended as an indication of the gravity with which a particular power viewed a crisis and the consequences which would follow if another power persisted in a line of policy of which it disapproved.

Throughout the period from 1815 to 1914 all the great powers, for many different reasons, regarded the prospect of a general European war with some apprehension. British governments believed that such a war would be long and expensive, the three eastern autocracies were convinced that it would probably result in the disintegration of the social order and provide their disaffected subject nationalities with an excellent opportunity for revolt. French governments before 1848 feared that a general war would inevitably see a revival of the four-power coalition against them or that it might provide the radical republicans with the

ideal circumstances for a *coup*. Above all, before 1848 there was a g
conviction amongst the great powers that a local conflict between two or
more powers would probably degenerate into a general conflagration.
This view derived from the conservative belief about the events of 1792;
that revolutionary elements in France had deliberately dragged the European powers into war to imperil their social and political systems. The
great dread of the social and political consequences of war acted as a
powerful restraint on a ruling class which felt itself beleaguered and which
was lacking in confidence. The revolutions of 1848 and the Crimean War
both proved that wars could be localized and temporarily dispelled the
fear of social collapse. Yet even then the dread of a general war remained
strong. Those powers which in the 1850s and 1860s embarked on wars of
territorial gain strove desperately to keep the wars localized, lest they be
robbed of the fruits of victory.

The fall of the Second Empire and the bloody events of the Commune
– both consequences of the war of 1870 – revived apprehensions about
even localized war as the harbinger of revolution, at least in Europe
east of the Rhine; and it was not long before doctrines of conservative
solidarity reminiscent of the neo-Holy Alliance reappeared in the Three
Emperors' League and the Three Emperors' Alliance. Further afield, the
Central Powers' diplomatic links with Italy and Spain in the 1880s were
conscious attempts to bolster up the monarchies in Rome and Madrid
against 'the dangerous idea of a republican brotherhood of Latin races'
centred on France. Franz Joseph's ambassador in St Petersburg was
convinced that there was in Europe 'a great revolutionary subversive party
just waiting for the crash and for the great conservative powers to weaken
and exhaust each other' in war; and as late as 1913 Berchtold was warning the German emperor of the dangers that would assail the Central
Powers if revolution broke out in Russia as a result of war. By the early
twentieth century, however, the exponents of conservative solidarity had
shifted their ground and were beginning to argue, as Bismarck had
done in the 1860s, that the problem of defending the social and political
order was one which each state must solve for itself and in its own way.
This was certainly the view in Berlin and St Petersburg. In July 1914 even
conservatives in Vienna were opting for violent solutions to local problems, albeit as a counsel of despair.

As a rule, however, nineteenth-century governments were content to
seek their salvation in diplomacy. In 1815 the common obligation to
uphold the treaty structure of Europe was given great emphasis by the
victorious allies, who regarded the General Act of the Congress of Vienna

as the foundation of the European territorial order. The British government came to hold an extremely legalistic attitude towards questions of treaty maintenance and treaty revision; and the Eastern Powers in the period from the revolutions of the early 1820s to the Crimean War were similarly disposed. There were specific reasons for this. The Second Peace of Paris was, as far as the four victorious powers were concerned, the legal instrument by which France was contained. The allies' insistence on the sanctity of treaties was another means of emphasizing their determination to keep France within the limits imposed upon her in 1815. Secondly, each of the three victorious continental powers had made valuable territorial gains in 1814 and 1815, and these they were determined to retain. In fact, therefore, the four powers elevated their common interests into a matter of high principle. The Eastern Powers also attempted to use the binding character of treaties as a means of preventing any change of which they disapproved, whereas the British, who cared less for the maintenance of the existing political order and were prepared to contemplate limited reforms, argued that treaties could be revised with the consent of all the contracting parties: this was the basis of Palmerston's policy towards Belgium in 1830 and towards Italy in 1848. In the 1860s British governments went further, arguing that treaties could be revised in the name of justice and humanity – it was on this basis that Britain recognized the new kingdom of Italy. But this new British formula was only selectively applied. Gladstone's attempt to revive it during the Near Eastern crisis of the late 1870s was only partially successful. Disraeli cared much more for the principle of contractual obligations.

The monarchs of the autocratic monarchies regarded treaties, particularly those which they had concluded with each other, as binding personal commitments which their honour and their duty towards God decreed that they must uphold. It was considerations of this sort that guided Nicholas I's approach to foreign policy. The French, by contrast, throughout the period from 1815 to 1870 consistently maintained that the treaties of 1815, which they condemned in their entirety, were an intolerable burden which they could not be expected long to tolerate. They claimed that France was not the only victim of the ambition and lust for conquest of the allies; the peoples of Italy, Poland and Belgium had also been sacrificed. Yet despite this general attack on the treaty structure, French governments found it convenient to pay lip service to the doctrine that the revision of treaties required the consent of the contracting parties: on three separate occasions between 1836 and 1863 French governments called for a congress of the powers to revise the Vienna settlement. In the late 1850s and 1860s the doctrine of treaty maintenance was either completely disregarded or cynically manipulated by those powers that sought treaty revision. Yet as soon as a state had made territorial gains, it sought to retain them by the revival of the principle of the binding character of treaties.

This was perhaps just one other respect in which 1871 marked the end of an interlude of upheaval and the return of the great powers to something resembling consensus. The London Protocol of January 1871, signed by all six powers, explicitly reaffirmed that treaties could not be legally altered without the consent of all the signatories – a principle that was successfully upheld when Russia had to submit the Treaty of San Stefano to the scrutiny of the Congress of Berlin in 1878; and one that proved a useful weapon in the hands of Austria-Hungary's opponents during the Bosnian crisis of 1908–9. Although Bismarck himself liked to say that treaties only had value so long as they suited the real interests of the contracting parties, in practice he had become the chief upholder of a European states system embodying the *status quo* of the Treaty of Frankfort. As this was acceptable to all except France and as she alone was impotent to change matters, the European states system based on the Treaties of Frankfort and Berlin, like that based on the Treaty of Vienna, in effect represented a tacit coalition against France. So long as France found no ally, the system was stable.

One of the most important elements in European diplomacy in the nineteenth century was the network of dynastic links, not only between the great powers, but also between them and the small states of Europe. Their effects were felt in several different ways. Firstly, there were the close family ties and personal friendships of the sovereigns of the great powers. The frequent meetings between the three autocratic monarchs were occasions for much diplomatic business to be conducted. No decade passed between 1815 and 1914 without at least one such meeting. The close family ties between the dynasties of Russia and Prussia were a significant factor within the alignment of the eastern powers. Both Alexander I and Nicholas I felt more closely attached to the Prussians than to the Austrians, and it was a matter of great regret to Nicholas that the Habsburgs refused for religious reasons to marry into the Russian imperial family. In the 1840s Nicholas I paid a state visit to Queen Victoria in order to consolidate the good relations he had established with the British during the Near Eastern crisis of 1839–40. Similarly Queen Victoria established close personal relations with both Louis Philippe and Napoleon III. The complex agreements on the Spanish Marriages were concluded during private visits between Queen Victoria and Louis Philippe. The affection felt by William I for his nephew, Alexander II, was a serious obstacle in the way of Bismarck's concluding the alliance with Austria-Hungary in 1879; just as the antipathy felt by Alexander III for William II helped to undermine the Reinsurance Treaty. Moreover, the ill feeling prevailing between William II and Edward VII did nothing for Anglo-German relations after the turn of the century.

Secondly, there was throughout the period a sort of monarchical 'trades unionism', rooted in the belief that monarchs must stand together or they would fall together. Edward VII, for example, was largely instrumental in delaying until 1906 British recognition of the regicide government established in Serbia in 1903; and George V's private secretary was sternly reminding the Foreign Office, as late as 1912, of the necessity 'in present revolutionary times for sovereigns to hold together. . . . We made too much of the French republic.' The German government, certainly, was gambling on feelings of monarchical solidarity in St Petersburg when they advised the Austrians to strike quickly at Serbia after the Sarajevo assassinations. Earlier in the century too, a Prussian monarch had written, when concluding an anti-revolutionary alliance with Austria in 1854: 'I shall not allow Austria . . . to be attacked by the revolution without drawing the sword on her behalf, and this from pure love of Prussia, from self-preservation.' The propaganda of French republicans, who called for a 'war of the peoples of Europe against the kings of Europe', and the widespread belief of conservatives in the existence of a general revolutionary conspiracy, did much to foster such attitudes. The activities of the Second International (established in 1889) and a spate of anarchist assassinations of crowned heads in the decades around the turn of the century sustained these feelings into the twentieth century.

Thirdly, it was widely accepted that a dispute between two states could be settled by the mediation of a third sovereign. The Austrian emperor successfully solved a territorial dispute between the dukes of Parma and Tuscany in the 1840s and in 1850 Nicholas I strongly urged the Austrians and the Prussians to compose their differences at Olmütz. In the later nineteenth century, this practice was less in evidence. It was the republican President Roosevelt who mediated peace between the emperors of Russia and Japan in 1905. Nevertheless, the Hague Peace Conferences of 1899 and 1907 were summoned in response to the personal wish of the Tsar; and the emperor of Austria was instrumental in persuading the Germans to submit to arbitration the potentially explosive Casablanca dispute with France in 1909.

Lastly, the great powers used dynastic alliances to cement their political agreements and symbolize their co-operation. The alliance of France and Sardinia in 1859 for war against Austria included a marriage compact between a daughter of Victor Emmanuel II and a cousin of Napoleon III. Neither Louis Philippe nor Napoleon III, who had gained their thrones by revolution, could secure marriage alliances with the ruling families of the other great powers; and they felt themselves outcasts. The monarchs of the other great powers did little to dispel these feelings. The animosity felt by Nicholas I towards both these monarchs affected Franco-Russian relations quite decisively. The Treaty of Björkö, signed on the occasion of an emotional meeting between William II and his cousin the Tsar in 1905, behind the backs of and contrary to the wishes of, their foreign ministers, was an extreme and, not surprisingly, abortive example of dynastic solidarity. Nevertheless William was more successful in his approaches to his Russian cousin at Potsdam in 1910, a move of which his government approved. The dynastic links between the Hohenzollerns in Berlin and Bucharest were an important factor in Germany's Near Eastern policy throughout the reign of King Carol, from 1866 to 1914: the fact that his heir was married to a strong-minded English princess was the source some dismay in Berlin. In the last resort, however, close family ties and monarchical solidarity were never allowed to stand in the way of a determined pursuit of state interests. There was undoubted truth in the remark made by Gorchakov in 1870: 'We are no longer in an epoch where family ties can lead to such great results as those of an alliance.' Moreover it must be remembered that in the course of the nineteenth century more monarchs lost their thrones as a consequence of the ambitions of fellow monarchs than as a result of revolution.

In the assumptions of their foreign policies and in their analyses of international relations the great powers differed significantly. The concept of the balance of power was hardly ever used except by British governments. The continental powers certainly did not consciously seek to uphold it. In the period before 1848 the three autocratic monarchies were determined that preponderant strength should be on the side of the forces of order and on the side of the coalition against France. The dominant concept of their foreign policies was 'security' against the great dangers that confronted them. In the 1880s and 1890s the maintenance of peace and the *status quo* depended on a preponderance of power centred on a conservative German empire and its associates, rather than on any genuine balance of power. Even in the era of two balanced blocs after 1907 it may be argued that behind Great Britain's devotion to the idea of the balance of power lay the harsh reality of a desperate need to stand well with France and Russia as much as any fear of Germany. Indeed, insofar as the continental states took the British theory of the balance of power into account, it had long been their custom to point to its inconsistency. Both the French and the Russians had insisted after 1815 that the aim of the British government was to create a military deadlock on the continent (which they then called a balance), while at the same time they jealously guarded their own naval hegemony. In fact, therefore, the association of the idea of the balance of power with British policy served to discredit it in the opinion of many continental statesmen. It was regarded as a justification for opportunism at the time when the conservative powers felt that a rigid adherence to fixed principles and loyalty to wartime allies were the surest means of maintaining the *status quo*.

In the 1850s and 1860s all the continental states, with the exception of Austria which took refuge in her treaty rights, began to justify the need for treaty revision and territorial expansion in terms either of the existence of unnatural coalitions against them or of national self-determination. In fact, therefore, both the Russians and the Prussians adopted after the Crimean War the very arguments which before the war they had so strongly opposed. The Russians adopted the French argument, that the humiliating treaty of 1856 had been imposed upon them by an 'unnatural coalition' which could not survive; the Prussians borrowed and modified the revolutionary doctrine that the state must fulfil the national aspirations of the German people. In the late 1860s the French abandoned the principle of national self-determination which they had earlier championed, and began to base their foreign policy on the old eighteenth-century notion of compensation: if other powers gained territory, then so must France. These two decades of aggressive policies, of hastily devised arguments for diplomatic expediency and short-term alliances for precise offensive objectives proved no more than an interlude. By the 1870s most governments – except the French – reaffirmed their commitment to the *status quo*. The British did not believe that the great changes of the 1860s rendered obsolete their attachment to the balance of power. For the most part, they had regarded it as directed against the expansion of France and Russia. There were many British statesmen who were convinced that the emergence of a large Germany strengthened a balance which had been weakened by the restless policies of Nicholas I in the Near East and Napoleon III in Italy and on the Rhine.

Russia and Austria-Hungary returned to the principles of the Neo-Holy Alliance as early as 1873, partly out of mistrust of Germany. When the latter power also declared for the *status quo* the stage was set for a whole series of conservative agreements in the 1870s and 1880s. These were intended like those of the period 1815–54 to be more or less permanent and to safeguard the lasting interests of the signatories in maintaining stability and order. Once again France was treated as the pariah and Great Britain was loosely linked to some of her erstwhile allies of the Fourth Coalition. It was only when Germany became a source of anxiety to her neighbours in the 1890s, that a counter-system of alliances developed. All the alliances concluded by the great powers in the years after 1879 with the exception of the Anglo-Japanese alliance of 1902 were strictly defensive – whatever suspicious observers may have thought. These alliances were intended to represent certain vital interests; and it was the clash of these interests that transformed the Austro-Serbian conflict into a general war in 1914. Nevertheless, the curious fact remains that, technically speaking, not one of the agreements concluded in the previous forty years came into operation in that final crisis.

In the century after the Congress of Vienna the foreign policies of the great powers were formulated and executed by a very small number of men. In 1815 only in England and France was there anything like a public and informed discussion of foreign policy. Yet by the 1860s even the Russian government was alive to the necessity of presenting a clear picture of its foreign policy to educated opinion, and in Austria and Prussia the press commented regularly on foreign affairs. By the time of the Franco-Prussian war all the great powers had adopted the practice of using newspapers as a means of influencing and regulating public opinion on international affairs. In central and eastern Europe the conduct of policy remained for the most part under the tight control of the sovereigns and their principal advisers. A report on the Russian foreign ministry in the 1830s described it as 'merely the faithful executor of the intentions of the Tsar'. It was only in England and France that the principle of ministerial control of foreign policy was properly established. In France this was abandoned under the Second Empire, and Napoleon III exercised as much personal control over the making of foreign policy as did Alexander II of Russia. After the 1905 revolution liberal and Pan-Slav elements were able to exercise pressure – sometimes effectively – on the Russian government through the Duma and the press. In constitutional Austria, as late as 1911, the emperor could declare that the foreign minister was simply '*Mein Minister*' carrying out '*Meine Politik*', and neither the Austrian nor the Hungarian parliament ever acquired a voice in the making of foreign policy.

Many foreign ministers retained their positions for decades. Metternich directed Austrian policy from 1809 to 1848 and Nesselrode served as Russian foreign minister from 1816 to 1856. His successor, Gorchakov, occupied the post for twenty-five years. Palmerston exercised a decisive influence over British foreign policy either as foreign secretary or as prime minister for almost a quarter of a century between 1830 and 1865, just as Salisbury did in the last quarter of the century. The foreign ministries of the powers were extremely small organizations, and as a rule ministers did not expect the permanent officials to provide them with political advice. For the most part they were clerks and copyists who performed menial tasks. The emergence of permanent official advisers on foreign policy was everywhere a development of the late nineteenth century. The aristocratic and landowning background of most nineteenth-century diplomats and their shared cultural and social assumptions did much to establish and maintain a unity of outlook and a common code of ethics amongst the diplomatic corps in the capitals of the great powers. Many diplomats, like foreign ministers, remained at their posts for decades: Barons Brunnow and Bunsen were respectively Russian and Prussian ambassadors in London from the 1830s to the late 1850s; Baron Calice represented Austria-Hungary at Constantinople from 1880 to 1906, and his successor, Markgraf Pallavicini from 1906 to 1918. The diplomats whom the great powers accredited to each other were always respected figures in the social and political life of the European capitals; Count Mensdorff, Austro-Hungarian ambassador at London from 1904 to 1914 was on intimate terms with his 'cousins' King George V and King Ferdinand of Bulgaria. In 1848 the provisional government in France decided to send prominent republicans as its envoys abroad, but Lamartine soon realized that this was a mistake and replaced them with more socially acceptable men. The diplomatic service of the Third Republic could also find use for a count or an admiral in posts like St Petersburg. Diplomacy was not regarded in the nineteenth century as a profession separate from politics. Many of the leading statesmen of Europe had at some stage of their careers been diplomats, Guizot, Clarendon, Bismarck and Bülow being notable examples. Ambassadors and envoys at the courts of the great powers certainly played an important part in the settlement of disputes, particularly in conference diplomacy. Their role was, however, usually restricted to the arrangement of details. It was this and the drafting of treaties that constituted what contemporaries regarded as 'the art of diplomacy'.

The steady improvement in communications that occurred in the nineteenth century, largely as a consequence of steamships, railways and the telegraph, did not in fact greatly alter the responsibilities of diplomats, at least as far as Europe was concerned. Major decisions about the relations of the great powers had always been taken at the highest level, although diplomats outside Europe were sometimes in a position to interpret more widely the political instructions they received from their governments. The main effect of better communications was to quicken the pace of diplomacy. Most of the great-power crises of the pre-Crimean War period lasted at least several months, and some for more than a year. It took the British and the Russians nearly nine months to reach agreement in 1839–40 on the settlement of the Egyptian-Turkish dispute. This was partly because it required at least eleven days for dispatches to be exchanged between the British and Russian capitals. It was not uncommon for minor diplomatic problems to drag on for several years, and in fact to be buried in volumes of correspondence. Ottoman governments were particularly prone to exploit this when harassed by the great powers – witness their largely successful rearguard actions against the attempts of the powers to introduce reforms in Macedonia and Armenia in the late nineteenth and early twentieth centuries. In the post-Crimean War period, crises were shorter and frequently accompanied by the exchange of recriminations between governments in newspapers and in parliamentary assemblies. There was much more emphasis on domestic propaganda and on casting opponents in the role of the aggressor: in 1914 each of the belligerent governments was able to persuade its subjects that it was fighting a defensive war. All realized that, in war, the mobilization of domestic resources, human as well as material, was vital: speed and surprise were at a premium, but the role of communications in sustaining the war effort and boosting morale was no less essential. The peace terms, too, which followed the great wars of the mid-nineteenth century, were also quickly negotiated: both the Armistice of Villafranca, which ended the war in northern Italy in 1859, and the preliminary Peace of Nikolsburg after the Austro-Prussian war of 1866, were negotiated in a matter of days. This was possible because of improved communications, and urgently necessary if the intervention of other powers were to be prevented. But these were changes of form rather than of substance. Even in the decades after the Treaty of Frankfort, despite the increasing prevalence of professional advisers in the foreign ministries of the great powers, the old *esprit de corps* and the cosmopolitan outlook of the diplomats, and the common 'unspoken assumptions' of the decision-makers about the nature and purpose of the European states system, survived. In fact, the European states system was still essentially that of the Congress of Vienna on the very eve of the First World War.

CHAPTER 2

The reconstruction of Europe and the Alliance, 1812–23

The peace settlement of 1814–15

By 1800, the European states system had been developing for just over three hundred years as a system of sovereign states, linked together by common traditions and interests, but retaining their independence as sovereign decision-making entities. For much of the first decade of the nineteenth century, however, most of the component elements of the system had been absorbed into the hegemonic empire of Napoleon I. It is true that by the end of 1812 that empire was seen to be no longer omnipotent; at one end of the continent, Napoleon had been unable to rid himself of the 'Spanish ulcer', as British forces advanced from Portugal into Spain; at the other, his failure to bring the Russians to heel had cost him his *Grande Armée*. Whether these setbacks were to be anything more than that, the year 1813 would show. The decision by the Russians to pursue the war beyond their borders and into central Europe was, of course, a momentous one; but much remained uncertain. Would it be possible for Napoleon's opponents in east and west to co-operate to any degree, and to what effect? how would the central powers, still formally Napoleon's allies, react to the intrusion of – from their perspective – sometimes uncomprehending, even threatening, flanking powers into the heart of Europe? would it be possible to bring Napoleon himself to accept the dismantling of his empire? and even if all this were achieved, would it be possible to re-establish something more akin to the states systems of the past, but more stable and enduring than those?

When the Russians, after expelling the *Grande Armée* from their soil, decided to pursue the war into central Europe this decision was in part a reflection of Tsar Alexander's view of himself as the divinely appointed saviour of Europe from the Antichrist, and of his desire to avenge the burning of Moscow by marching into Paris. It also included a strong admixture of traditional Russian expansionism and a determination to settle accounts with a France that seemed to stand everywhere in the way of Russia's aspirations. Not only was Napoleon the ally of a Sweden still smarting from the loss of Finland to Russia in 1809, and the abettor of the Turks in their resistance to the advances Russia had made towards the Caucasus and the Danube in the war of 1806–12; he had transformed both the Grand Duchy of Warsaw and Prussia's occupied eastern provinces into a vast arsenal threatening the security of the Russian heartland itself. By February, the Russians had secured the co-operation of Prussia. For some weeks King Frederick William III had been paralysed with fright at the thought of staking his country's existence on a commitment to either side; but as Napoleon uttered nothing but threats, while Alexander's threats were accompanied by prospects of territorial gains for Prussia at the expense of Napoleon's allies, and as his troops were now actually on Prussian soil, the King finally opted for the Russian side. The unspoken assumption behind the vague allusion in the Russo-Prussian Treaty of Kalisch (28 February 1813) to Prussia's receiving the 'equivalent' of her 1805 territories was that Prussia would abandon her former territories in the Grand Duchy of Warsaw, in exchange for compensation at the expense of Napoleon's ally, the King of Saxony.

This turn of events encouraged the British, so far of little weight outside Spain and Sicily, to new diplomatic efforts in central and eastern Europe. They had already been instrumental, despite strenuous French counter-diplomacy at Constantinople, in bringing about the Treaty of Bucharest (July 1812) that freed Russia from her Turkish entanglements. In March 1813 they managed – this time assisted by Napoleon's stubborn adherence to his Danish allies – to secure an alliance with Sweden, promising subsidies and support for the transfer of Norway from Denmark to Sweden in return for Swedish military action against the French in north Germany. With Prussia's change of heart the British foreign secretary, Viscount Castlereagh, saw the chance of transforming the whole balance of power in central Europe to Great Britain's satisfaction: 'To keep France in order we require great masses – that Prussia, Austria and Russia ought to be as great and powerful as they have ever been.' Two subsidy and alliance treaties with Russia and Prussia, endorsing the Kalisch programme, were followed on 27 June by the Third Treaty of Reichenbach, in which Castlereagh secured the support of his new allies for Great Britain's own war aims in Spain, southern Italy and the Baltic. Even so, the military setbacks recently suffered by Russo-Prussian forces at Lützen and Bautzen in Saxony made it seem doubtful whether the allies would even be able to clear the French out of Germany unless they could secure the co-operation of Austria.

The advance of Russian and Prussian forces into Saxony had placed the Austrian chancellor, Metternich, in a dilemma. He had been quick to withdraw Austrian forces from active co-operation with the French in January, but – whatever he was later to claim in his memoirs – he remained for the next eight months quite undecided about actually joining the allies. After all, as the French emperor's father-in-law and grandfather of the heir apparent, Francis I had of late established a tolerable *modus vivendi* with Napoleon. As ruler of a weak multinational empire he had certainly no interest in seeing French domination of the German states replaced by that of Austria's old rival, Prussia; and this would be especially unwelcome if Prussia was merely a catspaw of a Tsar who numbered among his advisers Baron Stein, with his plans for replacing the Napoleonic state structure of Germany by a centralised 'national' Germany that would leave little room for Austrian influence. All this would be, as Metternich's secretary, Gentz, observed, 'to exchange one scourge for another'. Metternich sought to manoeuvre, therefore, exploiting the power of Russia and Prussia to undermine French control of Germany without, however, allowing the northern powers to establish their own control of central Europe: to keep France in play as a factor in the balance of power, and to stop the war before Russia and Prussia became too strong. This was not an unrealistic objective as far as the latter powers were concerned. Indeed, so anxious were they to inveigle Austria into the war that they allowed Metternich to put to Napoleon peace proposals that amounted to little more that the restoration of Prussia and the abandonment of the Grand Duchy of Warsaw, and fell far short of what they had agreed with the British. That Metternich's plan failed was due entirely to Napoleon's refusal to make any significant concession whatever, either in his famous nine-hour interview with Metternich at Dresden in June, or in the subsequent Congress of Prague. It was only this that forced Metternich to join the allies in the hope of bringing Napoleon to reason by force of arms (12 August).

Even when Austria was in the war, Metternich's policy continued to be dictated by the desire to establish a balance between the belligerents.

True, he was now committed, somewhat embarrassingly, to fight for the allied war aims as defined by the Third Treaty of Reichenbach; and the Treaties of Teplitz of 9 September between the three eastern allies were disconcertingly vague in their allusion to an 'amicable agreement' that was somehow to be reached over the future of the Grand Duchy of Warsaw. After the allied victory in the Battle of the Nations at Leipzig (18 October) and the retreat of the French armies across the Rhine, therefore, Metternich was even more desperate for peace, and persuaded his allies (including the inexperienced young British ambassador, Lord Aberdeen) to offer the 'Frankfort proposals' to Napoleon in November. These envisaged a peace congress that would concede to France her 'natural frontiers' (including Belgium) and, although the Confederation of the Rhine was to be dismantled, would allow France to exercise in Germany 'the influence which every large state necessarily exercises over its smaller neighbours'. Meanwhile, Metternich had taken steps to secure Austria's particular interests against her allies. In a pre-emptive strike against Stein's plans, he concluded the Treaty of Ried with the king of Bavaria (8 October) envisaging a postwar Germany that maintained the existing sovereign states and was 'placed outside foreign [i.e. French or Russian] influence'; and further treaties with Baden, Hesse-Cassel and Hanover established a tier of Austrian satellites reaching from the Alps to the North Sea and cutting Prussia's territories in two. When the allies proceeded to invade France at the turn of the year, Metternich took care to send Austrian troops into Switzerland and establish a conservative regime there, much to the fury of Alexander, who was manoeuvring to become the patron of a liberal republic.

Two developments in January 1814 were to prove of enormous significance for the future peace. Firstly, the British foreign secretary himself went to the continent, where for most of the next two years he was to live in daily intimate contact with leading allied statesmen. In these critical months, British diplomacy was integrated into that of the continental powers to a degree unparalleled before or since – even in the later stages of the Second World War. Secondly, mindful of Napoleon's record in exploiting allied divisions in the past, the four allies agreed to act in their dealings with France 'collectively' and 'for Europe' – perhaps the first formal enunciation of that concept of a directory of leading powers that was to become such a feature of the nineteenth-century states system.

On occasion, Castlereagh was able to turn to good account the very difficulties facing the coalition: the growing distrust between Austria and Russia made both empires solicitous of British support; and sporadic French military successes in February that underlined the dangers of allied disunity. He managed to bring the Austrians round to his preferred solution of reducing France to her prewar frontiers – the 'natural' frontiers of the Frankfort proposals would have left Napoleon in control of Antwerp, that 'pistol pointed at the heart of England' – while he dissuaded Alexander from pursuing his plans to install a pro-Russian puppet regime in Paris. His greatest achievement was the four-power Treaty of Chaumont (9 March) defining the terms to be imposed on France and imposing on the allies a military commitment to uphold the settlement for twenty years. (It was still assumed that peace would be concluded with a vengeful Napoleon.) France was to be expelled from Spain, Italy and Germany, and was to be stripped entirely of all the gains she had made on her eastern frontier since the outbreak of the Revolutionary Wars in 1792. The final peace settlement was casting its shadow before; and the allied commitment to 'concert together' as to the best way of guaranteeing the continuance of the peace prefigured the Congress System of the postwar years. Napoleon's obstinate refusal, at the Congress of Chatillon, to take their proposals seriously finally convinced all the allies that he was 'the chief and only obstacle to peace'; and that the best hope for bringing France to settle down, both internally and within the proposed new European order, might be a Bourbon restoration under the old, pacific, Anglophile Louis XVIII. The latter, for his part, was ready to rule within the constraints of a constitutional monarchy and to respect the landholding and administrative changes wrought by the Revolution. True, Great Britain's success, both in the alliance negotiations and in those with the Bourbons, reflected the fact that her contribution, in terms of men and money, was exactly double that of each of her allies. But a success it was. As Castlereagh himself observed at Chaumont: 'What an extraordinary display of power! This, I trust, will put an end to any doubts as to the claim we have to an opinion on continental matters.'

At times, for example with the entry of Alexander I into Paris with the vanguard of the allied forces (31 March), in a demonstration of Russian military might that was to haunt the allies for a whole generation, it was Russia that dominated the peacemaking; and in an effort to ingratiate himself with French opinion, the Tsar took advantage of the absence of his allies to concede to the defeated Napoleon the extraordinarily generous Treaty of Fontainebleau (11 April) establishing him as sovereign in the island of Elba, dangerously close to the mainland of Europe. These terms the other allies felt constrained to endorse, in the interests of unity and the speedy departure of Napoleon from France. But the British soon regained the initiative in the negotiations leading up to the Treaty of Paris of 30 May, and in negotiating the details of the Belgian frontier Castlereagh took full advantage of the *carte blanche* conceded to him by the less directly interested eastern allies to push the French to the wall.

He was successful partly because, as far as the 'continental' aspects of the peace were concerned, he was acting as the executor of the allies in imposing the terms agreed by all four allies since Chaumont. Thus, France was forced to withdraw behind her 1792 frontiers (except for the sop of an addition of territory in the Plain of Savoy). Moreover, to safeguard the liberated territories from renewed French aggression, the treaty provided for a whole series of new territorial arrangements – past experience having shown those of 1792 to be inadequate: defenceless Genoa was to be incorporated into the Kingdom of Sardinia; the former republic of Venice, along with Milan to revert to Austrian control. The independence of Switzerland was reinforced by a European guarantee; the former Austrian Netherlands and the French-occupied Rhineland were to be divided between Holland and various German states, backed up by Prussia. Secret articles of the treaty obliged the French to agree in advance to all these arrangements, and to recognize the sole right of the four allies at the forthcoming Congress to implement these and other changes 'from whence a system of real and permanent Balance of Power in Europe is to be derived'. Clearly, much of what the British understood by that term had already been achieved.

What made the Treaty of Paris even more of an 'English' peace was the fact that, over issues affecting Great Britain's position as the leading naval and commercial power in the world, Castlereagh negotiated quite independently of his allies. He continued to maintain an adamantine resistance to any attempts either by France or by his allies (all erstwhile members of the Russian-led Armed Neutralities of 1780 and 1800) to question Great Britain's 'rights' to search neutral shipping. It was with the Dutch alone that he negotiated the purchase of the Cape of Good Hope; with France alone the cession of Malta and Mauritius, and a few islands of commercial importance in the West Indies; and with Spain alone the securing of Great Britain's commercial privileges in South America. It must be said that, considering the sacrifices Great Britain had made in the war, Castlereagh's demands were hardly outrageous; indeed, Napoleon termed them more appropriate to a defeated power. But the sum result of the treaties concluded in the summer of 1814 was that Great Britain had already secured what she considered to be her vital interests, political, strategic and commercial, on the continent and overseas; and this left her in a relatively strong position when in the autumn the Congress of Vienna assembled to complete the work of peacemaking in central and eastern Europe.

The Congress of Vienna (October 1814–June 1815) marked a further stage in the establishment of that great-power directorate that was to characterize the European states system in the nineteenth century. From the start, the four allied ministers were unanimous in their determination 'that the conduct of the business must practically rest with the leading Powers' and that 'the effective Cabinet should not be carried beyond the six Powers of the first order', that is, the four allies and France and Spain, who would promulgate the new order to the rest of Europe. The French representative, Talleyrand, took a different view, and demanded the immediate summoning of the full Congress – an attempt to revive the eighteenth-century traditions of French policy, and to pose as the patron of France's old clientèle of German and Italian rulers – particularly of the Kings of Naples and Saxony, both cousins of Louis XVIII. This was completely counter-productive and only confirmed the solidarity of the four allies in their determination 'to preserve the initiative within their own hands' – even if, as Castlereagh admitted, this might be 'rather repulsive to France'. As a result, although the Allies decided to assign certain specialized issues to auxiliary councils – such as that on the organization of the German states – and although they were prepared to allow France and Spain to join them in promulgating the final decisions of the Congress to the rest of Europe, the actual decision-making process at the Congress of Vienna was largely confined to the 'Cabinet' of four.

Many of the decisions of the Congress had been determined in advance, either by wartime agreements between members of the coalition, or by decisions taken at Chaumont and Paris concerning the territories bordering on France. One major question remained completely open, however: the destiny of the Prussian and Austrian territories from which Napoleon had created a client Grand Duchy of Warsaw under his most faithful German ally, the King of Saxony. Here, Metternich was soon to regret that he had not managed to commit his northern allies to anything more precise than the 'amicable arrangement' alluded to in the Treaty of Teplitz. Such an arrangement, it soon transpired, would be far to seek. The Emperor Alexander, inspired by his Polish adviser, Czartoriski, and fortified by the presence of half a million Russian soldiers in the Grand Duchy, was determined to transform it into an autonomous constitutional kingdom for himself. He was wont to plead his alleged duty to the Polish nation in justification of his plan; but it also made sense in terms of Russian ideas of the balance of power: the other powers had made, or were due to make, large gains in the west, and if Russia were to be compensated for her great sacrifices in the common war effort, geography dictated that that could only be in the Grand Duchy. And after all, Alexander had had good reason to expect, ever since the Treaty of Kalisch, that Prussia would concur in his plans, abandoning her former Polish territories in exchange for the acquisition of the remaining, German, territories of Napoleon's Saxon ally.

The Austrians were, of course, appalled at the prospect of such a drastic shift of the balance of power in favour of their northern neighbours. The disappearance of the kingdom of Saxony would double the length of the frontier Austria had to defend against Prussia, while the establishment of a Russian salient deep into the heart of central Europe would pose a threat, not merely to the Austrian province of Galicia (which had no natural defensive frontier to the north), but to the security of both Vienna and Berlin. It was the implications of the Russian plan for the independence of the two great German monarchies that most preoccupied Castlereagh: an Austria and Prussia permanently in awe of Russia could hardly provide in central Europe those 'great masses' that he looked to in order to keep France in order. On the Polish–Saxon question, the alliance had split down the middle.

At first, Castlereagh tried to find a solution within the framework of the alliance. (He had originally considered bringing the French into play; but he had found Talleyrand deeply suspicious of Austrian designs in Italy, and so concerned about the rights of Louis XVIII's Neapolitan and Saxon cousins that he even seemed prepared to abet Alexander's designs in Poland if he could thereby save Saxony.) For a few weeks in October, Castlereagh seemed to be succeeding, when he persuaded both Metternich and his Prussian counterpart, Hardenberg, to agree to a package deal: the two German powers were to reclaim their territories in the Grand Duchy, confining Russia behind the frontier of 1795, Prussia acquiring Saxony as a reward for her co-operation. On 3 November, however, this scheme collapsed, when Alexander, in a personal interview, prevailed on King Frederick William to stand by the Kalisch arrangement. From this point, the Grand Duchy of Warsaw was lost to Russia. There was no way in which peripheral Great Britain and feeble Austria could prevail in east-central Europe against a Russo-Prussian combination; and the two powers simply had to reconcile themselves to a 'Polish' settlement that did not accord at all with their ideas of a desirable balance of power.

To make matters worse, the Prussians now began to demand, in extraordinarily bellicose language, immediate recognition of their claim to Saxony. Not only did this portend a preponderance of the northern powers that would be completely intolerable for the Austrians; it also threatened to perpetuate and intensify that old rivalry between the two German powers that had given such opportunities for French and Russian meddling in the eighteenth century – the very antithesis of Castlereagh's objective of a strong central Europe to keep France in order. At this juncture, Castlereagh stood firm, telling the Prussians straight out that he was prepared to break up the Congress and return to London. His hand was strengthened by the news of the conclusion of peace between Great Britain and the United States that reached Vienna on 1 January; and on 3 January he joined with Metternich to conclude a defensive alliance with the French. As the issue now was not Poland, but simply the rights of the king of Saxony, Talleyrand proved amenable enough; and in the face of this display of determination, and finding that the Tsar, now satisfied in Poland, had deserted them, the Prussians gave way, agreeing to content themselves with the northern portion of Saxony. On this basis, a compromise could be achieved.

The settlement of the details of the Saxon question was a tribute to the untiring diplomatic activity of Castlereagh. In an exhausting series of personal interviews, he persuaded Metternich to concede to Prussia a better strategic frontier in Saxony than the military party in Vienna had been prepared to allow, while he brought Frederick William to abandon his claim to the 'trophy' of Leipzig. To reconcile the king to this crucial renunciation, he not only persuaded Alexander to return to Prussia a slice of her former territory (Posen) in the Grand Duchy, but provided further compensation in western Germany in the form of territories that had been earmarked for Hanover and Holland. The upshot was a German settlement that was tolerable for both leading German powers. A resurrection of the rivalry that had so weakened central Europe in the eighteenth century had been avoided. Indeed, the Prussians, now decidedly disillusioned with their erstwhile Russian partners, began to drift into the Austrian camp – to the extent that by 1818 Frederick William was routinely consulting Metternich even about such matters as the appointment of Prussian ministers. Similarly, in the south, Bavaria was reconciled to returning Salzburg and the Tyrol to Austria by the recovery of the Palatinate. Relations between the states of the planned German Confederation promised to be relatively harmonious while the reinforcement of Holland, Hanover and the Palatinate by the strengthening of Prussia in the west, together with the guarantee to Switzerland, meant that France was well and truly hemmed in – and gave some substance to Castlereagh's boast that 'a better defence has been provided for Germany than has existed at any former period of her history'.

The crisis in the alliance over the Polish-Saxon question had wide repercussions on the Vienna settlement in central and western Europe. In the first place, the character of the future German Confederation had been much affected by the quarrel between Vienna and Berlin at the end of 1814. Until then, the Austrians and Prussians had been virtually in agreement that the proposed confederation should have an effective central directory consisting of five leading German states under Austro-Prussian leadership. Now, the Austrians decided that Prussia could not be trusted, and aligned themselves with the middle states. The upshot was a confederation that was very loosely organized, under the formal presidency of Austria, and in which the emphasis was very much on the sovereign rights of the thirty-nine member states (and which even, as a further sop to the middle states, envisaged the establishment of constitutional régimes). In international terms the confederation, of which the federal forces could be mobilized only for defensive wars, suited the satiated, *status quo* powers, such as Austria and Great Britain, perfectly; and if the shift of Prussian power from east to west in the final stages of the Saxon negotiations implied that Prussia might some day take up the challenge to unite her scattered provinces, Prussia seemed ready enough, in the immediate aftermath of the crisis, to act as Austria's lieutenant in defence of the existing arrangements. These were further reinforced by the presence in the confederation of the kings of Holland and Denmark (as rulers of Luxemburg and Holstein respectively) and by its association with Great Britain through Hanover and the British acquisition of Heligoland off the north German coast. Notably absent from these arrangements were, of course, France and Russia, guarantors of the Treaty of Teschen of 1779 and authors of the great reorganization of Germany of 1803. Those days were clearly over; and although Alexander I, five of whose brothers and sisters were married into German ruling houses, might still hope to play the dynastic card if an opportunity arose, it seemed that the constitutional arrangements for Germany, like the territorial, provided Austria and Great Britain with a sound basis for defending what seemed to them an appropriate balance of power.

In the second place, as the crisis over Saxony saw the admission of France into the decision-making forum, it promised to have wide repercussions in south-central Europe too. Indeed, Talleyrand's belated

MAP 1 *Central Europe in 1815*

appreciation that France's best chance lay in exploiting the divisions between the allies, rather than in trying to pose as the leader of the excluded
powers against them, was rewarded, not only in Saxony, but in southern
Italy. For months, and despite British sympathy, he had made no progress
in his campaign on behalf of Ferdinand IV of Naples, still confined to his
Sicilian dominions while Napoleon's henchman Murat ruled in Naples
with the blessing of his new Austrian friends. To the latter, mindful of
prolonged conflicts with France and Spain over Italy in the eighteenth
century, Murat in Naples seemed infinitely preferable to a Bourbon. During
the bargaining over Saxony, however, Metternich gave way to the French
– he was in any case beginning to take umbrage at the hospitality accorded
by King Murat to a host of malcontents from the restored regimes in
north and central Italy. Castlereagh readily gave his blessing and himself
negotiated the final arrangements with the French: King Ferdinand was to
be restored in Naples and in return Louis XVIII would recognize Austrian
predominance in central Italy. The French king, it seemed, had managed
to do something for the legitimate interests of both his Saxon and his
Neapolitan cousins.

In the event, things turned out very differently. With the return of
Napoleon and the revival of the coalition, all Talleyrand's diplomatic
achievements went for nothing, and France's voice was not heard in the
final settlement of the German and Italian questions at Vienna. Murat
sealed his own fate by precipitately joining Napoleon; but, with Louis
XVIII in exile in Brussels and with no recognized government in Paris,
it was as an Austrian, not as a French client that King Ferdinand was
restored to his Neapolitan throne. In July the king signed a treaty with
the Austrians that put his kingdom in Austrian tutelage and committed
himself not to change its constitution without Austrian consent. In the
rest of Italy, meanwhile, Metternich was no longer in the least constrained
by any need to consider his erstwhile French partners. Habsburg client
rulers were restored in Tuscany and Modena; although the Treaty of
Fontainebleau had been invalidated by Napoleon's return, his Habsburg
wife, Marie Louise, retained Parma, to the exclusion of the Spanish Bourbons; and Metternich even managed to extract from an indignant Pius VII
the right to garrison the papal fortress of Ferrara. Austrian control of
Italy, backed up by British control of the Aegean islands across the Straits
of Otranto, indeed appeared complete. Again it seemed that Great Britain
and Austria had achieved the balance of power that suited them. Whether
they would be able to maintain it, given the deficiencies of Austria's
resources and the fact that the settlement both rested on and implied the

eclipse of France and the disappointment of her expectations, was an open question.

The French were soon to have even more pressing grievances as the disastrous consequences of the 'Hundred Days' episode became clear. As in 1813–14 the damage was self-inflicted; if, then, Napoleon's obstinacy had thrown away the opportunity of a relatively favourable peace, so now his new challenge to the allies vitiated all that Talleyrand had recently achieved by exploiting the divisions amongst them. The disintegrating coalition re-formed, for the express purpose of invading France and over-throwing Napoleon. His fall was speedily accomplished, by British and Prussian forces, at Waterloo (18 June); and Wellington, at the head of the army that took Paris, and therefore enjoying a position comparable with that of Alexander fifteen months before, made haste to restore the Bourbons immediately. The author of the Treaty of Fontainebleau, who had been toying with the idea of an Orleanist, or even a conservative republican, regime, found himself in turn presented with a *fait accompli*.

This contretemps apart, however, the British and the Russians were broadly of one mind as regards the international aspects of the restoration settlement; and this combination of the two leading powers was, not surprisingly, decisive in the peace negotiations. Indeed, their very rivalry served to consolidate their unity: both British and Russian negotiators were each concerned to avoid driving France into the arms of the other; and both viewed her as a potentially useful member of the states system. True, others were less far-sighted, and saw in France's prostrate condition only an opportunity for vengeance or booty. The Prussians, reviving their claims of 1792 to Alsace, led the small west German states and the Dutch in an annexationist campaign; and even Metternich, solicitous for Austria's position in the planned German confederation, felt obliged to pay at least lip service to demands for the permanent cession of France's frontier for-tresses to her German neighbours. Meanwhile, Castlereagh was striving to bring to reason a home government that talked of depriving France of everything she had acquired since the days of Louis XIV: 'It is not our business to collect trophies, but to try if we can to return the world to peaceful habits.' Fortunately for him, the big battalions were on this occasion on the side of the more statesmanlike approach. Metternich was instinctively for moderation and Castlereagh could always count on Russian support – especially when Talleyrand was succeeded as first minister by the Duke de Richelieu, a former emigré who had served Alexander for years as a successful governor of Odessa. Together, they prevailed over the Prussians, the German states and the government in London.

Indeed, the declared aim of the preamble of the Second Treaty of Paris (20 November 1815) was to restore 'those relations of reciprocal confidence and goodwill which the fatal effects of the Revolution and of the system of Conquest had for so long a time disturbed'. In territorial terms, France lost virtually nothing beyond the gains the First Treaty of Paris had allowed her to retain in Savoy. However, the allies' determination also to secure 'proper indemnities for the past and solid guarantees for the future' was reflected in certain symbolic stipulations for the return of plundered art treasures and the imprisonment of Bonaparte and in the rather more onerous provision for the payment of an indemnity of Fr. 700,000,000, part of which was to be spent on strengthening the border defences of the Netherlands, the German Confederation, and Savoy. As a further precaution, in case the French were still unwilling to mend their ways, the Treaty provided for the temporary occupation by allied forces of fourteen frontier fortresses and some eastern provinces of France. These terms reflected the prime concern of the allies with security, together with Alexander's desire to assume the role of France's protector, and Castlereagh's fear that harsher terms would only undermine the Bourbon regime and jeopardize the chances of France's settling down as a contented element in a stable states system.

The French, of course, saw things differently. For them, the central fact was that since 1789 all four allies had made extensive gains, either overseas, or, through the last three partitions of Poland, in Europe itself. For France now to be driven back to her prewar frontiers amounted to a major shift of the eighteenth-century balance of power to her detriment. Indeed, it was precisely in terms of a just balance of power that the French laid claim to Belgium and the Rhineland: this had been the French argument throughout the 1814 peace negotiations and it was to remain the argument of all French regimes, of whatever political complexion, for the next half century. The insuperable problem for all these regimes, however, was that every overt attempt to promote their concept of a just balance of power made its realization impossible, because it always revived against France that very coalition that had imposed the 'unjust' frontiers of 1815 in the first place. Indeed, however divided the allies might be over other issues, and however much they might wish to welcome a chastened France back into their community, they had all been taught by their experience of French hegemonial pretensions since 1789 that the new balance of power in the west was absolutely essential to the maintenance of peace and stability. The allies were certainly not indisposed to be conciliatory, as the Treaty of 20 November bore witness; but as even Castlereagh had ruefully to admit, 'nothing can keep France quiet and within bounds but the strong hand of European power'.

Quadruple Alliance and Holy Alliance, 1815–20

That Castlereagh's allies shared his determination to banish for ever the dangers that had plagued Europe for the last twenty years was demonstrated when, simultaneously with the Second Treaty of Paris, they adopted a proposal of Castlereagh's for a defensive Quadruple Alliance. This committed the four powers to immediate joint military action in the event of a Bonapartist restoration in France or a French attack on the frontiers recently established at Vienna and Paris. Should the French danger manifest itself in a less overtly expansionist form – some other internal upheaval in France, for example – the allies were only committed to joint consultations. It was a sign of the allies' seriousness of purpose – and rather novel – that they undertook these obligations against France for a period of twenty years. Even more novel, they went on to attempt to regulate their future relations with each other.

To this end, Castlereagh had originally hoped to include in the peace settlement a general guarantee of frontiers; but this had come to nothing, partly because Russia and Turkey had been in dispute ever since they had made peace in 1812, as to where their common frontier actually lay. Castlereagh still wished to do something, however, to enhance the durability of the settlement – not so much by creating new machinery, as by perpetuating those habits of co-operation that his experiences of coalition diplomacy had taught him over the past two years. In this, he was the precursor, not of the League of Nations, but of the summit conference. The passionate belief he had come to hold in 'the habits of confidential intercourse which long residence with the principal actors has established' make Castlereagh unique in the ranks of British statesmen and it was reflected in the famous Article VI of the Quadruple Alliance, which pledged the allies 'to consolidate the connexions which at present so closely unite the four sovereigns, for the happiness of the world, . . . to renew their meetings at fixed periods . . . for the consideration of the measures which at each of those periods shall be considered the most salutary for the repose and prosperity of nations and for the maintenance of the peace of Europe'. This last was, of course, a somewhat imprecise commitment, under which much could be done, or much refused; and whether it would in practice fulfil Castlereagh's hopes, remained to be seen.

After the war ended, allied unity was bound to come under strain, with the temporary removal of the French threat that had underpinned it, and the persistence of divergent attitudes amongst the allies towards the new balance of power. Great Britain, for example, had emerged from the peace settlement as a satiated power. Thanks to her own efforts and those of her allies she had attained her main objective – the containment of France; and even if, as her army was demobilized after 1815, Great Britain was to cease to be a land power of the first order, France remained hemmed in by a chain of buffer states backed up by Prussia in the north and Austria in the south, and further reinforced by the Quadruple Alliance of November 1815. In the world at large, moreover, in naval, strategic and commercial terms, Great Britain emerged as far and away the strongest power; and she had upheld her so-called maritime rights in defiance of protests from neutrals the world over. True, the new balance of power was not perfect, even in British eyes: the establishment of the Kingdom of Poland portended a continuation of the steady advance of Russian influence in central Europe; and nothing had been done to bring the ailing Ottoman Empire under the protection of the community of great powers. But despite these deficiencies, a combination of Great Britain and the two German powers might yet provide some security against both a revanchist France and an adventurist Russia; just as the Quadruple Alliance was to keep France in quarantine, it might equally well serve as a straitjacket to hold Russia to a common line of action – or inaction – with Great Britain and her German partners.

If the British strove to uphold the 1815 order because a balance of power and peace on the continent were considered essential to their position as the world's leading trading power, the Austrians pursued an identical objective from a rather more modest starting point. Like Great Britain, Austria emerged from the peace settlement as a satiated power, but also as a dangerously over-extended power. She had achieved, by dint of a skilful diplomacy that exploited both the combined efforts and the divergent interests of the allies in the war against Napoleon, a position in Italy and Germany that she could hardly maintain in the long run. In economic terms, the Habsburg Monarchy was a weak, agrarian power, unable to compete with France and Great Britain in terms of material resources, and lacking the manpower with which Russia made up for her deficiencies in that respect. The first years of peace, which saw a major financial crisis in Austria, with the revival of British industrial and Russian agrarian exports, soon revealed the hollowness of the domestic basis of Austria's great-power position. With a population of 30 million and an army of a mere 230,000, there could be no question of the Monarchy's attempting to maintain that position by sheer force against potential threats in Italy, Germany and the Near East. (Even the little expedition to Naples in 1821 was to throw the finances into virtual bankruptcy and undo much of the work of recovery since the Napoleonic wars.) As far as the Austrian empire was concerned, the argument of force, the *ultima ratio* that alone could give reality to the claim of any state to be a great power, was lacking. Hence, the efforts of Austrian statesmen on the one hand to establish legitimacy and respect for treaty rights as the basis for international relations, and on the other to perpetuate the power constellation that had created the order of 1815. Left to herself in a states system based on *Realpolitik* and naked power, Austria simply lacked the resources to maintain her position – as the 1850s and 1860s were to show.

Already in the years immediately after 1815, Austria faced a number of potential threats: in the west, from French revisionism, insofar as it was directed against Austrian control of Italy; from the expansion of Russian power generally, that made itself felt in Germany to the north, and in the Ottoman territories that bordered the empire to the south and east; and, worst of all, from a combination of the two 'flanking' powers. Like the British, however, the Austrians found security in the Quadruple Alliance of November 1815. On the one hand, it kept France in isolation; and to underscore this, and to ward off the dreaded Franco-Russian alignment, Metternich soon became very adept at depicting France as a hotbed of revolutionary dangers: 'It is in Paris, Sire,' he told the Tsar in 1818, 'that the great furnace exists from which the sparks of revolution fly.' On the other hand, the Alliance served to control Russia, a function which Metternich reinforced by exploiting – generally with Castlereagh's co-operation – those personal relationships that had grown out of the unusual degree of contact between the leaders of the coalition in 1814–15.

Even if Alexander himself, with his memories of the wartime coalition, was usually ready co-operate with Castlereagh and Metternich, his advisers, unencumbered by their master's emotional attachment to allied solidarity, were strongly averse to accepting Anglo-Austrian leadership of the alliance. The Corfiote Capo d'Istrias, for example, was personally extremely aggrieved at the refusal of the British to grant constitutional government to his compatriots in the Ionian Islands, and was beginning to see the best hope of the eventual liberation of the Greek people in a Russian alignment with France – an alignment ardently advocated by the

Corsican Pozzo di Borgo, Russian ambassador in Paris. The fact remained, moreover, that of all the victorious powers Russia was the least satisfied with the settlement of 1815, which all Russian statesmen, from the Emperor down, felt had failed to provide Russia with benefits commensurate with her exertions. Of all the continental powers, Russia had made the greatest military contribution to victory; and in the years between the entry of the Russian army into Paris and its defeat in the Crimean War – years when technology had yet to make its impact on the military balance – the myth of Russian invincibility still made its contribution to the Tsar's claim to a leading role in continental affairs. Not that Russian statesmen aspired to hegemony in a Napoleonic sense: indeed, all felt the need of a *point d'appui* in the west, whether in the wartime alliance as Alexander preferred, or in France as his advisers sometimes recommended. All Russian policy-makers were agreed, however, that the balance as established in 1815 was fraudulent: while a continental balance had been established that was largely acceptable to all the victorious powers, the settlement had quite failed to provide any check whatever on Great Britain's maritime predominance in the rest of the world. Overall, therefore, it was not a balance with which a world power such as Russia could rest content.

Certainly, on the continent itself, Russia was well placed to expand her influence further than ever before into central Europe – and could even dispense with that co-operation with France that had facilitated her interference in Germany in the generation after 1779. The Polish salient acquired in 1815 now ensured that her views would carry weight in Vienna and Berlin; and Alexander's close dynastic ties with Prussia, the Netherlands and the rulers of the south German states gave him a measure of influence in the confederation. Even in more distant Italy, where Metternich was belatedly attempting to make good an omission of the Congress of Vienna by subjecting the Italian states to a confederation on the German model, the Russians were able on several occasions to co-operate on an *ad hoc* basis with the French to frustrate him. But where could the Russian world-empire turn for assistance in its clash of interests with Great Britain, from Persia and the Ottoman empire to the coasts of California? Co-operation with the United States government, which shared Russia's indignation about Great Britain's arrogant assertion of her so-called maritime rights in the face of the united opinion of the world, was vitiated by the fact that Russia and the United States were themselves at odds over North Pacific claims; and although the Russians on several occasions pleaded for an international naval operation in the Mediterranean against the Barbary pirates, and although in 1816 the United

States actually sent a squadron to operate against them, it was the British who, with supreme contempt for these gestures, single-handedly took the matter in hand themselves in 1817. Certainly, the Quadruple Alliance, and its administrative organ, the conference of ambassadors at Paris, where Russia found herself constantly in a minority of one to three, could offer her no salvation. It was in vain that Pozzo di Borgo denounced the determination of Great Britain and Austria 'to keep France and Spain politically excommunicated in order to paralyse Russia', while his colleague in Madrid dismissed Metternich as 'le factotum de l'Angleterre sur le continent'. There was, however, a chance that Russia might break out of the constraints of the Quadruple Alliance and secure the support of other powers in establishing a genuine world balance: if something could be made of the seemingly meaningless Holy Alliance of September 1815.

In its original form, the Holy Alliance was hardly a practical diplomatic instrument at all. It arose from an admixture of doctrines of the Enlightenment, which Alexander I had imbibed from his tutors, and of a deeply personal Christianity, which had gained a hold over the emperor's mind during the war of liberation. Alexander's original draft spoke of the need to break with the diplomacy of the past and to found a new international order in which sovereigns and peoples would unite, merging existing states and armies into one, to defend the 'sacred principles which our Divine Saviour has taught to mankind'. The more sober final version, as amended by Metternich, eliminating both the condemnation of the past and the vision of a future merging of states and armies, was a simple alliance of sovereigns dedicated to the same noble ends. It was signed in the first instance by the rulers of Russia, Austria and Prussia, but all other states were invited to accede to it – although the Prince Regent of Great Britain, for constitutional reasons, could do no more than send an autograph letter endorsing the principles of the Alliance, and the Sultan of Turkey and the Pope refused to sign for religious reasons. In fact, neither Metternich nor Castlereagh regarded the Alliance as having any political significance whatever, the former dismissing it as 'a loud-sounding nothing', the latter as 'a piece of sublime mysticism and nonsense'. But after their experiences at the Congress of Vienna they welcomed the emperor's preoccupation with such visions, rather than with projects of expansion. Nor does the original Holy Alliance deserve its later reputation as an engine of reaction. Indeed, in 1816 the United States senate discussed joining it; and the Swiss Confederation actually joined; and it was significant that in Russia Alexander published the original text with its vision of a union of peoples.

It was not long, however, before the Holy Alliance developed a practical political function: as the basis of a states system resting, not on the four-power directory propounded by Castlereagh and Metternich, but on a general alliance of all powers, great and small. This function, while perhaps always inherent in the Alliance, really developed as a response to the Quadruple Alliance, signed two months later; and it reflected growing Russian resentment at the constraints imposed by the four-power directory, and the resentment of France at her exclusion from it. In a general alliance Russia might be able to bring other maritime powers, such as France, Spain and possibly the United States, into play, and to replace the 'fraudulent' continental balance of 1815 by a genuine 'world' balance of power. Whether this general alliance would be the Holy Alliance itself – which would bring Russia the added bonus of the self-exclusion of Great Britain and Turkey from the directing body – or some other general alliance in which Russia, France and their satellites would take the lead was fairly immaterial, and in these years, the use of term 'the alliance' was exceedingly imprecise. The essential issue, however – and it was to remain the issue until the emergence in 1820 of a third type of Alliance, the reactionary 'Neo-Holy Alliance' of the Congress of Troppau – was whether the European states system was to function on the basis of the Quadruple Alliance or of the Holy Alliance or some similar *alliance générale*.

Russian hopes of building on a Bourbon connexion as a counterweight to Anglo-Austrian domination of the international system were, of course, hampered so long as France remained in quarantine and constrained to dealing with the four occupying powers as a collective body. During the first three years of peace, while the question of the external status of France revolved round such issues as the army of occupation and the payment of the indemnity, which were handled by the four allies collectively through a conference of ambassadors in permanent session in Paris, the Anglo-Austrian combination was generally successful in establishing the international system on the basis of the Quadruple Alliance, in frustrating the efforts of Richelieu and Pozzo di Borgo to develop a special relationship between France and Russia, and, indeed, until the summer of 1820 in safeguarding both Austria's interests in central Europe and Great Britain's position as a world power.

Even in these years, however, the Anglo-Austrian position was exposed to serious challenge. The power relationships of 1815 were not frozen for ever in time; and already by 1817 the allies were agreed that France would soon have to be freed from the emergency controls imposed on her by the Second Peace of Paris. Her economy had recovered more rapidly than those of the allies and she was making rapid progress towards paying off the indemnity; while the continued presence of the army of occupation was, in Wellington's view, proving more an inflammatory than a stabilizing force. The allies determined, therefore, that these last relics of the recent conflict should be wound up in 1818 – the earliest date envisaged by the peace treaty; and that a congress, summoned in accordance with Article VI of the Quadruple Alliance would be the most convenient instrument both for ratifying these changes and for defining the future role of independent France in Europe. It was the necessity of adjusting to these changes that posed the first serious threat to the states system as organized by Castlereagh and Metternich. From the start, the French were quite adamant that the Quadruple Alliance must be transformed into a Quintuple Alliance with France as an equal member, or, ideally, abolished altogether. They were ably seconded by Pozzo di Borgo who reminded Alexander that the time had now come to revert to the principle of 'the independence of nations' and to put an end to 'this four-power Areopagus that arrogates to itself the right to decide the affairs of the rest of Europe'. Hence, the forthcoming congress should not be confined to the four allies and France, but should be open to all the states of Europe. Castlereagh and Metternich, by contrast, ever averse to opening doors to Franco-Russian co-operation or to conceding to those powers the right to meddle in the affairs of central Europe, stubbornly insisted in reply that 'the repose of Europe is intimately bound up with the maintenance of the Quadruple Alliance in its primitive integrity'.

In the event, the Anglo-Austrian view prevailed. It was, after all, the Tsar himself and not his advisers who determined Russian policy, and luckily for Castlereagh and Metternich, Alexander arrived at Aix full of goodwill towards his erstwhile coalition colleagues and declaring that any special Russian alignment with France would be nothing less than a 'criminal betrayal' of the Quadruple Alliance. The advantages of congress diplomacy as a method of settling matters of detail when the powers were already agreed in principle was amply demonstrated when the questions of the occupation and the indemnity payments were settled in a matter of a few days. Moreover, Castlereagh and Metternich were able to exploit their renewed contact with Alexander to thwart a number of offensives by the partisans of Franco-Russian co-operation elsewhere in the world. They persuaded him to abandon plans for an international naval operation against the Barbary pirates in the Mediterranean; to forbid his agents to support a French proposal for a European trade embargo against the rebellious Spanish American colonies; and to discountenance a proposal from the exceedingly active Russian minister in Turin for a frontier adjustment in favour of Sardinia.

It was ominous for the future of congress diplomacy, however, that when discussion moved on to a question about which the allies were not already agreed in principle, a fierce and prolonged debate ensued. When the question of the future position of France in Europe was raised, the Tsar seemed to waver and it took Castlereagh and Metternich some three weeks to get him back into line. In November, for example, Alexander permitted Capo d'Istrias to propose the establishment of an *alliance générale*, guaranteeing not only the existing territorial settlement between the states of Europe, but the established political order within them. From the start, Castlereagh was adamant in resisting this: he was fully prepared to stand by the commitments Great Britain had assumed at the end of the last war; but Parliament would not agree to any new alliance, let alone one of such a far-reaching nature. The Prussians, by contrast, worried about the obvious unpopularity of their rule in the recently acquired Catholic Rhineland, and even Metternich, conscious of the threat posed by revolutionary ideas to his master's fragile empire, had to admit that the proposed guarantee of thrones had its attractions. But Metternich's more immediate fear was of a possible Franco-Russian diplomatic combination, for which such a new alliance could all too easily provide an opening. In the end, he joined Castlereagh in insisting that the Quadruple Alliance remain the basis of the international order; and again the Anglo-Austrian combination won the day.

The upshot was that the Quadruple Alliance against France was explicitly renewed; and it was also agreed, as an isolated France might prove a source of trouble, to link her into the system by inviting her to attend any future congresses summoned under Article VI. To this extent, the Congress of Aix-la-Chapelle marked the transfer of control over the European states system from a four-power directory to a 'Pentarchy' of powers. It must be emphasized, however, that within the Pentarchy the Quadruple Alliance continued to fulfil its function of containing France and controlling Russia; French hopes of breaking out of isolation by establishing a special link with Russia had again come to nothing. The French certainly had no illusions about this, and Richelieu returned to Paris complaining bitterly about the inveterate suspicion of France that still characterized British and Austrian attitudes. True, the basis of Anglo-Austrian control of the alliance was Alexander's willingness to continue to give priority to solidarity with his wartime allies; and the tussle over the proposed *alliance générale* had exposed the fragility of this basis. For the present, however, it had been reaffirmed; and before he left Aix, Alexander gave Castlereagh permission to write to him personally about any problems that might arise in future – an extraordinary gesture towards a British foreign secretary, and one that Castlereagh was to make full use of. Castlereagh himself, undeterred by criticism from an increasingly isolationist cabinet in London (where Canning described the Aix agreements as 'new and very questionable'), readily reaffirmed, in the declaration of Aix-la-Chapelle, all Great Britain's existing alliance obligations. Indeed, the bases of the 1815 system had been reaffirmed in all their essentials; and Metternich, too, left Aix well content: 'Je n'ai jamais vu de plus joli petit congrès'.

The problem of revolution and the Neo-Holy Alliance, 1820–21

Anglo-Austrian domination of the system continued for the next two years and, indeed, seemed only to draw strength from signs of opposition to the order it represented. Of course, these were years of considerable social discontent, arising from the transition to peacetime commercial competition; and the discontent of the intelligentsia – Metternich's 'agitated classes' – assumed a variety of forms, ranging from liberal demands for the freedoms embodied in the French Revolution to a Romantic reaction, particularly in Germany, against both the imperialism of the Revolution and the betrayal of German aspirations by the compromises of the Restoration settlement. True, Metternich feared that certain lesser German rulers might pander to these elements by granting the constitutions that had been alluded to in Article XIII of the constitution of the confederation; and in peripheral areas such as Spain and Naples the liberals did indeed enjoy local successes by securing the support of elements in the army. Insofar as they were never in a position to overthrow the established monarchical-aristocratic order in any of the great powers, however, they never constituted a real threat to the system of 1815. On the contrary, the effect they had on the perceptions of the decision-makers only strengthened the hands of the defenders of the established order at a national and international level. In the first place, they helped to convince all governments of the need to stand together against the universal menace. Great Britain was no exception: these were the years that witnessed the Peterloo massacre, and which saw Canning even more eloquent than Castlereagh in denouncing 'the spoiler and the assassin'. In the second place, by helping Metternich to convince the Tsar that France in particular was infected with the germs of revolution – indeed, that a directing committee was co-ordinating the whole vast revolutionary conspiracy from its seat in Paris – they fuelled Alexander's suspicions of France and reinforced the Anglo-Austrian domination of the states system.

Metternich scored one of his most striking successes in the wake of a series of disturbances in Germany, culminating in March 1819 in the murder by an unbalanced student of August Kotzebue, a journalist writing in the service of Alexander I himself. Metternich determined 'to draw the greatest political advantage from the matter' and after making sure of the support of the King of Prussia at Teplitz in July, he spent the whole of August in meetings with representatives of the other German states at Karlsbad. The resultant 'decisions' were elaborated in further conferences in Vienna and were incorporated by the Diet into German Federal Law in 1820. They provided for greater control of intellectual activity; the redefinition in a strictly monarchical sense of the constitutional provisions of the Federal Act; and for the establishment at Mainz of a commission to investigate subversive individuals. The seriousness of the threat may be doubted: in a dozen years the Mainz commission discovered only 73 subversive individuals in the whole of Germany. But the 'Karlsbad decrees' were to set the tone for Metternich's control of the confederation on the basis of 'dualism': with an obedient Prussia in tow he could exploit 'federal obligations' to whittle away the 'state rights' of the third Germany. Certainly others suspected his motives. The French complained, and some of Alexander's relatives in south-west Germany raised questions in St Petersburg – which found an echo in a circular from Capo d'Istrias. But Alexander himself, increasingly worried by the spectre of revolution, did not respond while George IV's ministers in Hanover enforced the 'Karlsbad decrees' without demur. True, Castlereagh refused to accept Metternich's argument that the matter was also the concern of the Alliance and that Great Britain herself should endorse the new measures. Only in the case of France might Great Britain be obliged to take up a position on the internal affairs of another state; and the opposition in Parliament had been vocal in its criticism of the decrees. He made haste to assure Metternich nevertheless that 'we are always pleased to see evil germs destroyed, even if we are unable to give our approval openly'; and Metternich understood: 'he is like a man who hears good music in church: he would like to applaud but dare not'.

Until the summer of 1820 Anglo-Austrian domination of the states system extended even to the western periphery of the continent. When a military putsch forced the King of Spain to revive the extreme liberal constitution of 1812 the French made another effort to break out of the constraints of the 1815 settlement. Initially, they manoeuvred to promote French influence in Madrid through a regime modelled on their own: the policy of *exportation de la Charte* that they were later to pursue in Italy; but when this was scotched by the British, the French declared that the time had come for an international discussion of events in Spain, perhaps even for military intervention. When this idea was taken up in Russian diplomatic circles, Castlereagh and Metternich found themselves again confronted with a Franco-Russian bid for leadership of the states system.

The British were at once on guard: Wellington, on the strength of his experiences of the Peninsula campaign, expatiated on the uselessness of attempting to impose a regime on the Spaniards by military means, while cabinet discussions in London resulted in Castlereagh's famous state paper of 5 May 1820, defining the British position on intervention in the internal affairs of other states. While Castlereagh fully admitted the right of any state to interfere in the internal affairs of another state if its own interests were threatened, he rejected utterly the view that such intervention was a matter for the Alliance. The purposes of the Alliance had been clearly defined in the treaty of November 1815, renewed at Aix; they covered the case of intervention in France in certain circumstances, and Great Britain would continue 'to be found in place when danger threatens'. The Alliance was, however, 'never intended as an organization for the government of the world. . . . It was never so explained to Parliament.' Moreover, if Great Britain could not recognize any general right of intervention to uphold existing regimes, in the particular case of Spain, who was not threatening anybody, there was no case for intervention by any power. The effect of the state paper in Paris and St Petersburg was forceful enough to silence all talk of intervention for the time being; and it was significant that Metternich – who, much as he disliked the revolution in Spain, disliked the prospect of French or Russian troops marching to suppress it even more – gave Castlereagh his full support. 'Magisterial inaction', he sententiously observed, was the only practical course available to the powers in Spain. Anglo-Austrian domination of the Pentarchy seemed set to continue.

Within a matter of weeks Metternich was jolted out of his complacency, when a military putsch established a constitutional regime in Naples (1 July). Here, 'magisterial inaction' would not suffice: if the Revolution were allowed to triumph in Naples the example was bound to imperil the weak pro-Austrian regimes in central Italy, perhaps even the

Lombardo-Venetian kingdom and the Austrian monarchy itself. From the start, Metternich determined on military intervention; and both the general threat and the stipulations of the Austro-Neapolitan treaty of July 1814 (which forbade constitutional changes in the kingdom without Austrian consent) gave him a fair case in international law. These arguments were readily accepted in London, where Wellington urged on the Austrian ambassador the need for haste: 80,000 men could now settle what might take 200,000 later – 'it is time to make an example'; while Castlereagh gave what encouragement he could by ordering the strengthening of the British Mediterranean squadron.

On this occasion, however, the Anglo-Austrian partnership was not to have things all its own way. The French viewed events in Naples with a mixture of alarm and expectation. On the one hand, they had no wish to see Metternich repeat his recent success in Germany and 'make Austria the absolute mistress of Italy', 'on the pretext' as Pozzo di Borgo slyly put it, 'of punishing the revolutionaries'. On the other hand, France might hope to find in Italy the opportunity so recently denied her in Spain to break out of the constraints of the 1815 system, especially if she could promote the establishment of a moderate constitutional regime in Naples, under the protection, not of Austria, but of the Pentarchy. A French circular of 10 August duly announced that Louis XVIII, as head of the House of Bourbon, was the sovereign most affected by the revolution in Naples, which, moreover, ought to be discussed at a congress summoned under the terms of Article VI. Of course, international intervention with a constitutional objective was the very antithesis of the single-handed Austrian intervention to restore the *status quo* that Metternich and Castlereagh had had in mind; and Metternich tried desperately to head the French off by proposing confidential discussions between the Emperor Francis and the Tsar (who was about to attend the opening of the Polish diet) at Troppau, in Austrian Silesia – or, better still, an ambassadorial conference under his own chairmanship in Vienna. This was not to be: in Warsaw, Pozzo di Borgo and Capo d'Istrias, aided by a French delegation, prevailed on Alexander to write to Metternich on 28 August, insisting on a full congress in the style of that of Aix-la-Chapelle.

Metternich was now in a dilemma. The revolution in Naples could not be ignored like that in Spain; but Metternich was faced with a stark choice between taking single-handed action as recommended by London, and making any action a matter for the Alliance, as France and Russia were demanding. Even though the debate was essentially one over a point of theory, the latter option would certainly entail a break with the British.

Castlereagh's language to the French ambassador was perfectly clear: to involve the Alliance in the suppression of revolutions would be 'to pervert its essence (*principe*). It is the Holy Alliance as conceived by the Emperor [Alexander] and we cannot endorse it.' Indeed, rather than accept such a redefinition, 'England will be obliged to withdraw from the Alliance.' On the other hand, to line up with Great Britain in defiance of France and Russia could involve great risks: the entente between those two powers would be strengthened; if Russia were seen to be disapproving, revolutionaries everywhere would take heart; finally, it might be hazardous for the Monarchy to throw its armies into Italy in defiance of the formidable military power established since 1815 on its northern frontier (against which a naval power like Great Britain, however well disposed, could never offer material assistance). Metternich could not escape from the harsh realities of the 1815 settlement in central Europe. He decided, therefore, to let the French and Russians have their congress at Troppau, and to concentrate on trying to dissolve the developing entente between them and secure Russian endorsement for the kind of reactionary intervention he had in mind.

The Congress of Troppau (October–December 1820) was dominated by the struggle between Metternich and Capo d'Istrias and his French supporters for control of the mind of Alexander, who was to remain the guest of his Austrian allies for the next eight months. Apart from a few formal sessions, the diplomacy of the congress was conducted in secret negotiations, often *à deux* – a method ideally suited to Metternich, who spent many a long evening in the tiny Silesian town, in endless tea-drinking sessions with Alexander, preaching to him about the universal revolutionary menace emanating from the directing committee in Paris. He was fortunate in that the emperor himself was developing an increasingly reactionary cast of mind in these months; but he played skilfully on Alexander's disillusionment with his recent encounter with an ungrateful Polish diet, and exploited to the full reports of a mutiny in one of the crack guards regiments in St Petersburg. Metternich was also fortunate to find his French opponents less formidable than he had feared. The French position had become impossibly difficult once the British decided to make a show of their aloofness from the proceedings by only sending observers to the congress. The French, suspecting an attempt to win favour in the eyes of Italian liberals, also decided to confine their diplomats to the role of observers; but this only weakened their negotiating position with the eastern powers, while such tentative efforts as they made to plead for a compromise with the Neapolitan regime only widened still further the gulf that was beginning to open between France and Russia.

The upshot was the Preliminary Protocol of 19 November, drafted by Capo d'Istrias, amended by Metternich, and published by the three eastern powers as the Troppau circular of 8 December. This document declared that:

> *states which form part of the alliance and which have undergone a change due to revolution in their form of government, the results of which menace other states,* ipso facto *cease to be part of the alliance and remain excluded from it until their situation gives guarantees of legal order and stability.*

The signatories went on to pledge themselves, 'when the allies can take effective and beneficent action' – a condition inserted by Metternich to exclude the case of Spain – to apply, first, moral pressure and, if necessary, force, to bring erring states back into the bosom of the alliance. This definition of the function of the alliance produced an immediate rift with the British – as, indeed, Capo d'Istrias had perhaps intended. Castlereagh, totally impervious to the allies' claim to be saying nothing new, and their invitation to the British government to join them, issued a public refutation of their arguments and castigated the Troppau Circular as a breach of international law. But although Metternich's yielding to the Russians to the extent of making the suppression of revolutions a matter for the alliance had had embarrassing repercussions in London, it must be emphasized that this contretemps lay largely in the realm of political theory. In practice, the rapport he had established with Alexander had given him all he wanted: he had no difficulty in eliminating from the original draft Capo d'Istrias's allusion to the need to establish in Naples a regime that embodied a 'genuine national wish'; and he had every reason to hope, as the statesmen adjourned to Vienna for Christmas, to reassemble in sunnier climes at Laibach, with the king of Naples in attendance, that the result of any intervention would be the re-establishment of the strictly conservative pro-Austrian regime.

During the adjournment, events again played into Metternich's hands when the Neapolitan regime, ignoring frantic advice from Paris to adopt a French-style charter, opted for the extreme Spanish constitution of 1812. Metternich was relieved: 'the Neapolitans would have embarrassed us terribly if, instead of the constitution of the cortes, they had adopted the Charter.' As it was, Metternich found himself more in control of events at Laibach than at any time in his career. He had Alexander's full backing – Capo d'Istrias was now 'like a devil in holy water' – and he had no difficulty in brushing off French suggestions of mediation 'between vice and virtue': there could be no question of constitutional government for the Neapolitans, 'un peuple à demi africain et barbare'. The 'negotiations' with the King of Naples were the purest farce, a mere diplomatic fig-leaf for the sending of an Austrian force to Naples. True, this force was accompanied by commissioners from Russia, Prussia and France, to demonstrate that Austria was acting in the name of the alliance; but it was an Austrian victory all the same, and the Austrian army also took the opportunity to occupy strong points in the Papal states, and to suppress an attempt by part of the Sardinian army to establish a constitutional regime in Turin.

Austria's position in Italy seemed stronger than ever before. It was, moreover, now reinforced by Russian approval that had been lacking in October; and the British government too saw nothing to object to in this outcome, remaining quite unperturbed by pro-Italian speeches in the Commons. The French, by contrast, were bitterly disappointed, and rebuked their representatives at Laibach for failing to keep 'the scourge of war' from Italy. Their hopes of the previous summer of establishing, in entente with Russia, a French-protected regime in Naples, had collapsed utterly; and their discomfiture was complete when Castlereagh not only rebuffed their suggestion that Great Britain and France lend diplomatic assistance to the fledgling regime in Turin, but reported their suggestion to Metternich – who made excellent use of it with Alexander. Indeed, by the time the Congress of Laibach ended in May, the French once more found themselves completely isolated.

As regards the relations between the four Powers of the Quadruple Alliance, the Congresses of Troppau and Laibach bore witness to both change and continuity. The creation of an alliance pledged to the suppression of revolutions – the 'Neo-Holy Alliance' of the three eastern powers – was both a new phenomenon and one that was ominous for the future cohesion of the Quadruple Alliance. Castlereagh had made it abundantly clear that Great Britain would refuse to participate in such a system. On the other hand, the Franco-Russian challenge to Austria's right to determine the affairs of Italy single-handed had ultimately served to clarify and confirm certain power relationships that had hitherto only been implicit in the 1815 order. That Metternich should feel the need for external support before he could intervene in what was supposed to be Austria's own sphere of interest was indeed a striking confession of weakness. The French, British and Russians were to feel no need to seek the permission of others before intervening in Spain, Portugal or Poland in the next few years. For Austria, however, the hard fact was that it was only with the support of at least one of the 'real' great powers – Great Britain or Russia – that had raised her to greatness in 1815, that she could hope to survive even as a great power of the second rank; and as in the crisis of 1820 Russia had been better placed to harm Austria than Great Britain had been to help her, it was only natural that Metternich should have made the securing of Russian goodwill his prime objective. Even here, however, there were underlying elements of continuity with the preceding years: the recurrent nightmare of a Franco-Russian combination that posed the chief threat to the continued Anglo-Austrian domination of the states system had been banished yet again at Troppau and Laibach; indeed, Alexander now readily endorsed Austria's domination of Italy. Similarly, the disagreement between Castlereagh and Metternich had never extended beyond the realm of political theory. In terms of political realities, the British had no objection whatever to Austria's domination of Italy, and the identity of British and Austrian interests continued unimpaired. Indeed, a new question had arisen which was both to reinforce that identity of interests and, if it threatened for a time to set the Anglo-Austrian partnership in opposition to Russia, was to provide an opportunity for Metternich, working together with Castlereagh, to re-establish a tripartite system that secured for Austria the support of both her principal allies.

The Eastern Question, Spain and the Congress of Verona, 1821–23

The Ottoman Empire had never been really accepted as a part of a European states system. Indeed, from the sixteenth to the eighteenth centuries it had generally been regarded as a threat to it. Only the Most Christian kings of France had been inclined to make use of it, in their long struggle with the Habsburgs; but they had always shrunk from an actual alliance with it and even the old working arrangement had lost its *raison d'être* when Diplomatic Revolution had brought Bourbons and Habsburgs together in the 1750s. By the later eighteenth century the Ottoman Empire, faced after 1781 with an Austro-Russian coalition, was clearly a power on the defensive; indeed, after 1768 every war it engaged in against Russia ended with an Ottoman retreat, in terms of both territory and authority over the outlying possessions of the Empire. The problem was as much an internal as an external one: the steady weakening of the grip of the central authorities on the peripheral provinces was both cause and effect of a general breakdown of order, as Christian populations rebelled against the oppression of Muslim landowners and local officials – the Serbian revolt of 1804–13 originated in an uprising of this kind – and as local rulers tried to carve out independent fiefdoms for themselves in defiance of Constantinople: for years before the outbreak of the Greek revolt, the western Balkans had been thrown into confusion by the rebellion of the Albanian chieftain, Ali of Janina. All the same, these problems had sometimes been actively exploited by Russian rulers for their own expansionist purposes: in 1767 Catherine II sent agents to stir up a revolt in Montenegro, and to Greece three years later; and even less offensively minded rulers were drawn by a strong sense of honour and duty to take an interest in their Orthodox co-religionists within the Ottoman Empire. Although the Serbian rising of 1804 was by no means welcome to a Russian government deeply preoccupied with Western European problems, it was axiomatic in St Petersburg that Russia could never be indifferent to Serbia, 'because of the similarity of origin and of religion that exists between it and the peoples of Russia'.

It is true that Alexander I was in no position, either during the Napoleonic Wars or after, to attempt to realize the ambitious programme of Catherine II, who had dreamed of annexing the Danubian principalities, and even of taking Constantinople. At the same time, however, he was acutely conscious of having inherited from his grandmother a whole series of obligations towards the Orthodox peoples of the Balkans. For example, in the famous Article VII of the Treaty of Kutchuk Kainardji of 1774 Catherine had obliged the Turks to promise 'to protect constantly the Christian religion and its churches'; and Article XVI recognized Russia's right to a voice in the affairs of the Danubian principalities. These provinces, inhabited by Romanians and governed by Phanariot Greek officials, lay outside the Ottoman administrative system, and generally enjoyed freedom from Ottoman military occupation. Although nominally under Ottoman suzerainty, they constituted a kind of buffer zone between the Austrian, Russian and Ottoman empires and Alexander I took Russia's right to protect them from Ottoman interference extremely seriously. Not that he wished to incorporate them into Russia, as Capo d'Istrias advised: in the Treaty of Bucharest of 1812 he had been content to incorporate merely southern Bessarabia; but it had been Ottoman infringements of Romanian autonomy that had sparked off the war of 1806–12 in the first place. Less intense but also significant was the interest Alexander took in the connections established by his grandmother with the more distant

Greeks – an interest keenly encouraged by Capo d'Istrias who in 1820 persuaded the emperor to permit Alexander Hypsilantes, an officer in the Russian army, to assume the leadership of the Greek national propaganda society *Hetairia Philike*.

Not that Alexander and his advisers, any more than any other government in these years was actively seeking to precipitate an upheaval in the Ottoman Empire. On the contrary, even Capo d'Istrias felt that a long period of cultural and military preparation would be necessary before the Greeks could aspire to nationhood. He was genuinely horrified when in March 1821 Hypsilantes – who had promised to take no action without Russian consent – invaded the Danubian principalities in an attempt to spark off a general rising of Greeks. Alexander, too, dissociated himself from Hypsilantes, dismissing him from the Russian army; and the 'rising' in the principalities, where the local population was far more hostile to its Greek overlords than to Constantinople, soon petered out. It had two extremely serious consequences, however. The Sultan reacted by sending an army to occupy the principalities; and the Greeks of the Morea responded by massacring any Muslims they could lay hands on. This rising called forth Ottoman reprisals in turn, culminating in the execution of the Greek Patriarch of Constantinople. The latter, according to the British ambassador, was probably indeed guilty of treason: although an Ottoman functionary, he had concealed his knowledge of the revolutionary movement from his political masters. Even so, his public hanging, in full canonicals, from the door of his own cathedral on Easter Day 1821 caused considerable uproar in the Orthodox world.

Russo-Turkish relations were already plagued by a long-running dispute over the interpretation of the Treaty of Bucharest of 1812: the Turks were still occupying certain fortresses on the Danube, and demanding the return of some areas in the Caucasus which the Russians argued had not been annexed, but had voluntarily joined the Russian Empire during the late war. In this situation, the latest Ottoman actions in respect of both the principalities and the Orthodox Christians constituted challenges to the Tsar's honour that might well precipitate another Russo-Ottoman war. Capo d'Istrias, certainly, was determined to do all he could for his hard-pressed compatriots, while in St Petersburg an influential military party was keen to resort to force, as were those Orthodox and pietist circles who had of recent years secured such a hold over Alexander's mind. It was no wonder that the first news of the disturbances in the Balkans had filled Metternich with alarm: 'voilà le commencement d'une révolution immense'.

Although since the 1680s the Austrians had often been associated with Russia in her wars against the Ottoman Empire, and in the 1780s Joseph II had contemplated dividing the whole Balkan peninsula between Austria and Russia, these wars had of late been singularly unsuccessful for the Habsburgs. Indeed, Russia's inexorable advance to the Crimea and beyond, and indications of her future ambitions in the Danubian principalities, Greece, and, most recently Serbia, had given Vienna much food for thought. It was not just that Austria had traditional interests of her own to guard in the western Balkans – a two-hundred-year-old protectorate over the Catholics of Albania, and traditional links between the Serbs in Turkey and those in the southern provinces of the Monarchy. In strategic terms, given the advance Russia had made along the northern frontier of the Monarchy at the Congress of Vienna, Russian control of the Romanian and Serbian territories on its southern frontier would be doubly unwelcome. In fact, the Austrians were already coming to the conclusion in 1791, when Leopold II withdrew from the last Austro-Russian war against Turkey, that the safest neighbour for Austria in the south was the Ottoman Empire – a precept that was to be axiomatic for Metternich and almost all his successors. As regards the particular case of the Greeks they were doubly obnoxious in Metternich's eyes, both as a destabilizing element in the Balkans and as a branch of the international revolutionary movement: it was notorious that many refugees from the Austrian occupation of Naples had found asylum in Greece, 'that vast sewer open to all revolutionaries'; and Hypsilantes, who had sought asylum in Transylvania, ended his days in an Austrian jail. At Laibach, Metternich spared no pains in emphasizing this aspect of the affair to Alexander. For his chief anxiety concerned the possible implications of the 'révolution immense' for the states system as it had been managed since 1815: not only might Russia be drawn into a clash with her allies; she might be tempted to embark on a forward policy in collaboration with France – a combination that would represent a real challenge to continued Anglo-Austrian control of the states system.

At least Metternich could count on Castlereagh, who was equally dismayed at the prospect of a Russo-Ottoman war. He was, after all, the disciple of Pitt, who in the Ochakov crisis of 1792 had been the first British statesman to sound the alarm about Russia's seemingly inexorable advance along the Black Sea coast (although a pro-Russian commercial lobby in parliament had prevented his taking any action). During the wars the Russians, for their part, had been immensely irritated to find Great Britain standing in their way when they had attempted to liberate

Malta and the Ionian Islands from the French. Not that Mediterranean issues were, as yet, acute: the Russians, who had a healthy respect for the British and French navies and were worried about their vulnerability to amphibious attack, were less concerned to exercise influence in the Mediterranean than to keep other powers out of the Black Sea. The British likewise were willing to settle, in an Anglo-Turkish treaty of 1809, for the principle of the closure of the Straits to the passage of foreign warships in either direction. The Ottoman Empire was already performing that function of a buffer preventing clashes between the great powers that was to be such a notable feature of the nineteenth-century Eastern Question. Of course, it could only do so provided it continued to exist as an independent state. Its replacement by genuinely independent states in the Balkans might be equally compatible with British interests; but nobody in London thought such a development probable. Far more likely was an attempt by Russia to exploit her role as protector of dissatisfied elements either to establish a series of satellite states, or to acquire an overweening influence at Constantinople as she had tried to do in Warsaw and Stockholm in the eighteenth century. Indeed, the British particularly had good strategic and commercial reasons for opposing any Russian attempt to dominate either the Sultan or the Shah, as both the Ottoman and Persian empires ruled important stretches of territory on the British land route to India from the Mediterranean.

In Paris, the crisis aroused markedly less apprehension. There, the rising Ultra faction, proponents of the Alliance of Throne and Altar, viewed the Greeks primarily as fellow Christians worthy of support – although as Metternich scornfully observed, 'they forget that it is the Radicals who have raised the standard of the cross, in the hope of covering it, when the day comes, with a red cap'. Others saw the crisis primarily as a political opportunity: according to Metternich's informants, the Duc de Fitzjames had declared openly at the opera that 'nothing could be more advantageous for France than a war with Turkey. Russia would take what she wishes, Austria what she can, and we – 'turning to the officers present – we should recover our Belgium.' Such sentiments were widely echoed amongst former Bonapartists in the French foreign office, notably the influential political director, Rayneval, who urged Richelieu to seize the chance to establish an entente with Russia, break the Anglo-Austrian stranglehold over the states system, and revise the territorial settlement of 1815; and with the accession of an Ultra king in 1824 this train of thought was to influence French policy on the Eastern Question increasingly until the fall of Charles X in 1830. Meanwhile, for Richelieu, the prime consideration was that whatever settlement emerged, it must not be one from which France was excluded: a repetition of the 1772 partition of Poland or any further shift of the balance against France would be intolerable. For the moment, however, Richelieu decided to wait on events. Although he had become imbued, as Alexander's governor of Odessa, with the conviction that the Ottoman Empire was doomed, he had to take other traditions of French policy into account. The Ottoman Empire had served France well in the past and she might do well to try to prolong its life and cultivate long-standing French interests there – in the welfare of the Catholics of the Lebanon, or in Mehemet Ali's modernization work in Egypt, another area where France might take up the Bonapartist tradition and break out of the constraints of the 1815 settlement. Besides, after his recent experiences over Italy, Richelieu was reluctant to risk burning his fingers again by grasping after a Russian entente that might prove illusory: it was still not clear that Alexander could be relied on.

Metternich and Castlereagh faced the same problem. So long as Alexander was at Laibach he accepted Metternich's version of events, and in their final pronouncements at the end of the congress the sovereigns of Laibach assured the Sultan that they would give no support to the Greek rebels, who were acting contrary to the principles enunciated at Troppau. Castlereagh gave Metternich his full backing, writing privately to Alexander, on the strength of his invitation at Aix-la-Chapelle, and emphasizing that the Greek revolt was simply 'a branch of the organized spirit of insurrection'. On his return to St Petersburg, however, Alexander fell prey to very different advice – from military and Orthodox circles, from Capo d'Istrias and Stroganov, the violently anti-Turkish Russian ambassador at Constantinople. Indeed, on 18 July Stroganov presented the Turks with a formal ultimatum, drafted by Capo d'Istrias and demanding satisfaction on all Russia's outstanding grievances – over the Greeks, the Danubian principalities, and the Treaty of 1812. On the following day the Tsar observed to the French ambassador that it was 'Russia, and not Turkey, whom France should have as her ally'; and spoke of fighting the Turks 'in the name of Europe'. He was still reluctant to act without a mandate from his allies, however. While he was prepared to take a stand alone over Russia's treaty rights and the Danubian principalities, he had no stomach for attempting to tackle the Greek question single-handed. Not only did he have a realistic appreciation of British and French naval potential in the eastern Mediterranean; he was still convinced of the overriding importance of maintaining allied unity against the revolutionary threat. As he disconsolately remarked to Capo d'Istrias in August, 'if we answer the Turks with war the directing committee in Paris will triumph and no government will be left standing'.

Metternich and Castlereagh, for their part, were determined to keep Alexander firmly in line; and George IV's first visit to Hanover as king (21–29 October) provided them with a good opportunity, in meetings lasting over several days, to co-ordinate their efforts to restrain the Tsar. Both agreed that a congress would be useful as a means of 'grouping' Alexander; and in the meantime they agreed to ply him with further advice. Castlereagh wrote at length, warning the Tsar very firmly that he could not make any promises about Great Britain's attitude in the event of a Russo-Turkish war; and that he was not prepared to contemplate any 'new system in the East'. While he admitted that the sufferings of the Greeks were indeed deplorable, he pointed out that even more suffering would be caused by stirring up a war on their account – especially as they were quite incapable of self-government, as British experiences in the Ionian Islands had shown. Metternich concentrated on the desirability of disentangling the Greek question from Russia's other grievances against Turkey; and both statesmen promised to press the Turks to treat the Greeks with more humanity and to withdraw their forces from the Danubian principalities.

The battle was not yet won, however: in January 1822 the British ambassador in St Petersburg was still reporting that 'the labour and intrigues of Count Capo d'Istrias to bring on the war are inconceivable, and his enormous presumption still makes him believe that he can guide the politics of Russia and lead the revolutions of Greece at the same time.' In the spring, Alexander again asked London and Vienna for a mandate for action; but Metternich would only promise diplomatic support if the alliance were united (which he knew it would never be) and Castlereagh would not promise even that. Indeed, he turned the principles of Troppau neatly against Alexander, reminding him that if there were to be any intervention, it would have to be against the rebellious Greeks rather than against their legitimate sovereign in Constantinople. In the end, Metternich suggested handing the question over to a congress. To this, Capo d'Istrias was violently opposed, seeing it as an obvious ploy to procrastinate and tie Russia's hands; but when Alexander decided that the unity of the alliance must after all remain paramount and gave his verdict in favour of Metternich's proposal, Capo d'Istrias resigned himself to defeat and in July left Alexander's service. Metternich was triumphant: 'The principle of evil is uprooted, and Count Capodistrias is buried for the rest of his days.' Already, Castlereagh had secured the cabinet's permission to attend the proposed conference in person – in Vienna in September, immediately prior to a Congress on Italian affairs planned for Verona. The Anglo-Austrian entente that had so often served to control Russia and contain France within the states system was still proving effective as late as the summer of 1822.

In fact, the entente continued to function for some months after Castlereagh's mental breakdown and suicide (18 August), and the discussion of the Eastern Question at Vienna and Verona went entirely according to plan. Metternich, ably assisted by Lord Strangford, British ambassador at Constantinople, persuaded Alexander to settle for a diplomatic action by the alliance to bring the Turks to treat the Greeks more humanely and to withdraw their forces from the principalities; and the Austrian police foiled an attempt by representatives of the Greek rebel regime to secure admission to the Congress of Verona. In the concluding protocol of Verona, Alexander joined his fellow monarchs in regretting that 'the firebrand of revolution has been cast into the Ottoman Empire' and in condemning the Greek revolt as 'a rash and criminal enterprise'. Tension was further reduced when the Turks started to withdraw from the Danubian principalities in January 1823. Clearly, it was not due to differences over the Eastern Question that the Congress of Verona was to prove 'the last great liturgy of the cult of the alliance'.

Nor did Castlereagh's suicide presage any fundamental change in the functioning of the states system. It was a hard blow for Metternich, who had come to count on Castlereagh 'as a second self'; and the end of the ten-year partnership no doubt contributed to the ultimate defeat of Austrian diplomacy at Verona. On the other hand, the disappearance of Castlereagh had no immediate effects on the direction of British policy. There was no deviation from the decision that at Verona, the biggest international gathering since the Congress of Vienna, Great Britain was to be represented by a full plenipotentiary, not by observers as at Troppau; and in this respect Great Britain remained a fully committed participant in the 'congress system' until the end. It was also significant that, as Canning was not appointed to the Foreign Office until 16 September, the Cabinet in the interval selected Wellington, Castlereagh's chief collaborator in negotiations with the continental powers since 1814, to represent Great Britain at the Congress. (Canning himself would never have chosen a man so steeped in Castlereagh's 'new and very questionable' approach to foreign policy, and one so closely and for so long associated with continental rulers.) Most importantly, however, the instructions that Wellington took with him to Vienna and Verona had been drafted by Castlereagh himself, and it was these that defined British objectives at the Congress: to restrain Russia in the Eastern Question; to prevent the alliance from jeopardizing British trading interests by clumsy interventions in the conflict between Spain and her South American colonies; and to dissociate Great Britain from any proposals for active intervention by or in the name of the alliance in Spain itself. In this last respect, Wellington was only restating the British position on intervention that Castlereagh had set out in his state paper of 5 May 1820 and in his response to the Troppau protocol – to which Canning's famous dispatch declaring that Great Britain would not be a party to such intervention 'come what may' added nothing new at all.

It is certainly true that the prominence accorded at Verona to the question of intervention in Spain reopened the theoretical dispute over the nature of the alliance that had arisen at Troppau; and Alexander, who arrived at Verona declaring that 'the only aim of the Alliance is that for which it was founded: to combat revolution', made it no easier to heal. It is also true that, even though Alexander was genuinely anxious for intervention by the alliance in Spain, where civil war was looming and the king had appealed for French military assistance against the extremists, he was also intent on emphasizing the Spanish question precisely in order to revive the Troppau debate. This was, in fact, a calculated move to disrupt the Anglo-Austrian entente that was proving so restrictive of Russia's freedom of action in the Near East and to transfer domination of the states system from that entente to a Russia working closely with Austria – on the basis of Troppau – and possibly even with France. Metternich found himself again confronted with the dilemma he had faced in 1820; although now he was reluctantly admitting that something would have to be done about Spain, especially as a failure to act might discredit the alliance in St Petersburg and deprive him of his chief means of restraining Russia in the Near East. Even so, prospects for continued Anglo-Austrian co-operation were not hopeless. As in 1820, Metternich sought to seek to escape from his dilemma by admitting the Russian argument for intervention, while trying to steer it in a direction that was compatible with Austria's interests and that would not prove too disruptive of his links with the British. Nor was he entirely unsuccessful: although the four continental powers insisted, despite British objections, that the Spanish question was indeed the concern of the alliance, the congress stopped short of authorizing any military intervention. On that vexed question, therefore, it showed more restraint than the Congress of Troppau; and this issue cannot in itself account for the subsequent demise of the Anglo-Austrian partnership.

All the same, the Congress of Verona marked the beginning of the end of Anglo-Austrian domination of the states system. There, Metternich was far less in control than he had been in the more intimate discussions at Troppau. Quite apart from suffering a rebuff at the hands of France, Russia and the Italian states in his efforts to revive his plans for an Italian confederation, his apparent success on the main issue of Spain soon proved to be an illusion. True, while the congress lasted, his tactics of playing off Russia and the western powers against each other to smother any disruptive proposals seemed both ingenious and skilfully executed. He managed to exploit both French and British objections to seeing Russian troops marching across Europe to eliminate Alexander's visionary plans for an international expedition to Spain (and to sow mistrust between Alexander and the French); and he used British and Russian doubts about France's intentions and reliability to thwart the attempts of the French foreign minister, Montmorency, to secure an international mandate for a French expedition. (Here he was assisted by the fact that the French delegation was even more divided than at Troppau, while the prime minister Villèle was opposed to military action on the grounds of expense, and to an international mandate as derogatory to French prestige.) As a result, Metternich secured his desired compromise, a diplomatic demonstration: the allies would denounce events in Spain and break off relations with Madrid. This, he hoped would both render France harmless and satisfy Alexander's thirst for action sufficiently to keep him in the alliance, while not being so provocative to the British as to drive them out of it. That he had failed on the last score became clear even during the congress, when Wellington refused to associate Great Britain with the proposed *démarche*. Worse, however, once the congress had dispersed, Metternich's compromise was seen to rest on an equivocation: the diplomatic demonstration in Madrid that he had intended as a substitute for military action was regarded in Paris and St Petersburg as a first step towards it.

The outcome was, from Metternich's point of view, catastrophic. Even before the congress ended ministerial changes in Paris gave the lie to his hopes that France could be restrained by the alliance. When Montmorency returned from Verona to find his colleagues unanimous in their opposition to any kind of joint action with the allies, he resigned, to be replaced by Chateaubriand. The new minister injected an altogether more forceful and independent note into French policy, embarking on a series of gestures obviously designed to provoke war, and in April 1823 100,000 French soldiers duly crossed the Pyrenees, overthrew the revolutionary regime in Madrid, and re-established Ferdinand VII as an absolute monarch. For the first time in eight years, the French were acting independently beyond their borders, and the re-establishment of French predominance at Madrid was the first breach in the system of barriers constructed by the peace-makers of 1815.

It was also demonstrated that an important change had occurred in the states system and in the relations of the allies towards France and towards each other. In the aftermath of the Congress of Verona the Quadruple Alliance system that had served since 1815 to contain France and control Russia broke down completely. Of the allies, only the Austrians made an effort to continue the system of 1815. In a series of desperate appeals to London and St Petersburg, Metternich stressed the need for alliance control of French action in Spain: allied commissioners should accompany any expedition; the allies might install King Ferdinand of Naples as a temporary regent in Madrid. The problem for Metternich was, however, as it had been ever since 1815, that Austria was too weak to uphold the 1815 order without the support of one of the two 'real' great powers, Great Britain or Russia; and if Metternich had thus far managed to thwart French designs in Spain thanks to Castlereagh's support and Alexander's reluctant break with his wartime allies, he discovered in the spring of 1823 that neither the Quadruple Alliance nor the neo-Holy Alliance of Troppau could any longer be relied on.

In St Petersburg, Austrian warnings about the dangers of allowing France a free hand in Spain were received with derision as evidence of pusillanimity. Franco-Russian relations were improving markedly. Chateaubriand noted with satisfaction that 'our true policy is the Russian policy, by which we counterbalance our declared enemies: Austria and England' – after all, Russian support was essential to deter the British: 'let my Hon. friend Canning fume as much as he pleases, he is foiled.' The British were indeed greatly embarrassed. Austrian intervention in Naples, objectionable though the theoretical justification for it might have been, had in practice suited British interests, as it reinforced the order established in Italy in 1815. French intervention in Spain, by contrast, constituted an important alteration of the balance of 1815, and one that was particularly humiliating to the British who had been primarily responsible for expelling French influence from Spain. Logistically, however, there was nothing that Great Britain as a naval power could do against French military intervention in Spain; and a futile protest would simply underscore the humiliation. It is significant, however, that Metternich's last-minute attempts to mobilize his old friends to control Chateaubriand met with no more response in London than in St Petersburg. Unlike Castlereagh after his – rather more serious – disputes with Metternich over the Troppau Protocol, Canning had no desire to re-establish co-operation with Austria. Of course, he disapproved of the invasion of Spain; but he also noted with relief that it had not arisen from 'an assumed jurisdiction of the Congress'. Indeed, he rejoiced at Metternich's discomfiture, and viewed the disarray within the alliance with perfect equanimity: 'The issue of Verona has split the one and indivisible alliance . . . and so things are getting back to a wholesome state again. Every nation for itself and God for us all!'

The upshot was that after seven years of relative success, the alliance had in the end failed to contain France within the bounds of the 1815 settlement. This failure cannot be explained simply in terms of the strengths and weaknesses of congress diplomacy as a method of regulating the states system. Certainly, congress diplomacy could facilitate the smooth operation of the concert when, as in 1818, a broad measure of agreement had already been reached; but it could also exacerbate divisions in the concert, the Congress of Verona being a virtual textbook example of the dangers of resorting to congress diplomacy when no broad agreement existed. (As late as 1908 a British Foreign Office memorandum was to declare that it had been a principle of British foreign policy ever since the Congress of Troppau that Great Britain should not participate in congresses or conferences unless a measure of agreement had been reached beforehand.) Of course, the significance of congresses, for good or ill, in the functioning of the states system between 1814 and 1823 should not be exaggerated. Although they achieved more than their predecessors – the loosely organized peacetime congresses of the 1720s which, for want of any guiding directory of powers were characterized by years of futile wrangling – they did not really constitute a new system of international organization. Their place in the history of international relations is as precursors of the summit conference, not of the League of Nations.

Above all, they must be seen in the context of the whole complex web of interacting and conflicting interests that made up the substance of diplomacy in these years. Between 1815 and 1822 the chief issue in international relations was the struggle between the Anglo-Austrian and French and Russian interpretations of the international system, and the Congress of Aix-la-Chapelle was simply one aspect of that struggle. Equally, in 1820 Metternich decided, congress or no congress, that Austro-Russian co-operation offered a better chance of restraining Russia than Anglo-Austrian resistance, and this was reflected in the emergence of the Neo-Holy Alliance of the three eastern monarchies at Troppau and Laibach. But both the *rapport* he established with Alexander at Troppau and that he re-established with Castlereagh at Hanover failed him in the end; and in 1822–23 he suffered a signal defeat at the hands of a Franco-Russian combination that was to dominate European affairs for most of the 1820s. The congresses of 1818 to 1822 are really of a piece with the round-table talks between the allies in 1814 and 1815. They were essentially an expression of the desire of Metternich, Castlereagh and Alexander to manage their differences in peacetime by the methods that had served them so well in the wartime coalition; and their success depended not only on the continuance in power of these personalities, but on the continuance of the wartime diplomatic constellation, above all, the isolation of France.

Once the factors that had underpinned the wartime coalition – the common fear of French hegemony, and the financial dependence of the allies on Great Britain – ceased to operate, its disintegration had perhaps been inevitable. It was perhaps also unsurprising that, once Great Britain lost her pre-eminence as the other powers gradually recovered from the war, and the latter began to attempt to redefine the alliance to suit their own particular purposes – the reintegration of France into the system, or the struggle against the Revolution – this should give rise to increasing resentment in Great Britain, reinforcing deep-rooted isolationist attitudes in the ruling élite (of which Canning was a far more typical representative than Castlereagh). The distancing of Great Britain from the continental powers after Castlereagh's death was in this respect perhaps only a reflection of long-term trends, but these trends were also reinforced by personal and contingent factors. As Castlereagh's partners in the wartime coalition, Metternich and Alexander I, had shared his experiences and come to much the same conclusions, the coalition had continued in peacetime, in various guises, to give stability to the states system. For the best part of a decade, it had both contained the defeated power and mitigated conflicts between the victors – a greater achievement than those of its successors of 1919 and 1945. By the same token, however, the disappearance of two members of this triumvirate was bound to give more scope to tendencies which they had resisted or renounced. The potentially disruptive forces of French revisionism and Russian assertiveness had only been controlled, not eliminated, by the prolongation of wartime solidarity into peacetime. Whether these forces would continue to be controlled, after the disintegration of the alliance in 1823, and in a states system based on the nostrum of 'every nation for itself', remained to be seen.

CHAPTER 3

'Every nation for itself', 1823–30

Canning, Metternich and the control of the European states system

In terms of the foreign policy objectives of the great powers, the collapse of the congress system did not mean that the four allies had ceased to work together to contain France within the territorial limits imposed by the Second Peace of Paris; and certainly the essential aims of British policy, the containment of France in the west and Russia in the Near East, remained unchanged. In terms of the diplomatic devices the great powers employed to pursue their objectives, however, the 1820s witnessed a number of very significant changes. If the dispute at the Congress of Verona over the principle of intervention in Spain had revealed the limitations of the Quadruple Alliance as a mechanism for giving a co-ordinated direction to the policies of the Pentarchy, the sequel to the Congress – the actual implementation of intervention by France with the encouragement of Russia and in the face of the disapproval of both German Powers – had shown that the Neo-Holy Alliance was no longer in control of the situation either. Perhaps most significant of all, however, was the disappearance of the Anglo-Austrian entente, which Castlereagh and Metternich had employed to 'group' Russia and contain France. Even after Castlereagh's very public denunciation of the Troppau protocol, the Hanover meeting had demonstrated that this entente, based on a real community of interests, could survive differences over the theoretical purpose of the Alliance. (As the French complained, Great Britain and Austria were 'like college friends, who can say anything to each other without breaking up'.) Nor was there any inherent reason why the entente should not have survived the resurgence of the theoretical argument – in this case, less forcefully stated and less publicly aired – at the Congress of Verona. On this occasion, however, the Congress was not followed by any equivalent of the Hanover meeting, and the entente experienced no revival.

If Canning had found his hands tied while Wellington was expounding British policy at the Congress of Verona, on the basis of instructions drawn up by Castlereagh and approved by the Cabinet, once the Congress had ended he lost no time in demonstrating that he had no intention of restoring his predecessor's entente with Metternich or of confining British policy within the framework of 'the Areopagus'. Indeed, the disarray into which the latter had fallen over the French invasion of Spain was to him one of the few bright spots on the horizon; and if Europe really was 'getting back to a healthy state of things again, every nation for itself and God for us all', he decided that British interests could be best safeguarded by making separate agreements with France and Russia direct. This new approach was reinforced by personal factors, notably the violent antipathy that existed between Canning and Metternich. If Metternich had been dismayed to see Castlereagh, his 'other self', replaced by Canning, 'the revolution incarnate', and decided that Great Britain was now 'displaying herself naked to the world, gangrenous to the bone with revolution', Canning for his part had little desire to collaborate with 'the greatest rogue and liar on the Continent, perhaps in the civilised world'. In power political terms, however, the disappearance of the entente served to limit the effectiveness of both Powers. It is true that, faced with the threat of a Franco-Russian entente over Naples in 1820, Metternich had had to seek his salvation in a single-handed attempt, at Troppau, to influence the mind of Alexander I; and in the event of an actual conflict Great Britain as a west European naval power could never be of direct assistance to Austria – just as Austria's weakness limited her usefulness as an instrument of British policy on the continent. Nevertheless, in the day-to-day diplomacy of the states system between 1814 and 1822 the Anglo-Austrian entente had, on the whole, demonstrated the effectiveness of a combination of the two powers, both in 'grouping' Russia and in containing France. In the 1820s, the absence of the entente was to show that neither Great Britain nor Austria was strong enough alone to attain these objectives: by the end of the decade both Russia and France had broken free and seemed, indeed, to have seized control of the European states system.

The state most affected by these developments was Austria, a relatively weak great power dependent on the support of either Great Britain or Russia to maintain that eminent position in central Europe to which she had been elevated by the settlement of 1814–15. Despite the occasional scare over Russian adventurism backed by France, and despite differences with the British over alliance obligations in relation to revolutionary disturbances, it seemed by 1821 that Metternich had squared the circle, establishing a close entente with both the British and the Russians. Indeed, as far as the Eastern Question was concerned, even as late as the Congress of Verona Metternich, in co-operation with the British delegates, was managing to hold Alexander to a policy of restraint in harmony with his old wartime allies. Within weeks of the end of the Congress, however, Canning's ignoring of Metternich's desperate attempts to use the Alliance to restrain French intervention in Spain, and Alexander's open encouragement of this intervention, showed that, in the west at least, both Great Britain and Russia had escaped him; and he was reduced to trying, without British assistance, to hold Alexander to a conservative course in the Near East.

This was to prove a task beyond even Metternich's skill. The Anglo-Austrian entente, dubious though its value might have been in a war, had been based on a real community of interests that proved of immense value to Austria in day-to-day diplomacy; and with Castlereagh's support Metternich had generally managed to keep Alexander in line. An Austro-Russian entente, by contrast, however useful it might prove in war, concealed a fundamental conflict of interests in the Near East; and the imbalance between the power of the two parties was so great that Metternich's only hope of controlling Russia lay in such personal influence as he could continue to exercise over Alexander. This was to prove all too fragile; indeed, in the 1820s personal factors only weakened Austria's position still further. Even in the last years of Alexander's life, Metternich was to experience increasing difficulty in attempting single-handed to influence Russian policy in the west, and even in the Near East. The death of the emperor in December 1825 left the Austrian chancellor as the sole survivor of the triumvirate who had made the 1815 peace settlement and who had striven, despite all their differences, to sustain the spirit of co-operation that had restored Europe to order. Alexander's successor, Nicholas I, was as distrustful of Metternich as Canning was: 'Every time I come near him,' he wrote to his wife, 'I pray God to protect me from the Devil'; and the last shreds of Austrian influence over Russian policy disappeared. When Nicholas, with British, and then with French support, proceeded to go his own way in the Eastern Question, the underlying Austro-Russian conflict of interests was exposed to the light of day, as was the impotence of an isolated Austria to control events. Of course,

Austria's own inherent weaknesses had always condemned her to the role of a great power of the second rank: even the limited expense of the Naples expedition had thrown her finances into disorder; and at the height of the eastern crisis, in 1828, when penury had forced yet a further reduction in the size of the army, Austria was, the finance minister declared, 'armed for perpetual peace'. In these circumstances, no entente with Russia could offer Austria any lasting guarantee of security. The fact remained that if ever Russia should choose to make a forward move, there was little her entente partner could do to restrain her; and this was to be demonstrated repeatedly in the history of the Eastern Question – in the 1850s, the 1870s, the 1880s and in the last years of peace before 1914. Of course, if the Anglo-Austrian entente could be revived, however belatedly, Russia could be reined in – as was shown in the Crimean War, at the Congress of Berlin, and in the Mediterranean Entente of 1887; but when, as in the years after the Anglo-Russian agreement of August 1907, an Anglo-Austrian entente was no longer on offer, the Monarchy's international position was to be seriously endangered.

As early as the 1820s the perils of isolation were borne in on the Austrians, even in Germany and Italy, areas clearly assigned to Austria's sphere of influence by the 1815 peace settlement. As British, Russian and even Prussian support fell away, Metternich's achievements at Karlsbad, Troppau and Hanover became no more than distant memories. In Italy, for example, Russian support for Austria's position had never been unqualified. In 1820 the Russians had joined with the French to subject Austrian military intervention to alliance control; and at Troppau and Verona to stiffen the resistance of the Italian states to Metternich's tentative moves towards subjecting the Italian states to a federal organization on the lines of the German Confederation. Confronted with an extraordinarily violent denunciation of Austrian interference from the Papal delegate at Verona – 'the Italian population, almost without distinction of sect or party, detested Austria and groaned from the subjugation in which she held Italy' – Metternich had to retreat. There was, in fact, little he could do to influence Italian rulers who, although they were, more or less willingly, dependent on Austrian bayonets, proved deaf to his incessantly proffered advice to install centralized, efficient administrations staffed by professional bureaucrats. The regime of Marie Louise in Parma was relatively enlightened in a Bonapartist fashion, but for the most part, after Verona the rulers of the minor Italian states drifted steadily along the road to 1859. The Austrians, for their part, found themselves confronted with an unpalatable choice: between tolerating the progress of an international revolutionary conspiracy that threatened the established order in both local and international terms, and risking military intervention to prop up wayward and incompetent satellite regimes. Metternich was, of course, not the last statesman to fail to resolve the conundrum, which continues to perplex conservative great powers active in the third world to this day. In Germany, Metternich's problem was both different, in that the potential threat to Austria's supremacy came from a rival great power, and yet similar in that it was the sharp decline in Austria's authority on the international scene, consequent on her estrangement from her erstwhile British and Russian supporters in the eastern crisis of the later 1820s, that encouraged Prussia to take the first steps towards freeing herself from the domination that Metternich had established over her in the Karlsbad era. This danger – of an Austro-Russian estrangement leading to a weakening of Austria's position in Germany – was to present itself in even starker form in the 1850s. It was, however, implicit in the European states system even in the 1820s; and that it failed to materialize for the time being was due, not so much to any superior skill on Metternich's part, as to Prussian timidity and to the dramatic shift in the diplomatic kaleidoscope that followed the revolution of 1830 in Paris.

Iberian issues and South America

As a great power of the first order, Great Britain was less severely affected by the disappearance of the Anglo-Austrian entente. True, the 1820s were to show that Canning's policy of direct agreements with France and Russia was a less than adequate substitute for the entente as a means of defending Great Britain's continental interests within the Pentarchy; but the British were perfectly well able to act on their own initiative in their own recognized spheres of influence where their naval power could be brought to bear. Portugal, for example, was generally recognized to be one such British preserve. British influence in Lisbon rested on long-standing treaties of alliance dating back to the seventeenth, even the fourteenth, centuries; and in the early nineteenth century it found more concrete expression in the presence of a British squadron in the Tagus, and in the diplomatic support the British generally gave to Portugal in a series of frontier disputes with Spain in the peninsula and in South America. In his determination to uphold Great Britain's special position in Portugal Canning was entirely of one mind with his predecessor, who in 1820 had been quick to respond to the January revolution in Spain by reaffirming the British guarantee to Portugal; and, when a military *coup* established a constitutional regime in Lisbon in August, by preventing interference by the congresses in Portugal's internal affairs. In 1823 Canning displayed an equal firmness in extracting from the French a disavowal of any intention of going on from suppressing the constitutional regime in Spain to interfere with that in Portugal. True, this regime was to be engaged for some years in a running battle against absolutist opposition elements who were in receipt of arms and money from Madrid and moral encouragement from the Neo-Holy Alliance powers. But Canning made Great Britain's position perfectly clear. He consistently rejected Metternich's suggestions that the Portuguese conflict might be an appropriate subject for discussion by a congress, strengthened the Tagus squadron when the Lisbon regime was under acute pressure at the end of 1824, and dispatched a further 4,000 men to Lisbon at a critical moment two years later. In the face of this, the eastern powers had to accept that they could do nothing to influence events in Portugal; and during a visit to Paris in 1827 Canning also reached a *modus vivendi* with the French, whereby each government recognized the other's predominance in its respective sphere of influence in the Iberian peninsula.

South America was another area where British naval power could be brought to bear and where, in the peacemaking of 1814–15 Castlereagh had acted independently of the continental powers to safeguard British commercial interests by means of bilateral treaties with Spain. By the 1820s, the struggle of the Spanish American colonists for independence from the mother country was dragging on into its third decade, despite the fanatical determination of successive Spanish regimes to reject all compromise proposals put forward by the European powers and to crush the rebellions by force. It was not merely Spanish fanaticism, however, that denied the British the paramountcy in the Spanish American question that they enjoyed in Portuguese affairs, but the fact that the Spanish American question had wide repercussions within the European states system, and other members of the Pentarchy were determined to assert their interests in it. French commercial interests in Spanish America – largely confined to the wine and silk trades – might indeed be relatively modest; but every French government after 1815 displayed an enormous political interest in events in Spanish America, seeing in them an opportunity to undermine at least one part of the hated 1815 settlement by re-establishing French influence at Madrid. They attempted to bring a whole series of mediation proposals, generally favourable to Spain, before the conference of ambassadors in Paris and successive congresses, and were untiring in pressing Madrid to opt for the establishment in South America of independent states under Spanish or Italian Bourbons. These latter efforts Castlereagh condemned as 'the dregs of the old diplomacy' – in the mistaken belief that Paris was angling to put French Bourbons on Spanish American thrones; and he was as determined as Canning was later to be that whoever won the battle for influence at Madrid, France must not have Spain with the Indies.

The French threat was reinforced by the Russians who, although they had, of course, no direct interests in the question, sought in the years after 1815 to exploit it to further their general objective of drawing the Bourbon powers into their orbit to counter Anglo-Austrian domination of the Quadruple Alliance. It was with alarm that the British learned of the sale of a few Russian warships to Spain in 1817, imagining – again mistakenly – that Russia had been accorded a naval base in Minorca. At Aix-la-Chapelle Alexander's agents gave enthusiastic support to French proposals for mediation and the establishment of monarchies in the New World. They were thwarted when Castlereagh, with Metternich's assistance, managed to get Alexander back into line: 'Metternich est le factotum de l'Angleterre sur le continent', the Russian minister in Madrid observed in disgust. At the same time, the British faced a threat from outside the Pentarchy: from the United States, which had substantial economic interests in Spanish America, in terms of cotton exports, and even greater political interests. These were the decades of United States territorial expansion towards the south, with the Louisiana Purchase of 1803 and the acquisition of Florida from Spain in 1819. If Spain were expelled from the hemisphere altogether, the road to Mexico would lie open. While the French, therefore, sought to enhance their influence both in Spain and in Spanish America by resolving the conflict on a monarchical basis acceptable to both the colonists and Madrid, the United States had a simpler task, and worked single-mindedly to draw the colonists into their orbit by openly playing the republican card and encouraging the rebels to reject all compromise proposals emanating from the monarchies of the Old World.

British interests in Spanish America were primarily economic. During the years of the Anglo-Spanish alliance against Napoleon the Spanish colonies had been opened to British trade; and if the securing of this trade had been Castlereagh's prime concern in his separate negotiations with Spain at the end of the war, it assumed an even greater importance to Great Britain in the years of depression that followed. As regards the struggle between Spain and her rebellious colonists, Castlereagh strove for a *modus vivendi*, offering to mediate between the two sides, provided always that the open door to British trade with the colonies was guaranteed, and that there was no question of Great Britain's being involved in the use of force against the colonists. As for their future destiny, he adopted an intermediate position between France and the United States, broadly favouring the idea of monarchies in the New World, provided that they were not mere satellites of France. Yet although, in the years after 1815 he had a measure of success in fending off the attempts of France and Russia to interfere in Spanish America in the name of the Alliance, he himself made little positive progress in his negotiations with Madrid. The Spaniards, once they no longer needed a British alliance against Bonaparte, soon give full rein to their resentment of Great Britain's intrusion into what had been a Spanish trading monopoly, which they aimed to restore; they rejected the conditions attached to the British tender of good offices; and they were further exasperated by the support Castlereagh gave to Portugal in a number of frontier disputes with Spain. As for the future, neither the government of Ferdinand VII nor that of the revolutionary junta after 1820 showed the slightest interest in British offers of mediation, at Aix or at Verona, or in the idea of independent monarchical regimes in Spanish America.

Castlereagh for his part found the Spanish ministers, who were as ignorant as they were headstrong – they often had no idea where the territories they were so ferociously disputing with Portugal were actually situated – an impossible concern to deal with, and by 1820 relations between London and Madrid were decidedly cool. As a result, and spurred on by the embarrassment consequent on trying to develop trade with areas of the world that had no recognized government, Castlereagh decided to give priority to Great Britain's transatlantic trading interests regardless of the frowns of Madrid, and gradually moved towards granting commercial recognition to the rebel regimes. By 1821 the Trade and Navigation Acts had been amended to admit ships from the rebel colonies to British ports; in the summer of 1822 Castlereagh formally recognized a number of Spanish American states as belligerents; and he warned the Spanish ambassador that full diplomatic recognition was now only a matter of 'time and circumstance'. To the end of his life he refused to sacrifice British interests in the question to suit the continental powers, insisting, in the instructions he prepared for his mission to Verona that British Spanish American policy would be determined solely by British interests: it was a matter for Great Britain, Spain and the colonists alone; and it would not be determined by the other members of the Pentarchy. Not that the latter produced anything resembling a united view at Verona: Metternich remained opposed in principle to any mediation involving the revolutionary Spanish regime; a French mediation proposal designed to undermine Great Britain's trading privileges came to nothing; and the Spaniards continued to reject the notion of independent monarchies as advocated by Great Britain.

In the aftermath of Verona, however, matters came to a head, and the British found themselves confronted by a double threat. On the one hand, the restoration of Ferdinand VII in Madrid under French auspices might be followed by a French attempt to reassert their protégé's authority across the Atlantic; on the other, Washington seemed increasingly set on establishing the United States as the predominant power in Spanish America by granting full recognition to the rebel regimes. It was to counter this double threat that Canning, in a striking demonstration of the principle of 'every nation for itself', launched a double diplomatic offensive, in which he managed to play off Great Britain's potential rivals against each other to considerable effect.

In August 1823 he approached the United States ambassador in London, William Rush, with a proposal for a joint Anglo-American warning to the continental powers against attempting to interfere in the Spanish American conflict. Initially, this produced little: although President Monroe was not averse to co-operation, Secretary of State John Quincy Adams had no wish to play second fiddle to Canning; while the United States' counter-proposal, for immediate recognition of rebel republican regimes, seemed to Canning premature so long as there was a chance of establishing monarchies in the New World. The exchange nevertheless stiffened Canning to take a firm line with the French: when their ambassador in London, the Prince de Polignac, hinted at the desirability of a congress to take the Spanish American question in hand, Canning warned him straight out that any intervention by the continental powers would be met by immediate British recognition of the new regimes. At this, the French government backed off, confirming that it had no intention of intervening. Canning had called the French bluff and, as he hastened to inform both the United States and the colonists, all danger of intervention by the continental powers was at an end. This was certainly a success for Canning's diplomacy, and a notable step towards confirming Great Britain as the protector of the fledgling regimes. True, once the danger of Alliance intervention had passed, Washington tried to capitalize on the situation, proclaiming the freedom of the hemisphere from intervention by the powers of the Old World in Monroe's famous Message to Congress of 2 December. But this was essentially a sham: it was British action that had been decisive and the fact remained that it was on the strongest naval power of the Old World that the Monroe Doctrine depended for its enforcement.

Although Canning's approach to Rush may have been sincere enough as a response to a temporary alarm at the prospect of intervention by the continental powers, it does not seem to have been a bid for a long-term rapprochement with the United States. This power, in Canning's view, presented a grave threat to British interests in Spanish America. As Rush warned Washington: 'Mr Canning never liked the United States or their institutions nor ever will. He will watch all our steps with sharper and more active jealousy than any other English statesman living.' In one sense, Canning's Spanish American policy was a very good illustration of the successful operation – from the British point of view, at least – of the principle of 'every nation for itself': as he himself observed, 'the effect of the ultra-liberalism of our Yankee co-operators and of the ultra-despotism of the Aix-la-Chapelle allies, gives me just the balance that I wanted.'

In fact, suspicion of the United States ran like a red thread through Canning's Spanish American policy, and drove him on in the final stages of recognition. As the United States moved steadily towards recognition of the South American republics after 1823, Canning warned that 'sooner or later we shall probably have to contend with the combined maritime power of France and the United States. The disposition of the new states is at present highly favourable to England. . . . Let us not, then, throw the golden opportunity away.' That Canning was unable to persuade the Cabinet to seize the golden opportunity for another three years was due largely to the rearguard action fought by King George IV advised by a reactionary 'camarilla' that included the Austrian and Russian ambassadors. By 1826, however, he could declare with satisfaction, à propos the recognition of Mexico: 'The thing is done, . . . the Yankees will shout in triumph, but it is they who will lose most by our decision. The great danger of the time was the division of the world into European and American, monarchical and republican. . . . We slip in between and plant ourselves in Mexico. The United States have got the start of us in vain, and we link once more America and Europe.' Canning had, in fact, skilfully exploited the 'great danger' to the advantage of British interests. There were soon twenty new states in South America, and in the struggle for influence between Great Britain and the United States, it was the United

States who lost, failing completely in the Panama Congress of 1825–26 to establish a confederation headed by Washington. By the end of the 1820s the influence of Great Britain prevailed throughout South America, and her trade of some $80 million was more than three times as great as that of the United States. It seemed indeed that from the jaws of defeat in Spain itself Canning had snatched a clear victory in Spanish America, calling, as he himself boasted, 'the new world into existence to redress the balance of the old'.

The Eastern Question, 1821–33

Meanwhile, in the Old World the balance of power had shifted further to the advantage of the dissatisfied Powers, France and Russia. If Great Britain's pre-eminence as a naval power had ensured that, even acting in isolation, she could safeguard her interests in Portugal and South America, it was not an adequate basis for single-handed action in the Ottoman Empire. There Great Britain had to take seriously the intense interest displayed by other powers in the Eastern Question. After all, having de-mobilized her army after the end of the Napoleonic wars she was, in strictly military terms, among the weakest of the great powers, and in any continental combination simply lacked the military muscle to bend the other powers to her will. In fact, by the end of the 1820s the British were to be made painfully aware of the disadvantages of Canning's policy of 'every nation for itself'.

More immediately, it was Austria who suffered most from Canning's abandonment of Castlereagh's policy of controlling Russia within an Anglo-Austrian combination. After 1823 Metternich could rely only on his personal influence over the emperor Alexander, and this was to prove of very limited weight. In certain areas, it was of no weight at all: the Russians considered their own particular complaints against the Turks – whose military activities in the Danubian principalities and in Serbia were infringing Russian rights of protectorate established by treaty – as matters to be settled between St Petersburg and Constantinople direct (even though diplomatic relations had been broken off). In the Greek question, however, Metternich still had some scope for manoeuvre. In the first place, he was able to make something of the Russian emperor's reluctance to take action without a mandate from Europe. At a meeting with Alexander at Czernowitz in 1823 he managed, even without British assistance and to the dismay of the French, to hold him to the negative line on Greece recently proclaimed at Verona. In the second place, he found that the other allies were sometimes willing to join him in restraining Russia, even without a formal entente: as the Greek conflict sharpened in 1824, with the Sultan receiving very effective assistance from the Egyptian army and navy under Ibrahim Pasha, a Russian proposal to establish three small autonomous states in Greece was rejected in five-power discussions in St Petersburg. Both the British and the Austrians feared that such states would merely be Russian satellites; whereas the Greek nationalists rejected the plan as completely inadequate, and placed themselves under British protection. For Metternich the awkward fact remained, however, that there had been no revival of the Anglo-Austrian entente. Indeed, Canning now lost interest in further five-power discussions, hoping instead that Russo-Turkish relations might somehow be restored so that the question could be handled at Constantinople, where Great Britain would exert more influence than at a congress.

It was partly for this reason that Alexander's final attempt to secure a European mandate to enforce an Alliance solution, the Congress of St Petersburg in the summer of 1825, came to grief. The British simply boycotted the meeting. Only the Prussians, who had no direct interests at stake in the Eastern Question – but a considerable interest in standing well with Russia – were co-operative enough to earn Alexander's praise. The Austrians were by no means willing to concede to Russia a *carte blanche* for action, and all the congress produced was a number of anodyne resolutions which Alexander regarded as totally unsatisfactory. It was not merely Austria's increasingly open involvement on the anti-Greek side, as a supplier of armaments to the Turks, that led the Tsar to conclude that chasing after an illusory alliance unity was a thankless task. Reports of Metternich's vainglorious boasts – to the effect that he had Alexander in his pocket – completed his disillusionment. In August 1825 he declared that Russia would now cease her attempts to devise an eastern policy in concert with the allies and would henceforth consult her own interests. In concrete terms, he seemed to be thinking of an approach to the British. At any rate, even before Alexander disappeared from the scene in December 1825, leaving Metternich as the sole surviving relic of the triumvirate that had given direction to the European states system after 1815, it was apparent that the system had ceased to function as an effective restraint on Russia, and that the way was clear for a new configuration of powers in the Eastern Question.

The new emperor, Nicholas I, had none of Alexander's memories of working in close collaboration with the members of the wartime coalition:

he was twenty years younger than his late brother and had been only a teenager at the time of Waterloo. In personal terms, as the son-in-law of Frederick William III of Prussia and with brothers-in-law in several lesser west German states and in the Netherlands, he was certainly not inclined to take his cue from Metternich, and had no scruples whatever about acting independently of the alliance. The circumstances of his accession, amidst the confusion of the Decembrist conspiracy, might indeed have confirmed him as an even more fervent enemy of the Revolution than his predecessor; on the other hand, it was widely expected that the accession of a young emperor in such turbulent circumstances might well be the harbinger of a foreign diversion to distract attention from domestic problems. Certainly, Nicholas was less inclined to view events in Greece through Metternichian spectacles as a rebellion against a legitimate sovereign, than as yet another aspect of the Turks' disdain for Russia's obligations as the protector of the Christians of the Empire.

It was not so much the sufferings of the Greeks, however, who were covered only by a rather general reference in the Treaty of Kutchuk Kainardji to the Sultan's obligation 'to protect the Christian religion and its churches', that touched Russia's honour and reputation as the chief Orthodox power. Of far more importance to St Petersburg were Turkish infringements of the autonomous rights of the inhabitants of Danubian principalities and Serbia, which had been guaranteed by very specific articles in the Russo-Turkish treaties of 1774 and 1812. True, Russian indignation partly reflected a lack of accurate information since the rupture of diplomatic relations with Constantinople in 1821; but by February 1826, even the moderate Nesselrode, who had in the past so often acted as a brake on Capo d'Istrias, was advising the emperor to be prepared to use force against the Turks. The European powers would not object, he argued, so long as Russia made it clear that her aims were limited: that she was not attempting to destroy the Ottoman Empire or seize Constantinople. It must be emphasized that this plea for moderation was no mere tactical device but an expression of Nesselrode's considered view of Russian self-interest: if the Ottoman Empire collapsed, other powers might move to seize portions of it, and Russia might find herself confronting a number of great powers in the immediate vicinity of the entrance to the Black Sea. Hence, 'of all the powers that can occupy the Bosporus and possess Constantinople, is not the Porte the one from which Russia will always have the most means of securing deference?' Even so, this policy of restraint was nevertheless forcefully pursued, with an ultimatum to Constantinople in March 1826. Negotiations then followed which led to the restoration of diplomatic relations and the Russo-Turkish Treaty of Akkerman (July), which confirmed and extended the autonomous privileges of the Danubian principalities and Serbia and recognized Russia's rights as guarantor to supervise their future relations with Constantinople. No other power objected to the settlement by Russia and Turkey alone of these rather remote issues. Nesselrode's policy of the forceful pursuit of limited objectives had proved eminently successful.

At the same time, no one in Russia could imagine that the much publicized conflict in Greece could be handled as a bilateral Russo-Turkish question. As the Greeks came under increasing pressure from Ibrahim, who was rumoured to be planning to deport the entire Christian population of the Morea to Egypt, the cry for intervention arose in Philhellene circles all over the continent. The role of these circles in determining the course of events should not be exaggerated, however: in Great Britain, Byron's death at Missolonghi might cause a stir, but the attempt to raise a loan for the Greek cause in 1823 rather fizzled out amidst rumours of misappropriation of funds; in France, the propagation of the Greek cause as a struggle of Christians had its adherents among the proponents of the 'alliance of Throne and Altar' who surrounded Charles X; and, in terms of both numbers and influence, the Philhellene cause was strongest in the lesser German states, particularly in Bavaria (whose ruling house was to provide the first king of independent Greece in 1831), but none of these states was in a position to determine the course of the Eastern Question.

This was to be determined by the governments of the great powers. By 1826 Nicholas I had concluded that, if the policy of devising a common European line of action was bankrupt, there might yet be room for co-operation with an individual power; and that in view of the geographical location of the conflict, co-operation with the world's strongest sea-power would make sense. Canning, for his part, was rather attracted by the idea of an Anglo-Russian entente. Perhaps Castlereagh's policy of working with Metternich to 'group' the tsar would hardly have worked with Nicholas I, even if Canning had not been temperamentally averse to it. At any rate, it seemed to Canning that a separate entente with Russia might well be the best way to resolve the Greek conflict while averting the danger of single-handed action by Russia – and it would accord well enough with his ideas of 'every nation for itself'. It was to secure such an entente that the prestigious Wellington was sent to represent George IV at Nicholas's coronation in the spring of 1826. The upshot, the St Petersburg Protocol of 4 April, provided for an Anglo-Russian tender of mediation with a view to reconciling the Greeks and Turks on the basis of Greek autonomy within the Ottoman Empire; and the note of restraint was heard again in the disavowal by both parties of any intention to seek special advantages in terms of territory, commerce or influence. To this extent, the Protocol realized Canning's intentions; and the isolation and dismay of Metternich at the news of the Anglo-Russian rapprochement was no doubt a further cause for satisfaction in London. It must be admitted, however, that Wellington was no expert in the drafting of diplomatic documents and that Article III of the Protocol, which spoke of 'intervention, be it in common or separately' between the Porte and the Greeks, opened the door to that very kind of single-handed action that Canning had been most anxious to prevent.

Worse was to come. Canning's chances of exercising any effective control over Russian policy were further diminished when the Treaty of London of 6 July 1827 transformed the Anglo-Russian partnership into a tripartite combination with France. The French were intensely interested in the Eastern Question for a number of positive and negative reasons. On the positive side, they were in any case disposed to act with more confidence on the international scene since the success of their intervention in Spain had documented before Europe their capacity to engage in military action abroad without falling into revolution at home – thereby giving the lie to one of Metternich's favourite arguments for restraining France within the leading strings of the alliance. The resultant increase in French prestige was seen by the government as strengthening its hand against its liberal critics at home; and it whetted the appetite of an important section of the élite for further successes and for active co-operation with Russia to revise the order of 1815. On the negative side, even the cautious Villèle was sensitive to the argument that on no account must a question of such importance as the Eastern Question be settled without the participation of France: that would amount in effect to a repetition of the First Partition of Poland, when the ignoring of France by the eastern powers had had such catastrophic consequences for the prestige of the pre-revolutionary monarchy. Certainly, the St Petersburg Protocol had been greeted in the Quai d'Orsay with anxiety: France must herself seize the initiative if the injustices of the 1815 settlement in the west were not to be compounded by a further insufferable humiliation in the east. In the event, the Russian response to the feelers that now came from Paris was not unpromising. Although – as the French were later to discover to their chagrin – St Petersburg was not in the least interested in their ultimate objective of revision in the west, Nicholas I was very much alive to the advantages of bringing a co-operative France into the Anglo-Russian combination, if only as a means of strengthening his hand against British attempts to control Russian policy.

In the resultant Treaty of London – essentially an elaboration of the St Petersburg Protocol – the three powers agreed to pursue their search for a solution of the Greek question while extending the provisions for diplomatic pressure to include the possibility of opening direct diplomatic relations with the Greeks, and establishing a blockade to prevent reinforcements reaching the Egyptian army in the Peloponnese by sea. It was the attempt to enforce this last provision that led to an almost accidental encounter, on 26 October 1827, between an allied squadron and the Turco-Egyptian fleet in Navarino Bay, during which the Ottoman fleet was completely destroyed. Although the Russians seemed to have been hopeful that the Turks would now be prepared for concessions – it was for this reason that Nicholas decorated the Russian commanders – the Turks felt, not unnaturally, that the whole proceedings of the allies since the summer had been unfriendly to Turkey, and regarded Navarino as nothing less than an act of war. In an imperial rescript, the Sultan denounced Russia before the peoples of his Empire as a 'sworn enemy of Islam'; rejected allied demands in favour of the Greeks; revoked, by implication at least, the concessions already conceded to Russia at Akkerman, and announced that the Empire would have to fight for 'its faith and its national existence'. In a show of solidarity, the London allies broke off relations with the Porte, and both St Petersburg and Constantinople accepted that war was inevitable.

It is true that the British were sincerely dismayed by this turn of events. In November Navarino was described in George IV's speech to parliament as 'an untoward event'; and London was at pains to dissociate itself from Russia's formal declaration of war of 26 April 1828 – which cited Turkish violations of Russo-Turkish treaties without mentioning the grievances of the Balkan Christians. Even so, the striking feature of British diplomacy in these months was its complete inability to exert any effective control over Russian actions. Partly, this stemmed from the confusion in British domestic politics that followed the death of Canning in August and the subsequent disintegration of the Tory party. The new foreign secretary, Dudley, was completely ineffective, and eventually suffered a mental collapse; the prime minister, Wellington, was much preoccupied, ever since he assumed the premiership in January 1828, with the contentious question of Catholic emancipation; and the ministry was further weakened by the secession of the Canningites in May. Of equal significance, however, were political changes in France, where the cautious

Villèle fell from power in December 1827. The new minister for foreign affairs was none other than La Ferronnays, long-serving ambassador at St Petersburg and an ardent advocate of Franco-Russian co-operation as the key to the revision of the 1815 settlement. Throughout the spring of 1828, as Russia moved towards war, the British found themselves under intense pressure from the French, who argued that the only hope of influencing or restraining Russia lay in avoiding a breach with her at all costs; and this pressure, the much harassed British government proved unable to resist. By the summer, a conference in London had agreed to entrust the French with a military and naval mission to the eastern Mediterranean, which eventually expelled the Egyptian forces from the area; and by the end of the year the Poros agreement between the three allies envisaged the creation of an autonomous Greek state. Yet although the French military and naval presence and British political and economic contacts with the rebels might ensure them a measure of influence, an ambiguous solution based on autonomy might still have dangerous implications – as Canning and Metternich had objected in 1824 – in terms of giving Russia opportunities to meddle at Constantinople.

Admittedly, any Russian threat to British interests in the eastern Mediterranean was hardly imminent: on the contrary, even in the Danubian principalities, the Russians made very little progress in the 1828 campaign. In more general terms, however, the prospect was still a worrying one from the point of view of Great Britain's interests, and her position within the states system as a whole contrasted starkly with that of a decade earlier. Then, Great Britain and Austria, two powers with a recognized community of interests in upholding the *status quo*, had combined to constrain Russia to march in step with them: now, in the tripartite arrangement to which Canning had made Great Britain a party, and in which she was aligned with two powers with fundamentally revisionist objectives, it was Great Britain who was in a minority of one and who found herself virtually a prisoner of her new partners.

In fact, the issue was not so much one of particular changes in the Near East, as of the control of the European states system generally. By 1829 the Russians, frustrated by their military failures, uncomfortably conscious of British reservations, and stung by reports of gloating in Vienna, where Metternich was explaining that Russia had at last met her 1812, felt badly in need of friends. The hopes of French diplomacy rose accordingly, and Paris set its sights on nothing less than a diplomatic revolution, involving Berlin as well as St Petersburg. Prussia, the French told themselves, was, like France a 'puissance incomplète', with nothing to look for from association with *status quo* powers such as Great Britain and Austria. Indeed, she might be encouraged to turn against Austria in the traditions of Frederick II; and she might join with France and Russia in a new tripartite combination which could, Chateaubriand exulted, 'dictate to Europe'. Prussia's close dynastic ties with St Petersburg and the Tsar's forthcoming visit to Berlin were hopeful signs. France and Prussia should take advantage of the eastern crisis, helping Russia to her victory and taking their own rewards in the west. Growing domestic unpopularity pushed the French government in the same direction: Charles X speculated that 'perhaps a war against the court of Vienna would be useful to me, in that it would put an end to internal wrangling and bring the nation to act together as it desires.'

Throughout the Near Eastern crisis the French pursued their broader objectives with dogged determination and despite serious rebuffs. Nicholas I's visit to Berlin in June 1829 proved a bitter disappointment, fundamentally because the Russians were simply not interested in revising the 1815 order in the west, but also because the French had misjudged the German powers. Austria was indeed painfully isolated and Metternich was certainly not *persona grata* in St Petersburg; but the legitimist principles of the Neo-Holy Alliance still counted for something there. In a desperate manoeuvre reminiscent of the congress era, Metternich engaged Francis I to appeal personally to Tsar Nicholas, depicting France as a revolutionary power. The Prussians, too, failed completely to come up to French expectations, endorsing Austrian advice to the Tsar to make peace quickly 'in order to form an alliance of the three great continental powers against those whose internal agitations threaten to hurl Europe back into revolutionary upheavals'. The French, nevertheless, persisted, spurred on by public criticism of the king's new first minister, the Prince de Polignac, former French ambassador at London, who was accused of being both a hopeless reactionary and the dupe of the British – Nicholas spoke dismissively of the 'cabinet Wellington-Polignac'. Polignac's determination to counter these charges, together with sheer panic at the prospect of France's exclusion from a voice in the general settlement that loomed when the Russians achieved a sudden military breakthrough in the summer, produced a frantic spate of diplomatic activity in the Quai d'Orsay. In August, General Baron de Richemont urged in two long memoranda that Turkey's days were numbered, and that France must come forward as mediator to support Russia, 'notre allié naturel' against Great Britain and Austria 'nos ennemis vrais, implacables, éternels'. He proposed a general redistribution of territories, assigning Constantinople to Russia, some western Balkan territories to Austria, Holland to Great Britain, Saxony and Hanover to Prussia. France would take the Rhineland, as 'the Rhine is for France what the Bosporus is for Russia'. According to a revised version of 2 September – the so-called 'Polignac Plan' destined for the St Petersburg embassy – France was to take Belgium rather than the Rhineland, as it would be important to persuade Prussia to join with France and Russia in imposing the scheme on Great Britain and Austria as a *fait accompli*. But the ultimate objective was the same, and in line with the objectives of every French government since 1815: the reordering of the unjust 1815 settlement in the interests of a genuine balance of power.

The French were right about the urgency of the situation; but their assumptions about the possibility of co-operation with Russia were totally illusory. In fact, the fundamental incompatibility between the objectives of all three allies of the Treaty of London was as great as ever; and although the Russians were only too ready to take advantage of the connexion with France to override British objections to their activities in the Near East, they had no intention of rewarding the French by supporting their revisionist aims in the west. Even before the Polignac plan reached St Petersburg, peace negotiations had started between Russians and Turks. The latter had been greatly shaken by the Russian advance to Adrianople, within striking distance of the capital, and the British, who were equally alarmed, were urging them to make peace. The negotiations were facilitated by the relative moderation of Russia's demands. These reflected not merely the knowledge that the victorious Russian army was badly weakened by disease, but also the deliberations of the commission which Nicholas had appointed under Baron Kochubey to consider Russia's war aims, and which concluded, as Nesselrode had done before the war, and for much the same reasons, that 'the advantages of the preservation of the Ottoman Empire outweigh its disadvantages'. In the event, therefore, France was quite unable to secure a voice in the peace negotiations and the bilateral Treaty of Adrianople of 14 September provided for only the most minimal territorial changes in south-east Europe, while it left the door firmly closed on revision in the west.

The peace settlement brought Russia few gains of territory in Europe – the Bessarabian frontier was advanced to the mouth of the Danube – and rather more significant gains in Asia: Turkish recognition of Russia's annexation of Georgia and eastern Armenia complemented the strengthening of her position against Persia by the Treaty of Turkmanshei on the eve of the Russo-Ottoman war. Russia's chief gains at Adrianople were in terms of her increased influence at Constantinople: the constitutional arrangements of the Danubian principalities were revised and the privileges of the principality of Serbia were extended to certain hitherto disputed neighbouring districts, all of which changes enhanced Russia's opportunities for intervention at Constantinople as the protector of the minorities in question – a tactic she had used to some effect in both Poland and Sweden in the eighteenth century. In this respect, it must be emphasized that the corollary of Russia's decision to preserve the Ottoman Empire was that Russia should control it; and since the recent war, Nesselrode calculated, the Turks must realize that 'any serious difference with us would be a sentence of death'. Altogether, therefore, the decade had ended well for the Russians. They had freed themselves from the stranglehold of the Neo-Holy Alliance, and they had been able to exploit the embarrassments of the British and the ambitions of the French to secure a virtual free hand in the Ottoman Empire, without paying either of their allies anything in the west.

By the same token the Austrians, who in 1822 had seemed in a fair way both to staving off the extension of Russian influence along their southern borders while yet retaining Russian and British support for their own position in Germany and Italy, had suffered a series of setbacks. Metternich described the Treaty of Adrianople as 'a disaster'. It is true that the chief threat posed by the Near Eastern crisis to Austria's position in general European terms – the attempt by France to secure Russian and Prussian support for revision in the west – had in the end proved illusory; but Metternich had had to take the threat seriously, and in his efforts to hold on to St Petersburg and Berlin had had to pay a high price in terms of Austrian influence in central Europe. As late as 1824 he had managed, with Russian backing, to overcome the resistance of the south German states to a renewal of the federal obligations imposed on them at Karlsbad; but the isolation of Austria in the developing Near Eastern crisis changed all this, especially as the revolutionary threat seemed to diminish in the later 1820s and the rulers of the German states began to give reform priority over reaction. The investigatory Commission in Mainz was wound up; and moves were made towards developing the solidarity of the middle states as a Third Germany, independent of Austria and Prussia. The customs union established by Bavaria and Württemberg in April 1827 clearly had political overtones and was strongly disapproved of in Vienna; as were the efforts of the ambitious Prussian finance minister Motz, leader of an overtly anti-Austrian party at Berlin, to draw the middle states into the orbit of the tariff union that had been created in 1819 for Prussia's scattered territories, the *Zollverein*. In February 1828 Motz managed to pressurize Grand Ducal Hesse into a customs union with the *Zollverein*; and feelers were put out to the south German states. The Austrians, for their part, proved unable either to compete with or to oppose these tendencies. On the one hand, the Monarchy's economic backwardness precluded it from offering tariff reductions as a counter-attraction to the middle states; on the other, its diplomatic isolation made it seem essential to humour Berlin at all costs. It would never do, Metternich insisted, to allow 'our higher political relations with the Court of Prussia to be spoiled by a bit of true political rubbish'. The upshot, in May 1829, was the amalgamation of the Prussian and South German customs unions, imply-ing – in Motz's view at least – a new Prussian-South German political, as well as commercial, alignment. As R.D. Billinger observes, 'the basis for a *kleindeutsch* economic and potentially political solution to the German Question was being laid'. In sum, the 1820s had provided a salutary demonstration of the weakness of Austria's position when it was not underwritten by either Great Britain or Russia, the 'real' great powers; indeed, within less than a generation this weakness was to be revealed as a fundamental fault-line in the European states system established by the peacemakers of 1815.

The authority of Austria's erstwhile partner, Great Britain, had also been weakened as a result of Canning's abandonment of the entente in favour of an attempt to control Russia in collaboration with revisionist France. It was not so much the terms of the Treaty of Adrianople itself that worried British observers, most of whom fully appreciated that Russia was seeking to influence, rather than destroy, the Ottoman Empire. True, Russia's spectacular successes against both the Persians and the Turks were contributory factors in what was to prove in the next few years a sea-change in British attitudes towards Russia comparable to that which was to transform British attitudes towards Germany at the end of the nineteenth century. For the present, however, the British saw in the outcome of the Russo-Ottoman war not so much a pointer to Russia's possible future designs, as a dramatic demonstration of the fragility of the Ottoman Empire: 'this clumsy fabric of barbarous power', Aberdeen declared in November 1830, 'will speedily crumble to pieces from its own inherent causes of decay.' Moreover, whatever the implications of the recent crisis in the Near East, in terms of the functioning of the Euro-pean states system as a whole, one thing was clear: Canning's policy of working with France and Russia in order to restrain them had proved a failure. This was perhaps hardly surprising: whereas the Anglo-Austrian entente had embodied a real community of interests in 'grouping' Russia between two powers which both sought to preserve the order of 1815 in east and west, the combination of 1827 was essentially an unnatural one. Although, luckily for the preservation of the 1815 order in the west, at least, the French and Russians were also at cross purposes, the Treaty of London tied the British to two allies whose interests diverged widely from their own. As a result, the British, far from controlling their uncomfortable partners, had found themselves to a great extent their prisoners.

In these circumstances, the final settlement of the Greek question could be counted as a – rather surprising – success for British policy in the Near Eastern crisis. In contrast to the distant Danubian principalities and landlocked Serbia, the Peloponnese was one area where the British, ensconced in the Ionian Islands since 1815 and with a respectable naval presence in the eastern Mediterranean, had to be taken into account by both their partners. The Greek settlement was determined by the concerted action of all three parties to the Treaty of London – albeit, it must be said, in accordance with their own great-power interests, and without paying much regard to the view of the Greeks themselves. A joint protocol drawn up by the three allies in February 1829, when the Russo-Turkish war was still in a state of stalemate, had still envisaged the creation of an autonomous Greece; although even then the British, fearing that such a state might look to Russia for support in its disputes with the suzerain power in Constantinople, had sought to restrict its territorial extent as far as possible. After the Ottoman collapse of the summer, however, when it seemed that the days of the suzerain power were in any case numbered, the three powers agreed, in the London Protocol of February 1830, to create an entirely independent Greek state under their joint protection. As such a state was less likely to be simply a stalking horse for Russian influence, Palmerston eventually agreed to a fairly generous territorial settlement and the Russians, for their part, recognized that they could never aspire to exercise in Athens the kind of predominant influence they exercised in Bucharest. In these respects, the arrangements finally laid down in the London Protocol of February 1832 suited the interests of all three protecting powers well enough.

The Greeks themselves, who had no share in devising these arrangements, had perhaps less reason to be satisfied. True, the internal political situation was chaotic: local factions had proliferated even during the common struggle against the Turks; and when hostility to the precarious presidential regime established under Capo d'Istrias in 1828 culminated in the assassination of the president in October 1831, the country descended into virtual civil war. It was not entirely surprising, therefore, that the three protecting powers paid scant attention to local conditions in their final decisions, especially when the Russian emperor still despised the Greeks as rebels and the British, as governors of the Ionian Islands, held their political abilities in low esteem. The upshot was that although none of the three constitutions devised by the Greeks themselves in the 1820s had made provision for a monarchy, the protecting powers decided that Greece should have a strongly monarchical regime. Moreover, their eventual choice of ruler, the seventeen-year-old Otto of Bavaria, a Catholic, was hardly propitious for the future of his kingdom, which was from the start faced with dreadful financial problems that only foreign loans could alleviate. In fact, the new king was never able to establish much of a position for himself amidst the factions that dominated Greek politics and which revolved, not round the palace, but round the legations of the three protecting powers. As far as these powers were concerned, however, they could be content with the situation insofar as it offered all of them a degree of influence at Athens; and if the large measure of influence the Russians had been forced to concede to their partners confirmed them in their reluctance to further the process of replacing the Ottoman Empire by independent states, the British could take comfort from the fact, thanks to the St Petersburg Protocol and the Treaty of London, that at least the danger that had preoccupied them in the early 1820s, that of Russian control of the Peloponnese, had failed to materialize.

In the eyes of the French government, given the vastly exaggerated hopes it had entertained of a wholesale revision of the European balance of power, the outcome of the great eastern crisis, from which France emerged with nothing more than a voice, as one of three powers, in the settlement of the Greek question, was nothing short of a disaster. Far from establishing an entente with St Petersburg and Berlin to 'dictate' to France's 'eternal, implacable' enemies, Great Britain and Austria, the French had been treated as of no account by the Russians in the Adrianople settlement; and had naïvely connived at the extension of Prussian power over France's erstwhile protégés in south and west Germany – again for no reward. In desperation, the regime of Charles X cast around for an issue to restore its prestige and to counter the inevitable opposition attacks on the futility of its diplomacy. Finally, it hit on the idea of an expedition against the Barbary pirates of Algiers. Although an easy success beckoned and the international auspices were favourable – the German powers had no reason to object and the Tsar positively encouraged the French to occupy themselves in the western Mediterranean – this plan too was of a piece with recent French endeavours, being characterized by both hostility towards Great Britain and an obsessive concern to revise the 1815 order. It was widely expected in Paris that a move against Algiers would evoke a protest in London. But this would not only emphasize the isolation of Great Britain to the advantage of French prestige; it would – so at least the bolder spirits in the Quai d'Orsay calculated – provide an ideal opportunity 'at the first shot of an English cannon to seize Belgium pre-emptively and reoccupy the Rhine frontier'. In the event, with the establishment of French control of the city of Algiers in June 1830, the expedition was a complete success in local terms. In its wider purposes, however, as the British failed to react at all, the plan shared the fate of the other ambitious schemes of Charles X's regime. It was, moreover, to be the last attempt by the Restoration monarchy to find salvation in foreign diversions. By the end of July the king determined to tackle the opposition head on with the Ordinances of St Cloud. The resultant July revolution was to have significant consequences not only for French policy, foreign and domestic, but perhaps even more, for the relations of the European powers with France and with each other.

CHAPTER 4

From revolution to war, 1830–56

The European states system and the revolutions of 1830

The revolutions of 1830 were all protests against particular aspects of the peace settlement of 1814–15. The new order which the monarchs and statesmen of the great powers had imposed upon the states of Europe was condemned by liberals and nationalists as an old order, incapable of satisfying the aspirations of the peoples of Europe. This conflict of ideas which the revolutions of 1830 brought sharply into focus was, in the long run, more important than the revolutions themselves. By the end of 1832 the great powers had managed to contain the revolutions, but within forty years the idea of nationalism had totally destroyed the Vienna settlement. The peacemakers had worked on the assumption that states existed on the basis of dynastic rights and binding treaties. This was what they called the public law of Europe. From the 1830s onward a new class of politicians began to argue that states owed their existence to the will of people, and that the existing treaty structure enslaved the peoples of Europe. This was a profound conflict which admitted of no compromise and which could not be brushed aside. Liberal nationalists were confident that in the long run they would win the struggle of opinion. In fact, however, the problem was solved in a way that they had not anticipated: in the 1850s and 1860s some of the conservative monarchies ceased to cling to the treaty structure of Europe, separated liberalism from nationalism and appealed to the people over the heads of middle-class liberal politicians to legitimize their actions. In the 1830s, however, the conservative powers strove to maintain the existing order within their states and in international relations.

In the late 1820s the three eastern powers had drifted apart. To many observers it seemed that the Emperor Nicholas had abandoned the recently established policy of close co-operation with the two German powers when he indicated his willingness to work with England and France on the Greek question. Yet the Neo-Holy Alliance had survived, not only because Nicholas had been careful in the Treaty of Adrianople to avoid threatening Austria's Balkan interests; even more because both the Austrians and the Prussians remained alive to the need for Russian support against France and the revolution in Europe. Neither power felt able to dispense with it. Russia's apparent strength enabled her to offend her allies without seriously undermining her relations with them. Her guarantee to support them against their enemies had not been withdrawn during the Near Eastern crisis of the late 1820s. The French revolution of July 1830, raising as it did the spectres of both revolution and war, at once revived a sense of unity amongst the three allies. In August 1830 they issued the 'Chiffon de Carlsbad' in which they pledged themselves to maintain the 1815 settlement and warned the new regime in France to respect the established order in the rest of Europe. This was a measure of protection for central and eastern Europe rather than a challenge to France in the west. The three powers realized that they could not destroy revolution in France. Throughout the crisis of the early 1830s their aim was to prevent revolution from spreading eastwards.

The decision of the four erstwhile allies of Chaumont to recognize the government of Louis Philippe in France (the Orleans Monarchy) was essentially a bid for peace. They indicated their willingness to live with the new order in France if it would live with the existing order in the rest of Europe. The British government was the first to accord formal recognition to Louis Philippe; the Austrians and the Prussians quickly followed its example. Prussia wanted peace on the Rhine and Austria sought assurances that the new regime would recognize her dominant position in Italy. It was only the Russians who held out. They did not fear France to the same extent as the other three powers. To Nicholas, Louis Philippe was no more than a 'vile usurper'. However by January 1831 he gave in and recognized the Orléans Monarchy. By delaying recognition for six months he had clearly manifested his dislike of the new liberal order.

As regards the European states system, it was in the field of Franco-Russian relations that the July revolution made its most decisive impact. Whereas the restored Bourbon Monarchy had regarded Russia as its most likely ally, its successor saw Russia as its most inveterate enemy. The link between St Petersburg and Paris, by which Charles X and his advisers had set such store was now completely severed. It was not repaired until after the Crimean War. It was England and Austria who benefited most from the new antagonism between France and Russia; they no longer had to fear a Franco-Russian rapprochement for the revision of the 1815 settlement in Europe and for a forward policy by Russia in the Near East. Russia under Nicholas I was indisputably ranged amongst the *status quo* powers.

The appointment in November 1830 of a Whig government in England, committed to a measure of parliamentary reform, was regarded by many European conservatives, such as Metternich, as an event not very different in its consequences from the French revolution of July. It was regarded as another onslaught on the established order. Whig politicians were quick to take up the theme that the great powers were divided by the character of their political institutions into two rival groups; an eastern autocratic alignment and a western liberal entente. In England and France prominent politicians publicly suggested that their governments had a common interest in defending liberal ideas and institutions wherever they were struggling to establish themselves, and that they shared a common hatred of absolutist forms of government. This was the origin of the so-called 'liberal alliance' of the 1830s. Both British and French governments shared an exaggerated fear of Russian power and both were convinced that Russia entertained expansionist objectives in the Near East. Their criticisms of absolutism were mainly directed against Russian autocracy, particularly after its suppression of the Polish revolt of 1830. Attacks on the Austrian and Prussian versions of autocracy were much less frequent and less strident in tone. Each power saw the other as a potential ally against Russia. Nevertheless, the new Whig government soon showed itself just as anxious to contain France within the borders of 1815 as its Tory predecessors had been. If the image of France 'the friend of freedom' lingered on in certain Old Whig circles, the new Foreign Secretary, Palmerston, took an altogether less sentimental view of her: 'The policy of France is like an infection clinging to the walls of a dwelling, and breaking out in every successive occupant who comes within their influence.' Even so, as a true Canningite, he believed that France could best be contained by working with her rather than against her; and he found it easier to work with her in the early 1830s than Canning had in the mid-1820s. In foreign policy the revolution of 1830 was a setback for France. The new French government was acutely conscious of the great danger of isolation; it realized that one false step could easily revive the four-power coalition against France. The dread of isolation forced the new regime temporarily to abandon French revisionist objectives, and to work with Great Britain to avoid isolation. Palmerston exploited French weakness to the full; he attached strict conditions to his willingness to work with France: in Europe she must respect the Vienna settlement and in the Near East she must follow a British lead.

In the early 1830s England was in an ambiguous position. She was separated from her three allies by a clash of interest with Russia in the Near East and by a conflict of ideology in Europe, yet she still shared with them a common fear of French expansion. She was also linked to France by a common dread of absolutism. Palmerston exploited this ambiguity to great effect in the crisis over Belgium. He rightly claimed that he had used the three eastern powers to restrain France and France to restrain the three eastern powers. In August 1830 disturbances had broken out in Brussels that eventually turned into a movement against the union with Holland which the peacemakers had effected in 1815. The Catholic and largely French-speaking Belgians had become increasingly resentful of their subjection to the Protestant Dutch, their aspirations for a separate future were reinforced by traditions of a separate past. When the Dutch government appealed to the Prussians, who, as a result of arrangements made in 1815, garrisoned the fortress of Luxemburg (a possession of the House of Orange), for military assistance to suppress the revolt, Berlin refused to act without British approval. Wellington was convinced that Prussian intervention on the side of the Dutch would give the French a pretext for counter-intervention to protect the rebels, and he rightly believed that once the French army was in Belgium it would take a war to get it out. It was he who committed the British government to a negotiated settlement of the dispute by conference diplomacy in which the French were invited to participate. Like the recognition of Louis Philippe, this was a bid to maintain peace in the west.

The London conference opened in November 1830. By late December the five powers had agreed that Belgium should form an independent state. Palmerston's argument was that separation was the only solution calculated permanently to settle the dispute between the Dutch and the Belgians and to keep France within the borders of 1815. This, combined with the self-denying ordinance by which each of the five powers renounced any claim on Belgian territory (which in practice affected only France) was what persuaded the eastern powers reluctantly to accept that a popular revolt could result in treaty revision. In January 1831 the five powers assigned to Holland the frontiers of 1790, agreed to negotiate with the German Confederation a separate status for Luxemburg, and established the principle that the new kingdom of Belgium would be a neutral state, guaranteed by the five powers. Neutrality was intended to be the substitute for the barrier fortresses of 1814, most of which were demolished. In this way France was committed by new treaties to her own containment. Had the Dutch immediately accepted these terms, the Belgian question would have been settled by three months of conference diplomacy. Their refusal to do so prolonged the Belgian crisis for another two years and postponed the final settlement until April 1839 when all the parties involved signed the Treaty of London. In 1831 and 1832 the British and the French twice used force to coerce the Dutch into accepting the settlement. On both occasions the French attempted to gain something for themselves. With their troops actually in Belgium they felt in a better position to demand concessions. It was Palmerston who opposed them with the threat of war. Throughout the Belgian crisis England was the only great power which was not prepared to treat it as a matter for compromise. Palmerston insisted that such vital interests of security for Great Britain were at stake that no important concessions could be made to either the French or the Dutch. The eastern powers were forced to abandon their policy of suppressing popular revolts by vigorous great-power intervention in order to work with Great Britain for the containment of France, and the French were forced to relinquish their territorial ambitions to avoid the prospect of isolation and, perhaps, war.

Whereas the French government was convinced that a challenge to Great Britain on Belgium involved great dangers, in Italy the same restraints did not apply. Austrian policy was markedly anti-French. Metternich made no secret of his dislike of the new regime. Moreover, Austria in Italy was a weaker opponent than Great Britain had been in the Low Countries. In central Italy France sought to exert her legitimate influence as a Catholic power, which the non-Catholic powers were in no position to deny. Lastly, French objectives in Italy were political rather than territorial; they wished to act as the patron of the reform and anti-Austrian movements within the Italian states. The great-power conflict produced by the revolutions of 1831 in the Papal States and in the two outposts of Habsburg despotism, Parma and Modena, was less serious that the crisis over Belgium. There was no question of territorial revision, and the French were not prepared to go to war to uphold the doctrine of non-intervention in Italy. All they wanted was a striking diplomatic success. They were disposed to think that they could achieve it, first because Russia was preoccupied by the revolution in Poland and could give only moral support to Austria, and secondly because the Whig government in England would not assist

Metternich to shore up petty absolutisms in Italy. Austria without allies was the one rival the French felt they could confidently take on. They hoped to prevent Austrian intervention to suppress the revolts in central Italy by threatening counter-intervention. Metternich was not, however, prepared to abdicate Austria's authority in the peninsula. He did not want a war over Italy any more than the French did, but he was convinced that, whatever happened, Austria must defend her interests and her great-power status. Late in 1831 Austrian troops entered the Papal States; the French retaliated by a naval occupation of the papal port of Ancona. The government in Paris declared that when Austria evacuated her troops, France would withdraw her frigates and marines. This did not occur until 1838. Yet French intervention in Italy was much more of a disaster than a diplomatic triumph. The supremacy of conservatism in Italy under Austrian auspices was achieved despite the French; the Pope was horrified that a Catholic power should openly champion his domestic enemies; and the three eastern powers, alarmed by French action, agreed in 1833 on measures to forestall such counter-intervention in the future. French action in Italy was a policy of gestures rather than of confrontation. The major consequence these gestures secured was the strengthening of the conservative alliance against her.

In Poland, as in Italy, the new monarchy in France sought to appear as the patron of the oppressed. There was a large number of Polish émigrés in Paris and it suited the government, taunted by its republican opponents for its failure to liberate the enslaved peoples of Europe, to adopt a radical stand on an issue which fundamentally it was powerless to affect. Moreover, the Poles, like the French, had a case against the treaties of 1815, and all French governments from the Restoration to the Second Empire thought it looked less selfish to emphasize the grievances of others. In November 1830 a revolt broke out in Warsaw which quickly spread to the rest of Russian Poland. The French began to act as if there was a Polish question in European diplomacy; they condemned Russia's suppression of the revolt and suggested a meeting of the great powers to decide what measures of reform they should advise Russia to adopt in Poland. There was in fact no Polish question in European diplomacy, any more than there was an Irish question. The disaffected subjects of the strongest powers might gain much sympathy abroad, but they could not expect other states to take up arms on their behalf. By their protests to the Russians over the treatment of the Poles the French merely strengthened the repugnance in which Nicholas I held France. Palmerston received a deputation of Polish émigrés in London; he made clear his sympathy for them but equally he pointed out that he could do nothing for them. The British position was unequivocal: Russia ruled Poland by established treaty rights which accusations of misrule could not undermine. To attack them would be to strike a blow at the existing order throughout Europe. For the British government the Russian oppression of Poland was an integral part of the international order which contained France in the west. In the last resort there was no possible basis for Anglo-French co-operation on Poland. On this issue, as in Belgium and Italy, the French government pursued a policy which appeared to be radical but which in fact fell far short of a direct challenge to the Vienna system.

Holy Alliance and *Entente Cordiale*, 1833–48

The Near Eastern crisis of 1832–33 was a direct consequence of the Greek revolt. In late 1831 Mehemet Ali invaded Syria, which he claimed as the reward promised him by the Sultan for the assistance which the Egyptians had been asked to give the Turks in the Morea. In April 1832 the Sultan declared war on his vassal. This was followed by several months of negotiations in which both sides unsuccessfully attempted to gain the support of the European powers. In December 1832 the war was renewed and the Turks were decisively defeated at Konieh. The Sultan then turned to the British government to save the Ottoman empire from disaster. Palmerston did not really appreciate the gravity of the crisis in the Near East. He was reluctant to intervene, if only because to do so would require increased naval expenditure to fit out more ships, and this was regarded as impossible for a government committed to financial retrenchment. In the early nineteenth century British governments sought to maintain Great Britain's status as a great power by threats of increased expenditure rather than by actual increases. This was a powerful deterrent when the other powers could not afford to build large navies. Palmerston was equally reluctant to follow an Austrian lead and allow the crisis to be settled by conference diplomacy at Vienna. By these decisions he unwittingly paved the way for a Russian triumph.

The Turks, desperate for support, turned to their former enemies. Nicholas I readily offered the assistance which the British had refused. He had good reasons for doing so. He saw the crisis in the Near East as part of the revolutionary upsurge which had already disturbed Europe. To support Turkey against her rebel subject was consistent with his European policy of containment. Secondly, Nicholas was anxious to prevent the collapse of Turkey; in 1829 a committee had reported to the Emperor that it was in Russia's interest to support Turkey until such time as her collapse could be fully exploited by Russia. Lastly, Nicholas wanted to prevent Mehemet Ali from taking Constantinople and installing himself as sultan. He did not want an energetic and reforming ruler in control of the Ottoman Empire. Essentially Russian policy was directed towards the maintenance of the *status quo*, a weak Turkey always susceptible to Russian pressure. By the spring of 1833, with the Egyptian army only 150 miles from Constantinople, the Turks were dependent on Russian naval and military assistance. In July of that year this dependence was formally confirmed by the Treaty of Unkiar Skelessi. The treaty, which was to last for eight years, was a pact of mutual assistance in case of attack. In a secret article Russia relinquished her right to call on the assistance of Turkey in return for Turkish agreement to close the Straits to foreign warships. This too was a Russian attempt to maintain the *status quo*; it confirmed a long-standing tradition of Ottoman policy that the Straits were closed to warships of all nations. It applied as much to Russia as it did to the other powers. The British and the French were greatly alarmed by the treaty. They believed – quite wrongly – that the Russians had acquired the right to open and close the Straits at will, and Palmerston was genuinely convinced that the new Russian policy was a prelude to the partition of the Ottoman Empire. He refused to accept Nicholas's assurances that the treaty represented no fundamental change in Russo-Turkish relations. He and his cabinet colleagues could not conceive of a situation in which Britain and Russia were pursuing identical policies in the Near East.

After their triumph in the Near East, the Russians turned their attention to central Europe. Once again they sought to strengthen the *status quo* by specific agreements. Nicholas I realized that in order to place his relations with Austria on a secure footing he would have to offer Metternich assurances on the two great issues over which he was suspicious of Russian policy: the Near East and Poland. Nicholas and Metternich met at Münchengrätz in September 1833 and quickly concluded an agreement. The two powers agreed to act together to preserve the existing dynasty in Turkey, to defend the Sultan against the attacks of Mehemet Ali, to consult each other if the Turkish empire were to collapse, and mutually to guarantee their Polish possessions. This unequivocal Russian commitment to the maintenance of the existing order was intended to allay Metternich's fears that Russia sought expansion at the expense of her two weak neighbours. A month later the three eastern powers signed the Convention of Berlin, which was essentially a renewal, albeit in a modified form, of the principles of the Protocol of Troppau. Whereas Münchengrätz witnessed the Near Eastern and Polish agreement, the Berlin Convention established the basis for the future relations of the three powers in central Europe. This was in reality no more than the renewal of the Russian guarantee of support to Austria and Prussia against the Revolution and France. They agreed to assist their fellow monarchs to suppress revolution, and bound themselves to prevent the counter-intervention of a fourth power. It was this clause that was the most important result of the French occupation of Ancona. The Russians were well content with the various agreements they had concluded: 'all this seems to me' wrote the Emperor, 'to ensure our security and our defensive position'. The great strength of the eastern alignment was the inequality of power within it; both the Austrians and the Prussians were dependent on Russian support in case either or both were attacked by France or were overwhelmed by revolution. In German affairs, particularly where the stability of the smaller German states was concerned and in the affairs of the Confederation, Prussia was expected to follow an Austrian lead. In the last resort, the alignment was held together by Russia's willingness to respect Austria's interests in the Near East and by her vast military power. Palmerston, however, was convinced that 'the military organization of Russia's political fabric renders encroachment upon her neighbours almost a necessary condition of her existence'. He was determined to destroy the new Russian position in the Near East and to create a counterweight to Russian power in Europe. In the early 1830s the British government was convinced that the Russians posed an even greater danger to the peace of Europe than France.

The British and French governments reacted differently to the triumphs of Russian diplomacy in 1833. The French were more alarmed by the Convention of Berlin, which they believed was specifically directed against them; the British saw the greatest danger in the Near East where Turkey had been made unnaturally dependent on her most dangerous enemy. Talleyrand, the French ambassador in London, and leading members of the cabinet in Paris were convinced that the difference of outlook could be overcome by a general defensive alliance between the two powers whereby France would assist Great Britain to defend her interests in the Near East, and in return the British would support the French in Europe. Talleyrand's alliance proposal was rejected by Palmerston. Although he wanted French assistance against Russia in the Near East, he did not want to give the French security in Europe. The alliance which the French proposed would have placed the two governments on equal terms. Palmerston's aim was to perpetuate French fear of isolation and thus render them permanently dependent on British goodwill. He was convinced that, if ever they were freed from this anxiety, the French would revive their territorial ambitions. In fact, Palmerston sought to do in the west what Nicholas had done in the east: exploit the weakness and fears of his potential allies to force them to accept an agreement on his terms. In this Palmerston eventually succeeded. In January 1834 he finally refused the general alliance which the French offered. In March he offered instead a limited agreement designed to serve what were essentially British interests in the Iberian peninsula. The triumph of Russian diplomacy in 1833 in the Near East and eastern Europe was followed in 1834 by the triumph of British diplomacy in the west. There could be no doubt that these two powers dominated the European states system.

Canning's intervention in Portugal in 1826 had only been successful in the short term. After the immediate danger to the pro-British regime was past, the British marines were withdrawn, and in the following year the Portuguese government fell victim to those forces against which Canning had tried to protect it. By 1828, when the French withdrew their army of occupation from Spain, old-style absolutism had been restored in both Spain and Portugal. The two rulers, Ferdinand VII in Spain and Don Miguel in Portugal, looked to the three eastern powers for support, especially financial, and guidance, particularly after the July revolution in France and the appointment of a Whig government in England. In the early 1830s the British and French lost their positions as the patrons of the peninsular monarchies. Between 1830 and 1834 Palmerston made several attempts by diplomacy to destroy Don Miguel and his absolutism in Portugal. But all his attempts to restore Queen Dona Maria and the liberal constitution of 1826 failed. Ferdinand VII's determination to main-tain absolutism throughout the Peninsula was the greatest obstacle in the way of Palmerston's Portuguese policy. The death in 1833 of Ferdinand VII and the succession of his infant daughter Isabella II changed both peninsular politics and great power relations in the Peninsula. The late king's brother, Don Carlos, who was an exile in Portugal, refused to recognize his niece as Queen of Spain and began to gather together an army to invade Spain and claim the throne. The Spanish Regent, Queen Cristina, turned to England for support and offered to assist in the destruc-tion of Portuguese absolutism in return for British assistance in destroying the Carlist challenge to the new order in Spain. It was as a result of these realignments that the Quadruple Alliance of April 1834 was created.

Palmerston's aim was to associate France with the new treaty but to exclude her from the actual military and naval operations in Portugal. The French had little alternative but to accept the offer, first because they wanted an agreement with England and secondly because they saw British intervention in Portugal as a precedent for French intervention in Spain. Moreover, some French ministers hoped that some time in the future this limited treaty could be transformed into a defensive alliance. In late April and May 1834 British and Spanish forces quickly destroyed the military bases of the two pretenders in Portugal. The constitution of 1826 was restored and both Miguel and Carlos were forced into exile. Within two months Carlos returned to Spain and joined the Basque revolt. To the provincial insurrection was now added a disputed succession and a war of ideas, between Madrid liberalism on the one hand and clerical absolutism on the other. From the outset the eastern powers supplied the Carlists with arms and money, usually channelled through the lesser absolutist states. In July 1834 the British and French signed Additional Articles to the Quadruple Treaty in the hope of cutting off supplies to the Carlists and strengthening the new liberal regime at Madrid. Palmerston argued that although the letter of the treaty had been fulfilled by the expulsion of the pretenders from Portugal, the spirit of the treaty demanded that the two great-power signatories to the treaty were morally obliged to assist Spain to destroy the challenge of Carlism. From the outset Palmerston was determined that the new alliance should have a wider significance; 'the new confederacy of the west', he claimed, counterbalanced the 'triple league of the despotic powers'. The British government regarded its rivalry with Russia as the main problem of its foreign policy. 'There is', wrote Palmerston, 'the same principle of repulsion between Russia and us that there was between us and Bonaparte.' In the 1830s Russophobia became an important element in shaping British attitudes towards Europe. It combined a hatred of absolutism with a deep-rooted belief that Russia was an expansionist and aggressive power. The Russian government, by contrast, was never as overtly anti-British as the British were anti-Russian. As far as Nicholas was concerned, his main enemy was 'the Revolution', and he regarded France as the principal source of all revolutionary excitement. The Russians were far more anti-French than anti-British. Moreover, both the British and the Russians sought by separate means to maintain the territorial order, the British in the west, the Russians in central and eastern Europe. Equally, both powers strove to maintain internal order, the Russians by resolute opposition to political change, the British by promoting limited change from above. In fact the gulf between

Great Britain and Russia was not nearly as great as Palmerston supposed. The French soon realized that their British ally was as determined as the eastern powers to contain them. In the late 1830s they set out to destroy both the western liberal and the eastern autocratic alignment, and to create a new one centred around themselves.

In both England and France there were powerful influences opposed to the liberal union of the west. The Tory opposition in England condemned Anglo-French co-operation as a disastrous betrayal of the national interest, and in Paris many leading politicians regarded it as involving the sacrifice of the recovery of French honour and prestige to purchase the goodwill of England. The French resented British attempts to place themselves on a footing of equality with France in Spain. Although many French politicians were in fact opposed to the intervention of the French army in Spain to end the civil war, they sought jealously to guard their sole right to intervene and their political ascendancy at Madrid. The very issue on which the union of the two powers was cemented by treaty obligations became a matter of constant conflict between them. In the Near East too British and French policies were beginning to diverge. Palmerston was convinced that Turkey must be released from her unnatural dependence on Russia, while by the mid-1830s the Orleans Monarchy was beginning to cultivate good relations with Mehemet Ali. Moreover, throughout the 1830s the British watched anxiously French expansion in Algeria, and were determined to oppose further French conquests of North African territory. By the late 1830s French Mediterranean policy had reverted to its former anti-British bias. In 1836 Thiers, during his first ministry, attempted to reshape the European policy of France. This was grounded in the recognition that England as much as Russia was a barrier to French recovery. He believed that Austria and Prussia were as much prisoners of their alliance with Russia as the French were of their alignment with England. His aim was to secure some sort of an agreement with either or both. This was a French bid to assert her equality with her two great rivals: France must create her own alignment rather than remain the junior partner of another power. The favourable response which Thiers's initial overtures met in Vienna was merely a ploy on Metternich's part. He sought a public affirmation by the French of their dissatisfaction with the liberal alliance. This would destroy the illusion entertained by liberals and revolutionaries that they were protected by the two liberal powers, and Metternich hoped that it would incline England to look to her erstwhile allies for support against France. He had no intention of beginning alliance negotiations with the French. Foiled in his attempt to detach the

German powers from Russia, Thiers attempted to repeat the tactics of Chateaubriand and demonstrate French military power in the west by a slow build-up of French forces in Spain. This too was essentially anti-English. He wanted France to have all the credit for the destruction of Carlism, which was the surest way of reasserting French dominance at Madrid. In the autumn of 1836 this policy also collapsed as a result of disagreements within the French government and between Thiers and the king. By the beginning of 1837 the British and the French had ceased to co-operate in western Europe. Palmerston readily acknowledged this but he held on to the entente in the belief that it could still serve British interests in the Near East.

In the five years between the Treaty of Unkiar Skelessi and the out-break of the second Mehemet Ali crisis, the Near East was a source of constant, if low-key, tension between the powers. The basis of Palmerston's belatedly formulated Near Eastern policy was the wish to strengthen the Ottoman Empire to enable it to resist attack from either Mehemet Ali or Russia. He hoped that an extreme programme of reform would revitalize the Ottoman Empire and transform it into a modern and efficient state, able to look after its own interests. While it remained vulnerable to its enemies the British were prepared to afford it the protection it needed. Although the Russians had no desire to strengthen Turkey, neither were they prepared to allow Mehemet Ali to precipitate its collapse. Insofar as they were both opposed to Egyptian expansion, there was a real community of interest between the British and the Russians. All that was needed for actual co-operation was for the Russians to make clear the anti-Egyptian basis of their policy. Moreover, by the late 1830s both powers realized that no lasting settlement could be achieved in the Near East without some agreement between them. Palmerston was certainly prepared to work with the Russians in a great power conference if they would abandon the Treaty of Unkiar Skelessi.

The Near Eastern crisis of 1839–41 was precipitated by Turkey. The Sultan, who had long sought revenge for his earlier defeat, declared war on Mehemet Ali in April 1839. Within six weeks the Ottoman Empire was on the verge of collapse. In June the Egyptians inflicted the crushing defeat of Nizib on the Turkish forces. This, combined with the death of the Sultan, Mahmud II, the succession of a sixteen-year-old boy and the mutiny of the Ottoman fleet produced panic at Constantinople. After an unsuccessful attempt to reach agreement with Mehemet Ali, the Turks saw no alternative but to allow the great powers to intervene, and in August 1839 the Porte empowered them to reach a settlement on its behalf with Mehemet Ali. The first phase of the crisis – armed conflict in the Near East between Turkey and Egypt – was over. In the second and longest phase, the future of the Near East was only one of the problems involved.

In the period from August 1839 to November 1840 great-power diplomacy was dominated by the interaction of three problems: the search for a settlement in the Near East, the role of France in the European states system, and the future of great-power alignments. When the French raised the threat of war, it was on the Rhine and not in the Near East. Moreover, it was the French who prevented a speedy settlement of the second Mehemet Ali crisis by the concerted action of the five powers. By the autumn of 1839 the French began to argue that Mehemet Ali must not be robbed of the fruits of his victories, and that the expansion of Egypt did not of necessity threaten the security of the Turkish empire. The British claimed that this was a complete volte-face on the part of France. In fact it was only a question of emphasis. Since the mid-1830s the French had regarded their close relationship with Mehemet Ali as an integral part of their Mediterranean policy. Thiers, who returned to office in 1840, was not prepared to abandon Mehemet Ali and follow a British lead in the eastern Mediterranean. Palmerston regarded the French proposal that Mehemet Ali should retain Syria as compatible neither with the strengthening of Turkey nor with safeguarding the land routes to British India. The Anglo-French entente which Palmerston had never openly repudiated despite its breakdown in western Europe, in case it might be needed to restrain Russia in the Near East, had completely collapsed. It no longer served any British interest. Palmerston then turned to Metternich for support. He believed the Britain and Austria could co-operate in the Near East despite their different outlooks in Europe. Metternich gladly responded to Palmerston's approach; he saw it as an opportunity for Austria to take the lead in a settlement of the Near East, and to pave the way for the revival of the old four-power alliance. It was the Russians who denied Metternich the chance of such a diplomatic triumph. In September 1839 Nicholas I sent a Russian diplomat, Baron Brunnow, to London to seek Anglo-Russian co-operation for the settlement of the Near Eastern crisis.

In 1839 the Russians, like the French, changed the emphasis rather than the direction of their Near Eastern policy. Stability and order remained their basic objectives. The imperial government had already abandoned its right under the Treaty of Unkiar Skelessi to assist Turkey when it agreed, in August 1839, to seek an international settlement to the crisis. In fact the state of Russia's finances was such that she could not afford to assist Turkey; the greatest army in Europe was immobilized by an empty treasury. In 1841 the treaty would expire, and it was apparent to the Russians that the British government was determined to frustrate any attempt to renew it. This meant that the Russians had to seek other means to prevent the collapse of Turkey and to keep the Straits closed in time of peace to foreign warships. In addition to these Near Eastern objectives, Nicholas and his foreign minister, Nesselrode, sought to destroy the Anglo-French entente in Europe, isolate France and contain the forces of revolution by the revival of the four-power combination of Chaumont. This was his traditional policy in a new form. Palmerston's response to Brunnow's overtures was immediate and favourable. Just as Canning had worked with Russia on the Greek question to achieve a settlement acceptable to both powers, so Palmerston was prepared to do the same in the second Mehemet Ali crisis. In January 1840 Great Britain and Russia agreed to work together to confine Mehemet Ali to Egypt.

Throughout 1840 there were several determined attempts from within the British Cabinet to frustrate Anglo-Russian co-operation. Some of Palmerston's cabinet colleagues regarded the preservation of the Anglo-French entente as vastly more important than the question of whether Egypt or Turkey should possess Syria. In March 1840 Thiers formed his second ministry; he was disposed to believe it more likely that Palmerston would be forced by his colleagues to make concessions to France than that France would be forced to watch while Great Britain and Russia coerced Mehemet Ali. This was a serious miscalculation. In July 1840 the British and the Russians, supported by Austria and Prussia, concluded a series of agreements on the Near East. The new Anglo-Russian accord was given a solid basis by their mutual resolve to close the Straits to foreign warships in time of peace. This, like the Treaty of Unkiar Skelessi, confirmed the traditional practice of the Ottoman Empire. The four powers also agreed the terms they would offer Mehemet Ali if he submitted to them in ten days: the hereditary rule of Egypt, and the possession of southern Syria for his lifetime only. If, however, he refused these terms, the four powers resolved to drive him out of Syria and confine him to Egypt. If it became necessary to enforce the latter terms, Great Britain and Russia, the two naval powers, would undertake the task. Confronted by the Anglo-Russian accord, the French hoped to salvage something for Mehemet Ali and to recover their fast diminishing prestige by changing the issue. They began to suggest, first by hints and then by direct menace, that the coercion of Mehemet Ali could mean war on the Rhine. This alarmed the Austrians and the Prussians who would bear the brunt of any

French attack. Palmerston's pro-French colleagues urged the necessity of concessions to Mehemet Ali in the Near East to avoid war in Europe. Both Palmerston and Nicholas stood firm, the former because he believed that the French were bluffing, the latter because he knew that if the French attacked on the Rhine the British would offer him subsidies to put his army on a war footing. In August 1840 the British, Austrians and Russians began the coercion of Mehemet Ali against a background of war fever in Europe. By September some French newspapers were assuming that war was inevitable. It was at this point that Louis Philippe abandoned Thiers and the prospect of war and sought a new ministry which would work for peace. It was not difficult to find a new government which regarded peace in Europe as more important to France than the possession of Syria by Mehemet Ali. On 4 November the British Mediterranean fleet bombarded and captured Acre; as a result Mehemet Ali evacuated Syria and on 27 November accepted the terms offered by the four powers. With the change of government in France and the submission of Mehemet Ali, the crisis was effectively over. In July 1841 an agreement was concluded between the five powers on the Straits which confirmed the provisions of the agreement of July 1840. It was Austria and Prussia, rather than Great Britain and Russia, who were most anxious to bring France back into the concert. Their real concern was not the Straits but peace on the Rhine.

After the crisis was over, the Russian government offered the British a formal agreement which would place their co-operation on a permanent basis. It was a straightforward alliance proposal which was intended to be the final link in the chain of Russia's agreements. Palmerston politely refused it on the grounds that the two powers had a sufficient community of interest, in the containment of France and the maintenance of order in the Near East, to ensure good relations in the future. Russia's position in Europe was undoubtedly strengthened by the outcome of the crisis. Her relations with her two central European allies remained unchanged; to this united front of absolutist powers, the Russians could add a new stability in the Near East and good relations with England.

The fall of Melbourne's Whig government and the formation of a new Tory ministry under Peel, with Lord Aberdeen at the Foreign Office, did not jeopardize the improvement in Anglo-Russian relations. The Tories had been consistent critics of the liberal alliance, and had always urged a united front of the four allies of Chaumont to maintain peace and order. Aberdeen, however, soon came to the conclusion that good relations between England and France were as necessary as good relations between England and Russia. If the two great powers of western Europe remained at loggerheads it was quite possible that one of their many conflicts of interest, inflamed by the mutual hostility of public opinion in both countries, could lead to war. Aberdeen did not seek to revive the liberal alliance of the 1830s, which had in reality been directed against Russia, but to create an atmosphere of trust and understanding in which disputes could be avoided. His attitude was shared by Guizot, the new French Foreign Minister. He believed that Thiers, by bringing France to the brink of war, had also brought her to the verge of another revolution. Stability and order within France herself required peace between the powers, and the best way to achieve this was by sympathy and understanding between the leading statesmen of Europe. Whereas Thiers had attempted to defy the other powers, Guizot tried to persuade them to respect France. His aim was to reconcile France to the Vienna settlement and to her new status in Europe, and to reconcile the other great powers, particularly the autocratic monarchies, to the new order in France. He, like Aberdeen, was convinced that peace and stability in the west demanded good relations between France and England.

By the end of 1843 both Aberdeen and Guizot spoke of the existence of an entente cordiale between England and France. This was no more than an understanding between themselves, supported by a growing intimacy between the British and French royal families. In neither country was the new entente popular. It was strongly criticized in the parliaments and press of both countries, it was never wholeheartedly supported by all the members of the British and French cabinets, and it was frequently thwarted in its execution by British and French diplomats. The entente was in fact an extremely fragile instrument of co-operation. Its fragility was revealed on virtually every issue on which the two ministers sought to reach a compromise. The British were outraged by the treatment accorded to the British consul, Pritchard, in the Friendly Islands after the French annexation in 1842. This dispute dragged on for several months, and Peel publicly described French policy in the Pacific as 'a gross insult' to Great Britain. In 1844 the two powers clashed over Morocco; the British suspected the French of attempting to take control of the country whereas the French claimed that they were merely pursuing Algerian rebels who were using Morocco as a base for their activities.

The Moroccan crisis of 1844 coincided with the visit of the Russian Emperor to England, which was intended to demonstrate and consolidate the cordial relations which existed between the two powers. As far as Europe was concerned, the two powers soon found common ground; they both feared the growth of French naval power in the Mediterranean, and the Russians were easily convinced that the entente cordiale was not directed against them. On the Near East the two governments held discussions in early June which were confirmed in a memorandum of September. They agreed to co-operate if Turkey seemed to be on the point of collapse or was attacked by another power. This was no more than an agreement to do in the future what they had done in 1840. In the event of the complete collapse of Turkey, they pledged themselves to establish a basis for joint action. These discussions mostly reflected Russian anxiety about the state of the Ottoman Empire, but they also revealed the willingness of the two powers to discuss issues of common concern in a frank and open manner. Having settled their outstanding differences by the Straits Convention of 1841, all the two powers could do was to establish a fund of goodwill upon which they could draw when future differences arose.

In late 1844 and 1845 Aberdeen and Guizot tried to breathe life into their ailing entente by an exchange of views on Spain. The result was a series of informal agreements. The ostensible problem was the choice of a husband for the young Queen of Spain and her sister, the heiress to the throne. The real issues at stake were French prestige and the division of influence in the Iberian peninsula between the two great powers. Guizot was determined to secure from Aberdeen a clear admission that France was the great-power patron of the new liberal order in Spain. At the same time he was willing to concede that English influence should predominate at Lisbon. In the late 1830s and the early 1840s Anglo-French rivalry in Spain had fastened itself upon the conflicts within Spanish politics between the Moderados, the pro-French party, and the Progresistas, the pro-English party. In 1844 a *coup* by Moderado politicians and army officers destroyed the Progresista ascendancy established, under British auspices, in the late 1830s. Guizot wanted to arrange marriages for the Queen and her sister which would consolidate the Moderado hegemony at Madrid and thus strengthen the links between France and Spain. This would demonstrate that France, like the other great powers, enjoyed influence over her smaller neighbours. Aberdeen was content to follow a French lead on Spanish questions, thereby implicitly recognizing the predominance of France at Madrid. Unlike Palmerston, he saw no need to contest French influence in Spain. Aberdeen's only qualification was that France must not dictate to Spain on the marriage question. In 1845 he agreed to the marriage of the Queen's sister to the Duke of Montpensier, son of the King of the French, after the Queen had married and produced an heir. His insistence that the marriage should be delayed was an attempt to make the marriage merely a Bourbon family arrangement rather than a political issue.

In 1846 Guizot's policy on the Spanish marriages was threatened on two fronts. The Spanish government began to resent French dictation on the question, and in June the Peel government in England fell and was replaced by a new Whig ministry led by Lord John Russell, with Palmerston again at the Foreign Office. The latter was not prepared to accept the fundamental assumption of Aberdeen's policy that France should enjoy an indisputable preponderance at Madrid. He adopted a policy on the marriage question which enabled him to appear to be the champion of Spanish independence when in reality he was attempting to undermine French influence at Madrid. Guizot feared that he, like Thiers in 1840, would be outmanoeuvred by Palmerston. He abandoned the agreement he had concluded with Aberdeen and hastily concluded a double-marriage pact: the Queen of Spain would marry a Spanish Bourbon of impeccable Moderado credentials and at the same time her sister would marry Louis Philippe's son.

Palmerston was greatly alarmed by the arrangement. After an unsuccessful attempt to prevent the marriages, he concluded that the entente was in ruins and that England must look to the eastern powers to help curb the ambitions of France. Guizot believed that, in view of the hostility of England, he must cultivate good relations with Austria to prevent the isolation of France. From the autumn of 1846 to the revolutions of 1848 Great Britain and France were not only engaged in a bitter war of words and a struggle for influence over the small powers in the west, but they were also competing for the goodwill of the Eastern Powers. Palmerston looked to Russia, and to a lesser extent Prussia, for support whereas Guizot concentrated his efforts on gaining the goodwill of Metternich. The autocratic powers exploited this competition for their support. In the autumn of 1846 they extinguished the republic of Cracow, the last enclave of Polish independence, which had been a constant source of irritation to them. They claimed that it was the centre of Polish revolutionary activity, a danger to peace and order in eastern Europe. Although both the British and the French governments protested against the suppression of Cracow, their protests were muted and independent. Neither wished seriously to offend the eastern powers.

In the last year of his long stewardship of the Austrian empire, Metternich enjoyed a pre-eminence in European diplomacy which had been denied him since the Congress of Verona. He owed this importance not to his skill as a diplomat but to the many serious problems which

Austria faced. The challenge to Austria's authority in central Europe began in 1847. In 1848 the nature of the challenge was to change from protest to revolution, and to extend from a few to virtually all areas within Austrian influence. Metternich for his part sought to isolate each of his problems and to deal with them by a combination of coercion and diplomacy. This was his final legacy to the Habsburg monarchy: his successor Schwarzenberg was to restore Habsburg authority in 1849 and 1850 by using the same tactics.

In 1847 the two areas of crisis were Switzerland and Italy. In several Protestant cantons of the Swiss Confederation there were demands for radical reform of the Federal constitution, and in several Italian states there were protests against rising prices and inefficient government. Both problems could have been settled by Austro-French co-operation. Throughout the early part of 1847 Guizot claimed that he was just as anxious as Metternich to maintain stability and order in these areas. In fact, however, Metternich found it extremely difficult to persuade Guizot to work with him openly against the so-called forces of disruption. The French government wanted order restored in Switzerland under French rather than Austrian auspices, and moderate reform from above under French patronage rather than repression by Austria in central Italy. Fear of revolution in central Europe did not unite France and Austria; it merely intensified the competition between them. The French were never really prepared to ignore any opportunity to weaken Austria. In Paris Austria's difficulties were always regarded as France's opportunities. There were, moreover, domestic reasons why Guizot could not work with Austria alone; to do so would allow his critics in the Chamber to claim with justice that he had destroyed the entente cordiale and aligned the liberal monarchy with a reactionary power.

On Switzerland, Guizot saw a way out of this dilemma by attempting to lead a concert of all the powers. If France took the initiative, Guizot, not Metternich, would earn the credit for pacifying Switzerland, and in a combination of five the presence of England would guard him against the charge of working exclusively with the absolutist powers. In fact it proved impossible to create a concert of five on the Swiss question; the four continental powers openly sympathized with the Swiss conservative cantons, the Sonderbund, whereas the British government took the side of the radicals. Only Franco-Austrian intervention in the autumn of 1847 could have saved the Sonderbund from defeat. Guizot did not contemplate intervention until it was too late, and after the radicals had triumphed he could not permit unilateral Austrian intervention to rob them of their victory. By December 1847 the radicals were in a position to push through the Federal reforms they wanted, and both Guizot and Metternich were forced to accept that their Swiss policies had failed. Metternich was quite right when he said that Austria and France had worked against each other rather than with each other.

Italian problems in 1847 were much more serious than the Sonderbund crisis; Palmerston was convinced that they could lead to war. He feared that the intervention of the Austrian army in the central Italian states would result in French counter-intervention, and that the two armies would inevitably clash. By the end of the year the Austrians, the French and the British were each trying separately to prevent revolution and war in Italy. Metternich was determined to preserve Austria's dominance in the peninsula. As far as he was concerned there could be no alteration of the 1815 settlement and no compromise with reform movements which attempted to undermine the sacred principle of monarchical authority. Although he was prepared to consider the possibility of some modification in the administration of the two Austrian provinces of Lombardy and Venetia, he was nevertheless reconciled to the fact that repression might become a necessity. In the autumn of 1847 the British government sent a cabinet minister, Lord Minto, on a roving mission to Italy to urge the Italian rulers to reform their governments and the Italian reformers not to provoke Austria into military action. This British bid for the patronage of the Italian reform movements forced Guizot to make a counter-bid. French diplomats in the peninsula urged Italian liberals to look to France for guidance and support. The Austrians resented both French and British interference in Italian affairs, and the French resented the intrusion of the British. They regarded the anti-Austrian and the reform movements in Italy as exclusively under French direction. This pattern of great-power rivalry in Italy was interrupted, first by the February revolution in Paris and then by the Italian revolutions themselves. In 1848 it was the British government which took the initiative in the search for a new order in Italy which was both anti-Austrian and anti-French.

The revolutions of 1848 and the restoration of order

The French revolution of 1848 revived for a second time the fear that a revolutionary regime in France would attempt to destroy the 1815 settlement by a war of conquest and liberation. The fact that the new government was republican seemed to the autocratic powers to increase the danger. In their propaganda the republicans had consistently called for a war of the peoples of Europe against the kings of Europe. Lamartine's denunciation of the treaties of 1815 immediately after he assumed the post of head of the provisional government was regarded by many as a clarion call to war. Yet it soon became evident that republican France sought peace. Lamartine was in much the same position as Louis Philippe and his ministers had been in 1830: it was necessary to condemn the 1815 settlement to appease French public opinion, but it was equally necessary to respect the treaties in order to avoid war. War would have pushed the revolution leftwards, which the moderate republicans were extremely anxious to prevent; they believed that it would almost certainly result in the defeat of France and the imposition of a far harsher settlement than that of 1815. Lamartine's Manifesto, published in March 1848, was accompanied by private assurances to British politicians that the republic wanted peace. The four powers reacted to the revolution in France in 1848 just as they had done in 1830: they would not offend the new regime as long as it kept within its own frontiers.

In March the events of 1848 ceased to follow the pattern of 1830. On 13 March Metternich fell from power in Vienna, and with him collapsed the central authority of the Habsburg monarchy. In Hungary, Italy and Bohemia the revolutionary leaders turned their backs on Vienna and sought a separate future. Later in March, after riots in Berlin, the Prussian king, Frederick William IV, conceded constitutional reforms and appointed a new liberal ministry which declared that 'Prussia merges into Germany'. The only two great powers untouched by revolution were Great Britain and Russia. This fact brought the diplomatic dominance they had so long enjoyed into even sharper relief. For the next three years Palmerston and Nicholas I were the diplomatic arbiters of Europe. Neither the British nor the Russians had a single policy in 1848. They would have had if the revolutions had directly attacked their vital interests or if all the revolutions had been republican movements determined to destroy the institutions of monarchy and aristocracy in an attempt to construct a new social order. In those cases they would have defended themselves and the principle of monarchy. The diversity of the nature of the revolutions elicited flexible responses from both powers. The Russians in particular were prepared to wait upon events; throughout 1848 Nicholas adopted the pose of patient vigilance. He did not become 'the gendarme of Europe', the defender of the old order, until 1849 when the conservative forces in central Europe had already recovered their confidence and the political initiative from the divided revolutionaries. Palmerston, on the other hand, in Italy and to a lesser extent in Germany, sought to guide the forces of change and modify the territorial order of 1815. His efforts were much less successful. Nevertheless, both powers in their separate ways sought to prevent a European war arising out of the revolutions. They were determined to localize all the revolutionary and military conflicts and to prevent the intervention of any great power except themselves. In this they succeeded; the three wars of 1848–49, in Italy, in Hungary and in the two duchies of Schleswig and Holstein, were all kept distinct. Only in one, that in Hungary, were two great powers involved, and they fought on the same side.

Although Great Britain and Russia urged peace in the spring and summer of 1848, the revolutionary governments did not heed their advice. The German liberals attempted to incite the Poles to fight a war of liberation against Russia; they hoped that this would divert Russian attention while they attempted to reconstruct Germany. This was a false start, and the failure of the Polish revolution to materialize created consternation amongst high-ranking German liberals. They feared that Nicholas I would use his military power to destroy the revolution in Germany. It was the Italians who unleashed the first war of 1848. It was not strictly a revolutionary war, although the Italians found it convenient to depict it as such. In reality it was a war of aggrandizement of one monarch against another. Charles Albert, the king of Sardinia, sought to exploit the revolutions in northern Italy to acquire the two Austrian provinces of Lombardy and Venetia. He was the first monarch since Charles X in 1830, to seek territorial expansion as an antidote to revolution in his own state. In the next two decades others were to follow his example. In March and April a motley collection of regular troops and volunteers from other Italian states achieved some successes against the Austrians. Nevertheless in May the provisional governments of Lombardy and Venetia voted for union with Sardinia. These events convinced Palmerston that Austrian rule in Italy was bankrupt, and that the best way to secure the intended objectives of the Vienna settlement in Italy – a stable order free from French control – was by the creation of a new northern kingdom under the house of Savoy which would include Lombardy and Venetia. Palmerston offered British mediation between the belligerents on the condition that Austria would hand over her Italian possessions to Sardinia. He had high hopes for his projected settlement; it would end the war, strengthen northern Italy against France, safeguard British interests in the Mediterranean and enable the Austrians to concentrate on the recovery of their power in Hungary. It was, however, overtaken by events in northern Italy, over which Palmerston had no control. In July the Austrian forces, commanded by Radetzky, inflicted a major defeat on the Italians at Custoza; on 9 August Charles Albert concluded an armistice with the Austrians. The French government was greatly relieved by the collapse of the Italian war effort. Cavaignac, who had emerged as the strong man of the revolution after the June days in Paris, did not want the fragile republic embroiled in a war with Austria, nor did he wish to see Sardinia expel the Austrians without the assistance of France. This would mean revision of the 1815 settlement without French gains which would be a serious blow to the republic. In August Palmerston tried to salvage something from his plan for northern Italy by devising a scheme by which Great Britain and France would prevent Austria from recovering Venetia. This failed when his cabinet colleagues and Queen Victoria refused to support it.

The example set by Sardinia in taking up arms against the treaties of 1815 was followed by Prussia in northern Germany. The two duchies of Schleswig and Holstein, although predominantly German in population, were ruled by the king of Denmark. In April the inhabitants appealed to their fellow Germans for assistance to expel the Danes. The Prussian army entered the duchies, and by the end of April the Danish army had retreated into Denmark. The Prussians claimed that this was not an old-style war of conquest but a new-style war of liberation: a foreign king would be replaced in the duchies by a German prince. The Danes took their stand on treaty rights, and appealed to Great Britain and Russia to uphold the integrity of the Danish monarchy. The Russians merely denounced the attack by one monarch on the possessions of another, but they would not use their troops to defend Denmark or chastise the Prussians. Palmerston's response was more positive; he insisted that the Prussians should evacuate the duchies although, unlike the Russians, he had no means at his disposal to force them to do so. On northern Germany, as on northern Italy, the British had decided opinions; Palmerston believed that he knew what was best for both Austria and Prussia. His predecessor, Castlereagh, had realized that in central Europe Great Britain could not have an effective policy without allies. Palmerston had an ambitious policy but no allies; his various schemes consequently came to nothing. Although within a few months, the Prussians withdrew from the duchies, this was not as a response to the British request that they should do so. The withdrawal of his army was Frederick William's way of separating himself from the German liberal movement. This was not an isolated act of defiance by the Prussian king but part of the growing conservative reaction against revolution. In the last months of 1848 the old ruling élites in Europe recovered their confidence and used military force to recover their authority. As far as the territorial order of Europe was concerned, the revolutions of 1848 had had far less direct impact than the revolutions of 1830. A new state, Belgium, had emerged out of the upheavals of 1830; in 1848 the old frontiers were everywhere restored.

The recovery of monarchical and autocratic authority did not immediately result in the restoration of the old order in central Europe. In 1849 France ceased to be the only revisionist power; other states attempted to increase their power by jettisoning the work of the peacemakers. Both Austria and Prussia put forward extensive schemes of reconstruction for Germany, and Sardinia made a second bid for expansion in northern Italy. The old order was restored only after Austria had defeated Sardinia at Novara, recovered Hungary with the assistance of Russia, and eventually abandoned her own plan for the reorganization of Germany. Already with Russian backing, she had forced the Prussians to accept the revival of the German Confederation. The complete recovery of Austria was the most important development of the years 1849–51. It could not have been achieved without Russian military and diplomatic assistance. The moral of 1848 was that revolutionaries could not modify the settlement of 1815 by agreement amongst themselves; the moral of post-revolutionary diplomacy in the years from 1849 to 1851 was that the great powers could not do so either by agreement. In both Italy and Hungary short, localized wars were necessary to complete the recovery of the old order. British and French attempts to persuade the Austrians and the Sardinians to settle their differences by negotiation failed, and in March 1849 Charles Albert, pushed on by his radical parliament, renewed the war in northern Italy. Within a week he had been defeated at Novara, and he abdicated in favour of his son, Victor Emmanuel. Austria could defeat Sardinia, but England and France would not allow her to dismember so weak an opponent or to punish her harshly. The consequences of defeat for a small state with powerful protectors were less traumatic than for great powers. Sardinia could make war because she enjoyed immunity from disaster. This was an important asset which Cavour was later to exploit. Austria had to content herself with inflicting a mild rebuke on Sardinia in the form of a war indemnity which was finally agreed upon in August 1849.

Moreover, even before the northern Italian question had been settled, the French had seized the opportunity provided by Austria's preoccupation in Hungary and Germany to exploit the problems in central Italy. In November 1848 Rome had turned against the Pope. In April 1849 Louis

Napoleon Bonaparte, who had become President of the Second French republic in December 1848, sent an army to the gates of Rome. He could not decide whether to act as a good Catholic and restore the Pope or to pose as a good republican and protect the republic. This was a secondary aspect of the question; the real purpose of the expedition was to enable France to assert her power at last in the peninsula after having missed the opportunities for intervention afforded by two wars in northern Italy. In June 1849, after new elections in France had returned a majority of pro-clerical deputies, the French army destroyed the republic and restored the Papacy. The temporal power of the Pope now rested on the permanent presence of French troops in Rome rather than on the occasional intervention of Austria. In 1832 France had challenged Austrian influence in the Papal States; in 1849 Austria was in no position to challenge France. In effect, therefore, the French expedition to Rome significantly reduced Austrian influence in Italy. This was a profound change which was to have far-reaching consequences within a decade.

In Hungary the Austrians could not easily recover their authority without Russian assistance. The Hungarian question in 1849 was exclusively an Austro-Russian concern; neither the French nor the British wished to see Austria lose Hungary: without it she would have ceased to be a great power, and then there would have been no bulwark in central Europe to contain the expansion of Russia. Hungarian independence had no champions because it would have destroyed the system of five great powers. Changes in the hierarchy of power and small adjustments of territory in western and central Europe were developments which the powers were prepared to contemplate, but far-reaching changes in eastern Europe were opposed by all the powers. Great Britain and France feared that the collapse of Habsburg power in eastern Europe would strengthen Russia, Prussia feared that it would permanently concentrate the attention of Austria on her German interests. The Russians saw successful Hungarian defiance of Austria as a terrible precedent which the Poles might attempt to follow. In April 1849 the Austrian army was expelled from Hungary. In May the Russian army intervened in Hungary to save the Austrian empire from dissolution.

The Hungarian question only became a matter for the five powers after the revolution had collapsed. Kossuth and the other leaders of the revolt fled to Turkey, whereupon the Russians demanded their extradition. This resulted in the most serious Anglo-Russian disagreement since the mid-1830s. The British government was convinced that the Russians were using the refugee question to browbeat Turkey while the other powers were preoccupied by European questions. Louis Napoleon did not repeat the mistake of Thiers and separate France from England on a Near Eastern issue. In fact the two powers co-operated closely in stiffening Turkish resistance. Yet soon after the refugee question was satisfactorily settled, the Anglo-French accord collapsed when Palmerston intervened at Athens in support of the complaints of the Maltese Jew Don Pacifico, a slight to France and Russia, the other two 'Protecting Powers' of Greece. Although both the British and the French were profoundly disturbed by the increase in Russian power and prestige after the intervention in Hungary, they were not prepared to set aside their own interests to combine against Russia. In both London and Paris Austria was by 1850 regarded as little more than a client state of Russia. It was generally assumed that on all but local questions she would follow a Russian lead.

It was only in Germany that the crisis provoked by the revolutions of 1848 was prolonged beyond the end of 1849. In 1849 it was a three-sided conflict between Austria, Prussia and the liberal parliament of Frankfort and the Middle States, each with its own scheme of reconstruction. The latter two dropped out of the struggle when the King of Prussia contemptuously refused the crown of a 'small Germany', excluding Austria, offered by the liberal deputies at Frankfort, and when Prussia insisted on dominating, rather than assisting, the efforts of the Middle States to reform the Bund on a federal basis. Despite their common antagonism to the idea of a new Germany made by popular approval and consent, neither Austria nor Prussia wished to revive the old Confederation. The Austrians proposed an empire of 70 millions which included all the non-German possessions of the Habsburgs and in which Prussia would play an insignificant part. The Prussians put forward a plan for a small Germany from which Austria would be excluded and which the government at Berlin would easily dominate. Ideally both powers rejected a return to dualism. The Prussians pressed ahead with their plan for a new Germany, formed the Erfurt Union and in May 1850 held a congress of German princes at Berlin.

It was the Austrians who changed the nature of the struggle when they temporarily abandoned their plan for a reconstructed Germany. Almost immediately they gained the support of the German princes who saw the institutionalized rivalry of Austria and Prussia in the Confederation as the best guarantee of their own independence. Moreover, they brought the Russians, who had hitherto tried to remain neutral, over to their side. Nicholas wanted to repeat the tactics of the early 1830s and recreate the united front of conservative powers against France and the revolution. In order to achieve this Austria and Prussia must settle their differences, and by offering to revive the Confederation of 1815 the Austrians had – so the Russians believed – shown a commendable willingness to compromise. By the end of 1850 the Russians were actively supporting the Austrian argument that disturbances in the state of Hesse should be suppressed by the forces of the Confederation and not by those of the Erfurt Union. The Prussians had to decide whether they would resist Austria by war or yield to her by diplomacy. There was a war party in Berlin, but the king took the final decision to concede; he feared republican France more than he feared Austria, and he particularly regretted the estrangement between Russia and Prussia. The Prussians 'surrendered' at Olmütz in November 1850: the Erfurt Union was dissolved and the Confederation of 1815 immediately restored.

At first sight the Prussians had lost everything. In fact they had gained a great deal since 1848. In the revived three-power alliance Prussia was certainly treated as the equal of Austria, whereas in its earlier existence Prussia had been regarded as the least of the three. Moreover, if war had come, Prussia would probably have been forced to concede territory to France on the Rhine to purchase her neutrality. The king believed that this would have been a greater calamity than an agreement with Austria. Prussia was in no way weakened by her surrender; she had merely abandoned one plan for a new Germany, not her pretensions to its leadership.

The restoration of the 1815 order in central Europe and the revival of the three-power conservative alliance was above all a setback for republican France. Her Bonaparte President was denied the opportunity of seeking an alliance with another revisionist power, and there could be no doubt that the purpose of the Russian-dominated alliance was to isolate and contain France. Moreover, the fact that her new ruler was a Bonaparte enabled the Russians to create alarm at Vienna and Berlin about the intentions of France. It was easy for them to argue that sooner or later the nephew would attempt to emulate the uncle. By raising the spectre of war on the Rhine the Russians hoped to discipline their recently revisionist allies.

Their fears were not well grounded. Louis Napoleon's aims in foreign policy were limited. He did not want a war of revenge against the four allies of Chaumont such as was advocated by some Bonapartists and most left-wing republicans. He merely sought a modification of the territorial order in the west and equality with England and Russia in the hierarchy of the great powers. In fact he entirely adopted the assumptions, aspirations and fears of his Bourbon and Orleanist predecessors. Like them, he resented the containment of France and the loss of status and prestige which the military defeat of 1815 implied; he shared their fear of isolation and their dread of a war in which France would be opposed by the other four powers. There was nothing really new in his programme. Louis Napoleon used a few Bonapartist slogans to make his policy look different, but they were mainly for domestic consumption. In 1830 Louis Philippe said the Orleans monarchy wanted peace; in 1848 Lamartine said the republic sought peace; in 1852 Napoleon III said the empire meant peace; they all meant that France would not go to war until she had secured allies to guard against the danger of another defeat.

The Crimean War and the end of the Holy Alliance

It was his search for equality with Great Britain and Russia that led Napoleon III to take up the Near Eastern question. He had made a false start in Europe early in 1852 by appearing to threaten the independence of Belgium shortly after the *coup d'état* which made him Emperor. This had united the four powers against him. Palmerston raised the cry of French aggression to draw the four allies of Chaumont together. By turning away from Europe to the Near East Napoleon III sought to isolate and challenge Russia whom he regarded as the main obstacle to the recovery of France. He did not think in terms of war; he expected merely a conflict of prestige. In Europe the other four powers combined against France, in the Near East Prussia had no interests and neither Great Britain nor Austria had any interest in strengthening Russia. It was the contentious problems of the Near East which attracted Napoleon III. He chose to challenge Russia for two reasons: first, Nicholas I was extremely hostile towards France and the new imperial regime. After Napoleon's assumption of the imperial title Nicholas refused to address him as brother which was customary practice between sovereigns. Secondly, Napoleon III accurately assumed that the anti-French emphasis of the Russians was an attempt to provide the revived Holy Alliance with a unity of purpose which it would otherwise have lacked. Without Russian support Austria was weak, and freed from Russian control Prussia might revive her German ambitions. Moreover, the issue on which Napoleon III fixed his attention, the guardianship of the Holy Places, was likely to divide Austria, a Catholic power, from Russia, the leading Orthodox state. At the beginning of 1852 the French government demanded that the Ottoman government hand over the keys to the Holy Places in and around Jerusalem to the Catholic monks, thus denying the Orthodox monks the protecting role they had exercised for some years. This demand was followed by a series of overt threats; by the end of the year the Turkish government conceded.

The unconcealed irritation of the Russians with the triumph of French diplomacy at Constantinople was just what Napoleon III wanted. If the Russians had not reacted in this way the French would have worked hard for nothing. The Russian Emperor saw behind the conflict of prestige over the guardianship of the Holy Places a struggle between 'order' and 'revolution'. His aim was to strengthen the forces of order by a serious blow to French prestige. He would humiliate France in the Near East by demonstrating that Turkey feared Russia more than she feared France and that she must concede more to Russia than she had to France. In February 1853 Nicholas sent Prince Menshikov on a special mission to Turkey, first to demand the dismissal of the minister who had bowed to French pressure over the Holy Places, and secondly to secure the recognition of Russia's right to protect the Christian subjects of Turkey, a right allegedly based on the Treaty of Kutchuk Kainardji of 1774.

Prior to Menshikov's departure Nicholas had tried to reassure both the British and the Austrians that he would respect their interests in the Near East. In January 1853 he assured Seymour, the British ambassador, that if Turkey collapsed Great Britain would receive a fair share of the partition. This was a renewal of the assurance he had given on his visit to London in 1844 to Aberdeen, who had become Prime Minister in 1852. In the event, the Menshikov mission provoked a Near Eastern crisis in which the British and the Austrians as well as the French became deeply suspicious of Russian policy. As the crisis developed, the conflict of prestige between France and Russia was relegated to second place. The Turks resisted Menshikov's demands, and in May 1853 he left Turkey after the complete failure of his mission. In July the Russians occupied the two Turkish provinces of Moldavia and Wallachia and declared that they would withdraw only when the Turks conceded the demands which Menshikov had been instructed to make. Both the British and the Austrians were alarmed by Russia's action, the Austrians because the occupation of the principalities not only gave the Russians control of the lower Danube, the most vital trade route of the Habsburg empire, but exposed the entire eastern and south-eastern frontier of the Monarchy to Russian military pressure. The British could see no other explanation for Russia's occupation of the principalities than a determination to pursue a forward policy in the Near East. It seemed to many of the Whig members of the coalition government that their belief that strong despotic monarchies inevitably sought expansion was well grounded.

At the outset of the crisis both powers wanted a settlement which would enable the Russians to withdraw without damage to their prestige and by which Turkey could concede something to Russia without affecting her independence. In 1840 conference diplomacy had solved the Near Eastern crisis; in 1853 the Austrians were convinced that it could do so again. There was, however, a fundamental difference between the two crises: in 1840 the powers were responding to a crisis provoked by Egypt whereas in 1853 two great powers, the French and then the Russians, had themselves provoked the crisis. There was a profound difference between deciding on terms which Great Britain and Russia were agreed they would impose on Mehemet Ali and finding a solution to a Russo-Turkish conflict. A conference could only succeed if the Russians were prepared to retreat. It met at Vienna in July 1853; the representatives drew up the Vienna note which contained the concessions which the powers thought Turkey could reasonably be expected to offer the Russians. The Turkish government afterwards insisted upon amendments, but in September the Russians declared that the Vienna note gave them all they had demanded.

This 'violent' interpretation destroyed the concert. Whether, as Paul Schroeder has argued, the British were deliberately seeking a confrontation with Russia to destroy her prestige, in flagrant violation of the first commandment of concert diplomacy, 'Thou shalt not humiliate a great power', or whether they simply felt that Russia had shown that she could not be trusted, the concert's attempt to find a compromise solution had failed, and the British and the French turned to naval action to demonstrate their determination to defend Turkey. They had already advanced their fleets into Turkish waters. In September 1853 they ordered them through the Dardanelles. By opposing the Russians the British could not escape co-operation with France. Napoleon III realized that the British were trapped: if they advanced, France could advance with them; if they retreated, France would replace them as the protector of Turkey against Russia.

As it was, encouraged by these indications of western support, the Turks proceeded to declare war on Russia on 4 October 1853. Four days later the British cabinet decided to send their fleet up to Constantinople; it took the decision in ignorance of the fact that the Turks had already declared war. Its intention was to protect Turkey against Russia; its effect was to encourage her to begin hostilities. On 30 November the Russians destroyed the Turkish fleet at Sinope. This was a perfectly legitimate act of war but in the British and French press it was portrayed as a massacre. From the autumn of 1853 onwards there was a war fever in Great Britain and neither the British nor the French government could ignore the fact that public opinion – in Great Britain at least – wanted a decisive setback for Russia and the humiliation of the Russian despot. This could only be achieved by war, and in March 1854, after their ultimatum demanding Russian evacuation of the principalities was rejected in St Petersburg, war was duly was declared by Great Britain and France.

Meanwhile, Nicholas tried to secure his position in Europe before the hostilities began, sending Prince Orlov on a special mission to Vienna and Berlin in January 1854 to ask the two German powers for their armed neutrality. The Austrians and Prussians refused this reversal of roles: the purpose of the Holy Alliance was that the Russian army should protect Austria and Prussia in Europe, not that their armies should protect Russia in the Near East. The failure of the Orlov mission was a turning point not only in the Near Eastern crisis but also in the history of Europe: it confirmed the collapse of the Holy Alliance which for three decades had been the great bulwark of order in eastern and central Europe. The unity of the three conservative monarchies under Russian leadership had held France in check and given the Vienna treaty structure its security and strength. When Orlov returned to St Petersburg empty-handed one of the essential props of the Vienna system had disappeared.

It was the British and the Russians who sacrificed most by their refusal to compromise in 1854. The Crimean War brought to a close the era of Anglo-Russian domination in Europe. Great Britain, by fighting with France in the Near East, and Russia, by fighting against her, both conceded equality to her as a Mediterranean power. During and immediately after the war the French asserted a dominance in Europe which was made possible by the collapse of the Holy Alliance and then by the defeat of Russia. Moreover, French participation in the war made the issues at stake as much European as Near Eastern. Both the British and the Russians wanted a Near Eastern war which would not affect adversely the European treaty structure. They both fought for limited and localized objectives. The French, by contrast, fought for essentially European ends: to confirm the destruction of the Holy Alliance, and to deal a decisive blow to Russia's power and prestige in central Europe, in other words to create the conditions which would make revision of the 1815 settlement possible.

The outbreak of the Crimean War altered fundamentally the pattern of great-power relations. In the west France was no longer forced into a subordinate relationship with England. The liberal alliance of the 1830s was based on French fear of isolation in Europe; the alliance of the mid-1850s was based on equality in the Near East which the French intended to convert into primacy in Europe once the war was over. In eastern and central Europe the Russians had for three decades raised the spectre of French aggression on the Rhine and in Italy in order to persuade Austria and Prussia to follow their lead. This device worked only as long as the Russians made the maintenance of peace and order in Europe a higher priority in their foreign policy than the pursuit of their own interests in the Near East. The Crimean War reversed the order of priorities. The Russian obsession with their Near Eastern position changed their attitude towards France. From the early 1820s to the mid-1850s the Russians were determined to oppose French revision in Europe; after 1856 they saw it as a force to be exploited in the pursuit of their own revision in the Near East. By destroying the pattern of great-power relationships on which the Vienna treaty structure rested the Crimean War made territorial revision in Europe possible. Although not a shot was fired in Europe, it was certainly one of the most important European wars of the nineteenth century.

The outbreak of the war, meanwhile, had placed the Austrians in a terrible dilemma. Buol, immeasurably exasperated at the intransigence of all the belligerents, was determined to keep out of the war at all costs. On the one hand, he found Russia's latest pretensions absolutely unacceptable. In the long debate that ensued in Vienna, in the spring of 1854 he set his face firmly against suggestions from the pro-Russian military party at court in favour of making a common cause with Russia against Turkey and establishing Austrian control of the western Balkans, even though the emperor himself was quite attracted by the idea. Like every Austrian statesman after him, Buol considered the price of such co-operation prohibitive, both in terms of weakening Turkey, and of establishing a dangerous Russian strategic threat to the Monarchy in the eastern Balkans. In Buol's view, recent events showed that even the *status quo* of 1853 hardly gave the Monarchy adequate security: not only could there be no question of allowing Russia to make further advances in the Balkan peninsula; she must actually be pushed back from the position she had held in 1853. Austria must find her security in a permanent weakening of Russia in the Near East that would deprive the latter of any springboard from which she might launch further advances against Turkey, either militarily, or diplomatically, in the manner of the Menshikov mission.

To strengthen his hand for the impending confrontation with Russia, Buol managed to extract a limited degree of support from Prussia and, eventually, the other German states, in the form of a defensive alliance to maintain the *status quo* (April 1854). In July, he followed this up with an ultimatum to St Petersburg that forced Russia to withdraw her forces from the Danubian principalities. This gave the Monarchy immediate strategic security – especially as the theatre of war then moved to the distant Crimea – and at Turkey's request, the Austrians then proceeded to occupy the principalities themselves. The long-term consequences of all this for the Monarchy's position in the European states system were, however, to be very serious. In the first place, the rage it unleashed in St Petersburg finally set the seal on the destruction of the Austro-Russian alliance: 'The time has come,' Nicholas declared, 'not to fight the Turks and their allies, but to concentrate all our efforts against perfidious Austria and to punish her severely for her shameful ingratitude.' In the second place, it weakened Austria's position *vis-à-vis* Prussia within the German Confederation. Bismarck, now the Prussian representative in the Diet at Frankfort, astutely exploited the reluctance of the German states to be drawn into the conflict – in which their interests were, after all, hardly directly involved – to convince them of their common interests with Prussia in restraining the 'warmongers of Vienna'. The resounding defeat in the Diet, in February 1855, of an Austrian proposal to mobilize the forces of the Confederation, was a telling illustration of Prussia's enhanced position within that body. At the same time, Prussia's insistence on the strictly defensive character of the alliance of April 1854, and her interpretation of her own neutrality in a markedly pro-Russian sense – for example, her allowing Russia to use Prussian ports to evade the Anglo-French blockade – stood in stark contrast to Austria's threatening troop movements, which tied down so many of Russia's forces as to condemn her to a position of relative inferiority, and to humiliating defeat, in the Crimean theatre. In St Petersburg, these things were long remembered; and insofar as the Austro-Prussian struggle over the future of the 1815 settlement in Germany was as much an international as a purely German affair, the consequences for Austria's position in the states system were to be extremely embarrassing.

Buol's objective, meanwhile, was nothing less than the safeguarding of Austria's Near Eastern interests within the framework of a peace based on compromise and conciliation that would permit him to revive the concert after the war. Given the intransigent views of the belligerents, this task was to prove the equivalent of squaring the circle; but Buol seemed to be making some progress when he drew up with the French (who were hoping by accommodating him to draw Austria into the war) the so-called Four Points of 8 August, expressly designed to prevent any Russian advance in the Near East in future: the Russian occupation of the principalities was to be replaced by an international guarantee, and the Danube was declared a free river for navigation. The third point stipulated that the Straits Convention of 1841 should be revised 'in the interests of the balance of power', and the last demanded the renunciation by Russia of her claim to protect any Christian minorities whatsoever in the Ottoman Empire. Not only was Russia to be deprived of her capacity to threaten Turkey in the Black Sea, she was to give up protectorates – notably in Serbia and in the Danubian principalities – which had been established at considerable sacrifice of Russian blood and money, expressly sanctioned in international treaties, and implicitly recognized by Austria at Münchengrätz. The Four Points, by which Buol committed himself to altering the *status quo* in the Near East – in this case, of course, to Russia's disadvantage – showed that Austria too had finally broken with the policy of the Holy Alliance.

Buol's policy must seem all the more ambitious in that he was in no position to pursue it by military means. Although he was always prepared to consider diplomatic pressure, and even threatening military gestures, he was absolutely determined to avoid any commitment to support the western powers in actual war. After all, the Monarchy was still convalescent from the upheavals of 1848–49: several provinces were under martial law as late as May 1854, and at the end of 1855 the demands of financial stringency even forced the government to reduce its expenditure on the army. Above all, it was clear to everybody in Vienna that if Austria joined the war, it would be transformed from a Crimean war into a great European war – one that would be fought chiefly on Austrian territory, and in which the western powers could be of little direct assistance.

Once it was clear that there was no chance of war in the Balkans, the war in the Crimea began. In September 1854 the British and the French landed an expeditionary force of 50,000 men in the peninsula. Two months of inconclusive fighting followed; the western allies failed to take the fortress of Sebastopol, and the Russians failed to drive their enemies out of the Crimea. When winter set in there was military deadlock in the theatre of war. During the winter of 1854–55 the diplomats in Europe tried to do what the generals in the Near East had failed to do: end the war.

Once again the two Western Powers concentrated their diplomacy on attempting to secure new allies. In December, the Austrians signed a formal alliance with the western powers pledging themselves to work with them to implement the Four Points (and a secret agreement with the

French to maintain the *status quo* in Italy) but they still refused to commit themselves to fight. The Sardinian government, by contrast, alarmed by the news of the Franco-Austrian treaty, anxiously entered a war in which it had no direct interest. King Victor Emmanuel and his conservative advisers were determined not to let Austria outbid them for the favour of the western powers. Cavour, the prime minister, was more realistic; he believed that whatever attitude a small state like Sardinia adopted to the war in the Near East, Napoleon III would in any case seek to make use of its grievances against Austria and its ambitions for territorial expansion whenever he wanted to attack the 1815 settlement in Italy. In fact, it was the British who took the initiative, hoping that the appearance of a Sardinian force in the Crimean theatre would serve as a counterweight to the preponderance of the French (who had 200,000 troops in the Crimean theatre as opposed to 50,000 British) in the alliance. Cavour yielded to the king rather than resign, and as a consequence Sardinia agreed in February 1855 to send 15,000 men to the Crimea. The months from December 1854 to February 1855 were strictly speaking 'the Italian phase' of the Crimean War.

By the spring of 1855 Anglo-French tension over the conduct of the war was a subject of public comment. In France the war was unpopular, and Napoleon III was anxious to placate public opinion either by spectacular military successes or by a negotiated settlement. In England the war itself was popular but the belief that it was being mismanaged by the government aroused immense indignation. The fall of Aberdeen's ministry in January 1855 and the formation of a new government led by Palmerston was generally regarded as a commitment to a more vigorous prosecution of the war. In fact the new ministry was almost immediately forced to begin peace negotiations. It was the Austrians who took the initiative in bringing the belligerents to a peace conference at Vienna. French war weariness, the death of the Emperor Nicholas on 2 March and the accession of Alexander II, whose personal prestige was not committed to the war, seemed to provide a possible basis for compromise, and now that their interests were secure the Austrians had no objection to a negotiated settlement of the third of the Four Points. Indeed, a Russian offer to settle for an agreed balance of naval power in the Black Sea was accepted by the British and French representatives at the conference, but rejected in London and Paris. The British government wanted to punish Russia, Palmerston still insisting that 'small gains' would not be enough, and that there must be 'great territorial changes'. The French feared that without a devastating blow to Russian power and prestige, after the war was over in the Near East the 1815 order in Europe might remain stable and secure. The British feared that unless Russia was decisively defeated there would be no stability or security in the Near East. The western powers had left themselves with no alternative but to resume hostilities in the Crimea. In June they began the siege of Sebastopol and in September it fell.

The fact that French operations at Sebastopol had been strikingly more successful than those of the British deepened the rift between the two allies. Consequently, the British determined to redress the balance by an 1856 campaign in Asia Minor, using British, Turkish and Sardinian but not French forces, while confining the French to assisting British naval operations in the Baltic. Napoleon, however, was all too aware that neither prizes for the British in Asia, and certainly not the idea of 'mourir pour Kronstadt' would do anything to stem the growing unpopularity of the war at home. There, inflation had led to riots in the cities and the government had just been compelled to increase the Paris garrison from 30,000 to 40,000. Marxists were wrong: far from going to war in response to growing domestic discontent, domestic discontent was forcing Napoleon to make peace.

In exasperation, he turned to the Austrians, who were particularly anxious for a speedy conclusion to hostilities before the British could expand the allied war aims even further. Hence Buol's readiness in the agreement he reached with Count Bourqueney on 14 November, to toughen up the Four Points, hoping (rightly) to clinch the deal with the French, and (wrongly) to enhance Austria's security. Hence his endorsement, despite his original misgivings, of his allies' demands for the actual neutralization of the Black Sea – an unprecedented infringement on the sovereignty of a great power; hence his own insertion into the preliminary peace proposals of the allies of the demand that Russia cede to Moldavia the Bessarabian bank of the Danube, which Russia had held since 1812. The demand for the cession by Russia of southern Bessarabia, intelligible enough in terms of Austria's narrower commercial and strategic interests, was perhaps a fateful error. After all, since the 1820s Austria's great-power status had depended, not on control of the Danube delta, but on a good relationship with Russia. The cession of southern Bessarabia – the first loss of territory by Russia since the time of Peter the Great, and, to make matters worse, at the dictation of a power that had not even fired a shot – was regarded in St Petersburg as a greater stain on Russia's honour than any of the demands of her opponents on the battlefield. Hatred of Austria rose to new heights of intensity – and not only in St Petersburg, but at the

Russian embassy in Vienna whence the ambassador, Gorchakov, was about to assume the direction of Russian foreign policy.

At first, Palmerston, still set on his grandiose plans for 1856, was all for defying the allies – he 'did not give a fig for Napoleon' – and simply rejecting the Buol-Bourqueney terms; but the cabinet refused to back him up and agreed in December to Buol's putting them in an ultimatum to St Petersburg (albeit perhaps in the hope that Russia would reject it). Now it is true that, in that event, Buol was even now threatening only to break off relations, not to join the war: continuing colossal budget deficits had actually forced him to reduce expenditure on the army at this time. The Russians, however, decided to accept the terms: not only was the diplomatic horizon darkening – the news that Sweden had actually concluded an alliance with the allies on 21 November came to the Tsar as a tremendous shock; and a desperate appeal from his uncle in Berlin to make peace was hardly encouraging. Most important, the military and supply position was generally agreed to be so hopeless that another campaign in 1856 might see the loss of the borderlands, even a retreat to the pre-1721 frontiers. On the other hand, even if the Russians now found the idea of dealings with Austria totally abhorrent, they were certainly prepared to try to exploit the growing rift between the conciliatory French and the intransigent British to salvage something through diplomacy. On 16 January, therefore, a crown council in St Petersburg decided to accept the terms.

In the event, their calculations proved well founded, and neither the Congress nor the Treaty of Paris (30 March) was a total defeat for the Russians. True, the loss of southern Bessarabia was something they never forgave (Alexander II pointedly observing to Franz Joseph, no less than twenty years later, when Russia was about to recover the territory, that it was only thanks to Austria's 'treachery' that she had lost it in the first place). For the rest, however, the British largely isolated themselves by their extravagant demands, leaving Orlov and Morny ('the third Russian plenipotentiary' as the British put it) to establish an entente that allowed Russia to win the argument over a number of minor territorial points such as the destination of the village of Bolgrad or of the Isle of Serpents (over which the British nevertheless were quite inordinately exercised). They also managed to confine the neutralization of the Aland Islands (to relieve Sweden from Russian pressure) to a mere Anglo-Russian agreement that was not endorsed by the concert.

On the allied side, Napoleon III of course did not gain the revision of the 1815 settlement he so craved, the Austrians rejecting out of hand his offer of the Danubian principalties in exchange for Lombardy and Venetia (and also indignantly brushing off British criticisms of Austrian support for repressive regimes in Italy). As regards the original aim of bolstering up Turkey and protecting her from Russian bullying, rather more was achieved: Turkey was to carry out reforms and was to be admitted to the Concert of Europe with her territories guaranteed and further safeguarded by an additional Anglo-Franco-Austrian treaty of guarantee of 15 April. All Russia's special protectorates, dating back to 1774, were abolished and replaced by a general protectorate of the concert. Indeed, it was now established that the affairs of Turkey could only be handled by all the powers in concert, and not by bilateral negotiations. If, by the 1870s, the results of these measures were to prove disappointing, that was a problem for the next generation. More immediately, two barriers were created to give Turkey security by land and sea. The neutralization of the Black Sea relieved Turkey from any threat from that quarter (though it should be noted that Turkey was not allowed to fortify her position there either; and by forcing Russia to turn her attention away from the Black Sea towards bridgeheads in the Caucasus and Persia the British were ultimately increasing the Russian threat to India). The establishment of the Danubian principalities as autonomous units under the protection, no longer of Russia, but of all the powers, was intended to provide an obstacle to a Russian advance on Constantinople by land. At the same time, however, as radical elements in the principalities might seek to transform them into a Romanian national state, breaking away from the Ottoman Empire altogether, and perhaps even attracting Romanians living under Habsburg rule in Transylvania, the treaty had, at the insistence of Turkey, Austria and their British allies, prescribed the separation of the principalities.

The major consequence of the Near Eastern settlement of 1856 was to change the priorities of Russian foreign policy. The Russians were deeply humiliated by the exclusion of their naval forces from the Black Sea. They regarded it as an affront to their status as a great power. After the Peace of Paris the principal objective of their foreign policy was to rid themselves of this humiliation. Under Nicholas I Russia had been the guardian of the *status quo* in Europe; French revisionism in the west and the eastward spread of revolutionary ideas had been identified as the great dangers to the stability of the existing order. After 1856 the maintenance of order in Europe was relegated to second place. This was a profound change which significantly altered Russia's relations with the other powers. French desire for the revision of 1815 in the west was now a force to be exploited to achieve Russian revision of the treaty of 1856 in the Near

East. The Russians knew that they had only to wait a short time before the French would make overtures to them. Napoleon III in the late 1850s was, like Polignac in the late 1820s, anxious to link Russian dissatisfaction in the Near East with French dissatisfaction in Europe. In one important respect, however, he modified the legacy of Polignac: whereas the latter had wanted a Franco-Russian alliance directed against England and Austria, Napoleon strove to maintain good relations with England at the same time as he attempted to establish closer relations with Russia. This meant that he could not offer the Russians a direct and brutal bargain: French support for Russian revision in the Near East in return for Russian support for French revision in the west. The most he could offer was French support to rid Russia of the Black Sea clauses at another five-power congress. In fact, therefore, the two powers could not agree to work together; all they could do was to promise not to work against each other. This had important consequences for French diplomacy. If he had been able to offer a direct bargain to the Russians, Napoleon III, like Polignac, would have demanded Belgium. Denied this opportunity by fear of England, he was forced to pursue revision indirectly and encourage Sardinia to seek a new showdown with Austria. It was as much French weakness as Austrian weakness that resulted in a revival of 'the Italian question' in the late 1850s. The change in Franco-Russian relations fundamentally affected Anglo-Russian relations. In the decade after 1841 they had worked together in Europe to contain the French threat to the 1815 settlement. On most issues the other powers had been forced to follow either a British or a Russian lead. In the fifteen years after the Crimean War the British and the Russians ceased to co-operate; consequently they ceased to dominate Europe.

CHAPTER 5

The destruction of the Vienna Settlement in Italy and Germany, 1856–71

General characteristics of the period 1856–71

After 1856, forty years of peace between the great powers were followed by fifteen years of intermittent warfare. Between 1854 and 1870 all the great powers fought at least one war; Austria, France and Prussia each fought three. The object of all these wars, with the exception of the Crimean War, was the piecemeal destruction of the Vienna settlement. Each of the wars was followed by important territorial changes; the single most extensive revision of the map of Europe between the Congress of Vienna and the Versailles settlement of 1919 took place in 1866. In the 1830s and 1840s liberals and nationalists had condemned the Vienna settlement as reactionary, designed by the forces of dynastic conservatism to serve their own interests, yet in the 1850s and 1860s it was the conservative monarchies that actually destroyed it. They did so quite deliberately. Aggressive wars of national reconstruction and the identification of victory on the battlefield with national pride and regeneration were the means by which monarchical conservatism gave itself a new lease of life. Before the revolutions of 1848 the governments of the continental monarchies avoided war in order to strengthen themselves against their internal enemies; after the Congress of Paris some of them sought war for exactly the same purpose. In domestic politics the ruling élites abandoned the policy of total resistance to change; this had united all their enemies against them and produced the crisis of 1848. They realized that survival and a secure future required a more flexible response to the problems they faced. In the 1850s and 1860s the conservative ruling groups attempted to divide their opponents: they were prepared to make limited concessions to some in order to concentrate on weakening and isolating their most dangerous enemies. This process took different forms in different countries. In Sardinia the liberal monarchist Cavour worked with the conservatives to isolate the radical nationalists. In Prussia, and later in Germany, Bismarck, a conservative monarchist, succeeded in separating the forces of liberalism and nationalism. He borrowed from the programmes of both, and gave to both movements a new character and new aspirations. In France Napoleon III was, in the 1860s, prepared to concede some power to his liberal opponents in an attempt to save his dynasty and contain the republican challenge to his regime. Even the more traditionally conservative Austrian and Russian empires were forced, under the shock of defeat in war, to attempt to come to terms with fundamental problems: in Russia the social basis of the autocracy was modified by the abolition of serfdom, and in the Habsburg monarchy the political structure was changed by the compromise of 1867 with the Hungarians.

In the 1850s the emphasis on peace and order and on the maintenance of the existing treaty structure in Europe which had characterized great-power relations before the revolutions of 1848 was abandoned. So too was the fear of a general European conflagration arising out of military conflict in one area. Both the upheavals of 1848 and the conflict in the Crimea had demonstrated that wars could be limited and localized. Wars therefore ceased to be regarded as a great danger to the social order and became instead the means by which political changes within states were consolidated and given the seal of popular and patriotic approval. The localized wars of the period from 1856 to 1870 were limited in their aims: the great powers did not fight to destroy each other, merely to redistribute territory among themselves. There was a conscious effort to make the wars as short as possible. The rulers of the great powers believed that if war was prolonged and caused great hardship to the civilian population it could endanger the social order. The Paris Commune of 1870 proved them right in this respect. For the most part the politicians and the generals conducted their wars with a proper sense of restraint. Through the medium of the press governments were able to depict to their civilian populations war as a heroic spectacle which demanded respect and acclamation but not sacrifice.

The conduct of war in the mid-nineteenth century was fundamentally affected by economic and technological change. The Crimean War was fought with 'the weapons and tactics of the Napoleonic era' yet contemporaries did not doubt that England and France won the war because they were modern states with industrialized economies and sound systems of public finance, whereas Russia was a backward and inefficient state with an almost purely agrarian economy. (For his blind hostility to railway construction as liable to unsettle Russian society, Nicholas I now paid a terrible price; whereas British and French troops could be transported by sea to the theatre of war in a matter of three weeks, it took Russian soldiers marching from Moscow three months to reach the front.) By 1870 the armed forces of the great powers and the conduct of war itself had been profoundly affected by new technology. An efficient system of public finance and competent military and civilian administrations became acknowledged assets in the conduct of war. Before 1848 the continental monarchies had feared that war would impose an intolerable strain on their finances. Liberals in England and France had claimed that war was a crime against civilization. In the 1850s and 1860s most of the governments of the great powers believed that they could afford short wars without emptying their treasuries and saddling themselves with enormous debts. At the same time many intellectuals began to argue that war was an essential activity in the onward march of civilization. These were profound changes. The spread of daily newspapers made propaganda for a mass readership an essential activity of government in wartime. Most governments claimed at the outset of wars that they were the innocent victims of aggression and urged the people to unite in defence of their fatherland. Governments felt it necessary to conceal their very specific territorial ambitions behind general and idealized values. In 1866 Bismarck asked Germans to fight Germans not for Prussian expansion but for the sake of the fatherland; in 1870 Napoleon III called upon the nation to recover its glory on the battlefield, not to gain territory on the Rhine. There was real truth in the cynical prophecy of Napoleon I that 'rulers who call upon the people of Europe will be able to accomplish anything they wish'.

The fragmentation of the states system in aftermath of the Crimean War

The destruction of the 1815 order in Italy and Germany between 1859 and 1871 was only made possible by the fragmentation of the European states system in the aftermath of the Crimean War. By 1856, both the Quadruple Alliance and the Holy Alliance that had enabled that order to survive in all its essentials amidst the upheavals of 1848–50 had collapsed; and its two principal architects, Russia and Great Britain were beginning to withdraw, for a combination of ideological and practical reasons, from their commitments to uphold it. As early as 1857 one perceptive contemporary, the Bavarian minister in Vienna, could see what had happened:

> *the security embodied in the Alliance of 1815 consisted in the fact that it was designed to last beyond the achievement of its objective and to bring about a political unity in which every great power would subordinate its policy aims to the general interest and make sacrifices for the sake of the whole.... The present policies of the cabinets are no longer connected to the last peace treaty, but move along lines dictated by the individuality of each great power ... without having any common line in principle. The cabinets want peace, because they and Europe require it, and they work together in this direction at every opportunity, but more or less as their own interests demand and without having any common line in principle. That such a state of affairs is precarious is quite obvious. Many things are left to chance, many things to the boldness of one cabinet or another. The peace has no firm basis; it will last only so long as it remains a necessity for one power or another and so long as interests do not come all too openly into conflict.*

Over the next few years, to the gratification of the new generation of realists – Napoleon III, Cavour, Bismarck, even Gorchakov – intent on challenging the order as established by treaties, the era of long-term alliances based on general principles such as legitimacy and monarchical solidarity seemed indeed to have yielded to one in which alliances were to be short-term, revisionist, aggressive and directed to achieving specific concrete aims.

Of course, Russia's abdication from her role as policeman of Europe, was not merely the result of Gorchakov's narrowly obsessive desire to abolish the Black Sea clauses of the Treaty of Paris. It also reflected long-term weaknesses, notably Russia's precipitate fall from the position of leading continental power as a result of her exhaustion in the Crimean War. Nor, despite the reforms of Alexander II, was the gap between Russia and the west in terms of military capacity significantly closed – especially once a new power centre arose in the German Empire under Prussia, still virtually a vassal of Russia in the 1850s. In military terms, Russia was simply unable to keep up with her western neighbours; and even the cost of such efforts as she made to keep pace in the military field obliged her to abandon altogether her role as a major maritime power until the later 1880s. It was this enervating consciousness of Russia's relative weakness that underlay all the decisions of Alexander II and his ministers as they were confronted by momentous, and by no means agreeable, alterations to the states system in these years, and that explains in particular their acquiescence in the appearance on Russia's frontier of a mighty German empire – a situation that would have been quite inconceivable under Nicholas I.

In the European arena, therefore, the Russia of Alexander II was constrained to play a relatively self-effacing role. Not that Russia had no impact at all on the states system. It was ominous for Austria, for example, that Gorchakov and Alexander II abandoned Nicholas I's principled but unrewarding defence of the legitimist order in favour of a narrow concentration on such self-interested objectives as the revision of the Treaty of Paris. Between Austria and Prussia, if Alexander II, as the nephew of both Frederick William IV and William I, felt a genuine sympathy for Prussia, for Gorchakov it was a determination to weaken Austria as a pillar of the 1856 settlement, sharpened by personal rancour accumulated in his days as Russian ambassador in Vienna during the Crimean War that blinded him to the fact that Austria was after all, like Russia, a conservative legitimist power; and that led him to connive at her discomfiture at the hands of revolutionary Italians and a militaristic Prussia. With Great Britain there could, in Gorchakov's view, be no question of reviving that tacit collaboration that had stabilized the states system in earlier decades. True, the neutralization of the Black Sea had taken the edge off the old conflict over the Straits; and the consequent diversion of Russian activity towards the Caucasus and the central Asian khanates was not yet causing alarm in London. But in Gorchakov's view, Russia was still uncomfortably vulnerable to British naval power: 'In the Black Sea and the Baltic, on the coasts of the Caspian and the Pacific Ocean, everywhere England is the irreconcilable enemy of our interests, everywhere she shows her hostility to us in the most aggressive fashion.' Such an ingrained aversion to the British of course frustrated Napoleon III's hopes of transforming his entente with the British into a tripartite arrangement including Russia: 'Could we not agree à trois?', he asked the Russian ambassador, 'We should dominate Europe.' British fears of a Franco-Russian entente were, however, much exaggerated. Alexander II never felt he could quite trust Napoleon; and certainly never quite believed his tearful attempts to explain away the Tripartite Treaty of 15 April 1856 with Great Britain and Austria. He was prepared to go some way with him in order to divide the Crimean Coalition; and he did, thanks to Napoleon's support, score a few points in the wearisome negotiations over ambiguities in the Treaty of Paris. Alexander in turn was willing to connive at the weakening of Austria in Italy; but he was shocked by the fall of the minor Italian dynasties and virtually accused Napoleon of complicity in the revolution in Naples 'which overthrows all the principles of order and legitimacy on which all states are founded'. He was never in the least interested in Napoleon's wider plans for revision in the west; and if in 1858 he had taken umbrage when Napoleon had 'dared to mention Poland' to him in their meeting at Stuttgart, the Warsaw rising of 1863 finally finished off what had never been more than a fleeting and insubstantial phenomenon on the international scene.

The British, too, felt constrained to limit their commitments to the European states system in these years. Like Russia, Great Britain had to recover materially and psychologically from the Crimean War, in reaction to which parliament, throughout the later 1850s, refused to sanction an increase in military expenditure – which itself virtually precluded any effective action by the British to control the momentous changes that were occurring on the continent. In these years, Europe was simply not the chief priority of the world's chief financial and trading centre, and the feeling was growing that the country's military and naval resources were over-stretched. This feeling was compounded by the shock of the Indian Mutiny in 1857, and by a series of overseas commitments – the China wars, the Maori wars in New Zealand, serious disturbances in the Caribbean in 1865 – together with a whole host of problems arising from or exacerbated by the American Civil War, from the defence of Canada to the wearisome Alabama arbitration affair and the safeguarding of trade with South America. As late as 1869 it was still, according to the Foreign Secretary, Lord Clarendon, 'the unfriendly state of our relations with America that to a great extent paralyses our action in Europe'.

As far as the British could pay any attention to Europe, this was primarily focused on Russia and the Near East, and on the need to conciliate France – despite, or perhaps because of, her alarmingly fast-growing naval capacity and her equally alarming tendency to make common cause with Russia. Faced with this combination, the British had by 1858 drawn back from their Near Eastern entente with Austria and given up even the attempt to challenge the Franco-Russian interpretation of disputed clauses of the Treaty of Paris. Yet although, more generally, they would never go so far as to assist France and Russia 'to break out of those engagements which bind Europe together', and which according to Lord Malmesbury constituted 'the basic law of Europe', the fact remained that to join Austria in upholding the order established by treaty in the Near East or Italy, let alone in Germany, the British government would have needed both troops and a public opinion that it simply had not got. They were, of course, often driven to opportunistic shifts that seemed to supporters of the old order utterly unprincipled or hypocritical: 'egoism and self interest, these are the motives of England's policy', Count Apponyi declared. Short of the appearance of an actual hegemonic threat, however, the British could be fairly guaranteed to be neutral in any continental war in these years.

The role of France, by contrast, was dynamic and proactive. Even more than Cavour and Bismarck, Napoleon III could claim to be the chief instigator of the destruction of the Vienna states system. The central objective of his policy, the annihilation of the hated settlement erected on the ruins of his uncle's empire, was an *idée fixe* throughout his reign, indeed, an all-consuming obsession. As to the means of achieving it, he was to prove a man of extraordinary patience and flexibility: wars, congresses, cabinet diplomacy and the doctrine of self-determination of peoples were all pressed into the service of the cause. Once the Crimean War had demolished the alliance structure that had held France in check since 1815, the estrangement between Great Britain and Russia and their withdrawal from the centre of the stage permitted France to enjoy for a decade or so a somewhat artificial pre-eminence in the European states system. Yet as early as 1860 the re-emergence of Great Britain, skilfully playing the nationalist card herself to throw Napoleon's Italian plans into total disarray, demonstrated that any hopes he may have had of emulating his uncle as arbiter of Europe had been mere wishful thinking.

One problem, of course – and this reflected the disjointed nature of the states system of the 1860s as much as the distrust in which Napoleon was held and the many-faceted character of his foreign policy that offended so many interests – was that Napoleon, unlike the Prussians with their Russian alliance, could never find a partner to go with him though thick and thin. In the 1860s France's slide into isolation was accelerated by her activities in areas remote from Europe, from Cochin China to Mexico, which kept a sizeable portion of the French army occupied overseas, with correspondingly deleterious consequences for her authority nearer home. By the time Napoleon realized – in 1866 – that his labours for the king of Prussia (and the king of Sardinia) had brought their proverbial reward, it was too late. The creation of a united Italy and a formidable Prussian monarchy on France's borders had transformed the European states system and effectively put an end to French primacy. So long as the French refused to admit this, while yet, in the still fragmented states system of

1866, failing to find a partner to help them remedy their grievances, uncertainty persisted, until the war of 1870–71 inaugurated a new and more lasting hierarchy of powers.

At the opposite end of the political spectrum from Napoleon III and the realists, Austria was throughout these years the power least willing to accept the demise of the legitimist order – or, rather, Buol and Franz Joseph acted on the assumption that in place of the defunct Holy Alliance, a new legitimist system had actually come into existence, in which Austria and her friends would uphold the 1815 order in Europe and the 1856 order in the Near East as constituting the fundamental law of Europe. These friends, according to Buol, included Great Britain, Prussia and even, until Napoleon III began to connive at Russia's attempts to amend the Treaty of Paris, France. Perhaps it was partly a reflection of the young Franz Joseph's sense of honour and respect for the pledged word, perhaps an ingrained habit of thought from Metternich's day that automatically defined the interests of Europe as identical with the interests of Austria – at any rate Buol insisted that Great Britain would simply be bound, if not from conviction, then from self-interest as a legitimist power, to fight for Austria's position in Italy. He clung to this nostrum despite acerbic criticism from the British, at the Congress of Paris and later, of Austria's association with tyranny in Italy, and despite their pusillanimous failure to stand up to France and Russia in the Near East. This particular illusion was, of course, shattered in 1859; but the Austrians continued to blind themselves to the realities of the states system into the 1860s, imagining that Napoleon III would sacrifice his influence over Italy in order to help them to enforce the Treaty of Zurich; and that Prussia would be content to serve as their loyal lieutenant in Germany and even help them to recover their position in Italy. In the world of Bismarck, Cavour and Napoleon III, the Austrians with their notions of treaty rights, legitimacy and pledged words of honour were indeed babes in the wood. As Bismarck himself complacently observed: 'Austria will believe I am not serious until the very eve of the battle.' That Franz Joseph himself came to recognize this is clear from his own retrospective remark to his mother: 'We were very honourable, but very stupid.' It was only with the conclusive victory of Prussia in 1871, however, that the Habsburgs finally came to terms with the demise of the 1815 system in central Europe.

The fragmentation of the concert, and the consequent fragility of the international order of 1856, were well illustrated by the case of the Danubian principalities. In theory, the objectives of the Treaty of Paris and by extension of the Tripartite Treaty of 15 April that bound Great

Britain, France and Austria to uphold them, had been clear enough: to provide a barrier against a Russian advance while restraining nationalist tendencies that might threaten the integrity of Turkey or the Habsburg Monarchy. It was in line with these objectives that Turkish officials, with the connivance of British and Austrian consuls, tried, albeit rather clumsily, to obstruct the progress of the unionists in the Moldavian and Wallachian elections of 1857. At this point, a four-power diplomatic combination – of France, Russia, Prussia and Sardinia – suddenly appeared, and went to the extraordinary lengths of breaking off relations with Constantinople, whereupon the Turks gave up the struggle. Of course, no member of this quartet had any interest in the Romanian cause as such; but all of them saw in an unruly, ambitious state on the south-eastern frontier of Hungary a useful means of embarrassing Austria. After this, the nationalists made steady progress, establishing contacts with radical elements in Italy and Hungary and taking advantage of Austria's preoccupation with the Italian crisis in 1859 to advance the unionist cause still further by electing the same prince – Alexander Cuza – to head the administration in both principalities. It was significant that after a visit by Napoleon to Osborne in 1857, the British, too, had felt it politic to abandon Austria and fall in line with the Franco-Russian combination. According to one of Buol's colleagues, it was the fiasco of Buol's Romanian policy that cost him his career. Even so, his conviction that he could count on a concert of powers to uphold the established treaty order remained unshaken until well into the next Italian crisis, when it certainly did cost him his career.

The making of the kingdom of Italy, 1856–61

There was nothing about conditions in Italy itself in the aftermath of the Crimean War to suggest that within less than half a decade the 1815 order in the peninsula would be totally overthrown. Austria's position had been weakened despite her military triumphs in 1848–49; France had established her physical presence in Rome as protector of the Pope; and, thanks to the good offices of the western powers, the kingdom of Sardinia had managed to retain its constitution and emerge unpunished – and hence with enhanced prestige and confidence – from its disastrous assault on the established order of 1815. On the other hand, Austria's opponents in Italy were still in no position to challenge her with any hope of success. The Risorgimento had never been either a united movement or one that enjoyed the support of the masses; and although the events of 1848–49 had simplified matters by eliminating both the radical Republicans and Gioberti's pro-Papal Neo-Guelph movement as serious rivals to Sardinia's leadership, the realist Cavour was always acutely aware of the futility of the doctrine of *Italia farà da sé*. To him, the lesson of 1848–49 was all too clear: unless some external power could be enlisted to defeat the Austrian army, there could be no hope of challenging the order of 1815 in Italy.

Externally, too, Austria's position was weaker by the mid-1850s but it was by no means hopeless. Certainly, after the Holy Alliance had perished in the Crimean War, neither the Russians nor the Prussians would exert themselves to sustain their former ally's position in northern Italy. Indeed, both reckoned that they actually stood to gain from the weakening of their unco-operative neighbour. The British, too, were unremittingly critical of Austria's stubborn refusal to consider the slightest modification of her treaty rights, and her routine support for reactionary elements in the Papal States and the Kingdom of the Two Sicilies (which Gladstone had described as 'the negation of God erected into a system of government'). There was never the slightest chance that Great Britain, weakened and distracted as she was in the late 1850s, would be either willing or able to lend Austria material support to defend the order of 1815 against an external challenge. Even so Palmerston, who sometimes argued that it was Austria's duty to abandon the defence of the peninsula to the Italians themselves, while she concentrated on guarding her interests (and Great Britain's) against Russia in the east, was an extreme case. There was, in fact, as yet nobody in London who contemplated actively undermining Austria's position in Italy. Indeed, for the conservative foreign secretary, Lord Malmesbury, the treaties of 1815 and 1856 were 'the bases of the law of Europe'. As for France, the only power in a position to use effective military force against Austria, she seemed to Cavour an even less promising proposition. Although, as early as 1852 Napoleon had spoken of his desire 'to do something for Italy, which I love as a second fatherland', he had since shown little consideration for the kingdom of Sardinia, leaving it to the British to enlist Victor Emmanuel's support in the Crimean War, and after the war toying with his own particular ambitions in the south of the peninsula – for example, a scheme to enhance French influence in the Mediterranean by reinstating the Bonapartist Murat dynasty in place of the Neapolitan Bourbons. From Cavour's point of view, to use France to expel Austria from northern Italy while leaving Napoleon in control of Rome and Naples would indeed be using Beelzebub to drive out the devil.

Napoleon III's interest in Italy was, of course, only one aspect of his great political obsession, the destruction of the settlement of 1815. This objective was nearer attainment since the disruption of the Holy Alliance in the Crimean War; but a direct move against the 1815 settlement in the Rhineland or Belgium would still be all too likely to resuscitate the coalition that had destroyed Napoleon I and that had shown its teeth against Thiers and Louis Philippe as recently as 1840. The situation in Italy, by contrast, especially given the fragmented condition of the states system in the later 1850s, seemed to offer Napoleon the chance to start the revision of the hated Vienna settlement by a war against Austria alone. Neither Russia nor Great Britain, the two chief architects of the settlement, was likely to spring to Austria's defence. Gorchakov made this clear when he met Napoleon at Stuttgart in 1858, and even Alexander II was unconcerned at the idea of a weakening of Austria provided Napoleon could achieve this without unleashing a general revolutionary war. The British, feeling the pains of imperial overstretch even more acutely since the Indian Mutiny, and on particularly bad terms with Russia, were especially anxious to conciliate France at this time – witness Palmerston's uncharacteristically grovelling attempt to appease Napoleon by introducing the ill-fated Conspiracy to Murder Bill in response to Orsini's assassination attempt. This only convinced Napoleon that should he choose to move against Austria in Italy, Great Britain would be paralysed by 'une peur horrible de la guerre'. As for the German states, whereas Napoleon's mediation in the Neuchâtel affair had been much appreciated in Berlin, Austria's obstructive stance had rendered her chances of successfully summoning the aid of the German states in defence of her own lands outside the Confederation decidedly problematical. It was with a feeling of confidence, therefore, that in July 1858 Napoleon set out for his famous meeting with Cavour at Plombières.

The Pact of Plombières of 20 July initiated the first planned war of aggression in Europe since the days of Napoleon I. According to letters exchanged after their meeting, Napoleon and Cavour agreed that once Austria had been defeated, Sardinia would become the 'Kingdom of Upper Italy', annexing Lombardy, Venetia, the duchies of Parma and Modena, and the northern papal territory of the Romagna; in central Italy a new state under Napoleon's protection would be formed round the Grand Duchy of Tuscany, perhaps under a Bonapartist dynasty; the rest of the papal territories and the Kingdom of the Two Sicilies were to remain as they were, except that all four units were to join a confederation under the presidency of the Pope. Sardinia would pay France for her services by ceding, not merely the frontier territories she had acquired after the final defeat of Napoleon I, but the whole province of Savoy. In short, the objective of the war was to be the radical transformation of the 1815 settlement in northern and central Italy, but not the unification of the peninsula. No more than any of his predecessors did Napoleon have any wish to see a united Italian state sealing off France in the south-east. On the contrary, the future confederation was exactly the kind of permeable structure that would allow France, as the protector of the three weaker units against the Kingdom of Upper Italy, to exercise her influence throughout the peninsula. (Whether either the Pope or the French clericals would regard the new role assigned to His Holiness as fitting compensation for the despoiling of his states was a moot point.) Finally, the two conspirators agreed that, when it came to starting the war, it would be well if Austria could be made to appear the aggressor, so as to preclude her summoning aid from Germany under Article 47 of the Confederation regarding defensive wars. In January 1859 an additional treaty added Nice to the territories to be ceded to France.

Meanwhile, Austria's relations with Sardinia were fast falling into the pattern that was to characterize her relations with Serbia half a century later: an unbending, increasingly exasperated defence of unimpeachable treaty rights on the one hand, and a steady stream of irredentist provocations under the protection of a great-power patron on the other. Napoleon's unsolicited observation to the Austrian ambassador at his New Year's Day reception in 1859 – 'I regret that our relations are not so good as I could wish' – was generally understood, in terms of the restrained diplomatic language of the time, as a virtual public announcement that war was impending. It was in vain that Great Britain and Russia now moved to defuse the crisis, the former proposing mediation between Sardinia and Austria, the latter the summoning of a congress. In Paris, Lord Malmesbury, concerned at the same time not to 'drive Napoleon mad', confined himself to extremely guarded hints that Great Britain might not remain neutral; and these lost any force they might have had when opposition politicians in London informed Napoleon that Malmesbury was bluffing. Russia's congress proposal ground to a halt in the face of Buol's conditions – that Sardinia be excluded, and that any congress must only confirm the *status quo* in Italy. Meanwhile, the Austrians decided that the cost of their cumbersome and extensive mobilization measures to counter Sardinia's feverish war preparations was proving quite ruinous; and it was ostensibly for this reason that on 23 April they suddenly addressed an ultimatum to Turin, summoning Sardinia unilaterally to cease her military preparations forthwith; and when this was rejected, precipitately declared war on the kingdom.

Although it has often been alleged, with the benefit of hindsight, that the Austrian ultimatum reflected an irrevocable, even suicidally foolish, decision for war, exhaustive research by Katharina Weigand, the leading authority in the field, has demonstrated that that was not quite the case. In the first place, if Sardinia had submitted to the ultimatum, that is, submitted directly to Austria without trying to shelter behind the concert, the Austrians could have confidently consented to a congress that merely endorsed the *status quo*, and the crisis would have ended peacefully. It seems, moreover, that Buol had indeed taken this possibility into his calculations. Admittedly, these calculations were based, like Buol's whole policy, on a fatal illusion: the unquestioning belief that since the demise of the Holy Alliance, a new European 'system' had actually come into being, in which Great Britain and Prussia, accepting that an attack on Austria's position in Italy would amount to an attack on the whole 1815 order, and therefore on themselves, would rally to Austria's side. This would in turn suffice to overawe Napoleon into summoning Sardinia to submit to the ultimatum and the *status quo* would be secured. Of course, if Napoleon persisted in supporting Sardinia, the result would be a general conflagration in which Austria, Great Britain, Prussia and the other German states would crush the revolution incorporated in Napoleon and Cavour once and for all. That these calculations proved to be mistaken, owing to the fragmentation of a states system in which, as Buol lamented, 'all the states are following only the impulses of the moment' was indeed disastrous for Austria in the short term. It is worth reflecting, however, that Buol's successors made a similar miscalculation in their handling of Serbia and Russia in the infinitely more dangerous polarized states system of 1914, and with infinitely more disastrous consequences; and that the selfish indifference displayed by Great Britain and Prussia in 1859 at least re- stricted the dimensions of the conflict to one that Austria could survive.

Of course, the Austrian decision to take the offensive was disastrous enough, and plunged the Monarchy into total isolation. Any chance of even diplomatic support from the relatively friendly conservative govern- ment in London now disappeared, and Malmesbury could only lament helplessly that 'France having always been a curse to Europe, we look upon it as the will of God and resign ourselves to the torment.' Prussia had already been parrying Buol's legitimist arguments for some months – not that Buol had been prepared to listen: now Austria, as technically the aggressor, had sacrificed the right to invoke the assistance of the Confed- eration. These diplomatic errors were compounded by weaknesses at home that deprived the Monarchy of any advantages of surprise that might have accrued from its precipitate declaration of war. Not only were the finances thrown into total chaos, continued unrest in Hungary reflected in the unreliability of Hungarian forces in Italy had disastrous consequences on the campaign itself; and this was made worse by the timidity of mediocre Austrian commanders who failed to strike Sardinia down before French assistance arrived. On 4 June at Magenta, and on 24 June, under the command of Franz Joseph himself, at the exceedingly bloody battle of Solferino, the Austrians suffered major defeats. Meanwhile, central Italy was in turmoil: the Habsburg grand duke of Tuscany had fled on the outbreak of war, and by June insurrectionary groups encouraged from Sardinia had expelled the Habsburgs from Modena and the Bourbons from Parma and threatened papal rule in the Romagna, while Cavour's intrigues with rebel movements in Hungary raised the possibility of a general revolutionary war.

This was not to be. On 11 July hostilities suddenly ceased when, without consulting Cavour, Napoleon concluded the armistice of Villafranca with Franz Joseph. The terms were broadly along the lines of those Napoleon had agreed with Cavour at Plombières, but fell very significantly short of them. Franz Joseph agreed to cede to Napoleon (but not to Sardinia, lest he seem to be recognizing the principle of nationality) no more than the greater part of Lombardy, retaining, meanwhile, the important strategic position of the Quadrilateral fortresses that straddled the border between Lombardy and Venetia. Napoleon would hand the ceded territory over to Victor Emmanuel, who would also receive the duchy of Parma. The Habsburg rulers of Tuscany and Modena, however, were to be restored; and Franz Joseph successfully resisted an attempt by Napoleon to veto the use of force to this end. Franz Joseph was also to be a member, as ruler of Venetia, of the confederation that was to be established under the presidency of the Pope. If Cavour felt so betrayed by these terms that he resigned his office, Napoleon, for his part, felt in honour bound to renounce his reward of Savoy and Nice. Even so, although it paid scant regard to the wishes of the Italians, or of the other members of the states system, the north Italian settlement outlined at Villafranca was by no means unrealistic. At least, it reflected the interests of the two great powers most directly involved in the peninsula.

For Napoleon, Villafranca was really an attempt to secure at the negotiating table what he was increasingly unlikely to secure on the battlefield. Even in the theatre of war itself, for example, it was France who had made the great sacrifices – a month had sufficed to show how the Italians waged war – and after Solferino Napoleon found himself confronted with an Austrian defensive line, the Quadrilateral and the Mincio, that no army had ever broken: the really tough war had not even begun. Looking further afield, Napoleon was dismayed by the frantic activity of Sardinian agents, organizing movements for unity with the kingdom throughout central Italy. As he complained to Cavour after Solferino: 'je ne veux pas l'unité, mais l'indépendance'. Here, of course, it was Cavour, not Napoleon, who had abandoned the Plombières basis: Napoleon had never been committed to fight for the union of Sardinia with Tuscany, which he had intended as the kernel of a new central Italian state, possibly under a Murat or his own cousin Jerome. Moreover, the disturbances in the Papal States were stirring up a veritable hornets' nest among his clerical supporters at home, where the war had never been popular anyway. Finally, the international horizon was clouding over: Russia, ready enough to see Franz Joseph and his army humiliated and weakened, was voicing her disapproval of the overthrow of the central Italian dynasties, to say nothing of Cavour's contacts with Hungarian rebels, traditional allies of Russia's insubordinate Poles. Most alarming, however, was the possibility that Prussia might join the war. In reality, there was virtually no chance of this: if Berlin was indifferent to the wave of pro-Austrian feeling that had swept through the German Confederation, Bismarck at Frankfort even welcomed the prospect of Austria's defeat. In the military negotiations that eventually started in May, the Prussians exploited Austria's embarrassments ruthlessly: as the price of their support, they demanded not only equality with Austria in the Confederation, but Prussian command of its forces in the theatre of the war, and when Franz Joseph reluctantly conceded this, that the king of Prussia exercise his command in his own name, and not as the agent of the Confederation. At this, the negotiations came to an acrimonious end. In the course of them, however, Prussia had, as a bargaining ploy, mobilized six army corps on the Rhine; and Napoleon was not to know that the Austro-Prussian talks would ultimately fail. As he told Cavour on 10 July, 'in the present state of forces, France cannot possibly sustain a double war on the Rhine and the Adige.' He concluded the armistice on the following day.

Franz Joseph, for his part, was keen to end a war that had left the Monarchy in a terrible state internally and with no hope of salvation from any external source. Indeed, in the Army Order of Verona that followed the armistice on 12 July, Franz Joseph put the blame for Austria's defeat squarely on those 'oldest and most natural allies' in the Confederation who had deserted her. Prussia, certainly, was regarded in Vienna as something akin to a hostile power, especially when she compounded her disloyalty in the military field by treacherously making common cause with Great Britain and Russia in their diplomatic campaign to press for a mediated solution to the conflict. Not only did the Austrians suspect that, given the proven indifference of these three powers to Austria's treaty rights in Italy, their mediation would prove even more costly than a direct deal with Napoleon; the very notion of making concessions at the behest of non-combatants was quite incompatible with Franz Joseph's sense of honour. Whatever he might have to cede to Napoleon would have been lost fairly on the battlefield, whereas there could 'never' be any question of 'yielding to a European Areopagus'. Nor were Napoleon's terms particularly onerous: with Franz Joseph a member of the new Italian confederation, and his relatives restored in central Italy, he would have in the Quadrilateral and Venetia a useful springboard for the recovery of his lost territories in Lombardy. 'These', he confidently remarked, 'we shall take back in one or two years.'

Unfortunately for him, the Villafranca terms were to remain a dead letter, even though the three belligerents formally incorporated most of them into their final Treaty of Zurich on 10 November. The attempt by the imperial co-signatories to revise the order of 1815 by cabinet diplomacy was to be frustrated by a combination of the factors they had tried to ignore: Italian popular feeling and the states system. In central Italy, political activists backed by Sardinia remained in control of the duchies and the Romagna in defiance of the two emperors; but what really rendered Villafranca unenforceable was the support these movements received from the appearance on the scene of a third great power: Great Britain. On 10 June Palmerston returned to power in London, with Russell at the Foreign Office and Gladstone at the Exchequer. Not that the actions of this pro-Italian triumvirate were motivated simply by the romantic ideas of classically educated Englishmen, or even by Gladstone's indignation at prison conditions in Naples. As guardians of British interests, they were all profoundly suspicious of Napoleon III's intentions. Even in 1849, Palmerston had been unwilling to see Austrian influence removed from Italy if it had meant its replacement by that of France. Now, Russell was of similar mind: 'From 1815 to 1859 Austria has governed Italy. If the Italians had reason to complain, England had no reason to fear the employment of Austrian influence against British interests; but if France controls the united fleets of Genoa and Naples, Britain could have to look to the defence of Malta, Corfu and Gibraltar.' Ideally, the British wanted the peninsula to be free from both Austrian and French influence, and calculated that a politically united Italy leaning on Great Britain as a protection against France would be a most welcome new element in the Mediterranean balance of power. As Napoleon was equally determined to bring the peninsula under French influence, a kind of diplomatic auction now ensued, in which the British and French tried to outbid each other in an effort to ingratiate themselves with Turin. In the process the stipulations of Villafranca and – even before it was signed – the Treaty of Zurich went by the board.

First, the proclamation by the British of the principle of non-intervention, and its endorsement by France, Russia and Prussia, was a body blow to Franz Joseph's hopes of restoring the rulers of the duchies, who would clearly be unable to recover their thrones without external military assistance. It was in vain that the Austrians strove to cultivate their 'entente désirable' with Napoleon – after all their only hope of support – making concession after concession in the hope of salvaging at least something from the wreckage. For example, they reduced their demands in central Italy to restoration of a Tuscan state, without even specifying its ruler. It was all for nothing: on 25 November the British agreed to support the annexation of Parma, Modena and Tuscany by Sardinia, whereupon Napoleon hastily followed suit, and threw in the Romagna as well. It made no difference that the Pope and the Austrians now turned their backs on the idea of a settlement by a congress from which they could only expect further attacks on the legitimist order. The Austrians were simply not prepared to take action in its defence, as that would entail – as they confessed helplessly to Paris – a breach with the French, 'and that we do not want'.

Thus, in a laconic circular note of 30 March Sardinia simply informed the other powers of the annexation of the duchies and the Romagna, 'regardless', as a Bavarian diplomat observed, 'of the Treaty of Zurich signed only a few months before, . . . giving currency, in a way that makes a mockery of all international laws, to the new theory of the self-determination of peoples through so-called verdicts of popular votes'. When the French now proceeded to take their reward, annexing Nice and Savoy (also, like the Sardinian annexations, ratified by dubious plebiscites) this was denounced in London as a threat to the balance of power. In Vienna, Count Rechberg discerned a rather more profound threat, to the whole states system as it had been functioning since 1815: 'We have always opposed in principle the policy (système) of annexation, which has sought to replace treaties in which territorial stipulations have been agreed by the powers, by geographical necessities, popular votes or strategic guarantees. . . . This would be to deprive international relations of every element of security.'

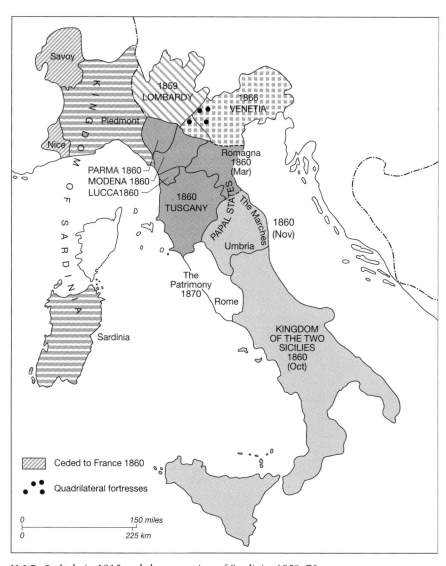

MAP 2 *Italy in 1815 and the expansion of Sardinia, 1859–70*

The sharpening of Anglo-French rivalry in the spring of 1860 played a vital role in the last phase of the creation of the kingdom of Italy, the annexation of the Kingdom of the Two Sicilies and the seizure of Umbria and the Marches from the Pope. Even more than in the central duchies the 'unification' movement was organized from outside. In Sicily, for example, the rising of April 1860 was of the traditional anti-Neapolitan kind, and included a number of disparate factions, Muratisti and Mazzinians as well as adherents of Cavour. Initially, Cavour may well have hoped that Garibaldi's expedition to Sicily might fail – after all, the Neapolitan army had beaten off a larger Mazzinian force in 1857. Certainly, few in Turin wanted him to succeed, D'Azeglio professing to fear an annexation of the backward south 'more than a second Novara'. It was at this juncture that Napoleon III's ambitions came into play, causing Cavour to have second thoughts. In June 1860 Napoleon came up with a mediation project to save the Bourbons of Naples: Sicily would become independent (under a Bourbon); Sardinia would sign treaties with both southern kingdoms, and Napoleon, as their protector, would establish his influence throughout the south. It was to this end that in July he proposed sending the French fleet to stop Garibaldi from proceeding from Sicily to Naples.

It was again British intervention that frustrated Napoleon's plans. Not that the British actually desired the annexation of the Kingdom of the Two Sicilies by Victor Emmanuel. They would have preferred to see it continue as a weak independent state dependent on British sea-power. In the summer of 1860, however, they were becoming increasingly apprehensive about Napoleon's ambitions in the Mediterranean. He had recently given his blessing to De Lesseps's efforts to obtain a concession from the Sultan to cut the Suez canal, and was perhaps planning to revive France's Egyptian ambitions of twenty years before. At any rate, he was already proposing to intervene in Syria in favour of Christian Maronites suffering under Muslim rule. Altogether, his activities in the eastern Mediterranean were disturbing the British; and rather than allow French influence to be established in the central Mediterranean through a satellite Neapolitan kingdom – perhaps with a Murat on the throne – they preferred to see the kingdom go to Sardinia. It was the British navy, therefore, that kept the Straits of Messina free for Garibaldi to proceed to the conquest of Naples. Cavour, whatever misgivings he may have felt, was at least relieved that he had not broken Austrian domination of northern Italy only to see French domination established in the south.

His alarm revived, however, when Garibaldi proposed to move on from Naples to attack the remaining papal territories, including Rome itself. This would obviously provoke a clash with the French troops guarding the papal capital and perhaps even, Cavour feared, Austrian military intervention. This latter danger was non-existent: the Austrians were still assiduously cultivating their '*entente désirable*' with France, if only because they had nowhere else to turn. Franz Joseph's meeting with the Tsar and the Regent of Prussia in Warsaw in October may have done something for personal relations damaged by the Crimean War; but however appalled Alexander II might have been by the revolutionary events in Naples, neither he nor the Regent felt there was anything the Eastern Powers could do about them, and their advice to Franz Joseph simply to accommodate himself to these disagreeable innovations showed that the Holy Alliance was indeed lost beyond recall. The prospect of Garibaldi's marching on Rome, by contrast, frightened Napoleon as much as Cavour: a bloody clash between French troops and the Italian national movement would turn what was already an uncomfortably enlarged neighbour into a hostile one. He agreed with Cavour that the only hope was for the Sardinian army to anticipate Garibaldi and occupy most of the Papal States, while taking care to give Rome itself a wide berth, his final advice being 'faîtes-le, mais vite!', The ploy worked, Napoleon judiciously joining the three eastern monarchs in demonstratively breaking off relations with Turin as a formal gesture of protest against Sardinia's latest illegal acts. It was, however, merely a formal gesture – despite Russell's feeling the need to respond to it with a blustering dispatch defending recent events – and when the new kingdom of Italy was formally proclaimed in March 1861, all the great powers apart from Austria accepted it readily enough into the European states system.

The creation of the kingdom of Italy was a textbook example of the dictum that wars and revolutions always give the lie to the expectations of those who instigate them. Even the Italians got more than they bargained for: the suppression of the subsequent anti-unionist rebellion in the south cost more Italian lives than all the wars against Austria combined. Napoleon III, certainly, had been disagreeably surprised to find himself faced, not with a grateful and politically divided peninsula entirely subject to French influence, but a united kingdom with a strong sense of grievance over the French garrison in Rome and, as the future was to show, perfectly ready to join with Great Britain or the German powers to the detriment of French interests. By the same token, the British, who had initially had nothing to do with the conflict, and whose role had been essentially reactive, even opportunistic (as Rechberg caustically observed, they had no intention of applying the doctrine of self-determination to the

Ionian Islands or India) had reason to welcome the final outcome of Napoleon's initiatives: a new kingdom, entirely free from Austrian or French domination, that might serve to strengthen British influence in the central Mediterranean, and that was not, in the event, to pose a threat to British interests until the 1930s.

Austria, by contrast, the object and victim of the Franco-Sardinian assault on the order of 1815, was a peculiar case. Indeed, so great had the shock been to the *mentalités* of decision-makers in Vienna that for the next few years they were quite unable to come to terms with realities. Certainly, their position – of refusing to negotiate 'except on the basis of the Treaty of Zurich, the non-execution of which lies at the root of the problems that preoccupy Europe' was impeccably legitimist. But as their constant talk of dispelling the 'phantom of Italian unity', even of enlisting French aid to 'demolish the whole edifice' of 1861, was to show, in a Europe in which all the other great powers had accepted the new order of things in Italy, Austria's 'legitimist revisionism' condemned her to total isolation. Moreover, if Franz Joseph's faith in France was fluctuating and in Great Britain non-existent, his continuing hope that a Prussian alliance might yet help him to restore his position in Italy was to be of crucial importance to the development of the German question that now moved to the centre of the stage.

The end of the 1815 order in Germany

An observer of the German political scene in the late 1850s would have been surprised to hear that within less than a decade the order of 1815 would be swept away. After all, even the momentous upheavals of 1848–50 had resulted only in the reinstatement of Austria as the undisputed head of the revived Confederation, with the active support of Russia, the approval of Great Britain, the acquiescence of France and, even, after Olmütz, of Prussia. It is true that Austria's attempt to increase her control at the expense of Prussia and the middle states in the Dresden conferences had been defeated, just as successive attempts by the middle states to gain more freedom of manoeuvre by constitutional reforms were to be frustrated – in fact, thanks to the solidarity of Austria and Prussia rather than to their rivalry. On the economic front, the Austro-Prussian commercial treaty of 1853 seemed to hold out the prospect of Austria's eventual admission into the *Zollverein*; while for Franz Joseph the concept of the Confederation as embodying the unity (rather than the unification) of Germany, led by Austria with Prussia as her loyal second in the struggle against the Revolution personified in Napoleon III and Cavour always remained the political ideal. Not for nothing did he proudly describe himself – three-quarters Wittelsbach by birth, nephew by marriage of the kings of Prussia and Saxony – as 'a German prince'; and from 1848 to 1866 all his ministers of foreign affairs without exception shared his 'Metternichian' vision of combining Austria's role as head of the Confederation with the cultivation of the partnership with Prussia. Yet, though the emphasis might shift between these two objectives, on one point the emperor and his successive ministers were agreed: Austria must uphold, if necessary to the point of war, that unquestioned headship of the confederation conferred on her in 1815.

By the end of the 1850s, this objective was becoming decidedly problematical. Already during the years of their alliance during the Crimean War, the divergent policies of Austria and Prussia towards Russia had ensured that in any future clash it would be Prussia and not Austria that would enjoy the patronage of the arbiter of Olmütz. In the years after the war Austria's position was further undermined by Buol's arrogant handling of both Prussia and the middle states, a reflection of his cavalier assumption that the dictates of self-interest ensured that Austria would always be able to count on their support to uphold the settlement of 1815. The Neuchâtel affair, for example, which started in 1848 with the seizure by Swiss revolutionaries of an enclave that had been a personal possession of the kings of Prussia since 1713, ended in 1857 with Frederick William IV's giving up his rights after Austria had joined with the western powers to pour cold water on his plans to send an army through southern Germany to defend them. Of course, in frustrating Frederick William's attempts to mobilize the support of the Confederation, Buol had unwittingly missed a chance to pin Prussia down to the principle of common defence of members' territories outside the Confederation that might have proved decidedly useful to Austria in Italy a couple of years later. It was perhaps even more ominous however, that the Prussians had turned to the mediation of Napoleon III to resolve the crisis; and the way in which Prussian-inspired newspapers now began to echo Sardinian and French criticism of Austria's position in Italy drove Count Rechberg, Austrian minister at Frankfort, and a devoted advocate of Austro-Prussian co-operation, to despair: this was 'unfortunately the natural consequence of Prussian policy which is pursuing, only with more restraint, in Germany the same policy as Sardinia in Italy. The former seeks to push Austria out of Germany, Sardinia to push her out of Italy.' The bill for Buol's miscalculations was presented, of course, in 1859; and with the

Army order of Verona blaming Prussian disloyalty for Austria's mis-
fortunes, relations between the two leading German powers took a further
turn for the worse.

Even so, Austria's prospects in the sharpening conflict with Prussia
over the leadership of the Confederation seemed far from hopeless.
On the one hand, the introduction of the February Patent in Austria in
February 1861 – a constitution that favoured the German liberal bourgeoisie – was not only a bid for their assistance in restoring the state's
finances, but a determined attempt to exploit Austria's image as a liberal,
centralized German state to enhance her appeal within the German Confederation as a whole. On the other hand, Prussia, who in 1862 ruthlessly
forced the other members of the Zollverein to endorse a commercial treaty
with France that lowered tariffs to a degree that virtually ruled out Austria's
future admission to the union, had demonstrated her determination to
exploit her leading position in the economic life of the Confederation
in a most disagreeable manner. Her image was further damaged by her
ruthless pursuit of army reform at the price of constitutional deadlock
and the appointment of Bismarck as Chancellor in 1862.

It is true that, on the political front, Prussia's ostentatious refusal to
co-operate in such reform initiatives as Franz Joseph's meeting with the
princes of the Confederation at Frankfort in August 1863 demonstrated
Austria's impotence to adjust the machinery of the Confederation to her
advantage by peaceful means. It is equally true, however, that Prussia
could not easily translate her commercial and military potential into political advantages. Her bullying of the other members of the Zollverein was
much resented in the middle states; and the absence of Prussia alone from
the Frankfort festivities only underscored her isolation from the centres of
political power within the Confederation. Indeed, whatever esteem Prussia
may have enjoyed among elements of the commercial and military élites,
she was undoubtedly less highly regarded than Austria in the eyes of
German opinion generally. There, liberal views prevailed, and since the
advent of Bismarck to power Prussia was increasingly regarded as a reactionary, militaristic state. Of the two popular organizations set up in the
late 1850s to promote German unity, the großdeutsch Reformverein, which
looked to Vienna and saw in the leadership of Germany by a multinational
empire a guarantee of the multifaceted diversity of German political
life, was making great strides; while the Prussian-oriented kleindeutsch
Nationalverein lapsed into embarrassed silence. Altogether, therefore,
insofar as Austria's position in the Confederation was a 'German' affair,
the leading role she had enjoyed since 1815 seemed secure.

From an international perspective, however, it was equally clear that Austria would be left very much to her own devices in defending it. Certainly, after the disintegration of the 1815 coalition during the Crimean War, it was unlikely that any other power would be prepared to assume the burden of military operations to uphold the Vienna settlement in either Italy or Germany; and the Austrians deepened their own isolation by the unyielding legitimist stance they adopted on all fronts. If their rigid defence of their rights in Germany and of the Near Eastern settlement of the Treaty of Paris cut them off from their former allies in Berlin and St Petersburg, their isolation from all the other powers was encapsulated in their stubborn refusal to recognize any of the changes that had occurred in Italy since Villafranca, and which had been recognized by all the other powers as an acceptable, if not particularly welcome, feature of the new international order. Ideally, the Austrians would have liked to reverse these changes, replacing the kingdom of Italy by the confederation envisaged at Villafranca and Zurich. But not only could they find no support elsewhere for such a programme; they had to fight off a series of proposals that Venetia, too, should be handed over to Italy. Napoleon III, for example, desperate to re-establish control of his erstwhile protégés in Florence, even offered the Austrians an alliance if they would cede Venetia to Italy (and perhaps Galicia to a Poland to be liberated from Russia). Not surprisingly, such harebrained schemes were as ill received in Vienna as the advice from Great Britain, France's rival for influence in Italy, that Austria should simply sell Venetia to Italy for much needed cash.

Austria's stubborn defence of her treaty rights in Venetia was not simply a matter of economic or strategic interests. It is true that Venetia was one of the richest provinces of the Monarchy (and worth far more than the barren Danubian principalities that Napoleon III was constantly urging on Vienna as an object of exchange); and if Venice was an important naval base dominating the northern Adriatic, the Quadrilateral fortresses salvaged from Lombardy at Villafranca were still the military gateway into Germany. The real issue for the Austrians was simply that of legitimist principle, which they considered, in the last resort, vital to the credibility and survival of the Monarchy as a great power. This had been the issue in 1859 and it was to be so again in 1866 and in 1914. As Franz Joseph's foreign minister put it to the British ambassador in 1866:

What was the Austrian Monarchy? It was an empire of nationalities. If she gave up Venetia today to please King Victor Emmanuel . . . where would his ambition lead him? Would he rest satisfied before he had wrested all the Austrian possessions in the Adriatic from their rightful owner? . . . The prince of Hohenzollern might some day find out that there was a considerable Romanian population in Transylvania, and that therefore it would be right that it should be added to Moldo-Wallachia. The prince of Serbia might also claim the Serbs in Austria. . . . in fact, . . . we are determined to take our position in defence of our principles and our rights, which are based on treaties, and if war should be the consequence, we shall do our best to protect the various possessions and interests of which the Empire is composed.

In short, it was not simply, as the Austrians sometimes complained, the 'non-enforcement of the Treaty of Zurich' that lay 'at the root of the problems that preoccupy Europe'. The Monarchy could never accept 'the principles upon which the Italian state is founded'. As events were to show over the next half century, there was a certain bleak realism in this analysis. In terms of the priorities and preoccupations of the other components of the states system in 1866, however, it was totally divorced from reality.

Any residual hopes the Austrians might have had of enlisting the other powers in defence of the legitimate international order were finally dissipated by the repercussions of the revolt that broke out in the Russian kingdom of Poland in January 1863. Admittedly, it was technically Prussia who transformed a Russian internal problem into an international issue by foisting upon a rather reluctant Alexander II the Alvensleben Convention of 8 February, providing for Prussian co-operation in policing the Russo-Prussian borders. Far more embarrassing to the Tsar, however, was the reaction of the Western Powers and Austria, with their pleas for moderation and amnesty (and, in Palmerston's case, threatening language about the forfeiture of Russia's right to Poland under the Treaty of Vienna). Not that these moral demonstrations seriously impeded Russia's suppression of the revolt: they had been in all cases very much sops to liberal opinion at home; and none of them was backed up by the remotest inclination to resort to force. In November, a final attempt by Napoleon III to use the affair as the starting point for a general revision of the map of Europe by proposing a congress with a disturbingly vague agenda ended only in the humiliation of its author. Not only the Russians and Prussians, but the Austrians, fearful of seeing the Venetian question raised again, and the British, ever suspicious of Napoleon's designs on Belgium, turned the proposal down flat. (The British refusal, of which Napoleon first learned from the newspapers, was considered particularly wounding in Paris.) By the end of the year, therefore, Russia and Prussia had drawn closer together, while Austria had compounded the error of the Crimean War, enraging Russia without really drawing closer to the Western Powers. Indeed, the signatories of the Treaty of April 1856 were now in complete disarray: with all three having demonstrated their ineffectiveness, with Austria on poor terms with both her erstwhile partners, and with Napoleon III barely on speaking terms with the British, the Crimean coalition was clearly in no shape to play a directing role in the crisis which directly opened up the German question in November 1863.

It was, in fact, a revived Austro-Prussian coalition that determined the course of the Schleswig-Holstein crisis of 1863–64. This confirmed the exclusion of the peripheral great powers and ensured that the war against Denmark remained localized and, in terms of the European states system, of relatively transient significance. In theory, the two leading German powers were acting against revolutionary challenges – from the Danish monarch, whose constitution of November 1863 violated the legal position established by the five-power Treaty of London of 1852, and from the German Confederation, whose espousal of the Duke of Augustenburg's claims was equally devoid of legality. Indeed, in theory the Austro-Prussian alliance of January 1864, proclaiming their principled determination to uphold the Treaty of London was in the best Metternichian traditions of the two leading German powers acting in the name of treaty rights and legitimacy. In practical terms, too, both powers had reason to fear the consequences of doing nothing. After all, here was an issue over which German opinion of all shades was united; and if the Austrians' claim to the leadership of Germany was to mean anything, there could be no question of their allowing Prussia to act alone in defence of the German cause as in 1848. Besides, even if they had no fundamental objection to the creation of a new middle state in North Germany, potentially an ally against Prussia in future debates at Frankfort, they had no relish for the humble role of executors of the 'revolutionary' demands of the middle states of the Confederation. The Prussians, for their part, were even less willing to contemplate an independent Schleswig-Holstein on their borders, and readily joined in alliance with Vienna to resolve the question over the head of the Diet. It is true, that insofar as the Austro-Prussian alliance left open the future of the duchies if the treaty of 1852 could not be enforced, it left Prussia dangerously free to aspire to control of the duchies for herself; but by the same token the Austrians had kept their hands free for a possible alliance with the middle states should Prussia play them false. For Franz Joseph, however, such doubts counted for nothing against the apparent realization of his great ideal: a conservative-legitimist alliance with Prussia against the Revolution.

Certainly, the 'revolutionaries' of 1864 were swiftly brought to heel, the German Liberals finding the dispute taken unceremoniously out of their hands by the cabinets of Vienna and Berlin, the Danes being defeated on land and at sea by Prussia and Austria respectively. Nor were the non-German powers either able or willing to impose a settlement by the concert. In the first place, Russia, France and Great Britain all found themselves hamstrung by the claim of Austria and Prussia to be acting in the name of the five-power treaty of 1852. On the one hand, the legitimist tsar, in any case somewhat in awe of his venerable German uncle – whereas Frederick William IV had been the uncle by marriage of Franz Joseph, his successor, William I, was the uncle of Alexander II – felt the king of Denmark to be acting beyond his rights. At the other end of the spectrum, Napoleon III felt the German case to be the stronger in terms of the principle of nationalities; and as injured pride still ruled out any approach whatever to the British, and as a large part of his army was engaged in Algeria and Mexico, there was little he could do to influence the combined German powers. As for the British, it is true that Palmerston had famously declared that if challenged Denmark would not stand alone; but it seems that this was intended as a veiled warning to the German powers not to arouse such sleeping dogs as the Scandinavian Union movement, a favourite brainchild of the king of Sweden. There was after all, nothing that the British could do – it was at this time that Bismarck remarked that if the British army landed in Germany he would send the Berlin police to arrest it. In any case, not only did Queen Victoria favour the cause of her Prussian son-in-law over the Prince of Wales's Danish relatives, Palmerston himself admitted that a Prussian victory would be hard for Denmark but good for Europe:

With a view to the future, it is desirable that Germany, in the aggregate, should be strong, in order to control those two ambitious and aggressive Powers, France and Russia, who press upon her West and East. As to France, we know how restless and aggressive she is, and how ready to break loose for Belgium, for the Rhine, for anything she would be likely to get without too great exertion. As to Russia, she will in due time become a Power almost as great as the old Roman empire. She can become mistress of Asia, except British India, whenever she chooses to take it. Germany ought to be strong in order to resist Russian aggression, and a strong Prussia is essential to German strength.

In this situation, it was exceedingly ill advised of the Danes, at the conference that was summoned to London to seek a solution by the concert, boldly to reject out of hand any settlement based on the Treaty of 1852. This left the two German powers to impose their own solution by force of arms, and by the Treaty of Vienna of August 1864 Denmark simply ceded the duchies to Austria and Prussia jointly.

Of course, as the Austro-Prussian victory over Denmark still left the long-term future of the duchies unsettled, and as Bismarck was now determined that Austria must be forced to yield to Prussia, not merely her 1864 position in the duchies but her 1815 position in Germany, the contest for control of the Confederation was soon resumed. And insofar as it was a contest among the members of the Confederation, it was a contest that Austria was to win. Bismarck's attempts to secure his ends by negotiation came to nothing for a number of reasons. For example, when he met Rechberg at Schönbrunn in October 1864, he made him a bold offer: if Austria would retire from Germany, Prussia would assist her in recovering her old position in Italy; and Rechberg, eager as ever to hold on to the Prussian alliance, was certainly prepared to consider it. William I, however, refused to be dragged into Austria's Italian illusions and rejected the Schönbrunn draft; and he went on to allow his ministers, against Bismarck's advice, to administer a final crushing rebuff to Rechberg's desperate attempts to negotiate a new Austro-Prussian commercial treaty. Rechberg's consequent resignation only strengthened the position of those in Franz Joseph's counsels who had always maintained that Rechberg's policy of conciliating Prussia was barren and undignified; and the emperor himself had rejected the Schönbrunn draft, being no more inclined than in 1859 to yield one iota of his rights in Germany in exchange for support in Italy.

Rechberg's successor, Count Mensdorff, was a conservative army officer inclined by temperament to an accommodation with Prussia, but he lacked the strength of character to stand up to the hard liners in the Ballhausplatz. Indeed, not until Berchtold in 1913–14 was an Austrian foreign minister to prove so unresisting to the advice of his officials. At any rate, Austria and Prussia henceforth moved inexorably towards confrontation. The Gastein compromise of August 1865, which assigned the administration of Holstein to Austria and that of Schleswig to Prussia (while conceding to Prussia extensive military facilities in Holstein that would make it impossible for Austria to maintain her position there by force of arms) was not really the concession it seemed. For the Austrians were now beginning to base their position, not on local conditions in the duchies – though even there public opinion was on their side – but on their stronger position in the Confederation as a whole. In February 1866 they finally abandoned the Prussian alliance in favour of an alignment with the middle states, and openly began to espouse the cause of the Augustenburg claimant. Faced with such an open challenge, the Prussians began to prepare for war, not just to seize the duchies for Prussia, but to expel Austria from the Confederation once and for all. That Bismarck had been driven to abandon hope of a negotiated solution was in itself an eloquent testimony to the strength of Austria's position within the framework of the Confederation, and to the continuing viability of the 1815 settlement in terms of satisfying most of its members. Even though the Austrians, embarrassed as in 1859 by the logistical problems of mobilization, were the first to undertake preparatory military measures, the Confederation was not deceived as to the source of the challenge to the established order. In the final confrontation at Frankfort over the future of Schleswig-Holstein in June, not a single state of any significance voted with Prussia.

The real problem for Austria, however, was that ever since 1815 – or 1779, or even 1648 for that matter – the German question had been not simply a German, but a European question. The position enjoyed by Austria in Germany since 1815 had been the result of an unusually favourable constellation in Europe, and her retention of that position depended on at least the continuing passive approval of the powers who had helped to establish it. It was in these terms, in terms of the European states system, that Austria had just as decisively lost the battle as in local terms she had won it.

Russia had ceased to underwrite Austria anywhere since the Crimean War, since when she had found Prussia to be an accommodating ally worth fostering – all the more so in view of Austria's dangerously liberal proclivities in respect of the Poles, and her stubborn refusal to purchase security in Germany and Italy by supporting Russian demands for the revision of the Treaty of Paris. The conservative government in London, whose aloofness from continental politics had been confirmed by the fiasco of Palmerston's blustering in the Schleswig-Holstein affair, were to be preoccupied throughout the later 1860s by a legacy of disputes from the American Civil War that had rendered their relations with the United States decidedly precarious. Even if not everyone in London would have agreed with the verdict of the prime minister, Lord Derby, on the war of 1866 – 'there never was a great European war in which the national interests of England were less concerned' – and some genuinely deplored a conflict in Germany that might jeopardize the strong central Europe that they themselves had done so much to construct in 1815, they were all in the last resort prepared to see in a Prussia strengthened at the expense of Austria and the middle states an adequate substitute barrier against France. In short, of the two main architects of the states system of 1815, it was clear that Russia would not, and Great Britain could not, do anything to help Austria and her German allies to maintain the old order against Prussia.

It was equally certain that the Italians, with whom Bismarck had on 8 April concluded an offensive alliance pledging the two powers to fight together if war should break out within three months, were prepared actively to assist Prussia in her assault on the order on 1815. True, the alliance was itself a flagrant violation of the fundamental laws of the Confederation, especially insofar as it envisaged the transfer to a foreign power of the territory (Venetia) of a member state: but for Bismarck, as for Victor Emmanuel, might had always been right; and in Moltke's view, a Prussian victory was absolutely dependent on Austria's being distracted by a second front in the south. That the Austrians made no attempt to frustrate Prussian plans by a direct offer to Italy (which would certainly have secured her neutrality) is surprising only in the light of hindsight. Before the war, there could be no question of attempting to buy Italy off in this way, not only for reasons of principle and precedent, but because the Austrians had an even higher opinion of their own military capacity than Moltke, believing themselves quite capable of holding their own against Prussia and Italy combined. Even if correct, this would have been a dangerous assumption, because even the Austrians admitted that they could not possibly defeat a combination of Prussia, Italy and France. In effect, therefore, the result of Franz Joseph's stubborn refusal to contemplate the 'scandal' of negotiations with Italy was to place the destiny of Austria, indeed, of the states system of 1815 in Germany and Italy as a whole, at the mercy of Napoleon III.

Napoleon's campaign to revise the 1815 order in favour of France had started well, with the shattering in the Crimean War of the Quadruple Alliance, that great bastion on which the old order had rested; but subsequent events had brought only disappointment. Instead of a weak and divided Italian confederation dependent on France and contributing to her domination of the Mediterranean, he was faced with an ambitious neighbour with a grievance against him that looked, if anywhere, to Great Britain for protection. Meanwhile, the two great powers he had most sedulously cultivated, Russia and Great Britain, had proved singularly uninterested in revising the states system as he had planned. By the mid-1860s, however, it was beginning to seem that the sharpening conflict between the two German powers might yet provide an opportunity to realize at least some of his dreams. Not that there could be any doubt in Napoleon's mind as to which of the two German powers he favoured. He had regarded Prussia, ever since 1859, as the power of the future that could help him to ward off one of his chief nightmares, a revival of Austrian power in central Europe. Like so many of his contemporaries, until 1866 he regarded Austria as the stronger of the two German powers; and since 1859 her imperviousness to his blandishments and her exasperating adherence to outworn treaty rights in the face of events had convinced him that she was indeed a hopeless case. It must be emphasized that it was only under the impact of the shock of Austria's sudden collapse at Sadowa that Napoleon III turned away from Berlin and towards Vienna. Before this, his policy was profoundly anti-Austrian: as late as May 1866 his famous Auxerre speech – 'je déteste ces traités de 1815' – was nothing less than a *ballon d'essai* for a war against Austria. If a German conflict destroyed the Confederation, after all 'organisée principalement contre la France', so much the better; and a long drawn out conflict that weakened both Austria and Prussia would enable Napoleon, even with his army distracted overseas, to extend his influence in central Europe against both, resuming his uncle's role as the protector of the middle states and – by compelling Austria to cede Venetia – re-establishing his reputation in Italy.

Hence Napoleon's busy activity in 1865–66 that was to have such far-reaching consequences – albeit, as usual, not at all those intended by Napoleon – on the European states system. On the German front, in fairly non-committal talks with Bismarck at Biarritz in October 1865, he was assiduous in egging the Prussians on with assurances of French neutrality in a German war; and the fact that no specific compensations for France were mentioned testifies not so much to Bismarck's duplicity as to Napoleon's unwillingness to limit his claims in advance. On the Italian front, he continued to press the Austrians to cede Venetia to Italy, suggesting in March 1866 that they might take advantage of disturbances in Bucharest (where a revolution had broken out that eventually replaced the native ruler by Prince Charles of Hohenzollern-Sigmaringen) to indemnify themselves by annexing the Danubian principalities. This incident merged into the German question when Napoleon, in an attempt to put pressure on Vienna, engineered the sending of the Italian diplomatic mission to Berlin that resulted in the Italo-Prussian alliance of 8 April. This in turn, while not making any direct impact on Vienna, ensured that when, as the

German crisis came to a head in June, Napoleon also threatened the Austrians with war, they had no choice but to submit to his terms.

The upshot was the much derided treaty of 12 June, whereby, in return for the promise of French neutrality, the Austrians promised in the event of victory to cede Venetia to Napoleon. (In the event of defeat their enemies would take the province anyway.) Even before the war, therefore, the Austrians had resigned themselves to the destruction of the 1815 settlement in Italy. In other respects, however, the treaty was by no means a total defeat for Vienna: by ceding Venetia to Napoleon rather than to Victor Emmanuel, the Austrians had managed to evade any recognition of the national principle; the treaty even provided for the transformation of the kingdom of Italy into a confederation, in which Austria would play a role, as envisaged at Villafranca and Zurich; and Napoleon agreed to Austria's revising the 1815 frontiers in Germany (for example, taking Silesia from Prussia), provided due regard was had for the balance of power.

Although within weeks the 1815 order in central Europe was indeed to be revised, this was not to be in accordance with the views of the signatories of the treaty of 12 June. For the second time in his reign Napoleon III was to find himself baffled by the outcome of a war from which he had confidently hoped to profit. On 14 June Prussia, outvoted in the final confrontation in the Diet at Frankfort, simply declared the Confederation dissolved, overran the unco-ordinated armies of Austria's bewildered German allies, and threw three armies into Bohemia. There, thanks in great part to the diffidence and sluggishness of mediocre Austrian commanders, the Prussians secured a crushing victory at Sadowa (Königgrätz) on 3 July. In the southern theatre, by contrast, the Austrians inflicted equally crushing defeats on the Italians on land and sea – which made the cession of Venetia all the more galling, especially as nothing more was heard of the Italian confederation, and events in the north had ruled out all hope of compensating gains in Germany. Faced, however, with quite new demands from Napoleon to hand over Venetia regardless, Franz Joseph could do nothing but submit to the 'damned robber in the Tuileries'. Even so, if the Austro-Italian Treaty of Vienna of 12 October, in which Austria, as the last of the powers, recognized the kingdom of Italy, set the seal on the destruction of the 1815 order in the peninsula, it also provided the opportunity for a fresh start in Austro-Italian relations, which soon became surprisingly amicable. It is, moreover, often forgotten that the Austrian victories in 1866 had been of momentous importance, in restricting Austria's losses to Venetia and preventing any repetition of the avalanche of 1859–60. Indeed, the Habsburgs were to hold on to the

South Tyrol and the Adriatic lands they had recovered at the Congress of Vienna until the final collapse of the Monarchy in 1918.

In the north too, although Austria was finally forced to renounce her role in Germany, some remnants of the old order survived the destruction of the Confederation of 1815. It was not simply because the Austrians, after their victories in Italy, began to transfer troops to the northern theatre that Bismarck decided to ignore his sovereign's demands for a march on Vienna and offer concessions to Austria for the sake of a speedy peace. There was also reason to fear that if the war dragged on the peripheral powers might intervene to restrict Prussia's freedom of action by mobilizing the concert of Europe. True, the isolationist British showed no inclination to resume the leading role they had played in the creation of the German Confederation; but France and Russia, since the seventeenth and eighteenth centuries respectively self-styled (and in 1779 even officially recognized) protectors of German liberties, were making disturbing noises. While Napoleon III tried to come forward as a mediator, making embarrassing references to Biarritz and the restoration of the 1814 frontier in the Rhineland, Alexander II expressed his concern for the dynasties threatened by Prussia's victory, and even talked of summoning a congress. It was in his haste to propitiate these importunate neighbours, as well as in the interests of a speedy peace with Austria, that Bismarck concurred in the important Article IV of the Treaty of Prague. This affirmed the 'independent international existence' of the three states south of the Main, Bavaria, Baden and Württemberg, and of Hessen-Darmstadt, geographically situated north of the Main, but homeland of the Tsarina. Article V alluded to an eventual plebiscite in northern Schleswig. For the rest, however, Bismarck ruthlessly exploited Prussia's military victory to annex a number of states and cities (most importantly the kingdom of Hanover) to make Prussia one contiguous territory stretching from East Prussia to the Rhineland, and to subjugate such independent states as survived north of the Main to the constitutional straitjacket of his new North German Confederation. Meanwhile, the secret treaties that he imposed on the four south German states even before the Treaty of Prague was signed, obliging them to co-ordinate their military and economic organization with that of Prussia, showed that from the start their 'independent international existence' rested on an equivocation.

For the most part, the great powers accommodated themselves readily enough to the new order as defined by the Treaties of Prague and Vienna. The Austrians, bankrupt and defeated, could for the immediate future be content if only nothing worse – such as Prussian expansion south of the

MAP 3 *Central Europe in 1867*

Main – should befall them. Franz Joseph was thoroughly disillusioned with the feeble performance of his German partners in the war, confiding to his mother that he felt himself well rid of them. Indeed, he concluded, after his experiences with Bismarck and Napoleon III, that his whole campaign to uphold with honour the 1815 order in Germany and Italy had been 'stupid'. Certainly, the final renunciation of Austria's Italian mission made for greater stability; and in 1868 the cancellation by the liberal government in Vienna of the Concordat of 1855 further improved relations with Italy. If Italy was to be a problem at all, that was to be for France: the compromise settlement of 1864 whereby Napoleon had withdrawn his troops from Rome on the understanding that the papal dominions would be secure, came to an abrupt end with Garibaldi's attempt to take the city in 1867. With the return of the French garrison, the Roman question again became a running sore in Franco-Italian relations. However, on the German front Napoleon III, while undoubtedly disconcerted by the speed and extent of the Prussian victory, was still thinking in terms of bargaining for compensations; and he was at least appreciative of Bismarck's moderation in respect of the German states south of the Main. As neither of the two flanking powers had any particular reason to challenge the new order of things, it seemed that the remodelling of central Europe in 1866 might yet bring a new stability to the states system.

The German question and the peace of Europe, 1866–71

It is all too easy, with the benefit of hindsight, to regard the period from 1866 to 1871 as a mere hiatus or interlude, with the Treaty of Prague as no more than a temporary resting point on the march towards the final unification of Germany. Yet to treat the events of those years as leading inexorably towards the dramatic denouement of 1870 is perhaps even more misleading than to portray the last few years before the outbreak of war in 1914 as leading inexorably towards that catastrophe. For whereas by 1908, or certainly by 1911, the states system was moving steadily towards polarization, culminating in the the general conflagration of 1914, the period from 1866 to 1870 was for the most part, and for most of the great powers, very much one of *détente*. It is true that the system still lacked any overarching ideological and political bonds such as had made for coherence and stability in the decades after 1815. Indeed, the system that emerged from the demise of the Quadruple Alliance in the Crimean

War might fairly be described as anarchical. After 1866, however, with agreed, if not exactly consensual, solutions having been found to the German and Italian questions, and with the arch-disturber of the old order, Napoleon III, cured by bitter experience of his more visionary notions, there were signs that the great powers were beginning to opt for circumspection and restraint in the pursuit of limited objectives, and developing the habits of co-existence.

In 1866, perhaps for the first time since the Crimean War, none of the members of the states system felt its deficiencies to be so intolerable as to demand a remedy even at the cost of war. Certainly Franz Joseph, his empire bankrupt and in the throes of constitutional, military and economic reorganization, firmly told his new foreign minister, the Saxon, Count Beust, that all idea of war must be given up 'for a long time'. True, as Austro-French negotiations in 1868–69 were to show, if a turn of events almost bordering on the miraculous were to present a safe opportunity for cutting Prussia down to size, there were courtiers and military men in Vienna who would be keen to seize it. Franz Joseph himself, however, had no desire whatever to resume the leadership of Germany, even if the Magyars, his new partners in government under the Ausgleich of 1867, obsessed with the Russian menace in the east, would have tolerated his doing so. For Beust and his master, Austria in the late 1860s was still very much a convalescent power. Even though the final settlement with Italy had brought much needed relief in the south-west, the Monarchy still had to guard against potential threats from the north and south-east, should Prussia establish herself south of the Main, or Russia, as patron of the Orthodox subjects of the sultan, in the Balkans. The Russo-Prussian diplomatic combination being the only effective power-grouping in these years, and there being no question of Austria-Hungary's confronting it single-handed, circumspection would have to be the order of the day in Vienna. Resentful, even vengeful, though many of its traditional ruling élite might be, therefore, the Dual Monarchy presented no threat to the continued peaceful functioning of the states system in these years.

As for Prussia, in the circumstances of 1866 Bismarck was well content with the tripartite division of Germany that emerged from the war: the exclusion of Austria, the isolation of the south German states, and unfettered Prussian control over Germany north of the Main, this last proving a feature of the European states system until 1919. Internally, too, the somewhat theoretical concessions Bismarck made to federalism in formulating the constitution of the North German Confederation – to the authority of the surviving dynasties and the autonomy of their territories – saved the

Confederation from much of the friction that was later to plague the more centralized Weimar Republic. Even so, in practice, the constitutional arrangements of 1866 (taken over into the Empire of 1871) entrenched the Prussian ruling élite in power for the next half century: although the Reichstag was elected on the basis of universal male suffrage, the Chancellor was not responsible to it and its legislative power was limited, and balanced by an upper house controlled by the member states, especially Prussia, where the three-class voting system guaranteed a permanent conservative majority. The Liberals, for their part, who had in 1866 granted the victorious Bismarck an indemnity for his past constitutional transgressions, still hoped to transform the North German Confederation into a genuine constitutional system, and only suspended their attacks on Bismarck in the hope that he might yet proceed to complete the unification of Germany. Indeed, by the end of the 1860s, as they began to despair of this outcome, their attacks on him became quite vociferous, and were only temporarily stifled by the military triumphs of Prussia in 1870–71. This is not to say, however, that Bismarck engineered the war for this purpose. That cannot even be said of his resolution in 1870 of the second piece of unfinished business left over from 1866: the status of the south German states.

Initially, like the constitutional arrangements of the North German Confederation, the independence of Germany south of the Main seemed to provide a viable basis for an enduring settlement. On the one hand, Bismarck had no desire to incorporate the south German states as full members into the North German Confederation. Their Catholicism, particularist traditions and dynastic pride all suggested that their exclusion was as much a condition of Prussia's domination of Germany as the exclusion of Austria. After all, the military and commercial treaties Bismarck had imposed on them in his hour of victory seemed, by obliging them to co-ordinate their military systems with that of Prussia, to fight alongside Prussia in future defensive wars, and to participate in the *Zollparlament* that was to take over from the *Zollverein*, to give Bismarck all the control over them that he could wish for. It was not long, however, before particularist feeling in the south German states threatened to undermine Bismarck's system of clandestine control: the expenditure involved in military reform sharpened south German criticism of Prussian methods – 'Steuerzahlen, Soldatwerden, Maulhalten' ('Pay your taxes, become a soldier, and keep your mouth shut'); and the *Zollparlament* elections of 1868 saw a triumph of anti-Prussian candidates south of the Main. In March 1870 the replacement of the pro-Prussian liberal cabinet of Prince Hohenlohe in Munich by a Catholic particularist administration under

Count Bray, former Bavarian minister at Vienna, was a further blow to the Prussophiles – underscored by reports that the Wittelsbachs were seeking to enhance their international standing by putting forward a candidate for the vacant throne of Spain. Not that Bismarck could easily counter these disturbing developments by peaceful means; his sharply negative reaction to the attempt by the Liberal deputy, Lasker, to promote the entry of Baden, the closest to France and the most pro-Prussian of the south German states, to the Confederation reflected not only his reluctance to truckle to votes and majorities, but his conviction that such a move would only deepen the rift between Prussia and the remaining south German states. If union was to be the ultimate solution, all four states would have to come in together. For the moment, however, there was precious little sign of any desire on their part to do so; and the one thing Bismarck could not do was to resort to force against them.

This was absolutely ruled out by the configuration of the European states system in the later 1860s, in which the very lack of firm ties between its members ensured that any power that attempted arbitrarily to alter the *status quo* by force would have to do so unaided – in which case an attempt by Prussia to seize the south German states could only be disastrous, both for her image in the German world and for her position in Europe. Even in Russia, for example, the most pro-Prussian of the great powers, if Alexander II was the respectful nephew of the king of Prussia, he had his wife's relatives in Darmstadt to consider – quite apart from Russia's general interest in upholding the tripartite division of Germany that she had helped to salvage from the wreckage of the old Confederation. As for France and Austria, they were absolutely determined to oppose by force any Prussian advance south of the Main; and Beust was untiring in reminding the south German states of their obligation, *vis-à-vis* not themselves but the powers of Europe, to maintain their independent international existence. Napoleon III told Lord Clarendon straight out that if Prussia crossed the Main 'alors, les canons partiront d'eux-mêmes'; while the Austrian war minister declared that 'Prussia on the Inn means the end of Austria'. With no assurance of Russian support, even Bismarck shrank from a war against France and Austria combined that would put all his recent gains in jeopardy. This being the case, unless some turn of events brought about a change of mood south of the Main, there really was little that Bismarck could do to remedy what he felt to be the deficiencies of the 1866 settlement in Germany.

In fact, the power most likely to attempt a violent assault on the *status quo* in these years was France. True, if Napoleon III had been disconcerted by the speed and completeness of the Prussian victory over Austria, he had by no means despaired of securing compensation. French public opinion, by contrast, unversed in the emperor's labyrinthine schemes, was absolutely devastated by Sadowa. If it had been for decades generally more pacific than the government, and had given a decidedly frosty reception to Napoleon's Auxerre speech as late as May 1866, it was quite transformed by the outcome of the war. Immediately the cry went up – and it was to be heard again in 1870 – 'revanche pour Sadowa': France must accept no more humiliations from Prussia. At the same time, however, this same public opinion was never willing to make the material sacrifices necessary to equip France for action against Prussia. Its incessant opposition to the cost of the government's attempted army reforms, eventually implemented in mutilated form in 1869, must give French public opinion a large share of the blame for the catastrophe of Sedan. Meanwhile, if it remorselessly obstructed the government's efforts in the military field, the public's vociferous demands for prestige successes pushed Napoleon III into frantic, and ultimately disastrous, efforts in the field of diplomacy.

Even in the immediate aftermath of Sadowa Napoleon had been disappointed with the results of his Biarritz policy, when Bismarck not only crushingly dismissed his oblique hints about a possible restoration of the 1814 frontier in the Rhineland, but made use of them to scare the south German states into accepting the military treaties of August 1866, with all their damaging implications for that 'independent international existence' by which France set such store. Bismarck's alternative proposal, that France compensate herself in Belgium, was, of course completely unrealistic, given the sensitivity of the British on the subject; and it was incautious of Napoleon to allow Benedetti, his ambassador in Berlin, to incorporate it in a draft treaty that came to rest in the Prussian archives. The following year, the humiliating fiasco, in the face of a public outcry in Germany, of Napoleon's scheme to purchase Luxemburg from the king of the Netherlands – on which occasion Bismarck again demonstrated his unwillingness to lift a finger for the sake of good relations with France – destroyed any lingering illusions Napoleon may have had of Prussian goodwill, and finally turned his thoughts towards securing his ends by force.

The problem for Napoleon was, however, in an era of loose alignments when the other great powers were broadly content to live with the *status quo* of 1866 and none had any desire to make sacrifices to help France to change the existing order to her advantage, that this was the route to isolation and frustration. Indeed, this was both demonstrated and exacerbated by the fact that throughout the later 1860s French diplomacy experienced one disaster after another. In Mexico, 1867 saw the final débâcle of French policy, and the execution of the Emperor Maximilian in June, on the eve of Napoleon's meeting with his imperial brother in Salzburg, was particularly unfortunate. The return of French troops to Rome after the failure of Garibaldi's coup soured relations with Italy. In 1869 Napoleon's former entente partner, Great Britain, reacted to rumours of French plans to take over certain Belgian railways with virtual threats of war. Less spectacular but also disheartening was the failure of Napoleon's repeated attempts to lure Russia away from her long-standing alignment with Prussia by supporting – despite the frowns of Great Britain and Austria – Russian efforts on behalf of the oppressed Christians of Crete. On the contrary, Russia proceeded in 1868 to conclude a formal military convention with Prussia. Although, as late as 1869, Napoleon, all too aware of France's military weakness, was reminding General Niel that there could be no question of war unless Prussia provoked one, the general feeling of exasperation against Prussia that had characterized French public opinion since 1866 had permeated the highest echelons of the regime. Indeed, the general opinion in Paris that France was 'in danger of losing her position among the great powers' was perhaps the most ominous feature of the international scene in the summer of 1870.

Not that the French had been able to secure any external support whatever for their posture. Ever since 1866 France and Austria had been in complete agreement about the necessity of preventing a further Prussian advance across the Main; but ever since 1866 they had been completely at cross purposes as to how this was to be done. Whereas the French wanted an offensive alliance focused on Germany, with a view to territorial gains in the Rhineland, Franz Joseph repeatedly objected that he could in no circumstances summon his ten million German subjects to support an invasion the objective of which was to subject German soil to French rule. The Austrians wanted an alliance focused on the Near East, possibly supporting the Ottoman Empire against Russia and confronting Prussia with the awkward choice between abandoning her ally or supporting her in an unpopular war, without the backing of German national feeling, in which event France and Austria, if victorious, would be free to make what changes they liked in Germany. This, Napoleon turned down flat, in the erroneous belief that he would be able to lure Russia away from Prussia by supporting her efforts on behalf of the Christians of the Ottoman Empire. In 1869 an attempted alliance *à trois* including Italy came to grief over the continued presence of French troops in Rome; and although the French and Austrian military planners got on famously, a visit by

Archduke Albrecht to Paris in February 1870 being noted with particular concern in Berlin, a political agreement remained as far off as ever. In June 1870, for example, when General Lebrun came to Vienna, Franz Joseph was again most emphatic: only if France went to war to defend the south German states against a Prussian attack could Austria join her. For the rest, 'je veux la paix, si je fais la guerre il faut que j'y suis forcé'.

Yet despite the mounting tension in Paris in the summer of 1870, the states system of 1866 had a number of positive features. It was not only one in which the freedom of most of the powers from any binding commitments continued to make for the localization and limitation of conflicts, but also – unlike that of the first half of the decade – an era of partnerships of restraint. If Napoleon's insistence on conciliating Russia held the Austrians back from confronting her too openly in the Near East, Austrian sensitivity to public opinion in the German lands served as a warning to France against rash moves in the direction of the Rhine; and Paris made it perfectly clear to the Italians that any entente must be based on their good behaviour over the Roman question. Similarly, the Russo-Prussian military convention of 1868 was a purely defensive agreement: the Prussians were not obliged to assist St Petersburg in any forward moves in the Near East; just as the Russians offered Berlin no encouragement whatever to advance south of the Main. After all, the ousting of Austria from her residual role as a protector of the independence of the south German states would be doubly unwelcome to St Petersburg – as finally destroying the German balance that Russia had been cultivating since the eighteenth century, and as forcing Austria to concentrate even more on the Balkans. In short, whatever tensions might be developing in Paris and Berlin, the states system of 1866 served to mitigate rather than to exacerbate them.

Indeed, the powers were able in these years to manage even the Eastern Question, source of the last great war that had destroyed the Vienna system, and, half a century later, of the general conflict that was to destroy the nineteeenth-century states system altogether. True, in the 1860s the problems of the Ottoman Empire were themselves relatively manageable and confined to the periphery. In Crete, sporadic rebellions of Greek Christians drew encouragement from Athens, while autonomous Serbia chafed under the remaining relics of Ottoman suzerainty. The situation in the Danubian principalities, was, if anything, more embarrassing to the Habsburgs than to the Sultan. There, since 1866 Prince Charles (Carol) of Hohenzollern-Sigmaringen presided over an irredentist regime under Ion Bratianu, which made no secret of its territorial ambitions in Hungarian

Transylvania, and which, thanks to a steady inflow of arms from Prussia, was rapidly turning itself into what Beust termed a 'living arsenal' on the southern frontier of the Monarchy. On the whole, the powers managed to act in concert to resolve these problems, prevailing on the Turks to withdraw their garrisons from Belgrade while firmly discountenancing Serbia's wider irredentist ambitions; and meeting in conference to secure an autonomous regime for Crete that satisfied Russia and France, while sufficiently respecting the Sultan's rights to reassure Great Britain and Austria-Hungary. Only in the Danubian principalities in 1868 did the Austrians feel it necessary to show their teeth, Beust hinting at a pre-emptive strike against the 'living arsenal'. When Bismarck, his bluff called and his Russian partners obviously indifferent to the Romanian cause, hastily abandoned his machinations and even prevailed on Prince Carol to dismiss Bratianu, this crisis, too, faded away.

It was Prussian involvement, little over a year later, in the candidature of Carol's brother, Prince Leopold of Hohenzollern-Sigmaringen, for the throne of Spain – perhaps, as in the case of Prince Carol, a Bismarckian ploy to put a potential opponent at a strategic disadvantage – that finally brought the latent hostility between France and Prussia to a head. As usual, Bismarck's motives were complex: on the German front, if he could both forestall a Wittelsbach candidature and render the southern frontier of France insecure, this could only enhance Prussia's authority in south Germany; while if the French preferred to go to war rather than tolerate a Hohenzollern regime south of the Pyrenees, well and good – at least the war would not have arisen out of a Prussian threat to the south German states. In fact, the Hohenzollern candidature – as Beust was indeed pleased to note – was not all that good an issue for Prussia to fight on: a Prussian dynastic issue to which German national sentiment was largely indifferent. On 6 July, however, Beust's complacency turned to utter dismay when Napoleon's foreign minister, Gramont, made an extraordinarily bellicose speech to the chamber that suddenly transformed the issue into a question of national honour between the two leading powers of western Europe; and when after Prince Leopold in panic withdrew his candidature, Napoleon again forced the pace, seeking to crown his triumph with a humiliating demand for guarantees of the withdrawal from the Prussian monarch himself. It was only this that enabled a despairing Bismarck to pluck victory from defeat by devising the Ems telegram that precipitated the French declaration of war on Prussia of 19 July.

This outcome resulted, of course, from the clash of two offensive strategies: Napoleon III had been disappointed by Leopold's retreat, and had pressed on in the firm conviction that he was responding to a public demand for war; and Bismarck had rephrased the Ems telegram in the full knowledge of the effect it would have on inflamed opinion in Paris. Chance and contingency, too, played their part, but Bismarck's miscalculations and desperate improvisations were worlds away from the clouds of emotion and illusion that enveloped the French decision-makers in the critical days. Gramont, for example – almost incredibly for a former ambassador at Vienna – had convinced himself that Austria-Hungary would have no choice but to fight alongside France, told the Austrian ambassador so straight out, and flew into a rage when the latter mentioned the word 'congress'. In the circumstances Franz Joseph, as he had always predicted, could do nothing and France found herself fighting alone. If her actual declaration of war convinced the outside world generally that she was the aggressor, Bismarck's publication in *The Times* of the Benedetti draft treaty relating to the annexation of Belgium absolutely destroyed what was left of Napoleon's reputation in London. The French decision to launch their invasion through the Bavarian Palatinate in the hope of separating the north and south German forces was particularly ill judged, both failing militarily and actually precipitating that union of north and south Germany that Bismarck had been unable to achieve and that no other member of the states system had desired. Suddenly, in south Germany the wearisome acrimonious debate about the *casus foederis* under the military treaties of 1866 was silenced as the southern states unanimously fell into line behind Prussia to fight the traditional foe.

Not that the French had been alone in their illusions. In fact, as in 1866, the general expectation outside Germany had been that Prussia would be defeated. That these calculations proved mistaken was not so much due to the inferiority of the French army as such, or even to Prussia's superior organization and speed of mobilization, as to bad French strategic planning and the confusion and corruption of the Second Empire that prevented France from realizing her full potential. At any rate, within less than a month of the first Prussian victories on 4 August, Napoleon III had been taken prisoner along with his army at Sedan, and on 4 September a revolution in Paris replaced the Second Empire with the Third Republic. In the long run, this was to prove a momentous and lasting change: France, who since the defeat of Russia in the Crimean War and the subsequent self-effacement of Great Britain, had been the leading power on the continent, had yielded her primacy to Prussia, now indisputably the leading military power in the European states system.

In the short term, the new regime in France had yet to be convinced of this, and Gambetta organized a *levée en masse* that led to four more months of guerrilla warfare. By November, Moltke had to confess himself baffled: 'almost the entire French army has been taken prisoner, and yet we have more men under arms against us than at the beginning of the war.' By dint of draconian methods, however, such as shooting non-uniformed combatants out of hand, and a prolonged siege of Paris, he managed by February 1871 to compel the republican government that had retreated to Versailles to accept an armistice. This was denounced by the Left in control of Paris, that declared its intention of fighting to the bitter end, duly establishing a radical and violent regime (the Commune) that proceeded to horrify the whole of monarchical Europe. It was only after the Republic had suppressed it (even more violently) that peace could be formally concluded by the Treaty of Frankfort of 10 May.

These were anxious months for Bismarck, desperate to settle both the peace with France and the future constitution of Germany on his own terms before third parties could intervene. Beust, for example, was known to be touting mediation proposals in London and St Petersburg, and to be intriguing at Munich, reminding the Bavarians of their obligation to uphold their independent international existence in accordance with the Treaty of Prague. In south Germany, Bismarck acted swiftly, summoning the rulers of all four states to Versailles, well away from Austrian influence, and getting the three smallest states into line before using them to bring overwhelming pressure on Ludwig II (who was also heavily bribed). Even then, he had to make important concessions to particularist feeling: the Bavarians refused point blank simply to subordinate themselves to Prussia by joining her North German Confederation. Hence, Bismarck's invention of the title 'German Emperor' for King William, who would exercise his imperial power over all the German states without distinction, including (to the dismay of old Prussian conservatives) the kingdom of Prussia, now technically mediatized too. The Chancellor, too, could be chosen from any of the states of the Empire; and the federal features of the 1867 constitution were taken over into the new regime. With the formal proclamation of the Empire at Versailles on 18 January 1871 the constitution of Germany was settled for the next half century. Getting the French to acknowledge the loss of their primacy was a more difficult task, but the verdict of the battlefield was ultimately unanswerable. Bismarck believed, perhaps rightly, that France would resent her demotion anyway, whether she lost any territory or not; and his insistence on a substantial indemnity and on the cession of Alsace and part of Lorraine was simply a move to

MAP 4 *Central Europe in 1871*

render France incapable of waging a war of revenge (and perhaps also to exalt the Prussian military monarchy in the eyes of opinion at home). At any rate, the Franco-German frontier as established by the Treaty of Frankfort was to be as enduring a feature of the international scene as the German Empire itself.

That Prussia could implement such momentous changes without interference from other members of the states system reflects its loose, fragmented nature in these years. In contrast to 1914, in 1870 no power felt its interests to be so closely bound up with those of a belligerent as to warrant facing the risks of intervention. Even the Austrians, who after the French had most to lose from a Prussian victory, only toyed with the idea of joining a victorious France, and that only for a few days at the beginning of the war. As news came in of the Prussian victories – or the 'frightful catastrophes in France', as Franz Joseph termed them – circumspection became the order of the day for the Habsburgs, who had everything to fear from a confrontation with German national feeling in full flood. Beust's tentative efforts to lure Great Britain and Russia to join him in restraining Prussia by 'mediation' failed as dismally as his attempts to stiffen the south German states to stand up to Bismarck. By December he resignedly informed Berlin that he would now cease to uphold 'the formal logic of the Treaty of Prague' against 'the weight of mighty events' that had conferred the leadership of Germany on the Prussian crown. Over the next few months, his forlorn hopes of French resistance gradually disappeared, and in May 1871 he confessed, in an important policy memorandum for Franz Joseph, that the new German Empire was there to stay: and that being the case, and as, if crossed, it could prove a dangerous neighbour for a Monarchy that contained so many Germans, the emperor would do well to establish amicable relations with it.

Initially, Russia's neutrality had been distinctly pro-Prussian. Prussia was, after all, Russia's only friend in Europe and Alexander II was afraid that a French victory would see the Polish question back on the agenda – hence, when France declared war, his decision to station 300,000 troops on the Austrian border. As envisaged in the Russo-Prussian military convention, this certainly helped to restrain Vienna from joining the war against Prussia, although it roused a mighty wave of anti-Russian feeling in Budapest. With the fall of the Second Empire, however, new fears alarmed the Tsar – the spectre of the Revolution, and, more immediately, the end of the division of Germany that had given Russia security on the western border for so long. In August 1870, therefore, Alexander twice approached the Austrians with remarkably far-reaching proposals:

Austria-Hungary and Russia should cease their military preparations against each other and co-operate to establish a balance of power in Germany in which south Germany would fall under Austrian control. Such was the intensity of feeling against Russia in Budapest, however, where she was even suspected of planning to overrun the Danubian principalities, that Beust and Franz Joseph could only respond to Alexander's offers with lame evasions. Yet another opportunity to check Prussia's advance south of the Main had fallen victim to the inability of members of the states system to act together, even when they shared an urgent common interest. At any rate, after this rebuff the Russians decided that there was nothing they could now do to stave off the disagreeable changes impending in the west, and that they might at least compensate themselves by taking advantage of the general crisis to pursue their own interests in the east. On 31 October Gorchakov, egged on by Bismarck, who welcomed anything that would keep the other powers at odds, announced in a circular that Russia would henceforth refuse to be bound by the Black Sea clauses of the Treaty of Paris.

If this move caused outrage in Vienna, it also embarrassed London, where since Gladstone's return to power in 1868 the principles of international law had assumed greater importance in British foreign policy. Not that this had really enhanced Great Britain's authority on the international scene: as a military power, Great Britain was simply not in the same league as either of the belligerents; and Gladstone had inherited from his predecessor a public opinion that was 'thoroughly bent on incurring no fresh responsibilities on the continent'. So far, he had confined himself to extracting assurances from both belligerents that they would respect the neutrality of Belgium guaranteed by the Treaty of London of 1839; and although after the disappearance of Napoleon III British opinion became rather more sympathetic towards France there could be no question of coming forward with mediation proposals that would only be rejected by Prussia. Besides, once confronted with Gorchakov's circular, Gladstone was anxious for Prussia's assistance in bringing her wayward Russian friends back on to the path of legality.

His hopes were not ill founded, and he was pleased to discern in the London Conference of January to March 1871 a gratifying revival of the Concert of Europe. Certainly, a consensus was facilitated by the fact that Gorchakov's declaration was of no more than theoretical significance; the Russians were still finding it difficult enough to raise the funds for urgent military reforms, let alone for fortifications and battleships in the Black Sea. In fact, the situation there was to remain quite unaffected by

Gorchakov's circular until the end of the 1880s. The confrontational line that the Austrians had been forced by Hungarian pressure to adopt (that if Russia refused to retract her circular, the western powers should station permanent countervailing squadrons in the Black Sea), therefore found no supporters; and, with Prussia and France both cultivating Russia, and Gladstone primarily interested in the point of principle, a sensible compromise could be reached. On 13 March, the great powers ratified the abolition of the Black Sea clauses of the Treaty of Paris, the London Protocol of 17 January, having laid down the principle for the future that international treaties could only be altered with the consent of the contracting parties. Thus, Russia's illegal action had paved the way for the proclamation of an important new article of international law.

This was not the only sign that legality and legitimacy still counted for something in the European states system. In fact, the triumph of the German Empire over the French Republic enhanced the prestige of monarchies and the political Right everywhere. It was 'in the name of His Majesty the German Emperor' that the Treaty of Frankfort proclaimed to the world the transfer of Alsace-Lorraine from France to Germany. The treaty made no reference whatever to the views of inhabitants, or to plebiscites purporting to test the wishes of populations, or to the principle of nationalities. These notions, which only ten years before had seemed to portend the overthrow of the whole international order based on treaty rights now went into eclipse; and (apart perhaps from a few rumblings in the Balkans) the doctrine of self-determination of peoples was to play no further role in decision-making in the European states system until the collapse of the great monarchies in 1918. For the moment, these monarchies could also take comfort from the fact that the disappearance of Napoleon III had deprived a host of international troublemakers – Italian, Serbian, Romanian, Hungarian and Polish – of his patronage; and events in postwar France were conspiring to increase their confidence further. On the one hand, the bloody regime of the Commune had sounded the tocsin against the revival of the Revolution: the only war that could now be waged in Europe, William I insisted to Franz Joseph, was the war against the Socialist International. On the other, the establishment of the Third Republic in France was welcome to Bismarck as confirming her isolation and her impotence to challenge the new order.

At the same time, France's erstwhile protégé and the latest addition to the ranks of the great powers, the kingdom of Italy, had abandoned her and was making steady progress towards conservative respectability. After all, the kingdom owed its existence to the sensitivity of its rulers to the prevailing trends in the states system. From being in the early 1860s the very embodiment, under the protection of the western powers, of liberal doctrines that struck at the very roots of the international order based on treaty rights, Italy had by the end of the decade moved towards an entente with conservative Austria. True, in September 1870 the military triumphs of the Prussian monarchy that led to the evacuation of French troops from Rome and the completion of the unification of the kingdom, were welcomed by Italians of all shades of opinion. The Left, however, underwent a radical change of heart once the despised regime of Napoleon III was replaced by a republic: the troops whom Garibaldi had gratefully eulogized on 7 September as 'German brothers' had by 7 October become 'Prussian hordes'; and Garibaldi himself went off to France to fight alongside the guerrilla resistance. (The Germans, for their part, had had enough of Garibaldi, the Prussian General staff deciding that, if captured, he should be shot.) The House of Savoy, by contrast, with those instincts of self-preservation that were to serve it so well, decided – as it was to do again in 1915 – to fly to the assistance of the victorious power and seek cordial relations with its mighty neighbours in the north. In 1873 Victor Emmanuel's state visit to Berlin, following closely on those of Franz Joseph and Alexander II, seemed to mark his acceptance into respectable ruling circles, and set Italy on the road that was to end in the Triple Alliance.

Yet if the Treaty of Frankfort stood at the beginning of a new era in which the European states system was again defined in conservative-legitimist rather than popular-liberal terms, the turbulent years from 1859 to 1871 had left enduring scars. The war of 1870 was the third Bismarckian war, but nobody in 1871 was to know that it was to be the last. Indeed, the hard lesson to be drawn from all the wars of the 1860s was that ultimately states must rely for their security on armed might, not on treaty rights. Certainly, the viability of the Treaty of Frankfort depended entirely on Germany's continuing to retain her military superiority over France. For all their beneficent, stabilizing aspects, the arrangements of 1871 always lacked that basis of general great-power consensus that had underpinned the settlement of 1815. True, most of the powers found the 1871 settlement tolerable enough, even if they had not been allowed any share whatever in constructing it; and Marx was perhaps being too gloomy when he declared that the Treaty of Frankfort had 'made war an institution'. Even so, it certainly made the long peace of 1871–1914 much more of an armed peace than the long peace that Europe had enjoyed in the more consensual states system of 1815.

CHAPTER 6

The testing of the new order, 1871–79

General characteristics of the period 1871–1914

In terms of the European states system, the 'long nineteenth century', between the end of the Napoleonic era and the outbreak of the First World War may conveniently be divided into three periods. The forty years between the Congress of Vienna and the outbreak of the Crimean War constituted the longest period of peace between the great powers since the states system emerged at the beginning of the sixteenth century. Whether it reflected simply a primitive instinct for self-preservation in an era when the experience of the immense destruction and instability of the Revolutionary and Napoleonic Wars still exercised a hold over the minds of statesmen, or whether it embodied more far-sighted motives of enlightened self-interest and an appreciation that in the exercise of restraint by the individual members of the states system lay the best guarantee of the security of all, the post-1815 system, based on compromise, balance, and respect for a legitimate order established by treaties gave Europe forty years of peace. In terms of the alignments of the powers, the peace was upheld by a broad consensus between the members of the victorious coalition, centred on Austria. This weak, *status quo* power that depended on respect for legitimacy and treaty rights for its very existence, was able to serve effectively as the keystone of the system, so long as it could count on the support of one, or, ideally, both of the 'superpower' members of the coalition, Great Britain and Russia. It was the co-operation of this preponderant and fundamentally conservative group of powers that maintained the peace for a generation after 1815 and that defeated the assault launched on the established international order by the revolutionaries of 1848.

Yet the triumph of the forces of order in 1848–49 ultimately undermined the conservative consensus on which the 1815 system was based. In the first place, the fear of 'the Revolution', now so resoundingly defeated, lost much of its effectiveness as a restraint on the actions of governments as did the concomitant fear of war as the midwife of revolution. Consequently the resurgent absolutist regimes that emerged in France and central Europe in the 1850s were much more prepared to consider recourse to war than their pre-1848 predecessors had been; and Napoleon III was actually prepared to espouse the revolutionary doctrine of self-determination against the legitimist doctrine of treaty rights in a deliberate challenge to the order of 1815 that was infinitely more serious than anything his Bourbon or Orleanist predecessors had devised. At the same time, the three great conservative powers of the old coalition, all at odds with each other over the eastern crisis of 1853–56, ceased to co-operate to uphold the 1815 order – indeed, Great Britain and Russia actively connived at its destruction. The upshot was that the years 1854 to 1871 saw the great powers involved in no fewer than five wars that witnessed the end of the 1815 settlement in central Europe and the establishment of a kingdom of Italy and a German empire.

All the same, the last of these wars marked a return to stability, and the Treaty of Frankfort was followed by an even longer period of peace between the great powers than the Treaty of Vienna. The wars of 1854–71 had modified the international order but had not abolished it. The ranking of the great powers within the European states system had been radically altered; but an international system still survived, based on the co-existence of a number of sovereign states, in which the great powers continued to assert their traditional claim to pre-eminence. The German Empire might have replaced the French Empire as the 'predominant' or leading power within the system, but it was far from being a hegemonial power like the France of Napoleon I, which had treated the other continental powers simply as satellites and had represented the absolute negation of a system of independent sovereign states. True, the new order was uncomfortable for France: Prussia's seizure of Alsace-Lorraine was never to be forgotten; the statue of Strasbourg in the Place de La Concorde was to remain draped in black crêpe until 1919; and the impossibility of a combination between France and Germany was to be henceforth the fixed point in the shifting alignments within the states system. The other powers took a less melodramatic view of the new order, however: France had launched the war of 1870 in the face of universal disapproval, and to the other powers the Treaty of Frankfort was perfectly acceptable – provided always that Germany too saw in it the basis of a stable new order and not a springboard for further expansion. Their forbearance was not ill-founded as far as Bismarck was concerned, who wanted nothing more than the maintenance of the continental *status quo*; and even though new developments revived old anxieties after the turn of the century, it was not until the July crisis of 1914 that a great power felt sufficiently threatened to plunge the states system into war.

The stability of the post-1871 states system, like that of the post-1815 states system, was enhanced by a renewed emphasis on legitimacy and treaty rights as the basis of the international order. Whereas in the upheavals of the 1850s and 1860s the disruptive force of national self-determination had wrought havoc with an international order based on legitimist principles, the new order of 1870–71, despite the element of coercion inherent in it, represented a return to a conservative order grounded in monarchical authority. The adjustments made in these years – the incorporation of Alsace and part of Lorraine into Germany, the entry of the south German states into the new Empire, the transfer of the capital of the kingdom of Italy from Florence to Rome – were all changes imposed by constituted monarchical authorities without recourse to the plebiscites and appeals to the popular will that had characterized the diplomacy of Napoleon III and Cavour. The London Protocol of 1871, reaffirming the principle that international treaties could only be modified with the consent of the signatory powers was another sign of the revival of legitimist principles; and it was vindicated in action at the end of the decade when the Russians had to abandon their attempt to reorder south-east Europe by the bilateral Treaty of San Stefano and acquiesce in a settlement imposed by the powers in concert at the Congress of Berlin, a settlement that reflected the preoccupations of the governments of the great powers and one in which the aspirations of the Balkan peoples were very much a secondary consideration.

In the military field, too, lessons drawn by decision-makers from the violent readjustment of the states system in 1870–71 served for a time as a stabilizing factor. It is true that the example of spectacular success of Prussian arms, coupled with the prevailing doctrine of the overriding importance of the offensive, of getting in the first blow if war should be come inevitable, led to a general increase in nervousness: except in Great Britain, conscription became the order of the day, and the military expenditure of all the continental powers grew steadily right down to

1914. But even so, Karl Marx was exaggerating when he declared that the Treaty of Frankfort had 'made war an institution'. Certainly, it had helped to make armaments races an institution; but armaments races do not necessarily lead to wars, or even to an increased danger of war – witness, for example, the Anglo-French naval arms race in the later 1880s. In fact, a determination on the part of a group of *status quo* powers to maintain an armed preponderance – such as in fact existed in Europe until the 1890s – can be rather a guarantee of peace. Indeed, the collapse of the international order in the 1930s might be seen as an object lesson in the failure of the *status quo* powers to maintain an adequate level of armaments. And already before this, in the first decade of the century, when Great Britain moved to the Franco-Russian side, a balance of armaments resulted that was perhaps more equal, but, in the polarized states system that was developing, was certainly more dangerous: as every crisis became a trial of strength between two blocs the idea gradually gained ground in military circles in the central powers that an increasingly desperate situation could only be saved by preventive war.

Even so, for many years after 1871 the experience of the Franco-German war seems, like the experience of the Napoleonic Wars, to have had a stabilizing effect by making governments fearful of a new war. After all, by 1871 the war had precipitated a revolution in France that had ended in the terrifying spectacle of the Commune; and Prussia's victory over the army of Napoleon III had led, not to a speedy peace, but to a *levée en masse* and prolonged guerrilla warfare. This new type of warfare, the *Volkskrieg*, or total war, was to Moltke and his contemporaries a most awesome phenomenon. In the words of the Austro-Hungarian chief of staff, arguing against a resort to war in the eastern crisis of 1878, the wars of 1866 and 1871 had shown that 'long wars cannot be sustained by a modern civilised state using universal conscription'; and as Moltke himself explained to the Reichstag in 1890:

The days of cabinet wars are over. . . . We have only the Volkskrieg, *and no rational government can easily decide to start such a war with all its unforeseen consequences. . . . The existence of the Empire would be at stake, perhaps even the continued existence of the social order and civilisation.*

Although Moltke toyed with the idea of a preventive war as a solution to the problem of a two-front war that never ceased to oppress him – as indeed, perhaps, Bismarck did in the 'War in Sight' crisis of 1875 – by the end of the 1880s they had both settled for a simple deterrent theory: to build up Germany's armaments to such a degree that no power would dare to start a war with her. It was perhaps only at the end of the century, when Germany had ceased to be a *status quo* power content with the degree of preponderance she had enjoyed since 1871, and when Moltke's successors tried again to make war a practical instrument of policy by devising strategic plans for a controlled cabinet war in the age of the *Volkskrieg*, that the European states system was really set on the road to disaster.

In the decades after 1871 political considerations, too, inclined the ruling élites of Europe towards caution and conservative solidarity. The Paris Commune had revived anxieties reminiscent of those that had plagued governments after 1815, namely, that war between the great powers might give the Revolution its chance. It was significant that at the three emperors' meeting at Berlin in September 1872 that marked the end of twenty years of rivalry and conflict between the two German monarchies, William I adjured Franz Joseph that the only war that could now be waged in Europe was that against the Communist International. The Holy Alliance and Münchengrätz found distinct echoes in the Three Emperors' League of 1873–78 and the Three Emperors' Alliance of 1881–87, and monarchical solidarity remained a strong element in the policies of all three eastern empires until the early twentieth century. As Franz Joseph's ambassador at St Petersburg observed in 1885, 'there is in Europe a great revolutionary subversive party just waiting for the crash and for the great conservative powers to weaken and exhaust each other in the conflict, and then the radical reform can begin.' In Western Europe, too, the Triple Alliance of 1882–1915 between the central powers and Italy, was expressly designed 'to fortify the monarchical principle and thereby to assure the unimpaired maintenance of the social and political order within their respective states'. The association of Great Britain and Austria-Hungary with Italy and Spain in the Mediterranean Agreements of 1887–96 was in part an attempt to bolster up friendly monarchical regimes against bullying by republican France; just as both London and Vienna tried to put in a word for Spain at Washington on the eve of the Spanish-American War of 1898. Again, by the early twentieth century, this cement of the states system too was beginning to weaken. Only in Austria-Hungary did Archduke Franz Ferdinand remain fanatically devoted to the doctrine of monarchical solidarity and absolutely opposed to all notion of war with Russia; and as S.R. Williamson has emphasized, the violent removal from the scene of the head of the Austrian 'peace party' was a key element in precipitating the catastrophe of the old European states system in more ways than one.

In Berlin and St Petersburg, by this time, ideas of monarchical solidarity counted for less than considerations of national honour and even racial solidarity – although the fate of all three empires by 1918 would seem to suggest that the apprehensions of earlier generations of decision-makers had not been without foundation.

Although both the internal stability of the post-1871 European states system as reordered in 1871 and the attitudes of the statesmen in charge of it tended to restrain the Powers from actually resorting to war, the period between 1871 and 1914 was no different from any other in that it witnessed intense rivalries and manoeuvring for position within the states system. This was, after all, the Age of Imperialism, and much great power activity reflected the growing involvement of the members of the European states system in the rest of the world. Indeed, it would be no exaggeration to say that until the twentieth century most of the actual disputes between the great powers arose from their extra-European activities. Moreover, these extra-European disputes could sometimes have serious repercussions on the alignment of the great powers in Europe: after the French seized control of Tunis in 1881, rivalry over territories on the southern shores of the Mediterranean led to twenty years of hostility between France and Italy; the estrangement between France and Great Britain after their quarrel over Egypt in 1882 lasted even longer; Anglo-Russian rivalry over central Asia; the scramble for China in the 1890s; the trials of strength between France and Germany over Morocco in the early twentieth century, and the repercussions of Italy's seizure of the Ottoman province of Libya in the Balkans and the eastern Mediterranean were only the most notable examples of this phenomenon. At the same time, however, one of the most striking features of all these extra-European rivalries was that none of them led to an actual armed confrontation between the great powers. They were all resolved peacefully; in 1914 Great Britain actually found herself allied to her chief opponents of the age of imperialist expansion; and the power that started the war, Austria-Hungary, was the power that had been least involved in these extra-European conflicts.

True, the indirect and cumulative effect of these activities on the alignments of the powers within the European states system was indeed a factor in the collapse of that system into general war in 1914. Even in the Austrian case, for example, the mood of desperation prevailing in Vienna by 1914 at the Monarchy's declining ability to maintain its position in the ranks of the great powers was certainly not alleviated by the failure at this time – thanks to the opposition of its own alliance partners – of an Austro-Hungarian scheme to stake out a colony in Asia Minor. More importantly, Germany's repeated clashes with France over Morocco had had a profound effect on British perceptions of Germany's general object-ives that certainly affected British assessments of the German intentions in 1914; just as the decision of the British to stand by France and Russia in the July crisis reflected their determination to hold on to their extra-European agreements with those powers at all costs, if only for fear of a revival of the old struggles with them in Africa and Asia. Italy's imperial-ist war with Turkey in 1911–12 had perhaps the most direct effect of all, in the contribution it made to the Balkan Wars, the expulsion of Turkey from Europe, and the overthrow of the whole Near Eastern balance from which the Great War arose.

On the other hand, it must be emphasized that extra-European ques-tions were never in themselves important enough to cause war between the great powers. Although once the conflict had broken out in 1914 the acquisition of enemy colonies became a war aim for all the belligerents, it was not the cause of the breakdown of the long peace. The previous forty years had shown that the world was big enough for all the great powers to pursue their imperialist objectives in peaceful competition. Indeed, extra-European questions had sometimes served as lightning conductors diverting the attention of the powers from more dangerous conflicts of interest that existed within the European states system itself. It was for very good reason that Bismarck had cherished the hope after 1871 that France might be reconciled to her new position in Europe if she could 'convalesce in Africa'.

Infinitely more risky, by contrast, was his calculation that Germany's exposed position in the centre of the continent would be alleviated if Russia, Austria-Hungary and Great Britain could be encouraged to busy themselves at the periphery of the continent in the Near East – as he himself came ruefully to realize towards the end of his life when he remarked to a friend: 'I shall not live to see the great war, but you will, and it will start in the Near East.' What was indeed to prove fatal to the continued peace-ful functioning of the European states system was its failure to cope with the Eastern Question, which in 1913 developed in such a way – in a way that no extra-European question could – as to threaten the vital interests of the great powers, namely, their standing as great powers within the system. By 1914 the Near Eastern situation posed a direct threat to the great-power status of Austria-Hungary and Russia, and an indirect threat to the great-power status of the other powers whose fate was bound up with the survival of Austria-Hungary and Russia as great powers. After forty years of peace, the European states system collapsed in war.

A decade of loose alignments, 1871–79

The creation of the German Empire in 1871 had repercussions throughout the whole European states system. The old German Confederation,
for all its faults and its proven inability to satisfy or contain the demands
of German nationalism, had been a stabilizing element in international
terms. It had been strong enough, in defensive terms, to check the ambitions
of the restless powers, France and Russia; but its complex and cumbersome
federal structure prevented its organization into a state that might pose
an offensive threat to its neighbours. Like the Ottoman Empire later, the
Bund of 1815 was a passive element, a shock absorber, in the international
system. The new German Empire was very different. Already, in terms of
population, military capacity and industrial development, the strongest
power on the continent, it was inspired, controlled, and, above all organized by a Prussian élite that had just proved its determination and efficiency in three successful wars within seven years. Bismarck himself had
acquired an alarming reputation; and Russian fears as to where 'the
Minotaur in Berlin' might strike next were widely shared in Europe. From
being a constitutionally inert buffer, Germany had become a dynamic
element in the system, with a potential for exerting pressure outwards
on its neighbours that was bound to cause them a degree of concern.
Even so, the long peace from 1871 to 1914 showed that the problem
was not unmanageable: the war of 1914 to 1918 showed that it had not
been solved.

So long as Bismarck remained in control at Berlin, the problem was
eased by the fact that German policy was eminently conservative and
pacific. After all, Bismarck had now achieved his ideal German Empire,
and a small group of Prussian, conservative, Protestant, Junkers controlled the most powerful state on the continent. Bismarck's aim after 1871
was simply to perpetuate this state of affairs. Any change must be for the
worse: hence his opposition to Pan-German dreams of Great Germany,
involving the incorporation of ten million Austrian Germans, potentially
a rival element who might combine with the South Germans to wrest
control of the empire from Prussia; hence his hatred of internationally
minded Social Democrats and of 'doctrinaire' Liberals, who sought to
make the Reichstag an effective force in German political life and rejected
a constitutional system that simply glorified the Prussian national monarchy and left the imperial Chancellor largely independent of Reichstag
control; hence his ruthless persecution of 'alien' elements – Danes, Alsace-
Lorrainers, Poles – Hanoverian patriots, with their almost treasonable

links with foreign ruling houses, and even ultramontane Catholics: none of these people really ever had any place in Bismarck's Germany. Bismarck's career after 1871 was one long rearguard action in defence of the agrarian Junker élite – and later of their allies in industry – against this host of 'enemies of the Empire'. Yet although his intentions may have been conservative at home, he adopted tactics which, especially when taken further by his successors, led ultimately to Germany's ceasing to be a conservative and conciliatory power abroad. He himself later came to regret the irremediable damage done to Franco-German relations by his decision to take the trophy of Alsace-Lorraine, in an attempt to enhance the standing of the new Empire in the eyes of the German people. Even more serious, his support of Junker economic interests was eventually to damage Germany's relations with Russia beyond repair; his device of using colonial policy for domestic electoral purposes was, in the hands of more vigorous and less skilful successors, to do untold harm to Germany's relations with the western powers; and altogether the tradition he established of resorting to war scares and foreign adventures to escape from mounting difficulties at home, was in the long run to prove disastrous both for Germany and for Europe. Indeed, according to Professor Wehler, the roots of all Germany's later problems with 'encirclement' can be traced back to traditions established by Bismarck. In the 1870s, however, Bismarck still appreciated the need for caution and conciliation if he was to avoid provoking the formation of hostile coalitions, and to secure the acceptance of the German Empire into the European states system.

Equally, in the 1870s almost all of the other powers were prepared to accept the new order of things, or at least to reserve judgement on the new Empire. Only France was irreconcilable and vengeful: no French politician could accept the Treaty of Frankfort as the last word. But at the same time, the French fully realized that, even when they recovered from the war, they would never be able to reverse the verdict of 1871 without the assistance of an ally; and an alliance was hard to find. In France itself, the proponents of alliances with Austria, Russia and Great Britain, were all at odds with each other; and the monarchist government's quixotic and emotional attachment to the Papal campaign against the kingdom of Italy made the task of French diplomacy no easier. Altogether, the political system of the Third Republic, with its kaleidoscopic parliamentary alignments and its lack of any experienced directing hand in foreign affairs put France at a disadvantage in competing with the military-aristocratic empires of the east, where policy remained firmly in the hands of the monarch and a few expert advisers. Even when the *Intérêts* – the financial and commercial circles who controlled the politics of France behind the scenes – ousted the monarchists and established the République des Affaires in 1877, their utter opportunism produced only one unstable coalition government after another, sometimes with disastrous consequences for the position of France as a great power – for example, the sudden fall of Gambetta in January 1882 was to bring her twenty years of trouble over Egypt. In short, the isolation and impotence of France in the 1870s was due as much to conditions at home as to the machinations of Bismarck.

The other powers were more ready to accept the new Germany into the international community, but always with one proviso: that she did not seek to expand any further. Italy, for example, had welcomed Prussia's victories over Austria and France, which had brought her a rich province and a capital city; but she still had reservations about the even more astronomical rise of Prussia herself. The right-wing Northern professionals who dominated the Italian Foreign Office, and whose ideas largely determined the character of Italian foreign policy whatever government was in power at Rome, were firm believers in the Piedmontese tradition: that Sardinia had risen to greatness not by virtue of her own strength – indeed, in their eyes Italy, with fewer material resources than Belgium, could never be a great power in her own right – but by skilfully exploiting the rivalries of others. Obviously, if one power ever dominated the continent, Italy would lose her freedom of manoeuvre; so although Germany might be useful, France and Austria must also remain in play. Of the last two, Austria was the less dangerous, so on the whole Italy inclined towards the central powers – who as the stronger combination offered better chances of pickings in any case; and the demands of the Left for an irredentist policy at Austria's expense were given short shrift. This trend was particularly marked under Crispi, after 1887. As a southerner, Crispi was more interested than the traditional Piedmontese politicians in expansion in North Africa to relieve the surplus population problem of the south; and he also hoped to make his name as the founder of a new Roman Empire straddling the Mediterranean. He was always totally indifferent to irredentist claims, except possibly at the expense of France, Italy's Mediterranean rival; and he was more rigidly committed than any other Italian politician to a close alignment with Great Britain and the central powers. But even his predecessors since 1871 had had no reason to regret or disapprove of the creation of the German Empire.

If any power might have been expected to resent it, it was Austria-Hungary, who had been striving since 1866 to prevent it. But in the event, the prevailing uncertainty about Prussian intentions, and in particular the fear of another *Blitzkrieg* and the loss of Austria's German territories, determined Vienna to prefer discretion to valour and to seek to conciliate the new Empire. After all, Austria's expulsion from Germany and Italy in the 1860s was now clearly irreversible; and Austria-Hungary now had other preoccupations: the avoidance of a third defeat, in the South, at the hands of embryonic South Slav and Romanian nationalist movements which had already taken on a disturbingly anti-Habsburg tinge and which might, especially if they secured Russian backing, eventually threaten the existence of what was left of the Monarchy. Rather than tolerate a repetition of 1859 and 1866 in the Balkans, Austria-Hungary would fight to the death. In this sense, in terms of the peace and stability of the European states system, south-east Europe already harboured explosive material. True, left to itself, the Monarchy was a distinctly conservative power. It had no territorial ambitions, and would be content if the Ottoman Empire and any national states that emerged from it remained open to Austro-Hungarian trade and cultural and political influence. Necessity, as much as choice, dictated a passive policy. The Monarchy was still essentially a military-aristocratic state, relatively backward in terms of economic development, and hamstrung by a complex constitutional structure that both technically and psychologically worked against an active foreign policy. In the early 1870s it lacked confidence and needed support; and although Andrássy remained firmly opposed, like the rest of Europe, to any further increase of German power at the expense of France, he did in fact hope initially that the new Empire might be persuaded to join a coalition to hold Russia in check.

In fact, the Russian government was rather less concerned with stirring up Balkan nationalism than the Austrians imagined, and usually managed to ignore Pan-Slav pressures at home. Since the Crimean War, the Tsar was convinced that he was facing a British offensive on a worldwide scale. Russia's efforts to establish her position in the Caucasus and in central Asia in the 1860s were certainly in part an attempt to prepare for a renewed British onslaught; and even the 'threat to India' that the British perceived therein was partly a defensive move, calculated to deter a British attack on Russia in an area where she was still painfully vulnerable – at the Straits. There, certainly, Russia's chief opponent seemed to be Great Britain. Despite the revision of the Treaty of Paris in 1871, it was to be almost twenty years before the Russians managed to build a fleet capable of defending their southern coast against a British incursion into the Black Sea – hence their obsessive insistence on the strictest interpretation of the rule of the Straits. But even if Great Britain remained Russia's main preoccupation, other problems were already beginning to appear in Europe. Admittedly, the traditional Hohenzollern-Romanov friendship had held good in the 1860s; Bismarck was keenly aware of his debt of gratitude to Russia – hence he was always to turn a deaf ear to Andrássy's proposals for an anti-Russian coalition; and Russia and Germany still had a common interest in suppressing Polish nationalism, where 'liberal' Austria had again broken ranks. But despite all this, the Russians were concerned at the exceedingly independent behaviour of their erstwhile Prussian protégés in 1871, particularly at their ignoring Russia's interest in a German balance of power based on the independence of the South German states. The decisive role Russia had played in German affairs for more than a century had clearly come to an end; the Treaties of Teschen, Vienna and Olmütz, documenting Russia's interest in the balance of power in central Europe, had been replaced by the Treaty of Frankfort. The shock was enough to make Alexander II at last implement the military reforms that had been under discussion since the Crimean War; and to convince him that Germany must certainly not be allowed to shift the European balance any further in her favour.

The preoccupations of the other world power, Great Britain, were more exclusively extra-European. The balance of power, anchored in a strong, conservative central Europe, had allowed Great Britain to concentrate her attention on her territorial Empire, especially India, and on her informal, commercial empire. Certainly, Great Britain would never shrink from involvement in continental affairs if they threatened to endanger the security of the empire: she had been quick to react to even the most tentative efforts of France and Russia to challenge the 1815 settlement; and she had allied with France, Austria and Sardinia, and fought a war against Russia to prevent Russian control of the Ottoman Empire, a vital link in Britain's communications with India. But by the early 1870s, Great Britain seemed almost on the periphery of the European states system. True, there was no pressing need for intervention: despite Russia's advance in Central Asia, India seemed relatively secure; and the Royal Navy had proved well able to assert British commercial interests against non-European powers such as China. But Great Britain's reserve was also a result of her unpleasant experiences with the continental powers in the 1860s, when Austria and Prussia, the great stabilizers of the 1815 system, had joined France and Russia as disruptive elements, inflicting a particularly galling diplomatic defeat on Great Britain in the Danish war. A general revulsion of popular feeling against involvement with the selfish and immoral diplomacy of the continental powers was certainly one element in the isolationism of British governments until well into the 1870s. In any case, the Russian threat, such as it was, lay outside Europe; with the fall of the ambitious schemer Napoleon III, France had ceased to be a threat at all; and there was no reason to fear the new German Empire, Protestant, apparently liberal, and with no extra-European ambitions – provided always it did not strike out on a path of continental domination.

In sum, therefore, provided the new German Empire did not have designs to expand any further, it could be accommodated easily enough within the European states system. Indeed, the system as ordered in 1871 was inherently more stable than anything that had preceded it. The order of 1815 threatened by revisionist France and messianic Russia, had had to be secured by positive action, in the form of long-term alliances – the Quadruple Alliance including Great Britain, the Holy Alliance without her; the later 1850s and 1860s had witnessed the formation of a number of short-term, *ad hoc* alliances for the specific purpose of revising aspects of the 1815 settlement. After 1871 most powers were broadly satisfied with the international order. Moreover, whereas the 1815 settlement, resting on a weak power, Austria, and her somewhat variable supporters, had been a constant temptation to dissatisfied powers to make alterations in it to their advantage – and such alterations had indeed been made in the decade after 1856 – the states system as reordered in 1871 rested on the most powerful military state in Europe. No other power was strong enough to threaten it. The 1870s, therefore, proved to be a period of relatively low tension, when no powers felt threatened or aggrieved enough to form binding alliances to overturn the international order or committing them to support each other to the death.

In these years of loose alignments, almost of anarchy, in the best sense of the word, there was little risk of local disputes producing general wars. Franco-German hostility might be an immovable obstacle to real harmony; but it was not a threat to peace. France in isolation was too weak to attempt to overthrow the 1871 settlement; and no other power had any desire to do so. Equally when Bismarck created a war scare in 1875 and talked of weakening France further, he found the rest of Europe combined against him in an overwhelming show of unity: if the British and the Russians called Germany to order publicly, the Austrians and the Italians made it clear enough through private channels that they were of the same mind. In preventing any further weakening of France by Germany, all the powers had a common interest; and so, as Bismarck's hasty retreat demonstrated, on the German side too, Franco-German hostility presented no serious threat to the peace and stability of the European states system.

The same could not be said, however, of the other potential area of friction, the Eastern Question, which, as the powers themselves had conflicting interests in it, presented a more intractable problem.

The Eastern Question concerned the future of the Ottoman Empire, a future which appeared increasingly problematical as nationalist feeling developed amongst the Empire's subject peoples in the Balkans. These subject peoples constantly sought to drag in the great powers, whose support they sought, not only for their complaints against the Ottoman government, but for their own mutually incompatible territorial claims against each other. Yet although the powers, for their part, had interests of their own at stake, and were usually concerned to preserve the integrity of the Empire, it must be admitted that the attempts of even Turkey's self-styled friends to prolong the existence of the Empire were largely ineffective, if not actually counter-productive. By the Treaty of Paris they had, indeed, freed the Empire from the incubus of Russian interference, but only to subject it instead to the supervision of the Concert of Europe; and the – albeit well-meaning – intervention of the great powers in the following years seemed only to have the effect in practice of reducing the sultan's authority. In the Danubian principalities a series of steps were taken between 1858 and 1862 towards the creation of an autonomous Romanian state; in the Lebanon, an autonomous regime under great-power protection was established in 1860; disturbances in Serbia in the early 1860s were rewarded by the powers' persuading the Turks to withdraw their last remaining garrisons from the principality; and a revolt in Crete in 1867 secured for the insurgents a constitutional regime guaranteed by the powers. By the 1870s Ottoman rule had ceased to be more than nominal in Romania and Serbia. In the Bulgarian-inhabited provinces of the Empire the establishment by the Turks, in 1870, of an autocephalous ecclesiastical organization – the Exarchate – independent of the Greek Patriarchate at Constantinople had, indeed had the effect (as the Turks intended) of promoting dissension between the orthodox subjects of the sultan; but at the same time the national-religious pro-paganda so passionately promoted at the grass-roots level by Exarchist priests and schoolmasters boded ill for the authority of the traditional Muslim ruling élite.

It is true that the undermining of Ottoman authority was partly due to indigenous causes – to miscalculations on the part of the Turks (as in the case of the Exarchate), and even more to their sins of omission, notably their failure, despite their promises of 1856, to implement reforms to satisfy their Christian subjects: the revolts in the Herzegovina and Bosnia that started the crisis of 1875–78 were primarily the result of the seemingly unending oppression of the peasantry by the landowning beys. On the other hand, it must be said that local circumstances did not make the government's task an easy one: on several occasions in the past when Constantinople had attempted to stave off peasant disturbances by reining in the landowners, it had been faced with even more formidable rebellions of the beys and their armed retainers. Over the past half century Bosnia had gained the reputation of a land of seemingly endemic lawlessness and a plague, not only for the government in Constantinople but for that in the neighbouring Austrian monarchy, which had to bear the costs contingent on repeated incursions of fleeing Christian rebels or of Muslim bands in pursuit, into its south Slav borderlands.

Not that Austria-Hungary or any of the great powers was consciously seeking to undermine the Ottoman Empire. After all, so long as the Empire existed, it provided for the interests of all the great powers a safeguard, not ideal for any, but tolerable for all. Within the confines of that inert and labyrinthine power structure there was room for all the powers to manoeuvre, and for all to maintain a measure of influence. So long as the Empire continued to exist as an independent state, it offered each of the powers a measure of security and served to postpone a clash of great-power interests which were in the last resort incompatible. Thus, the Empire gave the British some security against a Russian advance towards the eastern Mediterranean and overland route to India; for Austria-Hungary, it prevented the establishment in the Balkans of national states with territorial claims against the Monarchy and potential allies of Russia; and Russia saw in the Empire, as guardian of the closure of the Straits to foreign warships, an obstacle to a British incursion into the Black Sea. The powers had demonstrated their interest in the continued survival of the Empire very clearly in the Treaty of Paris, when they had formally admitted Turkey to the Concert of Europe and, by abolishing Russia's special rights of protectorate and transferring the responsibility for supervising the well-being of the Sultan's Christian subjects to the concert as a whole, they had established the principle that the affairs of the Empire were the concern of all the powers. On the other hand, none of the other great powers can be absolved of all blame for the increasing instability of the Ottoman Empire. Indeed, insofar as its continued existence depended not so much on sporadic displays of interest shown by distant Christian powers as on the maintenance of the authority of the Ottoman government, the actions of the European powers were in many respects anything but conducive to its survival.

For example, although the Ottoman Empire had been formally admitted to the Concert of Europe, it was in no sense treated as an equal by the other powers. Whatever their differences with each other, the Christian powers were always united in their tenacious insistence on their rights under the 'Capitulations' (a series of concessions granted by the Porte to Christian states at various times since the sixteenth century). Not only did these arrangements confer on the subjects of the great powers within the Empire extra-territorial privileges – such as the right to use their own consular courts and postal services – that limited the power of the sovereign authority to a degree that would have been inconceivable within the European states system. The capitulatory provisions that forbade the Turks to raise their customs duties without the consent of the great powers had resulted in an artificially low import tariff that not only deprived the Ottoman government of much needed revenues, but, by holding the Empire in fee to the advanced economies of great powers intent on developing their export markets, was certainly one factor retarding the development of the indigenous Ottoman economy. Meanwhile, even such attempts as the powers made to strengthen the Empire by encouraging it to undertake reforms were from the Turkish point of view no mixed blessing. Ottoman efforts to modernize the administration – the setting up of western-style ministries in the 1850s, for example – contributed to the financial difficulties that led by 1875 to the bankruptcy of the Empire and the establishment by the great powers of the Caisse de la Dette Publique to administer up to a fifth of the revenues of the Empire in the interests of the bondholders. Perhaps most serious of all, the attempts of the great powers, however well intentioned, to stabilize the Empire by appeasing the grievances of the Sultan's Christian subjects had the effect of encouraging the latter to look to their external protectors for salvation and made them all the less willing to seek an accommodation with the Ottoman government. Since the Treaty of Paris, the concessions extracted from Constantinople by Turkey's self-styled protectors – concessions which far exceeded anything Russia acting alone had been able to extract before – on behalf of the Sultan's subjects in the Danubian principalities, in Lebanon, Serbia and Crete, all served in the end to undermine the authority of the Sultan and to whet the appetites of the subject peoples. To this extent, the creeping disintegration of the Empire was very much a function of its proximity to and its involvement in the European states system. The disintegration of the Empire remained a real possibility; while the efforts of the powers to defend their conflicting interests within it led ultimately to dangerous divisions between them.

In itself, the Eastern Question was of no direct concern to Bismarck: Germany, alone of the great powers, had no interests at stake in the territories of the Ottoman Empire. Indirectly, however, as a matter of vital concern to Austria-Hungary and Russia; and as a potential source of conflict between these two powers which might yet provide France with an ally, the Eastern Question was to present Bismarck with a dilemma that in the long run defeated even him.

It was, moreover, a problem that – like the other insoluble problem of French revanchism – had been exacerbated by Bismarck's own actions in the 1860s. In 1866 Austria had been driven out of Germany and Italy at one blow; and 1871 put an end to her hopes of recovering her position in either area. Henceforth, it was a fundamental tenet of Habsburg foreign policy that there must be no repetition in the south of that fatal combination of an irredentist threat backed by a great power that had proved so disastrous in 1859 and 1866. Potential irredentist threats were not far to seek – in the claims of various nationalist elements, in Serbia to the south Slav lands, in Romania to Transylvania, and in Italy to the Adriatic territories of the Monarchy. Certainly, the Imperial and Royal Army was strong enough to cope with all these threats; but if an irredentist state should ever receive the backing of another great power, the Monarchy would be in mortal peril.

Hence, the broad strategy of Habsburg foreign policy, pursued more or less successfully until the revolutionary overthrow of the Near Eastern power constellation in 1912–13, was to prevent or, failing that, to counteract the fatal combination of an irredentist movement supported by a great power. As far as prevention was concerned, alliances or ententes could be made with Russia and with the rulers of the irredentist states themselves committing those governments to uphold legitimacy and the monarchical principle against nationalist currents amongst their subjects. Alternatively, if these efforts seemed to be failing, the Monarchy could try to construct a wider combination of other powers, such as Germany, Great Britain and Italy, to resist the local threat. But even though the purpose of such diplomatic combinations could be seen, from an Austrian point of view, as defensive – to ward off an irredentist threat, to prevent the Balkan states serving as extensions of Russian military power encircling the Monarchy in the south, or simply to prevent the creation of a great South Slav state dominating the Balkans and cutting the Monarchy off from its traditional markets – they also had, necessarily, more far-reaching implications. Insofar as an increase in Austro-Hungarian economic influence in the Balkans implied, as everybody recognized, an increase in political influence; and insofar as the Monarchy's Balkan alliances were expressly designed to provide security by establishing its political control of the governments concerned, even the limited 'defensive' aims of Austro-Hungarian policy had disturbing implications for Russia.

After all, it had long been a fixed tenet of policy in St Petersburg that the Balkans and the Straits must not be allowed to fall under the control of a potentially hostile power. This was not so much an expression of the Pan-Slav creed that Russia should herself liberate and take control of the Balkans; or that, as General Fadeyev put it, 'the road to Constantinople lies through Vienna'. Even the sober conservatives in the imperial government recognized that a power that controlled the Balkan peninsula would be in a position to cut Russia off from access to the Mediterranean through the Straits. This waterway was vital for the grain exports of southern Russia; and insofar as the revenues from these exports were essential for the servicing of the loans that financed Russia's military and industrial development, freedom of passage through the Straits was vital for Russia's prospects of survival as a great power. Hence, no potentially hostile power, whether Austria-Hungary, Great Britain, or, in 1912, even Russia's protégé Bulgaria (let alone, in 1914, Germany) must be allowed to control Constantinople and the Straits. By the later nineteenth century the Straits question was assuming increasing importance in Russian foreign policy; indeed, in the volatile situation that developed after 1912, it became its chief concern.

It was the fact that the clash of Russian and Austro-Hungarian interests in the Near East was really a clash of two defensive strategies that made the problem so dangerous, and so intractable. Had it been a clash of two expansionist imperialisms on the offensive, it would in fact have been easier to manage: the Habsburgs had survived the collapse of their overseas expansionist ambitions in the eighteenth century; and Russia was able to withdraw from her Far Eastern adventures after 1905 without endangering her security. But in the Near East, neither power believed it could allow the other to achieve complete security without fatally jeopardizing its own security. Of course, so long as the Ottoman Empire existed as a buffer – and the Sultan was always too astute to throw in his lot with any one power – the question was manageable. Once the Empire was expelled from Europe after 1912, neither Russia nor Austria-Hungary could afford to put its own great-power status at risk by abandoning control of the resultant power vacuum to its rival. If the question were ever put point blank, it could be resolved only by force, and this was the issue in 1914.

Already for two generations it had been clear to the chancelleries of Europe that the Eastern Question, with its grave implications for the great-power status of Russia and Austria-Hungary, posed a far more serious threat to the stability of the European states system than any west European question or the extra-European activities that absorbed so much of the attention of the powers. Even when relations between the two most interested powers seemed harmonious, there was always the danger that developments in the Near East beyond their control might provoke one of them to make a bid for security – for example, the Russian threat to occupy Bulgaria in 1886 – that the other could not accept, and that the result would be war.

For Bismarck, the implications of an Austro-Russian war were simply horrific. In the first place, France would at last find an ally. In the second, Germany would find herself confronted with two equally unacceptable alternatives. One the one hand, she might stand aside and allow Austria-Hungary to go down to defeat and probably dissolution, whereupon the German inhabitants of the Monarchy would seek to unite with their brothers in the north (as indeed, they were to do in 1919). This, however, would pose a threat to Prussian control of the German Empire, to its very *raison d'être* in Bismarck's view. Bismarck simply did not want any more Germans in the Empire – especially not not Habsburg Germans with their traditions, since the days of Prince Eugene, of a German mission in the Balkans; or southern Catholic Germans, potential allies of Munich or the Vatican against Berlin. That would be to undo the work of 1866. However much the Pan-Germans, in Berlin or in Vienna, might rave about the need to complete the work of unification, Bismarck set his face steadily against them; and his successors too remained true 'Prussians' in this respect. When there was talk of the impending break-up of the Habsburg Monarchy in the great Hungarian crisis of 1905, for example, a circular from Bülow to all German missions abroad formally disavowed any desire to see the Austrian Germans incorporated into the Empire. The option of simply letting Austria-Hungary collapse was, therefore, never seriously considered by Bismarck. The existence of Austria-Hungary was essential for the preservation of a Protestant, Junker-dominated German Empire, and in the last resort Germany would have to fight rather than let the Monarchy collapse – as Bismarck, in fact, admitted to Andrássy in 1872. To this extent, the Dual Alliance of 1879 said nothing new.

On the other hand, the thought of going to war with Russia in defence of the Habsburg Monarchy was almost equally abhorrent to Bismarck. Germany had no conflict of interests with Russia: she had no significant interests of her own whatever in the Balkans and the Near East before the reign of William II. On the contrary, she shared a great common interest with Russia, in the suppression of Polish nationalism (in contrast to the Austrians, who were irritatingly cultivating their Polish subjects as one of the three 'master races' of the Empire). The dynastic link, too, still counted for something: William I was genuinely fond of his Russian nephew, and given that the Chancellor, under the constitution of 1871, depended solely on the Emperor for his position, an attempt by Bismarck to start a war with Russia might simply result in his dismissal. Bismarck, for his part, was always convinced that war with Russia could not conceivably be of any advantage to Germany. As he reminded the military in 1888, even if Germany were victorious over Russia, indeed, even if she dismembered her, Russia could not be destroyed for ever. Russian national feeling was so strong that the dismembered limbs would be bound to come together again: the only result of such a war would be to give Germany an eternally hostile (and possibly revolutionary) neighbour.

Faced with this insoluble dilemma, Bismarck, far from pushing himself forward in the thankless role of honest broker, took refuge in simply retreating from the scene, in the hope that, left to themselves, Austria-Hungary and Russia might somehow be able to reconcile their interests in the Near East without obliging Germany to choose between them. True, by the end of the decade the disadvantages of this *laissez faire* approach had become painfully clear, Austro-Russian hostility having reached such a pitch that Bismarck was forced to come forward and attempt to reconcile the contending parties through a system of formal alliances centred on Germany. For most of the 1870s, however, Bismarck, far from seeking a hegemonial, or even a directing, role for Germany within the states system, strove to keep her safely and discreetly in the background, and preferred to leave the shaping of great power alignments to the initiative of others.

Of course, such was the pre-eminence of Germany's position, that even a strictly abstentionist attitude on Bismarck's part was bound to have some influence on the decisions of the other powers. For example, his negative attitude towards Austro-Hungarian plans for a grand alliance to oppose Russia's supposed Balkan designs was an important factor in Andrássy's reluctant decision to examine the possibility of co-operation with Russia. On the other hand, the change of heart in Vienna was also a result of Andrássy's failure to enlist the support of Gladstone's government, which at this time was attempting to reach an accommodation with Russia in Central Asia. Perhaps even more important, however, was the attitude of Russia itself. When Alexander II, worried by the news of Franz Joseph's impending visit to William I in September 1872, secured an invitation for himself and Gorchakov to Berlin at the same time, the occasion was transformed from the demonstration of Austro-German solidarity intended by Andrássy into a general demonstration of monarchical solidarity. More than this, the meeting of the three emperors marked an important turning point in Austro-Russian relations. Andrássy was very pleasantly surprised when the Russians assured him that they harboured no designs against the *status quo* in the Near East, and were even prepared to acknowledge Austria-Hungary's commercial interests in the area. With both Austrians and Russians in agreement on the dangers inherent in any attempt to tamper with the Balkan *status quo*, and with no immediate crisis to arouse their mutual suspicions, the way was clear for a return to the spirit of Münchengrätz. A formal written agreement eventually followed, on the occasion of Alexander II's visit to the Vienna international exhibition in the summer of 1873. In the Schönbrunn Convention of 6 June the two emperors, recognizing the need to guard against surprises and to avoid drifting into positions from which they could not retreat, pledged themselves to keep in touch about developments in the Near East and, above all, to reach agreement before taking any action in the area. The rapprochement was crowned by a very successful Austrian state visit to St Petersburg in January 1874, when Franz Joseph made amends for his sins of the 1850s by doing homage at the deathbed and tomb of Nicholas I.

It is true that, already in the autumn of 1873, when William I acceded to the Schönbrunn Convention, an imposing Three Emperors' League had been created that harked back, ideologically, to the Neo-Holy Alliance; and that all this was most welcome to Bismarck – Austro-Russian tension was subsiding and the French Republic was totally isolated. (When Victor Emmanuel II visited Berlin in September, Italy too was also loosely associated with the new monarchical bloc.) On the other hand, the isolation of France was hardly an objective of the original architects of the League, Gorchakov and Andrássy. On the contrary, both of them were more suspicious of Germany than of France in 1873, and the Schönbrunn Convention itself had distinctly anti-German overtones. Article I, which pledged the Austrian and Russian monarchs 'to maintain the peace against disturbances from any quarter whatever', was obviously directed, not against impotent France or isolationist Great Britain, but against incalculable Germany. The accession of Germany in October perhaps blunted the edge of this article, but Germany, after all still the power least interested in the

Eastern Question, remained very much an accessory party. The Three Emperors' League was essentially an Austro-Russian instrument and in no sense part of any 'Bismarckian system' of alliances.

In fact, Austro-German relations grew no closer at all in the next few years. In Austrian court and military circles, memories of 1866 lingered on; Franz Joseph vetoed exchanges of information about naval technology with Prussia; he shrugged off repeated Prussian requests for the nullification of Article V of the Treaty of Prague (that committed the Prussians to hold a plebiscite in North Schleswig); and the court of the exiled king of Hanover continued to reside at Gmunden in Upper Austria. More seriously, the Austrians showed no sympathy for Bismarck's chief anxieties in these years – his dismay at the rapid recovery of France and his alarm at the strength and bellicosity of the French royalists, whom he imagined to be plotting with the Vatican to stiffen his opponents in the *Kulturkampf* at home and engineer a coalition of Catholic powers against Germany abroad. (Andrássy noticed, in a conversation with Bismarck, how the blood always flushed to the rims of the Chancellor's eyes at the very mention of the Pope, whom Bismarck declared to be an even more dangerous enemy of all governments than the Communist International.) Whereas Bismarck wished to see the Republic continue in France, to intensify her isolation in a monarchical Europe – and even destroyed the career of a German ambassador to Paris who dared to disagree with him – Franz Joseph made no secret of his principled preference for the French royalists. He also deplored Bismarck's anti-Papal diatribes and roundly declared that there would be no *Kulturkampf* in his own dominions. In Austrian eyes, the maintenance of France as a great power was still a European interest, and Franz Joseph made a point of telling the French ambassador this during his visit to St Petersburg in 1874.

The Russians took the same view. Already in July 1872 Gorchakov had made haste to assure Paris that '*a strong and wise France* is precisely what Europe needs; strong in order to maintain the balance'. He was no doubt strengthened in this sentiment by the injury done to his own vanity by Bismarck's meteoric rise to the position of Europe's most successful statesman; and both political and personal considerations played a role in Gorchakov's reaction to the 'War in Sight?' crisis of May 1875. This diplomatic firework exploded when the Berlin *Post*, taking umbrage at the French government's plans for military reforms, hinted that Germany might have to resort to preventive war. In the ensuing diplomatic flurry Bismarck found himself, for once, completely outmanoeuvred. The French seized the chance to depict themselves as the injured party, whereupon all the other powers adjured Bismarck to keep the peace – the British and Russians in official *démarches*, the Austrians and Italians privately – and Bismarck's reaffirmation of his pacific intentions brought the affair to an end. There had never been any serious danger of war, but the incident threw an interesting light on the tenuous nature of relations within the Three Emperors' League: Gorchakov's spectacular appearance in Berlin to announce to the world that 'peace is now assured' showed that 'the Chancellor's War' had by no means ended. 'Bismarck will never forgive him' Andrássy gleefully declared – and did three hand stands on his study table. But he was at the same time careful to keep his own relations with Gorchakov in good order. This was important, as a really serious crisis was about to break in the Near East that would put the Three Emperors' League to the test. For Bismarck, if the 'War in Sight Crisis' had confirmed both the acceptability to the other powers of the balance established in 1871 and the danger of isolation threatening Germany if she tried to enhance her position further, the outbreak of disturbances in the Near East that might distract the attention of the other powers away from Germany and towards the periphery of the continent, might bring a welcome relief.

The Eastern crisis of 1875–78

The summer of 1875 saw a revival of the Eastern Question, with rebellions in the Ottoman Empire leading within two years to a war between Russia and Turkey and eventually to a confrontation between the great powers. This crisis was rather different from the last great Eastern crisis, in the 1850s, which had focused on the resistance of the western powers and Austria to Russia's attempt to assert her domination over the government at Constantinople – essentially an attempt to revive in an extreme form the 'protectorate' policy of the Treaty of Unkiar Skelessi. On that occasion, the threat to the territorial integrity of the Ottoman Empire from the aspirations of its subject peoples had played a relatively insignificant part. The crisis of the 1870s, by contrast, resembled the crisis of the 1820s: it was sparked off by a nationalist revolt within the Empire and Russia assumed the role, not of protector and patron of the Sultan, but of liberator of the Balkan Christians.

Certainly, in Bosnia and the Herzegovina external factors seem to have played a role in fanning the smouldering grievances of the indigenous peasantry into flame in the summer of 1875. It was perhaps no coincidence that, immediately to the east, Prince Milan of Serbia had conducted a triumphal progress through his principality in June; and that a month

earlier the Emperor Franz Joseph had paid an unusually prolonged ceremonial visit to Dalmatia, in the course of which he had been pleased to
receive the respects of numerous delegations of Catholics from the neighbouring Ottoman provinces. (The murder by the Turks of a Herzegovinian
monk who had been granted an audience by the Emperor was later put
forward as a pretext for the rebellion.) Certainly, the Christians of the
Herzegovina and Bosnia seem to have been expecting help from outside
when they rose in revolt against their Muslim masters at the beginning of
August. Help was to be slow in coming, however, and the Bosnian rebellion was still unresolved in the spring of 1876 when the Bulgarians staged
a revolt of a more overtly national-political character, perhaps less deeply
rooted in the socio-economic grievances of the peasant masses than the
Bosnian revolt but nonetheless formidable in that its ecclesiastical and
intellectual leaders had at their command an organization of some two
hundred secret revolutionary committees. When the Turks suppressed this
rebellion in a welter of blood – the so-called 'Bulgarian horrors' – when a
series of palace revolutions paralysed the government in Constantinople,
and when Serbia and Montenegro proceeded in July from clandestine
support for the rebels to formal declarations of war on the Sultan, the
powers found themselves confronted with a full-scale crisis that might
indeed portend the collapse of the Ottoman Empire in Europe.

As in previous eastern crises, the British were generally inclined to
uphold the integrity and independence of Turkey against Russian encroachments. By the mid-1870s this attitude was reinforced by new considerations: a Russian advance towards the Mediterranean was now doubly
unwelcome to the British, given the growing importance of the Suez Canal,
completed in 1869, as an additional (if for Great Britain still not the
main) route to India; and in 1875 British interest was further heightened
by the Disraeli government's purchase of the khedive's shares in the Canal
Company. Added to this was a general feeling that British prestige had
declined in the 1860s. The cumulative effect of the humiliations suffered
in the Schleswig-Holstein affair, the abrogation of the Black Sea clauses
of the Treaty of Paris, and the long drawn out wrangle with the United
States over the *Alabama* affair perhaps accounts for some of the excitement that now seized the British, leading to the cry that Great Britain
must not be ignored any longer. On the other hand, circumstances still
conspired to make it difficult for the British government to take action.
The behaviour of the Turks, their failure to reform, and above all, reports
of their brutality – Disraeli's attempt to dismiss them as 'coffee house
babble' was unconvincing in the face of Gladstone's 'Bulgarian horrors'

campaign – made it much more difficult than in the 1850s for the British government to back Turkish integrity through thick and thin – as the Turks were to discover to their cost at the Congress of Berlin. Even more restrictive of British freedom of manoeuvre, however, was the diplomatic constellation in Europe at this time. So long as the Three Emperors' League operated the British were simply unable to find a continental partner. As in the mid-1830s, an alignment of the three northern courts implied the exclusion of Great Britain from an effective role in the Eastern Question. This had always been a nightmare for the Foreign Office; indeed, Disraeli was later to boast that the main aim of his diplomacy in the crisis had been to disrupt the Three Emperors' League. As it was, however, until the League came to grief for quite other reasons in 1878, British policy in the Near East was doomed to be largely ineffective.

In Austria, the advocates of action seemed to be in a stronger position. It was not merely that the Bosnian revolt focused attention on the need to do something about the unending disorder on the southern frontiers of the Monarchy. The danger was now apparent that if the rebellious provinces slipped from Turkey's grasp they might contribute to the formation of a large south Slav state sealing off the Monarchy in the South and perhaps even harbouring irredentist ambitions as a Balkan Sardinia. Military and naval circles had been arguing ever since the 1850s that the possession of the Bosnian hinterland was essential to the security of the Dalmatian coastal strip and – particularly since the loss of Venice in 1866 – to the Monarchy's standing as an Adriatic power. The Emperor, who had so far only managed to lose territories, was certainly attracted by the idea of adding something to his dominions; and during his Dalmatian tour in 1875 vouchsafed to General Mollinary that he would be put in charge of the occupying force in Bosnia if the time for action came.

On the other hand, these views were not those of Andrássy, who once remarked to the Empress that 'the Emperor does not understand the Eastern Question and will never understand it.' As a Hungarian patriot who had been given asylum in Constantinople when he had been burnt in effigy in Budapest in 1849, Andrássy was both pro-Turkish and anti-Slav. He shared Metternich's view that an innocuous Ottoman Empire was the best possible neighbour for Austria-Hungary; and he certainly had no desire to endanger the privileged position the Magyars had enjoyed since 1867 by bringing more Slavs into the Monarchy. Certainly, he was concerned, in broad terms, to guard against Russia's taking advantage of the crisis to establish her influence throughout the Balkans, complementing her 1815 position in Poland by encircling the Monarchy in the South; and this meant in particular preventing the creation of a big south Slav state under Russian protection. Equally, the creation in Bosnia of a weak independent or autonomous state was deemed unacceptable: given the racial and religious mix of the populations there, this would simply be a recipe for perpetual chaos, or even civil war, on the Monarchy's southern borders. If Turkish rule there finally collapsed, it would have to be replaced by some kind of Austro-Hungarian control. While always keeping a wary eye on the possible implications for the domestic structure of the Monarchy, therefore, Andrássy was coming to adopt the position of his predecessor: 'Bosnia must be either Turkish or Austrian; a third possibility simply does not exist.'

Russian intentions at this time were in fact less threatening than the Austrians feared. In contrast to the 1850s, when an over-confident Russian government had taken the lead in forcing matters to a crisis, Russian policy in the 1870s was eminently cautious. True, Pan-Slav liberationist currents were detectable among the intelligentsia, in influential circles in the army and even , thanks to the tsarevich, at court. Alexander II and Gorchakov, however, were still mindful of Russia's weakness relative to the other powers and above all concerned to avoid a confrontation with Austria-Hungary or Great Britain that might drive those two powers together or, worse still, end in war. The Austrians, too, preferred to avoid a confrontation. They had nothing to gain from a war with Russia: if Napoleon had not been able to destroy her, Austria-Hungary alone certainly could not. Nor was there any prospect of finding a satisfactory ally: Bismarck was clearly not disposed to confront Russia over the Eastern Question; as for a British alliance, the objections that had made Buol shy in 1854 were still valid – the Monarchy would risk being simply used as a battering ram by a naval power that could be of no assistance on a central European battlefield. Above all, the harsh fact remained – and this had been the case for at least a century – that if the Habsburgs actually went to war in defence of Turkey they would forfeit the sympathies of the entire Slav world, creating trouble for themselves with their north and south Slav subjects at home, and creating the worst possible scenario abroad by driving the whole of the Christian Balkans into the arms of Russia. As the the crisis developed in the summer of 1875, therefore, it suited the decision-makers in both Vienna and St Petersburg to seek a compromise solution by diplomacy within the framework of the Three Emperors' League.

Until 1878 the Three Emperors' League was in fact successful in containing the crisis, and proved itself to be far more than the fair weather system some historians have alleged it to be. Russia and Austria-Hungary, acting in the spirit of the League, collaborated successfully, if not to solve the conflicts within the Ottoman Empire, at least to prevent an infinitely more dangerous conflict between themselves. This, of course, suited the third party to the arrangement, Bismarck, who was only too happy – and this was typical of his attitude towards the Three Emperors' League – to allow Russia and Austria-Hungary to take the Eastern Question in hand. He had no desire to see Germany directly involved in issues that were not worth the bones of a Pomeranian musketeer; and that might only involve her in a choice that would alienate one of her partners should they prove unable to agree; and provided tensions could be contained – and herein, admittedly, lay a risk – it was all to the good if the attention of the other great powers could be directed towards the periphery of Europe, allowing Germany to remain quietly in the background.

In local terms, the results of Austro-Russian co-operation were meagre. The pacificatory recommendations of the so-called Andrássy Note, agreed between Andrássy and Gorchakov in December 1875, were accepted by the Turks but rejected as completely inadequate by the rebels. The turbulent events of the spring threatened briefly to disrupt Austro-Russian co-operation when Andrássy and Gorchakov met under Bismarck's auspices at Berlin and when the Russians proposed far-reaching concessions to the Bulgarian rebels and the creation of an autonomous Bosnian state. This, Andrássy rejected out of hand as 'a noose which they are trying to put round our necks'; but Gorchakov proved extraordinarily accommodating, allowing Andrássy to redraft his proposals as the anodyne Berlin Memorandum (13 May) which simply asked the powers to press Turkey to grant an armistice to the rebels and a number of reforms. Even this was too much for the British, who saw in any proposal for pressure on Turkey a risk of strengthening Russian influence at Constantinople, and who were in any case suspicious of anything that emerged from the Three Emperors' League. In the face of their objections, the Memorandum was dropped. The powers were not coming up with many solutions, but they had at least managed to avoid a confrontation within the European states system.

The escalation of the crisis in the summer saw a further meeting between Gorchakov and Andrássy at the Bohemian castle of Reichstadt in July, where some progress was made towards eliminating the war between Turkey, Serbia and Montenegro as a possible source of conflict between Russia and Austria-Hungary. Again, the aim was not so much to devise a solution to the conflict in the Balkans as to prevent its causing a conflict between the two most interested great powers, and the interests of both the Balkan peoples and of the other members of Concert of Europe were given short shrift. According to the Reichstadt agreement, if Turkey were victorious, she was to be prevented from profiting from her victory and changing the *status quo* to her advantage – a telling comment on the peculiar status assigned to Turkey in what was, after all, a Christian states system; whereas if she were defeated she was to be virtually expelled from Europe, while the Balkan Christians would have to be content with small territorial concessions and varying degrees of self-government. The interests of Russia and Austria-Hungary were well taken care of: Russia was to be allowed to recover the strip of southern Bessarabia lost to the Danubian principalities in 1856, while Austria-Hungary would take control of Bosnia and possibly the Herzegovina. Confident in these guarantees against the creation of a big independent Slav state, Andrássy was even prepared to allow Serbia and Montenegro to advance to a common frontier in the Sanjak of Novibazar. In broader European terms, it was significant that although the Germans were initiated into the agreement in August, the other powers were left pretty much in the dark. In fact, whereas the Andrássy Note and the Berlin Memorandum had been drawn up for presentation to the other powers, the Reichstadt agreement marked a notable step towards the withdrawal of Russia and Austria-Hungary from the Concert of Europe. It was not concert pressure, for example, but a Russian ultimatum that forced the Turks to grant an armistice to the defeated Serbs in October.

Whatever the shortcomings of Austro-Russian diplomacy in the eyes of the contending parties in the Balkans and the British, there was no danger of conflict between the great powers themselves so long as Austria-Hungary and Russia could continue to co-operate within the Three Emperors' League; and it must be admitted that the alternative arrangement – the Concert of Europe – proved itself even less efficacious. This was thanks in large measure to the intransigence of the Turks, who were no more prepared to make concessions to the concert for the sake of the peace of Europe now than they had been on the eve of war in 1853. In the aftermath of the Russian ultimatum of October 1876 the British, anxious lest Russia might be seeking to exploit the crisis to secure a dominant position in Turkey, managed to revive the Concert of Europe in the six-power Constantinople Conference. Initially, this seemed to be very successful, and the powers quickly reached agreement on far-reaching concessions to the Balkan Christians: Serbia, Montenegro and Romania were to become independent; the territories of the Bulgarian Exarchate were to become autonomous but were to be split in two. To this extent, the Austrians were secured against the creation of a big Slav state. On the other hand, they found themselves in a weaker position in negotiations *à six* than in bilateral negotiations with Russia, and had to agree to the inclusion of an autonomous Bosnia on the programme. The whole proposal soon came to nothing, however, in the face of Turkish resistance. In December the Sultan suddenly announced the establishment of a constitutional regime and handed the whole question over to a Council of Notables which promptly rejected the concert's proposals. Even when, in a last desperate effort to keep the peace the other powers persuaded Russia to acquiesce in the anodyne London Protocol of 31 March, which whittled down their proposals to a mere recommendation that Turkey adopt some reforms, the Turks turned this down flat. This at last provoked the Russian government, long under pressure from exasperated Pan-Slav opinion at home, to declare war on Turkey on 24 April.

Even this escalation of the crisis was peacefully contained within the states system, thanks to a revival of Austro-Russian co-operation. Already before the failure of concert diplomacy at the Constantinople Conference, the Austrians had been sounding St Petersburg with a view to safeguarding their most vital interests in the event of a Russo-Turkish War. The idea of actively coming to the defence of Turkey against the Russian colossus was unanimously ruled out in Vienna: neither militarily nor financially was the Monarchy in a condition to sustain such a conflict, even if there had been any prospect of assistance from Germany or Great Britain (which Bismarck and Salisbury had both recently made clear there was not). The Russians, for their part, were reluctant to launch their armies towards Constantinople unless they could be sure of a benevolent Austria-Hungary on their flank. In the event, Austrian and Russian anxieties were well catered for in the Budapest Convention of 15 January 1877: the Russians promised to keep their military activities away from the frontiers of the Monarchy, to refrain from unleashing a revolutionary Slav crusade or from creating a big Slav state in the Balkans; while the Austrians promised to observe a benevolent neutrality and to obstruct any interference by the concert or any attempt by the western powers to invoke in Turkey's defence the Tripartite Treaty of April 1856. As deadlock at Constantinople dragged on into the spring a supplementary Convention of 18 March dealt in more detail with possible territorial changes if a Russo-Turkish war should actually precipitate the collapse of the Ottoman Empire. The settlement would follow broadly the terms agreed at Reichstadt – although Andrássy now took the precaution of adding that if Serbia and Montenegro acquired the Sanjak they were to guarantee to Austria-Hungary commercial access to its Balkan markets.

In the event, the relatively cautious character of Russian military and diplomatic activity for several months after the outbreak of the Russo-Ottoman war seemed to testify to the value of the Budapest Convention and the efficacy of the Three Emperors' League. Admittedly, this moderation owed something to the surprisingly stubborn resistance Russian troops were encountering at the siege of Plevna (July–December). Throughout the summer Andrássy continued to trust in Russian good faith – at any rate, he showed scant inclination to consider any alternative alignment, and treated soundings coming from London with extreme reserve. The British, faced with this combination of the two most interested powers, were helpless. It was not the first or the last time that British statesmen had reason to fear 'the Alliance of the Three Northern Courts'. So long as this combination operated, the concert was paralysed; but the Eastern crisis was contained.

Everything was changed at the end of the year when Plevna fell and the Russians advanced to within striking distance of the Ottoman capital. By the preliminary peace of Adrianople (31 January 1878), drawn up by Ignatiev, the Russian ambassador at Constantinople, the Turks were compelled to agree to grant independence and cessions of territory to Serbia, Montenegro and Romania (while the last was to cede southern Bessarabia to Russia). The most striking feature of the peace terms was, however, the the creation of a large Bulgarian state, to be occupied by Russian forces for two years. Clearly, this Russian satellite – which with its Aegean coastal strip would cut the Ottoman Empire in Europe into two – would both dominate the Balkan peninsula and constitute a direct military threat to Constantinople. Bosnia and the Herzegovina, now completely cut off from Constantinople, were to govern themselves as an autonomous state. This drastic redrawing of the Balkan map cannot simply be ascribed to Ignatiev's ignorance of Gorchakov's agreements with the Austrians. It seems that the government in St Petersburg itself was also carried away in the elation of victory. At any rate, Alexander II dismissed the protests that now came from Vienna as 'based on irrelevant assumptions and prejudices', while Gorchakov blandly described the creation of Big Bulgaria as the result of 'force of circumstances'.

The British saw in the preliminary peace terms a Russian bid to control the Ottoman Empire; and they would never admit the implied Russian claim to settle single-handed a question which the Treaty of Paris had formally declared to be the concern of the Concert of Europe, or to override the stipulations of the London Protocol of 1871 regarding the alteration of treaties. In February the British fleet entered the Straits and the more forceful Salisbury replaced Derby at the Foreign Office. The Austrians were more equivocal. Of course, they were horrified by the Bulgarian and Bosnian stipulations of the peace, which portended the annihilation of Austro-Hungarian influence in the Balkans. On the other hand, an attempt to oppose Russia by force appeared extremely hazardous, given the financial and military weakness of the Monarchy; while as far as diplomacy was concerned, the Austrians had themselves connived at the elimination of the concert throughout 1877, and they could not, technically, invoke the Budapest convention as the Ottoman Empire had not actually collapsed. They made a last attempt to bring Russia to reason by bilateral negotiations, but when this failed and the preliminary peace terms were enshrined in the definitive Russo-Turkish Treaty of San Stefano of 3 March the Austrians at last despaired of the Three Emperors' League and rediscovered their loyalty to the concert. By this time, euphoria was beginning to give way to realism in St Petersburg: Russia was, after all, quite isolated in her defence of the San Stefano terms; her army, with its lines of communication still over-extended, was exhausted, and her vulnerability to an attack in the Black Sea had in practice hardly diminished since 1871. In these circumstances the Russians were perhaps even less willing than their western opponents to risk an armed confrontation and under British and Austrian pressure consented to submit the Treaty of San Stefano to revision by all the powers at a congress. As neither Vienna nor St Petersburg was generally acceptable as a venue, it was decided to hold the congress under Bismarck's auspices in Berlin.

To Bismarck the suggestion that the Congress might meet in Berlin was not particularly welcome. If since the outbreak of the crisis he had been basking in the illusion that the attention of the other powers had been conveniently diverted away from Germany to the periphery of the continent, this had proved to have been a profound error. The tensions had returned from the periphery to the centre with a redoubled intensity, and the danger had again arisen that Germany might find herself estranging one or other of the great powers and providing France with a partner. As it turned out, however, Bismarck did not have to come forward and make any momentous decisions, thanks largely to the fact that all the interested parties preferred a diplomatic compromise, whatever its inconveniences, to the risks of a showdown. The Russians, deciding that their best chance lay in dividing their opponents and in squaring the stronger of them, reached a preliminary agreement with London at the end of May that put the worst of the British fears to rest: Big Bulgaria was to be drastically reduced in size so as to leave the greater part of Turkey-in-Europe intact. Austrian fears on the score of an autonomous Bosnian state were substantially relieved by an Anglo-Austrian agreement of 4 June, in which the British promised to propose Austrian control of Bosnia and the Herzegovina to the Congress. Finally, British fears about Russian designs in Asian Turkey were eased by the Cyprus Convention (4 June) by which the Turks in their desperation entrusted the island to the British and, in return for a British guarantee of their territories in Asia Minor, promised to implement reforms there under the supervision of British consuls.

All these preliminary agreements between the most interested great powers ensured that the Congress of Berlin was a success – at least as far as the concert was concerned. Indeed, it completed its labours in exactly one month (13 June–13 July) and, like the Congress of Aix-la-Chapelle, demonstrated the efficacy of congress diplomacy for reconciling differences between great powers who had reached a broad measure of agreement beforehand. (The fiascos of Verona in the previous generation and Algeciras in the next were equally clear demonstrations of the dangers of resorting to congress diplomacy without any such preliminary agreement.)

As far as the great powers were concerned, the Treaty of Berlin (13 July 1878) was at least a tolerable arrangement. The Big Bulgaria of San Stefano was divided into three parts: the principality of Bulgaria under Ottoman suzerainty, from which Russian troops were to be evacuated within nine months; the autonomous Ottoman province of Eastern Rumelia – designed to give Turkey a defensible frontier in the Balkan mountains – under a Christian governor-general and an Ottoman military occupation; and the Macedonian provinces of Big Bulgaria which were returned to direct Ottoman rule (Map 5). The independence of Serbia, Montenegro and Romania was confirmed, the two Slav states receiving rather smaller additions of territory than had been envisaged at San Stefano; and the exact delimitation of their new frontiers and those of Greece was left for future negotiation. Bosnia and the Herzegovina remained formally part of the Sultan's dominions but were entrusted to an Austro-Hungarian military occupation and administration without limit of time. The Sanjak of Novibazar continued under Ottoman rule as a corridor separating Serbia from Montenegro and the Adriatic, while Austria-Hungary acquired the right to have garrisons there and military and commercial routes through it to secure her commercial access to the western Balkans, Salonica and the Aegean. Russia had less reason to be satisfied: after all her expenditure

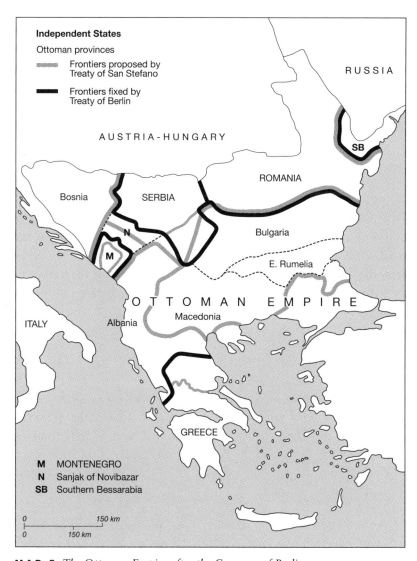

MAP 5 *The Ottoman Empire after the Congress of Berlin*

of blood and money she emerged with little more influence in Bulgaria than any of the other powers; but she had recovered southern Bessarabia and even managed to retain some small gains in the region of Batum on the east coast of the Black Sea (although an additional Russo-Turkish treaty forbade her to fortify this port). The British emerged with the Cyprus Convention and, according to Disraeli, 'peace with honour'.

As far as the European states system was concerned, the Congress of Berlin showed that it was still firmly under the control of the great powers. The principle that the Eastern Question was a matter for all the powers in concert had been triumphantly vindicated. In more general terms, if Russia's single-handed redrawing of the Balkan map at San Stefano had recalled the redrawing of the map of Italy in 1860–61, when again an opportunistic great power had attempted to exploit the principle of national self-determination to set at nought the treaty rights of the other powers, the Congress of Berlin marked a reaffirmation of the authority of the great powers acting in concert to reorder south-east Europe on the basis of a treaty concluded between legitimate governments. As a demonstration that changes to the international order would only acquire legitimacy if they were made by the great powers acting in concert and in accordance with their own, great-power, priorities, the Berlin settlement marked a return to the principles of 1814–15.

Like the 1815 settlement, it was not entirely welcome to small powers and vocal groups who found themselves excluded from the decision-making. During the Congress itself, Bismarck had been brutally frank in reminding both the Turks and the Balkan governments of the irrelevance of their aspirations. As a result, although the Treaty of Berlin to a great extent succeeded in assuaging the threatening conflict between the great powers, at a local level in south-east Europe it perpetuated, even exacerbated, the original causes of instability. True, the fundamental problems there hardly admitted of a compromise solution: the racial and religious structure of the Balkans was so hopelessly confused that no treaty could ever have been devised that would have met with general approval. In the Balkans, only force could determine frontiers, as was to be shown in 1913, 1919 and on various occasions since 1945. Even so, it might well be argued that the original Treaty of San Stefano, for all its deficiencies in terms of the norms of behaviour in the European states system, and for all it had whetted the appetites and sharpened the rivalries of the Balkan peoples, had reasonably well reflected both ethnic realities and the wishes of many of the local populations – whose cries of disappointment were to give the powers no peace for the next forty years. The Treaty of Berlin, by contrast, reducing the Big Bulgaria of San Stefano and handing Macedonia back to the Turks, while at the same time – perhaps unwittingly – fostering the belief in the new Balkan states that recourse to violence could still bring rewards of Ottoman territory, created an exceedingly intractable Macedonian problem for the future.

As far as the great powers were concerned the 1878 settlement, like that of 1814–15 was tolerable for all, but viewed with very varying degrees of satisfaction. The '*status quo*' powers, as in 1815, were Great Britain and the Habsburg Monarchy, who had combined to check Russia's inordinate pretensions, had strengthened their position as counter-balancing powers in the Near East, and who now posed as the patrons, not only of Turkey but of the non-Bulgarian Balkan states. However much some of the latter might regret certain decisions of the Congress – for example, the exclusion of Serbia and Montenegro from the Sanjak – the nightmare prospect of the Big Bulgaria of San Stefano had driven them all for the time being into the Austrian camp. The Austrians were determined to build on the advantages they had gained (such as Serbia's commitment to contribute to a railway link between Vienna and Constantinople) and to co-operate with Great Britain in forcing Russia to respect the Bulgarian provisions of the Treaty of Berlin. In London, Disraeli and Salisbury were of similar mind, and worked hard to persuade the Turks to see in Great Britain and Austria-Hungary with their new territorial commitments in the area twin pillars – the Austrians in the Balkans, the British in Asia Minor – upholding the Ottoman Empire against its eternal enemy, Russia. An Anglo-Austrian gentlemen's agreement of May 1879, committing the two powers to take no steps in the Near East without consulting each other marked the closest degree of co-operation between them since the days of Castlereagh. Certainly, the Three Emperors' League was a thing of the past, and Andrássy was beginning to think in terms of that great defensive bloc against Russia that he had sketched out in 1871.

All these schemes were to come to nothing. As far as Turkey was concerned, the Sultan was by no means inclined to co-operate with his two self-styled protectors, who had, after all, appropriated more Ottoman territory to themselves than even Russia had. In Asia Minor the Turks showed scant inclination to implement the reforms envisaged by the Cyprus Convention; and in Bosnia they actively encouraged native opposition to the Austro-Hungarian occupying force, which had to fight a regular campaign against fierce Muslim resistance. Indeed, it was the expense and scale of this operation that caused the constitutional upheaval in Austria that brought Andrássy's tenure of office to an end: criticisms voiced in the

Austrian parliament by elements of the ruling German Liberal party led Franz Joseph to appoint a conservative-clerical-aristocratic ministry under his childhood friend, Count Eduard Taaffe, and it was the prospect of having to work with such uncongenial colleagues that in August determined the Liberal Andrássy, apparently at the height of his career, to tender his resignation.

An even more serious obstacle to the creation of an effective anti-Russian bloc was Germany. Bismarck, who cared nothing for the Balkans but a great deal for harmonious relations with Russia was by no means inclined to join in an Anglo-Austrian combination against her. On the contrary, at the Congress of Berlin the 'honest broker' had been above all concerned to spare Russian susceptibilities – even to the extent of making a secret appeal to the Austrians to renounce their plans for Bosnia. In the aftermath of the Congress, however, it appeared that his pains had been ill rewarded. Indeed, by the summer of 1879 Bismarck's chief preoccupation was the deepening crisis in Russo-German relations.

Certainly, this had much to do with domestic developments in both Russia and Germany. In 1878 the Russians, in their drive to force on their own industrial development, had increased the tariff on imports of equipment from Germany. At about the same time Bismarck, switching from his alliance with the free-trading Liberals in the Reichstag to a protectionist alliance with conservative landowners and industrialists, had raised the tariff on grain imports from Russia. There, this measure caused immense resentment: the revenue from grain exports was rightly seen as vital for servicing the state loans that underwrote Russia's military and industrial development, indeed, her very status as a great power. Of course, the Eastern crisis had made its contribution to the development of anti-German feeling in Russia. It was perhaps all too understandable in psychological terms that many Russians, who had felt they could expect little better from inveterate opponents such as Great Britain and Austria-Hungary, should ascribe the chief blame for their recent humiliations to the allegedly lukewarm support of ungrateful Germany – a power whose own rise to greatness in the 1860s had owed so much to Russian goodwill. At any rate, Bismarck was in turn irritated by Russia's apparent lack of appreciation for his efforts, by her constant complaints about relatively trivial incidents arising from the enforcement of the Berlin settlement, by her endless armaments and by the anti-German diatribes of the Russian nationalist press. On 15 August 1879 Alexander II sent a further list of grievances – the so called 'box-on-the-ears' letter – to his imperial uncle in Berlin, hinting that the deterioration of Russo-German relations might some day end in war. When the news of Andrássy's impending resignation arrived at this juncture, Bismarck's neurotic fear of coalitions at once revived: the new Austrian government might complement its pro-Slav domestic policy by a pro-Russian, anti-German foreign policy; worse still, the clericals might bring in Catholic France as well, to create that combination most deadly to Prussia, a 'Kaunitz' coalition. Altogether it seemed to Bismarck's fevered brain in the summer of 1879 that the animosities of the great powers that for most of the 1870s had been safely diverted to the periphery of the continent were returning to the centre and imperilling Germany's existence.

Bismarck's answer was to be the Dual Alliance of 1879 – in the short term a device to gain control of Austro-Hungarian policy and to bring the Russians to their senses, but in the long term a manoeuvre to reconcile Austria-Hungary and Russia and control them both within a Three Emperors' Alliance. The old Three Emperors' League had been, essentially, an Austro-Russian affair, which had enabled Germany to take refuge in a quietist policy while France remained isolated and the other powers busied themselves on the periphery of the continent. The new Three Emperors' Alliance was to be very much a Bismarckian instrument. The alignments that eventually emerged from the great Eastern crisis seemed to show that the loose diplomatic arrangements characteristic of the 1870s could not give Germany adequate security. Now Bismarck would have to come forward himself, take a view on the Eastern Question, and, eventually, try to take diplomatic control of the European states system. A new era was dawning, of formal alliances binding most of the continental powers to Germany. Not that this in itself threatened the peace of Europe. On the contrary, revanchists in France would be more helplessly isolated than ever. Nevertheless, the years 1879 to 1882 mark a decisive change, when the European states system moved from the loose, almost anarchical arrangements of the 1870s to a system in which one power and its satellites were clearly preponderant, a system that lasted until the mid-1890s.

CHAPTER 7

The conservative powers dominate the states system, 1879–95

The first Bismarckian alliance system, 1879–87

One of the most important consequences of the great Eastern crisis of 1875–78 was that Bismarck came gradually to the conclusion that the loose alignments of the 1870s, which had for a decade permitted him to stay passively in the background while international tensions were safely deflected to the periphery of the continent, could no longer give Germany security. Although the Congress of Berlin had temporarily resolved the crisis, it had left the concert deeply divided, the Three Emperors' League in ruins, and Germany in an acutely uncomfortable position between Austria-Hungary, now set on working with Great Britain to enforce the new order in the Near East, and a deeply resentful Russia. Indeed, by the summer of 1879 Bismarck was beset by a host of fears: on the one hand, he was afraid that Andrássy's impending resignation might herald a reorientation of Austro-Hungarian policy in the direction of an alignment with Russia, or even France; on the other, he was, for the first time in his career, beginning to feel unsure of Russia, even threatened by her. All this pushed Bismarck to come forward himself and attempt to establish his control of the European states system.

How far he would succeed would depend, of course, on how far decision-makers in other capitals, and even in high quarters in Berlin, were prepared to go along with his plans. The German Empire might well be the strongest power in Europe, but it was not a hegemonial power, and Bismarck was in no position, at home or abroad, to adopt the tone of

Napoleon I. He was relieved, therefore, on meeting Andrássy at Gastein on 28 August, to find him willing to agree in principle to the idea of linking Austria-Hungary and Germany in a formal alliance. This had, after all, been a dream of Andrássy's ever since 1871. For Bismarck, it would banish the danger of a change in Austro-Hungarian policy after Andrássy's departure; and he even toyed with the idea of giving the alliance permanence by incorporating it into the constitutional structure of the two states, recreating, in a sense, a community of German peoples such as had existed before 1866, or even 1806. More immediately, and for both parties, an alliance would provide security in the event of a Russian attack. The long-term objectives of the two parties, by contrast, did not coincide. Bismarck, for whom the chief enemy was still France, was hoping by means of a general defensive alliance to commit the Austrians in the west; and, far from envisaging war against Russia, was hoping, by offering to protect the Monarchy against her, to secure a degree of influence over its policy that would allow him to steer Austro-Hungarian policy towards a reconciliation with Russia. Even before the alliance was signed he was calculating that its effect would be to give pause to warlike spirits in St Petersburg and to prepare the way for a restoration of the Three Emperors' League, directed this time from Berlin. For Andrássy, however, the alliance was essentially an anti-Russian device, and he was determined to remain aloof from any Franco-German conflict and, above all, from any 'warmed-up Three Emperors' League'. That would only, like its predecessors, give umbrage in the western capitals, to the detriment of the Monarchy's working partnership with Great Britain and its amicable relations with France. These differences took five weeks to resolve, and Bismarck had twice to threaten resignation before he could overcome the misgivings of the Emperor William, set on a reconciliation with his Russian nephew and deeply averse to any alliance with Austria-Hungary, let alone one specifically directed against Russia. On 7 October, however, the Dual Alliance was signed in Vienna.

One of the most striking features of the Austro-German alliance, concluded in the first instance for five years but destined to be the longest lasting of all the alliances of the era, was the very limited character of its stipulations. The two signatory powers pledged themselves to support each other with all their forces in the event of an attack from Russia, or from another power supported by Russia, and to observe benevolent neutrality in the event of any other wars. In deference to the narrowly anti-Russian perspective of Vienna, Bismarck had had to give up his ambitious plan for a general defensive alliance; and insofar as he had admitted as early as 1872 that in the last resort Germany could never permit the Dual Monarchy to be destroyed by Russia, the alliance did not perhaps represent anything new at all as far as Germany was concerned. Even in concrete military terms the alliance did not at first amount to much: at any rate, it was not until 1882 that the German and Austro-Hungarian general staffs started to discuss the practical implementation of their commitments. Nor did the alliance have any economic infrastructure: for Bismarck, high policy and economic policy moved on completely separate planes, and in the years immediately following the conclusion of the alliance the Monarchy's exports of livestock to Germany were subjected to the full rigours of Bismarck's protectionist tariff. Like much of Bismarck's diplomacy, the Dual Alliance was very much an *ad hoc* reaction to a temporary panic; and in this case it served its purpose: news of the conclusion of the alliance (although its specific terms were kept secret) did indeed have a sobering effect in St Petersburg, and, as in 1872, Alexander II, confronted with the threat of an Austro-German bloc, immediately sought to repair his relations with Berlin. Whether this would come to anything, and what effect the alliance would have, once the threatening emergency had passed, on the day-to-day diplomacy of the contracting parties, was as yet completely uncertain. Indeed, from the moment the alliance was signed, a struggle broke out between Vienna and Berlin over these issues.

Certainly Bismarck had been unduly sanguine when he assured the Russian ambassador that with the alliance he had succeeded in 'digging a ditch between Austria and the Western Powers'; and if he intended to exploit his newly acquired status as an ally to force the Austrians into a reconciliation with St Petersburg that would banish the danger of a Near Eastern conflict for good, he found Vienna extraordinarily resistant to his advice. Andrássy's successor, Heinrich Baron Haymerle, a former ambassador at Rome and, as Andrássy's assistant at the Congress of Berlin, something of an expert in the Eastern Question, was firmly resolved to continue his predecessor's co-operation with the British to force Russia to respect the Berlin Treaty. Indeed, as far as the future of the Dual Alliance was concerned, he hoped to develop it, in association with Great Britain and Italy, into a formidable anti-Russian bloc; and he further asked Bismarck to extend its terms to cover a possible threat to the 'military capacity' of the Monarchy, such as a Russian occupation of Romania. It was in vain that Bismarck raged against Haymerle's stubborn refusal to talk to the Russians – 'Baron Haymerle always utters an emphatic "No" three times on waking up in the morning, for fear of having undertaken some commitment in his sleep' – that he rejected any commitment to

Romania out of hand; that he poured scorn on Austrian suggestions that Italy might prove a valuable ally; and that he told Vienna straight out that the Dual Alliance was 'not designed to support any Balkan policy whatever'. Franz Joseph, for his part dismissed the professions of good faith that were now beginning to come from St Petersburg as utterly worthless, and Haymerle was equally unmoved: 'So long as our interests in the Near East are so closely parallel with those of the English', he concluded in February 1880, 'we should be unwise to abandon England.'

Harsh realities were soon to force Haymerle to recognize, as Andrássy had had to recognize a decade before, that a weak great power such as Austria-Hungary was in no position to dictate the course of European alignments. It was not simply that his hopes of establishing an effective entente with the British to defend the Ottoman Empire and the Treaty of Berlin against Russian encroachments were vitiated by the deep suspicion harboured by the Turks, still smarting over Cyprus and Bosnia, against their self-styled British and Austrian protectors. In March, Haymerle's hopes were dealt a further blow by accession to power of Gladstone in London. By the summer, the British were adopting a distinctly pro-Christian and anti-Turkish line at the Berlin ambassadors' conference on the unfinished business of the Congress, notably the definition of the frontiers of Montenegro and Greece. In the former case they treated with supreme disregard the appeals of the Albanians (whom the Austrians wished to protect as a barrier to Slav domination of the western Balkans) and in the latter they actually combined with Russia to coerce the Sultan into making concessions to Greece. Even in Bulgaria, the Austrians gloomily surmised, Gladstone could hardly be counted on to join in upholding the Sultan's rights if Russia encouraged the principality to unite with Eastern Rumelia in defiance of the Treaty of Berlin. Meanwhile, Bismarck, who suspected Gladstone of seeking to draw Russia away from Germany by accommodating her over Afghanistan and encouraging her on a path in the Near East that might lead to a conflict with Austria-Hungary, increased his pressure on Vienna to come to terms with St Petersburg. By now, in fact, even Haymerle was prepared to consider 'the advantages of standing well with Russia, particularly since England is so actively trying to undermine Turkey and can no longer be counted on'. When he met Bismarck at Friedrichsruh in September 1880 he declared himself ready at least to investigate the possibility of securing Austro-Hungarian interests in the Near East by a formal agreement with the Russians.

It was perhaps naïve of the Austrians to entrust the handling of the negotiations with St Petersburg to Bismarck – on the assumption that their interests would be better safeguarded in trilateral than in bilateral negotiations; and they were certainly unduly sanguine in expecting that Bismarck would pay serious attention to the list of desiderata they sent to Berlin (including a German guarantee of Romania and recognition of Austria-Hungary's right to annex not only the occupied provinces of Bosnia and Herzegovina but the Sanjak of Novibazar). For Bismarck's main objective was an agreement that would satisfy St Petersburg, and as his nervousness increased in the atmosphere of uncertainty that followed the assassination of Alexander II in March 1881, he bullied the Austrians mercilessly into lowering their terms. Consequently, it was German and Russian preoccupations rather than Austro-Hungarian, that were to the fore in the final Three Emperors' Alliance treaty of 18 June. In contrast to the Austro-Russian-dominated Three Emperors' League of 1873–78, the Alliance was very much a Bismarckian instrument, and, like the Dual Alliance, it was much more specific in its terminology. The first two articles of the Treaty pledged each of the three governments to observe benevolent neutrality if either of the others were engaged in war with another power, although they were obliged to reach a prior agreement in the event of war with Turkey, or of territorial changes in the Ottoman Empire. In Article III the German powers promised to uphold the strict Russian interpretation of the rule closing the Straits to foreign warships (as opposed to the flexible interpretation enunciated by the British at the Congress of Berlin).

Matters of immediate practical importance were dealt with in a secret annex to the Treaty, and here the Alliance, in attempting to make specific and positive provision for future eventualities, echoed the Austro-Russian agreements of 1876–77 rather than the original League of 1873. Austria-Hungary's right to annex Bosnia and the Herzegovina – but not the Sanjak of Novibazar – was recognized; and Austrian anxieties about an eventual union between Bulgaria and Eastern Rumelia were temporarily assuaged: the Sultan was to be dissuaded from occupying Eastern Rumelia as prescribed by the Berlin Treaty, but in the event of any union Austria-Hungary's commercial interests in Bulgaria were to be safeguarded, and the union was not to be instigated by Russia, nor accompanied by any further Bulgarian expansion into Macedonia. Finally, Russian and Austro-Hungarian agents in the Balkans were to be instructed to refrain from intriguing against each other, and even to co-operate.

As for the general significance of the Alliance, which A.J.P. Taylor characterized as 'a practical agreement about the Near East, without even a monarchical flourish', it is indeed true that, unlike the League of 1873, it was signed by diplomats, not by sovereigns; and that the text contained no explicit reference to the the doctrine of monarchical solidarity. On the other hand, in practical terms, the revived consensus between the three Eastern Empires certainly gave the new Tsar a welcome breathing space to consolidate his regime; it accorded well with the marked shift to the right in the domestic politics of both German powers at this time; and to judge by the incessant references to monarchical solidarity in the correspondence and meetings of the three emperors in the next few years it would seem that monarchical solidarity was certainly one of the unspoken assumptions of the Three Emperors' Alliance – in which respect it might indeed be seen as a successor to the Holy Alliance, Münchengrätz and the Three Emperors' League. In another respect too it re-echoed those agreements: in the isolation of Great Britain. The exclusion of Gladstone's influence from the Near East was one thing on which all three governments were agreed; and even if the isolation of France was primarily Bismarck's preoccupation, and if Gladstone's contribution to the destruction of the Anglo-Austrian entente had been perhaps even greater than Bismarck's, the Three Emperors' Alliance had undoubtedly 'dug a ditch between Austria and the Western Powers'.

As in the case of the Dual Alliance, indeed of all alliances, the gains and losses were assessed differently by the parties involved. Although the Austrians had hoped for more, the limited terms of the Alliance in turn put no serious restriction on their own freedom of action. Neither they nor the Russians would accept Bismarck's argument that the Alliance implied a division of the Balkans into two distinct spheres of influence: the Austrians were still no more prepared to consign Bulgaria and Romania to the status of vassals of Russia (with disastrous implications for the defence of Hungary) than the Russians were prepared to give up their traditional interest in the fate of Serbia and Montenegro. In fact, Austro-Hungarian interests in the Balkans were now in some respects more secure. In Bulgaria, for example, the Treaty did nothing to disturb Austria-Hungary's ascendancy, based on the prince, Alexander of Battenberg, and the national-minded commercial bourgeoisie; the commitment to refrain from anti-Austrian agitation threatened to deprive Russia of her chief weapon – Pan-Slav propaganda – against this ascendancy; and if the Treaty restricted Russia's freedom to take military action in the Ottoman Empire (which technically still included Bulgaria), it imposed no restrictions on Austrian activity in independent states such as Serbia and Romania. Indeed, within a matter of days after the conclusion of the Alliance, Haymerle proceeded to conclude a secret alliance with King Milan of

Serbia, quite independently of the Monarchy's allies – the Germans were not even informed of it until 1883 – that made the principality a political and commercial dependency of Austria-Hungary. In the wake of this, the Vienna–Constantinople railway line through Serbia and Bulgaria, envisaged in the Treaty of Berlin, was eventually completed in 1888. Although Austro-Russian relations were perhaps only correct rather than cordial, given the Monarchy's relatively exposed position in the European states system, Haymerle, and his successor the arch-conservative Kálnoky – who had even less liking for Gladstone – could be content to work within the framework of the Three Emperors' Alliance.

The Russians, for their part, whatever conditions the Alliance might have prescribed for a long-term union of Bulgaria with Eastern Rumelia, did not feel themselves restricted in their day-to-day proceedings in the principality, where they were engaged in a wearisome and entirely counter-productive political campaign to assert their control over Prince Alexander and his ministers. Nor did Alexander III feel in the least obliged by his new alliance obligations to abandon for ever his long-term objective: control of the Straits and the creation of a Slav federation centred on a liberated Constantinople. For the time being, however, he was content to support his cautious and ultra-conservative foreign minister, N.V. Giers, a devotee of co-operation with the Central Powers and the maintenance, at least for the time being, of the territorial *status quo* in the Ottoman Empire. Moreover, in the context of the states system generally, the Straits clause of the Three Emperors' Alliance was quite invaluable to Russia: it gave her security against what continued to be her great nightmare, at least until the building of a Russian Black Sea fleet in the late 1880s, an incursion by the British fleet into the Black Sea; and it allowed her to continue, unperturbed by the frowns of London, her drive through Central Asia towards Afghanistan.

For Bismarck, its chief architect, the Three Emperors' Alliance was a great diplomatic achievement that came near to achieving his ideal. Not only was Germany now safely *à trois* in a Europe of five powers, the isolation of France was reaffirmed, as was the elimination of Gladstone's influence – if Russia now proceeded to embroil herself with Great Britain in Central Asia, so much the better: that would only confirm what was perhaps the chief advantage accruing to Germany from the Treaty, the reduction of Austro-Russian tension over the Near East. Now, as in the 1870s, Bismarck's great nightmare was still a war between the two Eastern Empires that would force Germany to make an unpalatable choice between them at the risk of providing France with an ally; and faced with that nightmare Bismarck found the solution offered by the Three Emperors' Alliance, of a reconciliation of Russia and Austria-Hungary under German auspices, infinitely preferable to the prospect of taking up the cudgels on behalf of his Dual Alliance partner in a war that could bring Germany no conceivable gain. In this respect it was significant that in every Balkan crisis in the 1880s Bismarck took the side of the Russians, exploiting his status as an ally to summon the Austrians to acquiesce. This reflected not merely the fact that these crises happened to focus on Bulgaria, which in Bismarck's view lay firmly in Russia's sphere of influence, but Bismarck's overriding concern to hold on to Russia at all costs. Indeed, in terms of the functioning of the European states system the Three Emperors' Alliance was always more important to Bismarck than the Dual Alliance. Of course the two alliances were not so much contradictory as complementary, being predicated on two quite different scenarios in Austro-Russian relations; and both alliances were designed to influence those relations. But so long as the Three Emperors' Alliance functioned, the Dual Alliance was in effect redundant, its role being reduced to that of a reinsurance treaty, a defensive military agreement for use in the unlikely event of war. The Three Emperors' Alliance, by contrast, designed to establish German control of the day-to-day relations of the powers, constituted the true cornerstone of the first Bismarckian alliance system.

Even so, relations between Berlin and St Petersburg were never to return to the cordiality of the 1860s. Fundamentally, the problem was that Russian policy-makers could never really reconcile themselves to the creation in 1871 of the German Empire, no longer Russia's junior partner, even protégé, but the strongest power on the continent; and the conclusion of the Dual Alliance of 1879, proof in the eyes of the Russians that Germany would in the last resort always support their rivals, made matters even worse. In a sense, there was little that anybody in Berlin could do about Russia's underlying sense of grievance: the German Empire was there to stay; and although Bismarck made every effort to reassure St Petersburg about the strictly defensive nature of the Dual Alliance, he refused to abandon it as the Russians were demanding – it was, after all, his chief means of controlling the Austrians. Ironically enough, therefore, that same Dual Alliance that Bismarck had so successfully exploited to coerce Vienna into a rapprochement with St Petersburg was to constitute an insurmountable obstacle in the way of his ultimate objective, the establishment of relations of real confidence between St Petersburg and Berlin.

More immediately, developments in the Near East pointed to other weaknesses in Bismarck's diplomatic edifice. If Vienna resented Russian encouragement of the anti-Austrian Radical party in Serbia, St Petersburg ascribed the failure of its clumsy efforts to browbeat Bulgaria to Austria-Hungary's encouragement of the nationalist bourgeoisie in the principality, and truculently demanded from Bismarck a degree of effective support he was in no position to give – the Austrians were no more prepared to abandon their interests in Bulgaria than Bulgarian politicians were prepared to listen to advice from distant Berlin. Indeed, the whole problem of Austro-Russian relations was exacerbated by the increasingly intractable behaviour of the Balkan states. This was, of course, a problem that had confronted the powers ever since the Greek War of Independence, and one that was to have fatal consequences for the system in 1914. Already by the 1880s, however, Balkan monarchs, under growing pressure from their nationalist subjects, were increasingly unwilling, indeed, unable, to accept the role of mere pawns of the great powers. At the same time, the governments of Russia and Austria-Hungary themselves, however conservative, were exposed to constant pressure from wilder nationalist elements. Unlike the Austro-German Alliance, which was generally popular in both empires, the Three Emperors' Alliance was very much a matter of cabinet diplomacy that never really struck roots in the hearts of the peoples of the signatory Powers. In Budapest, Andrássy denounced the whole idea of co-operation with Russia: 'whereas the Congress of Berlin led Russia out of the Balkans, my successors have brought her back in again'. In St Petersburg, influential journalists such as M.N. Katkov inveighed against the Alliance that had made Russia the dupe of the German powers. True, these currents were resisted: at the highest level monarchical solidarity remained the order of the day. But, as the far-reaching consequences of the Bosnian revolt of 1881–82 were to show, decision-makers could never entirely ignore them.

In October 1881 a revolt broke out in Bosnia against the introduction of conscription into the occupied provinces, and for the next six months the Austro-Hungarian army was engaged in a regular campaign to suppress it. In one respect, the affair provided striking proof of the value of the Three Emperors' Alliance: on an international level, the attitude of the Russian government, which ostentatiously abstained from all criticism of the Austro-Hungarian authorities, was impeccably correct. On the other hand, the tribulations of the Bosnians provoked a tremendous effervescence in the Russian press, which the minister of the interior, the Pan-Slav N.P. Ignatiev, seemed to do nothing to restrain; and from January 1882 General M.D. Skobelev made a series of fiery speeches, in St Petersburg, Belgrade and, finally and most alarmingly, Paris, denouncing

Austro-Hungarian atrocities and advocating a Franco-Russian alliance to fight the central powers. Yet it was not the fact that such sentiments existed in certain circles in Russia that caused concern in Vienna and Berlin, so much as the fact that the Russian government seemed afraid to restrain Skobelev. Despite repeated appeals from his allies, the Tsar did not recall Skobelev to Russia for nearly six months. True, Kálnoky was relieved in June to hear of the sudden death, in a Moscow brothel, of 'the one man in Russia who might have prevailed against sensible people'; but the Tsar's timid reaction had left him with the worrying thought that, however correctly the imperial government might behave, 'no one can say whether the dam of the state's authority might not one day be swept away'. In short, the very crisis that had demonstrated the tactical usefulness of the Three Emperors' Alliance had shown equally clearly that it could provide no absolute guarantee of security. The upshot was a general tightening of the security system of the central powers to cope with the contingency of the failure of the Three Emperors' Alliance. Most immediately, the Skobelev affair precipitated the formation of the Triple Alliance.

If the Triple Alliance of 20 May 1882 was for both central powers, like the Dual Alliance for Bismarck, not so much the realization of a long-term plan as a makeshift measure to cope with an emergency, this was not the case for Italy, for whom the Alliance represented the fulfilment of a long-cherished aspiration. Until 1882 relations between Italy and the central powers had been problematical. Indeed, throughout the 1870s the relations between the new kingdom of Italy and all the established great powers had been deeply ambivalent. Since the acquisition of Rome, in the wake of the collapse of of the Second Empire, Franco-Italian relations had been decidedly cool: to many in Italy, France appeared as an obstacle to their ambitions on the south coast of the Mediterranean, particularly in Tunis; and irredentists on the Right still cast their eyes on Corsica, Nice and Savoy. The same people, by contrast, saw in Austria-Hungary a valuable member of the European states system, to be preserved as a barrier against Russian or Slav control of Italian-inhabited lands on the *altera sponda* across the Adriatic. On the other hand, irredentists on the Left looked to the incorporation of territories still under Austro-Hungarian rule – an objective, in fact, that no Italian government could renounce for ever; and the refusal of the Pope to recognize the kingdom of Italy posed a further obstacle to close relations between Franz Joseph, Apostolic King of Hungary and Europe's leading Catholic monarch, and the House of Savoy. For most of the 1870s Italian governments tried to tack, pinning their hopes on a policy of *equidistanza* – cultivating friendly relations with all while undertaking binding commitments to none – as the best chance of enhancing their position in the community of great powers.

By the end of the decade, however, it seemed clear that *equidistanza* had not paid off. The Italians emerged humiliated from the Congress of Berlin, where Bismarck had openly encouraged France to turn her attention to Tunis (in an effort to divert her from Alsace-Lorraine); and where Andrássy had coldly snubbed their suggestions that south Tyrol might be an appropriate compensation to Italy for Austria-Hungary's advance into Bosnia. They decided, therefore, to abandon *equidistanza* in favour of an alignment with the central powers. In 1880, however, although they found Haymerle not at all disinclined to the idea of adding Italy to his planned anti-Russian bloc, they came up against Bismarck, solely intent on forcing Austria-Hungary to seek an accommodation with Russia. When, in May 1881, the Treaty of Bardo established a French protectorate over Tunis and caused a rift between France and Italy that was to remain a fixed point of the states system for almost twenty years, the Italians pressed their suit even more strongly in Vienna and Berlin – but to no avail. Indeed, the very crisis that spurred the Italians on only made them seem less attractive as a potential ally for the central powers. Bismarck had no desire whatever to prevent France from expending her energies in North Africa; and the Austrians, who had always refused to commit themselves against France – even to secure such a valuable prize as the Dual Alliance – were certainly not inclined to be dragged into a quarrel with her on Italy's account. Finally, the conclusion of the Three Emperors' Alliance in June relieved the pressure on both central powers, and made them even less responsive to Italy's importunities.

When the danger appeared with the Skobelev affair that the Three Emperors' Alliance might nevertheless be swept away, Bismarck and Kálnoky had to think again, and the terms of the Triple Alliance, negotiated between Kálnoky and the Italians with Bismarck's concurrence, were settled within a matter of weeks. Like the Dual Alliance, the Triple Alliance was a strictly defensive military agreement: in the event of an unprovoked French attack, the central powers were obliged to come to the aid of Italy, while Italy was obliged to come to the aid of Germany; and all three signatory powers were obliged to fight together if either or both the others 'without direct provocation on their part should chance to be attacked and to be engaged in war with two or more' non-signatory powers. Article IV committed the signatories to observe benevolent neutrality if a co-signatory found itself threatened by a fourth power 'and obliged on that account to make war on it' – that was the extent of Italy's obligations in the event of an Austro-Russian war. A supplementary 'Mancini declaration', to the effect that the alliance terms 'cannot . . . in any case be regarded as directed against England' took account of the peculiar vulnerability of the Italian coast to the Royal Navy.

This was not the only indication of the privileged position Italy enjoyed within the Alliance. Altogether, the Alliance represented a pure gain for Italy, who after a decade on the periphery of the European states system, had at last been fully accepted in the ranks of the great powers; and as the weakest and least stable of the three allied powers it was Italy who gained most from the preamble to the treaty, which declared the determination of the allies 'to fortify the monarchical principle and thereby to assure the maintenance of the social and political order in their respective states' – to which end they pledged themselves in Article I 'to exchange ideas on economic and social questions'. Certainly, it was also in Austria-Hungary's interests that the Italian monarchy should survive as a bulwark against revolutionary irredentism. Kálnoky was continually haunted by the fear that a republican triumph in Italy would herald the fall of the Iberian monarchies and a congeries of Latin republics grouped round France. Bismarck, too, had an interest in reinforcing the monarchical principle in Italy in order to emphasize the isolation of France; and for him the ideological aspect of the Triple Alliance was complementary to that of the Three Emperors' Alliance.

As for the military terms of the Alliance, Italy had secured the support of two great powers against an unprovoked attack from her only enemy; she was herself committed only to helping Germany against that same enemy; and her commitment to observe benevolent neutrality in the event of an Austro-Russian war was neither onerous nor in conflict with her own preference to see Austro-Hungarian rather than Slav domination of the east coast of the Adriatic. Clearly, Germany's interest in the military clauses of the Alliance was equal to that of Italy: an Italian thrust into southern France would be decidedly useful to Germany in the event of war on the Rhine; and Germany always took her obligations to Italy's military and economic welfare more seriously than the Austrians did. For the latter, provided Italy did not actually collapse into revolution, Italian military weakness and inefficiency were simply a further guarantee against an Italian stab in the back in the event of war in the East; and that was, after all, the prime Austrian interest in the Triple Alliance. Kálnoky was unperturbed by the imbalance in the military terms of the alliance: an unprovoked French attack on Italy was a most unlikely prospect; whereas

Vienna had no wish whatever to seek an equivalent promise of Italian military assistance against Russia – assistance that would be of negligible value, and that might only open the door to Italian claims to a voice in any peace settlement. Kálnoky was quite content to have increased the Monarchy's freedom of action in case the worst came to the worst in the east. Indeed, as he emphasized to the somewhat affronted Pope, his only reason for concluding the Alliance with the Italian monarchy had been 'the dreadful confusion prevailing in Russia'.

Yet if, in terms of specific military commitments the Italians had been able to achieve almost all they could hope for – thanks, of course, to the anxieties of the Central Powers about the general international situation in the spring of 1882 – they soon found they had less reason to be satisfied with the role accorded to the Alliance in the European states system. Even before the crisis had passed it became clear that for the Central Powers the Triple Alliance was merely one of a number of emergency measures they were holding in reserve against the possibility that the Three Emperors' Alliance might be swept away. The Dual Alliance, for example, was given more substance in these months, when the German and Austro-Hungarian general staffs at last made contact, the Germans revealing, to the Austrians' relief, that in the event of a two-front war they intended to concentrate their initial military effort in the east, and the two general staffs agreeing to co-ordinate plans for a pincer movement deep into Russian Poland. The Austrians continued to cultivate their alliance with Serbia and to develop their economic interests in Bulgaria; and when in the summer of 1883 rumours of an impending Russian invasion of Bulgaria frightened the Romanians into appealing for Austro-Hungarian protection, the Austrians seized the chance, not only to conclude a secret defensive alliance with King Carol but to secure German accession to it, thereby achieving that security in the south-east that Bismarck had been denying them since 1879. It was significant that the Italians were not even informed of the Romanian alliance. As far as the Central Powers were concerned, even in their 'emergency' network of defensive military agreements the Triple Alliance was not assured of pride of place.

This place was held by the Dual Alliance, which continued its existence parallel to, but completely separately from, the Triple Alliance. Italy had not, as is sometimes claimed, 'joined' the Dual Alliance. Indeed, the conclusion of the Triple Alliance did not affect the Dual Alliance in any way. In 1882 Austria-Hungary was no more committed to assist Germany in a war against France alone than she had been in 1879. For Austria-Hungary, and even for Germany, so long as the chief problem lay in the east, the Dual Alliance was always more important than the Triple Alliance; and the secondary significance of the Triple Alliance was underlined by the fact that the whole network of Germany's defensive military agreements – with Austria-Hungary, Italy and Romania – was itself in Bismarck's eyes very much a reinsurance system to be kept in reserve against the failure of the Three Emperors' Alliance.

The Three Emperors' Alliance remained the key to the first Bismarckian alliance system. As memories of the Skobelev affair faded and the tension eased between Russia and the Central Powers the network of defensive alliances moved into the background and both Germany and Austria-Hungary hastened to demonstrate their renewed faith in the Three Emperors' Alliance as the basis of their security system. Meetings between the three emperors at Skiernewice in 1884 and Kremsier in 1885 were accompanied by exchanges of messages reaffirming the principle of monarchical solidarity against the revolutionary menace; and at Skiernewice Kálnoky made the important concession of recognizing Russia's claim to an interest in the western Balkans, extending the Alliance's prohibition of unilateral military action or territorial alterations in the Ottoman Empire to cover the whole Balkan peninsula. So convinced was he that 'it is for Austria-Hungary a matter of life and death to avoid war with Russia' that when the Hungarian parliament presumed to disparage his achievements in the field of co-existence he even tendered his resignation. Franz Joseph, however, gave him his full backing, and Kálnoky, reassured on the main issue of relations with Russia, kept his nerve in the face of a number of blows to the Monarchy's position in the Balkan states arising from the growing political chaos in Serbia and friction with Romania (the result of Budapest's attempts to protect Hungarian agriculture from Romanian competition) that reached the proportions of a tariff war by 1886. Neither Kálnoky nor Bismarck was in the least inclined to run after the Italians, who in turn felt keenly their exclusion from Skiernewice. In 1885 Italy's expedition to Massawa, on the Abyssinian coast, evoked no support, or even sympathy, in Vienna and Berlin, where it was regarded – rightly – as lying outside the scope of the Triple Alliance, and as an unnecessary provocation of France. In the summer Bismarck and Kálnoky agreed that if the Triple Alliance were ever to be renewed – and that was not necessarily desirable – there could be no question of any further concessions to Italy. Despite the Alliance, Italy was still not recognized as an equal of the other great powers.

The years after Skiernewice were the heyday of the first Bismarckian alliance system, and of the domination of the European states system by the three conservative empires. Central to this was the Three Emperors' Alliance, which by establishing the framework for an Austro-Russian *modus vivendi* in the Near Eastern storm centre and by isolating revanchist France, seemed to provide the answer to all Germany's external problems. So long as this Alliance continued to function, the 'alternative' network of defensive military alliances could be held in reserve, and the Triple Alliance and Italy's concerns were relegated to a very subordinate role in the states system. Moreover, within that states system France and Great Britain occupied an even more peripheral position. As in the 1830s, if the three eastern powers could harmonize their policies they could dominate the affairs of east and central Europe and had no need of the West. For the Eastern Powers, indeed, the exclusion of the influence of the Western powers was an important common objective and itself served to reinforce their domination.

The isolation of France, where the consolidation of the republican regime was paving the way for a significant military build-up by the early 1880s, continued to be Bismarck's fundamental objective. Nor had the republic ever found favour with the ultra-conservative Alexander III. Even in Vienna, however, Andrássy's concern for the survival of France as a great power was now being eclipsed by Kálnoky's conviction that 'the long continued existence of a French Republic, recognized as a fully equal power, is a dangerous matter for the monarchical principle'. Indeed, should France ever defeat Germany, 'the republican and socialist menace would sweep through Europe like a flood when a dam has been broken'.

As for Gladstone's Great Britain, if the prime minister's anti-Turkish proclivities had estranged the Austrians, while his advocacy of a European states system based on the concert of Europe rather than on groups of powers aroused Bismarck's scorn and ire, he found himself in May 1885 in direct conflict with Russia, whose troops had appeared at Penjdeh, on the borders of Afghanistan. The crisis, like all the extra-European conflicts between great powers in the period, was settled by a compromise agreement, but it was instructive in the functioning of the European states system under Bismarck's control. When in desperation the British had considered attempting to call Russia to order by sending some warships into the Black Sea – the only area where she might be vulnerable to their power – the three eastern powers had united to remind the Sultan of his obligations to forbid this under the Straits Convention, whereupon the British had had to beat an ignominious retreat. As Italy had joined her allies and France had given the same advice at Constantinople, there was some truth in Lord Salisbury's jibe that Gladstone had at last achieved his beloved concert of Europe: the continental powers were all united against Great Britain.

In fact, the continental powers were far from united. The French stance in the Penjdeh crisis reflected not any reintegration of France into a German-led Europe, but simply the alienation of France from Great Britain that, like the frank hostility that now characterized Franco-Italian relations, was to remain a feature of European alignments for some two decades. Indeed, whereas in the 1830s a measure of Anglo-French co-operation had served as a check on the domination of the European states system by the three Eastern Powers, in the 1880s the dominance of Bismarck's first alliance system was enhanced by the disunity prevailing between the Western Powers. Yet if, within Europe, the consequence of this disunity had been to drive Italy into dependence on the Central Powers, and to hinder the creation of any Anglo-French counterweight against them, its origins lay in a burst of 'imperialist' activity outside Europe.

Extra-European activities: the disunity of the Western Powers

In a sense, it is not so much the often remarked outburst of 'imperialist' activity in the last quarter of the nineteenth century that demands an explanation, as the peculiar interlude of anti-imperialism in the preceding generation. Overseas empire-building had been a notable characteristic of the activity of west European states since the fifteenth century; and in the case of France it continued throughout the nineteenth century – witness the activities of Napoleon I in Egypt, of Charles X and Louis Philippe in North Africa, of Napoleon III from Indo-China to Mexico. Between 1830 and 1870, however, the attention of most powers was absorbed by crises in Europe over the Near East and the dismantling of the Vienna settlement in Italy and Germany. The British were in these years content to develop their 'informal' empire, based on trading links, without the military and administrative costs attaching to formal colonial rule; and as Great Britain, as a free-trading power, posed no threat to the 'open door' and to the trade of potential rivals, her imperial activities caused no particular concern to the other European powers.

By the end of the 1870s, however, the position was changing. A general depression that was to last until the mid-1890s led to the adoption of protection by most members of the European states system and the assumption spread that a power that did not secure political control of its markets through a colonial regime risked seeing those markets closed by powers that did – no one was then to know that Great Britain, the world's greatest imperial power, was to remain free-trading until 1931. In France, for example, Jules Ferry, an Alsatian industrialist and a firm believer in the necessity for protected markets if France was to compete with more advanced industrialist powers such as Great Britain and Germany, used his position as minister of education to send out an expedition to investigate the flora and fauna of the Congo basin; and the result was the establishment of the French Congo. A similar alarm over Italy's supposed political designs on Tunis precipitated the establishment of a French protectorate there in 1881. As other powers in turn discovered that wherever the French flag was established their own trade was excluded, something of a vicious circle developed. In short, *Torschlußpanik*, or 'fear of the closing door' was an important strand in the web of motives that drove the great powers – quite regardless of their alignments within the European states system – to move from a system of informal imperialism to the establishment of political control over most of the extra-European world.

Certainly, 'economic' theories of imperialism (in terms of a drive by 'advanced' powers to find markets for surplus capital) put forward by writers such as J.A. Hobson and Lenin, are too simplistic as an explanation of such a complex phenomenon as nineteenth-century imperialism. In the first place, some of the most active imperialist states, such as Portugal and Italy, were themselves acutely short of capital. In the second, in terms of national economies at least, the economic return on capital exported to the colonies was minimal: in 1901 Great Britain's trade with the whole of the vast empire acquired after 1880 amounted to a mere 2.5 per cent of her total trade, most of which went to the European continent and the Americas; while Germany's trade with her own colonies accounted in 1913 for a mere 0.1 per cent of her total trade. The trade of both powers with each other and with the Americas far outweighed their trade with their colonial empires. Indeed, although some Frenchmen saw in the acquisition of a colonial empire a means to restore France's great power status, the 'Scramble for Africa' was probably a deficit operation for the great powers involved, when the expense of acquisition and the costs of administration are taken into account. On the other hand, although trade with the newly acquired colonies might be minuscule as a proportion of national trade, it was nevertheless extremely profitable to the small groups of investors involved in it. These people were, moreover, well connected – whether in trading and exploratory organizations such as the British East Africa Company, backed by such notables as Chamberlain, Rhodes, and eventually Rosebery, and an influential lobby of Liberal imperialists; whether in the *Parti Colonial* with its network of members in the French assembly and the ministries; whether individual German trading houses with their connections and shareholders in the Wilhelmstrasse and the higher bureaucracy of the Reich. These dedicated enthusiasts constituted powerful pressure groups that could sometimes, if political circumstances at home were favourable, manipulate governments to further their ideals and protect their interests and investments.

Domestic political developments contributed to the imperialist activities of the powers in a variety of ways. Portugal's expansion in West Africa, for example, was largely an attempt by an embattled monarchy to fend off its parliamentary critics, and the Portuguese government was in fact relieved when it was able to abandon its pretensions under the cloak of compliance with the orders of the great powers assembled in the Berlin West Africa conference of 1884–85. In Italy, alarm about the stream of impoverished peasants emigrating from Naples and Sicily spurred the 'southerner' Crispi to seek to divert the population drain to a colony in North Africa; and in Germany Caprivi warned that unless the Reich developed its colonies to absorb German products, it would find itself exporting its population (although in 1914 the total German population in the colonies was still less than the German population of Paris). In many states imperialists were influenced by Social Darwinist theories, that interpreted international relations in terms of a survival of the fittest: according to Crispi 'Italy needs colonies for her future and for her trade, and this bourgeois habit of always counting the cost is unpatriotic; there is something greater than material interests, the dignity of our country and the interests of civilisation.' The French *Parti Colonial* was imbued with a similar spirit; and even Lord Salisbury spoke of the dawn of an era in which 'for one reason or another – from the necessities of politics or under the pretence of philanthropy, the living nations will gradually encroach on the territory of the dying.' Joseph Chamberlain saw in imperialist activity leading to greater prosperity and the imbuing of the working classes with enthusiasm for Empire – concepts that also figured prominently in the promotion of *Weltpolitik* in Germany – a prophylactic against the threat of stagnation and social revolution at home. In this context, imperialism indeed constituted a European, albeit many-faceted, phenomenon; but it was one to which the particular alignments of the powers within the European states system made no distinctive contribution.

Similarly, the external factors motivating the extra-European activity of the great powers had little to do with the shifts of the European

diplomatic kaleidoscope. The strategic concerns behind British involvement in Egypt and the Sudan reflected a determination to protect the
route to India through Suez and the Red Sea against all comers, whether
friend or foe in terms of European alignments. Expansion in terms of
the 'advancing frontier', when an imperial power that had established its
control of one area, found itself drawn further by the need to control
unruly elements beyond its new frontier – seen in the British advance into
the Sudan, and Russia's absorption of a whole series of central Asian
khanates – clearly had no more to do with developments in Europe than
had its moral counterpart, the 'civilizing mission' theory that contributed
to the British advance in East Africa.

The Egyptian case provided a good illustration of how a great power,
confronted by a chaotic situation, could find itself drawn into *ad hoc*
intervention without any clear long-term objectives at all. By the late
1870s the simple inability of the khedive's regime to cope with the influx
of foreign capital into Egypt had resulted in the establishment of the so-
called 'dual control' of the finances by the two most interested powers,
France, the chief bondholder, and Great Britain, since Disraeli's purchase
in 1875 of the khedive's holdings, the largest single shareholder in the
Suez Canal. In a series of hand to mouth efforts to protect the interests
of the bondholders against aggrieved indigenous elements (who, not
surprisingly, resented the austerity measures imposed by the dual control
at a time when 90 per cent of the khedivial revenues were being spent
on servicing the debt) the Gladstone government simply drifted into a
military confrontation leading, after Wolseley's victory over rebel forces
at Tel-el-Kebir in May 1882, to a full-scale British occupation of the
country.

Yet although the Egyptian affair, as far as its origins were concerned,
exemplified the autonomy of imperialist activity from the functioning
of the European states system, its impact on the latter was nevertheless
momentous. Although Gladstone had hoped to handle the affair in concert with the other powers, the reactions of the latter were tentative and
ineffective: the three Eastern Empires shrank from involvement in measures that seemed to pre-empt the Ottoman suzerain power; the Italians,
on the point of concluding an alliance with the central powers, declined
Gladstone's invitation to act, as did the French, embarrassed by a change
of government at the critical moment. It was, however, not so much the
fact that Great Britain had emerged, almost by chance, in sole occupation
of the country that made the Egyptian question such a contentious international issue. It was Gladstone's decision to continue the occupation

until order and stability had been established and – out of deference to his lofty ideal of the concert – to abolish the special position enjoyed by Great Britain and France under the dual control in favour of the control of Egyptian finances by all the powers acting together through the *Caisse de la Dette*. France was now alienated beyond all measure. The cordiality that had characterized Anglo-French relations in the 1870s came abruptly to an end and for the next twenty years the estrangement between the two leading western powers remained one of the great fixed points of the European states system, like the estrangement between France and Italy over Tunis. Moreover, just as Bismarck was able to take advantage of the latter when an alliance with Italy began to appear useful in 1882, so he was able to make use of the 'Egyptian lever' – Great Britain's need for support against France's frantic obstruction in the six-power control commission – in his relations with Great Britain and France.

The motives behind Germany's own colonial activities in the 1880s certainly appear to have been largely unconnected with the European states system. In itself, the idea of a German colonial empire was decidedly unattractive to Bismarck. Indeed, it threatened actually to weaken Germany's position as the leading continental power. For Germany, whose security lay in its military capacity, and in Bismarck's skill in manipulating the other powers to preserve Germany's dominant position amongst them, the acquisition of colonies would only be an expensive encumbrance if not – given Germany's total lack of the naval resources to defend them – a hostage to fortune. Against this sceptical attitude, which, fundamentally, Bismarck retained to the end of his life, colonialist pressure groups could at first make little headway. The sudden burst of colonial activity in 1884–85, when Germany acquired virtually every colony she was ever to possess, did not, however, reflect Bismarck's conversion to the views of the *Kolonialverein*, but simply the peculiar condition of the German political scene in those years. Bismarck's switch from an alliance with the Liberals to one with the agrarian and industrialist Right – the Alliance of Rye and Steel – and the introduction of protectionist tariffs had resulted in an increase in food prices that in the elections of 1881 cost his supporters their majority in the Reichstag. For the next six years, if he was to secure approval for his anti-Socialist Law, or for his programme of advanced social legislation to win the workers for the monarchy, Bismarck needed all the votes he could muster, and he could not afford to estrange potential supporters such as the *Kolonialverein*. On a more positive level, it seems that he was persuaded – briefly – by colonialists in high places that colonies were a commercial proposition and could be made to administer themselves at no cost to the imperial government. An additional bonus was the chance that any friction that might arise with Great Britain would discredit Bismarck's liberal enemies, notably the Crown Prince and his English wife. It was this complex – and short-lived – combination of motives that lay behind Bismarck's sudden willingness to assume the protection of Luderitz's trading company in Angra Pequeña (leading eventually to the creation of German South West Africa), and to anticipate the French, British and Americans in the Cameroons, East Africa and the East Indies. Significantly, with the victory of the Alliance of Rye and Steel in the elections of 1887, the death of Frederick III after a reign of only three months in 1888, and the discovery that colonies did in fact entail financial burdens that threatened to increase the dependency of the government on the Reichstag – with the exception of the Cameroons, all the colonies were eventually to be farmed out to private companies – Bismarck's interest in colonial activity disappeared as quickly as it had been aroused.

Now it is true that the effects of Germany's colonial activity were felt, at least at the periphery, in the European states system. On the other hand, A.J.P. Taylor's treatment of the actual origins of Germany's colonial activity in terms of the states system – as an attempt to engineer a quarrel with Great Britain in order to draw France into the orbit of his alliance system – has been challenged by H.A. Turner, who has emphasized that for Bismarck, colonial policy, like commercial policy, moved on a completely different plane from the high politics of the states system. It is true that Bismarck did ocasionally engage in co-operation with France against Great Britain in Egyptian affairs, if only to embarrass the hated Gladstone; that he was immensely irritated by London's fumbling response to his suggestion that Great Britain might assume the burden of protecting Luderitz's trading post; and that he joined with France to oppose the Congo Treaty of 1884 between Great Britain and notoriously protectionist Portugal (against which even British trading houses were protesting). However, all this was entirely understandable in extra-European terms, and had no significant repercussions on the alignments of the powers in Europe. The Berlin Congo Conference of 1884–85 reduced the likelihood of friction over extra-European questions between all the powers, insofar as it agreed certain guidelines (the principle of effective occupation, the internationalization of the Congo and Niger rivers) for colonial activity in future. But it produced no Franco-German entente in Europe. On the contrary, it revealed that the interests of Germany, as an advanced industrial power, coincided more closely with those of free-trading Great

Britain than with those of protectionist France. The French, for their part, might toy with the idea of co-operation with Germany outside Europe to embarrass the British, but they were never interested in an entente with her in Europe. Indeed, it was just at this time that the Tonkin disaster led to the fall of Jules Ferry, and a resurgence of nationalist feeling against all talk of collaboration, even in the colonial field, with Germany – who after all, as Déroulède put it had 'taken two children and offers us twenty domestic servants'. In sum, the Berlin Conference ended leaving both Great Britain and France equally remote from the alliance network that dominated the European states system.

Nor was the contribution of the Western Powers more than peripheral in the transformation of the European states system in the later 1880s, that saw the replacement of the first Bismarckian alliance system by one in which Germany was aligned with her erstwhile opponent in the extra-European arena, Great Britain. True, the revival of nationalism in France gave a new sense of urgency to Bismarck's efforts to ensure the isolation of that power; and with the replacement of Gladstone by Salisbury, who, like Bismarck, preferred to think in terms of groups of powers with common interests rather than the amorphous concert, it began to seem at least conceivable to Berlin that Great Britain might some day be integrated into a conservative system. The crucial factor in the shift in the European states system was, however, a crisis in the area most central to the functioning of that system: the Near East. It was the conflict of interests that developed between Bismarck's chief alliance partners, Austria-Hungary and Russia, that destroyed the first Bismarckian alliance system.

The Bulgarian crises of 1885–87 and the second Bismarckian alliance system

In September 1885 a *coup* in Philippopolis, the capital of Eastern Rumelia, proclaimed the union of the province with Bulgaria, while the strength of national feeling in the principality forced Prince Alexander to acquiesce in this flagrant violation of the Treaty of Berlin. The resultant international crisis demonstrated yet again the centrality of European affairs to the functioning of the European states system, and was ultimately to have far more serious consequences for the alignments of the powers than any extra-European developments. It also demonstrated, as the *coup* was carried out in defiance of the Tsar (who had become thoroughly ill-disposed towards his insubordinate cousin in Sofia), the impotence of the great

powers in the face of increasingly wilful nationalist elements in the small
Balkan states – a phenomenon that was to have even more explosive
consequences after the turn of the century. At the same time, however, it
showed that the problem was not necessarily an insuperable one in terms
of the functioning of the European states system. It was, in fact, one of the
most striking features of the crisis that the Three Emperors' Alliance, like
the League before it, proved to be a good deal more than a fair-weather
system. So long as its members acted with restraint, co-ordinating their
policies and ignoring British attempts to drive a wedge between them, the
Three Emperors' Alliance, like its predecessor, proved perfectly well able
to cope with the issues raised by the small powers. Throughout the 'first'
Bulgarian crisis, of 1885–86 – over the union and the resultant Serbo-
Bulgarian war – the three Eastern Empires continued to dominate the
European states system.

Once it was clear that Russia had not engineered the Philippopolis
coup the Austrians fell in line with their allies in demanding the rescinding
of the illegal union, especially as it threatened, by provoking a host of
claims to compensation from Bulgaria's neighbours, to throw the whole
peninsula into chaos. At the ensuing Constantinople conference the British,
who attempted to defend the union – having reached the conclusion
that a strong independent Bulgaria provided the best barrier to Russian
influence – found themselves isolated and helpless. But although the three
eastern powers managed to preserve their unity, they proved no more able
than the British to direct the actual course of events in the Balkans. In
an attempt to assert their claim to compensation the Serbs, despite the
advice of their Austrian allies, launched an attack on Bulgaria, only to
be defeated at Slivnitza by the Bulgarians, who in turn invaded Serbia.
Although the reckless way in which the Austro-Hungarian envoy to
Belgrade, Count Khevenhüller, carried out his mission to restrain Prince
Alexander (threatening him with a Russian invasion of Bulgaria) aroused
indignation in St Petersburg and exposed the underlying fragility of the
Austro-Russian *modus vivendi*, Kálnoky strove tenaciously to keep in line
with Russia and contain the crisis. In the event, when peace was concluded March 1886 the Bulgarians refrained from claiming any Serbian
territory; but their victory had at least ensured that there could be no
question of revoking the union, which the great powers had now in effect
to endorse, recognizing Prince Alexander as ruler of Eastern Rumelia in
a personal capacity. To this extent, the Three Emperors' Alliance had
suffered a defeat; but more significantly, in terms of the European states
system, the first Bulgarian crisis showed that the disruptive activities of

Balkan nationalists had not broken the unity of the Alliance. The Austrians, as Kálnoky announced in August 1886, had 'no intention of weakening the relationship that was sealed at Skiernewice and Kremsier and which came into operation during the last Bulgarian crisis'. They even restrained themselves from taking up the cause of Prince Alexander when a Russian-inspired *coup* removed him from power a few weeks later.

At this juncture, however, the Tsar's decision to send a mission under General Kaulbars to Sofia to control the election of Alexander's successor marked the start of a second Bulgarian crisis which was an altogether more serious affair. Although there were some elements of continuity with the first Bulgarian crisis – the stubborn defiance of Russia by the majority of Bulgarian nationalists, for example – it was now not simply a case of the disruptive activity of small Balkan peoples but of the single-handed action of one great power taken with supreme disregard for the susceptibilities of another deeply interested, and allied, great power. The Austrians, thoroughly alarmed at the prospect of a Russian satellite state that would threaten both Romania's and their own security, now openly declared their opposition to Russia's claims to any position of special influence in Bulgaria; and in a speech to the Hungarian delegations in November Kálnoky virtually threatened Russia with war if she attempted a military occupation of the principality. When Salisbury backed him up with a speech in similar vein in the House of Lords Bulgarian resistance to Russian pressure received a tremendous boost, and by February 1887 the Russians despaired and withdrew the Kaulbars mission, an unmitigated and humiliating failure. The Tsar's rage, of course, knew no bounds; and the most serious consequence of the whole affair, in terms of the European states system, was that Alexander III now refused point blank to consider any more alliances with Austria-Hungary once the Three Emperors' Alliance expired in June. Just as surely as the Treaty of San Stefano had destroyed the Three Emperors' League in 1878, so now again a move by Russia beyond the parameters of her agreements had been thwarted by Austria-Hungary seconded by Great Britain, and the Kaulbars mission had destroyed the Three Emperors' Alliance.

The impending disappearance of the Three Emperors' Alliance forced the Austrians to consider alternative means of safeguarding their interests. Short of an actual Russian attack on Austria-Hungary – of which there was no sign – the Dual Alliance had nothing to offer. For some time Bismarck, increasingly worried by the revival of French military power symbolized by General Boulanger, had been even more than usually anxious not to offend the Russians. Throughout the crisis, to the exasperation of the Austrians, he blandly reiterated his spheres of influence theory, according to which Bulgaria lay in Russia's sphere; and on 12 January 1887 he publicly declared in the Reichstag that 'it is a matter of complete indifference to us who rules in Bulgaria and what becomes of her'. No more than in 1879 did the Dual Alliance have 'any Balkan policy whatever'.

The Triple Alliance, by contrast – which both Bismarck and Kálnoky had considered abandoning in the heyday of the Three Emperors' Alliance – now found more favour in Vienna; and in the negotiations that ended in its renewal in May 1887 the Italians were able, as in 1882, to exploit the anxieties of the Central Powers about the intentions of Russia and France for their own purposes. At no further cost to themselves they managed to extract from their allies a number of additional protocols, pledging the three powers to work to maintain 'the territorial *status quo* in the Orient, . . . on the Ottoman coasts and Islands, and in the Adriatic and Aegean seas'. An Italo-German protocol (incorporated as Articles IX–XI into the body of the alliance when it was again renewed in 1891) provided for German military assistance to Italy if the pursuit of her interests in North Africa should land her in war with France. An Austro-Italian protocol (which in 1891 became the famous Article VII) extended their co-operation – at Kálnoky's insistence – from the Ottoman coasts and Islands to the whole of the 'regions of the Balkans' – apparently an indication of Vienna's anxiety to secure Italian support in Bulgaria. It also laid down that if either of the two powers should be forced to 'modify [the *status quo*] by a temporary or permanent military occupation', this should be 'based on the principle of reciprocal compensation for every advantage territorial or other which each of them might obtain.' It was ironic that the North African agreements, which on the face of it implied a far-reaching modification of the strictly defensive alliance in an acquisitive, even offensive, sense, were never to be invoked or to cause difficulties with any power; and for the rest, the Germans had been careful, as usual, to avoid any commitment to oppose Russia in the Balkans. The Austro-Italian protocol, by contrast, while eminently conservative in its intentions, was deplorably vaguely worded and was to cause endless trouble between the two allies. It helped to kindle in Italy an interest – at first entirely artificial, even spurious – in the affairs of the *altera sponda* that was eventually to become a veritable obsession; and Kálnoky's insouciance in failing to specify in writing that any eventual compensation must not come from territories of the Monarchy was to deal a death-blow to the alliance in 1914–15.

More immediately, however, the association with Italy proved advantageous to the Austrians, in that it helped them to establish contact with the British. Already in February 1887 an Anglo-Italian exchange of notes had confirmed the determination of the two powers to co-operate to maintain the *status quo* – obviously against France and Russia – in the Mediterranean and adjacent seas. The Austrians acceded to this accord in March, and Spain followed in May. Certainly this 'First Mediterranean Agreement' was a somewhat unusual diplomatic edifice, in that it rested on no one agreed text: the British note was far less detailed than the Italian, while the Austro-Hungarian note of accession failed to specify to which of the two it referred. Nor did it contain any specific military stipulations. Even so, as it established an effective working arrangement in the field of day-to-day diplomacy it was an important element in the shift of alignments that followed the collapse of the first Bismarckian alliance system. It served to reintegrate Great Britain, after almost a decade of isolation, into a continental power combination, to give Italy more confidence to resist French pressure, and to compensate Austria-Hungary for the disappearance of the Three Emperors' Alliance.

For Bismarck, of course the disappearance of the Three Emperors' Alliance, the very keystone of his alliance system, was a devastating blow, all the more so in that it coincided with the rise of nationalist elements in France demanding a rapprochement with Russia and pressing the government to force Italy out of the Triple Alliance by such devices as a tariff war and the exclusion of Italian bonds from the French stock market. In these circumstances the Mediterranean Entente, while not a 'Bismarckian' construction, nor, as yet, part of any 'Bismarckian system', suited the German Chancellor well enough. In the first place, it stiffened the Italians and confirmed the isolation of France; in the second, it helped to contain the Eastern crisis: by giving the Austrians more confidence it reduced the risk that they might despair of diplomacy and plunge into war out of sheer desperation, as they had done in 1859 and 1866, and were to do again in 1914; and it served to restrain Russia without involving Germany in the task.

Indeed, it left Bismarck quite free to cultivate his own relations with the Russians and to conclude with them, when the Three Emperors' Alliance duly expired on 18 June 1887, a secret Reinsurance Treaty (of the existence of which Germany's allies were not even informed). Insofar as this Treaty committed Russia and Germany to benevolent neutrality if either were involved in war with a third power (although offensive wars against France and Austria-Hungary were excluded from this proviso) it relieved Bismarck of his worst nightmare – that Russia might actually support a French attack on Germany; and insofar as Germany expressly committed herself to support the Russian position in Bulgaria and at the Straits, Bismarck could continue to hope that, even if his ideal of a tripartite agreement reconciling Russia and Austria-Hungary had proved unrealistic, the Eastern Question could still provide a field for co-operation, rather than disharmony, between Berlin and St Petersburg.

As things turned out, a diplomatic battle royal was soon in progress at Constantinople, between the powers of the Mediterranean Entente on the one hand and Russia supported by her French and German suitors on the other. In this battle, as the Turks were generally averse to taking action that might commit them irrevocably to either side, the honours were fairly evenly divided. In Bulgaria, where the regents had elected Prince Ferdinand of Saxe-Coburg-Koháry to succeed Alexander, the Russians were pressing the Turks to deny him recognition and even to invade Bulgaria to depose him. (As a Catholic, a relative of Queen Victoria, and a former Austrian army officer Ferdinand was in Russian eyes the most objectionable candidate imaginable.) The powers of the Mediterranean Entente, meanwhile, pressed the Turks to grant Ferdinand recognition. In the event, the Turks took no action at all, and by 1888 the Russians gave up in disgust and withdrew all their agents from Bulgaria. In the Egyptian question, by contrast, the Mediterranean Entente suffered a defeat when French and Russian threats frightened the Sultan into abandoning the Drummond Wolff Convention, providing for the evacuation of Egypt on terms extremely favourable to the British (including, in certain circumstances, a right to reoccupy). Russia's influence at Constantinople was further enhanced by the construction, at last, of a Black Sea fleet; and as she began to reinforce this fleet with ships built in the Baltic, the Mediterranean Entente powers – who now adopted the strict interpretation of the rule of the Straits for so long propounded by Russia – protested in vain. In December, they reaffirmed their entente by a second exchange of notes, this time identical and directed specifically to resisting Russia's supposed designs in Sofia and Constantinople, and envisaging in certain circumstances, the possibility of military and naval action in the Ottoman Empire. Although the Second Mediterranean Agreement was, like the First, still only an 'agreement to agree' it was, as Salisbury put it to Queen Victoria, 'as close an alliance as the Parliamentary character of our institutions will permit'.

It was a very important feature of the Second Mediterranean Agreement that Salisbury had only been prepared to ask the Cabinet to undertake even such a limited obligation after he received a letter from Bismarck recommending the agreement and stating that in the last resort Germany too would be prepared to fight to preserve Austria-Hungary. Insofar as this letter implied a German commitment, albeit only a moral one, to the Mediterranean Entente, the latter could now be regarded as forming a part, together with the Reinsurance Treaty and Germany's defensive alliances, of a second Bismarckian alliance system. This system was in W.L. Langer's view Bismarck's greatest diplomatic achievement, the squaring of the circle: the Reinsurance Treaty maintained the wire to St Petersburg; the Mediterranean Entente confirmed the isolation of France and kept Russia within bounds; and the defensive alliances provided security if the worst should come to the worst.

In theory, this was all very well; but in practice the governments of the day were less enamoured of the new system. The Mediterranean Entente powers complained incessantly of Germany's tendency to support Russia in day-to-day diplomacy, which was 'the worst feature of the situation' at Constantinople. The Russians, for their part, still smarted over their defeat in Bulgaria and suspected Bismarck – quite unjustly – of collaborating with their opponents. It is true that there was in theory no contradiction between Germany's commitments to Russia and to her allies in the Dual and Triple Alliances; and technically Germany was not a party to the Mediterranean Agreements. In terms of the spirit of these various agreements there was, however, a serious contradiction between Bismarck's promises to the Russians in the Reinsurance Treaty and his role in the conclusion of the Second Mediterranean Agreement, specifically designed to oppose Russia in Bulgaria and at the Straits. So long as secrecy was maintained, and so long as Germany's partners were unaware of the extent of her various moral and legal commitments, the system did in fact seem to work to produce the uneasy stalemate between the other powers – all forlornly hopeful of German support – that Bismarck desired. But the success of the second Bismarckian system was only achieved at some risk. If a major confrontation had occurred, Bismarck could hardly have honoured all his commitments, legal and moral, to all parties; and even short of this, if the full story of his activities ever leaked out it would have a devastating effect on Germany's relations either with Russia or with the powers of the Mediterranean Entente. As Bismarck's successor was to remark, the Reinsurance Treaty in particular, cornerstone of the second Bismarckian alliance system, was 'a land mine under the Triple Alliance'.

Even discounting such risks, it could hardly be said that the Reinsurance Treaty fulfilled its prime purpose of maintaining the wire to St Petersburg.

Regardless of Bismarck's dogged support for Russia at Constantinople, Russo-German relations deteriorated steadily in the late 1880s. This was largely a result of economic and financial factors. As the agricultural depression continued Bismarck came under increasing Junker pressure for higher tariffs against imports of grain from Russia. Naturally, the Russians were alarmed: it was revenue from grain exports that funded Russia's industrial and military development, indeed, her very survival as a great power. As they retaliated by raising their tariffs against industrial imports from Germany, the commercial relations between the two empires drifted towards a tariff war. Bismarck was soon in an impossible position, caught between the irreconcilable demands of a conservative foreign policy based on solidarity with the tsarist empire, and a conservative domestic policy based on bolstering the position of Junkers and industrialists. In the last resort, he opted for the latter, which was, after all, fundamental to the very *raison d'être* of the Empire of 1871. Desperately, he took refuge in the fantasy that economic policy and high policy moved on completely separate planes; but the fact remained that in the end his much vaunted 'Primat der Außenpolitik' had had to yield to the demands of the 'Primat der Innenpolitik'.

Matters came to a head with the emergency measures taken by Bismarck in the closing months of the Eastern crisis, notably the so-called 'Lombardverbot' of November 1887, whereby the German government withdrew its guarantee to underwrite Russian bonds on the Berlin stock exchange, resulting in their virtual exclusion from the market. This move was partly a response to long-standing objections from the military to a policy of lending Russia money to build strategic railways that threatened the security of Germany's eastern provinces. At the same time, however, insofar as it was also a retaliatory gesture against a recent Russian *ukaz* restricting landholding by foreigners (largely Germans) in Russia's western provinces, it was an attempt by Bismarck to repeat the tactics of reconciliation through intimidation that had brought St Petersburg to its senses in 1879. It also seems to have been an attempt to restrain Russia from adventures in the Eastern crisis by keeping her short of money – on the assumption that she was solely and helplessly dependent on Germany: 'Paris is no market for Russian paper', Herbert Bismarck confidently declared. This assumption was totally mistaken. The French were quick to seize the opportunity (just as the Germans were to complete the financial 'diplomatic revolution', buying up the Italian bonds driven off the Paris *bourse* at this time) and the first of a series of French loans to Russia followed in 1888. As the Germanophile Giers was to lament five years later, the roots of the Franco-Russian alliance lay 'in the financial policy of Prince Bismarck'.

The operation of the second Bismarckian system was perhaps even more seriously obstructed by political changes in Germany after the accession of William II in June 1888. If the old Emperor had been content for nearly two decades to leave the control of all German policy, domestic, foreign and military, in the hands of the Chancellor, his grandson was determined to secure a role in decision-making both for himself and for other advisers, often military men. The new emperor was, moreover, not only wilful, but temperamentally very unstable; and his violent swings of mood introduced an element of instability into Germany's policy that was to be characteristic of the whole reign, and that seriously impaired Germany's position as a stabilizing element in the European states system. For example, he started off in a strongly Bismarckian mood, insisting, to the dismay of his Austrian allies, in honouring St Petersburg with the first state visit of his reign; but the dour Alexander III failed to respond to the effusiveness of this 'garçon mal élevé' and William had swung into a violently anti-Russian mood by the time of Franz Joseph's state visit to Berlin in July 1889.

The Austrian state visit was a notable landmark, in that it demonstrated, even before Bismarck's fall from power, that the Chancellor was no longer in sole control of German policy, and that for many in the highest quarters the bedrock of German security was not the Reinsurance Treaty but the Dual Alliance. Russia was definitely Germany's chief enemy, William II's confidant General Waldersee told the visiting Austrians; and Germany would even evacuate Alsace-Lorraine if the demands of a war with Russia required it. 'Your mobilization will be the signal for us to come in with all we have got' the war minister Verdy du Vernois declared; while William II himself assured Franz Joseph that 'whatever reason you may have for mobilizing, whether Bulgaria or anything else, the day of your mobilization will be the day of mobilization for my army, whatever the chancellors may say.' True, the value of such assurances from one so volatile as William II was questionable – as the Austrians were to discover on several occasions in the next twenty years. For the moment, however, it seemed that the Dual Alliance had at last acquired both a Balkan and a military policy. In March 1890 Austrian hopes that things really had changed for the better and that there was now no one with 'Russian sympathies' in office in Berlin were confirmed by the news of the resignations of both Bismarck and his son. As Franz Joseph's uncle wrote to the chief of general staff: 'Thank God, we are rid of the whole family.'

The *Neue Kurs* and the reactivation of French diplomacy

Bismarck's successor as Chancellor, General Leo Count Caprivi was a straightforward military man little versed in diplomacy who assumed, like most of the German military since 1871, that any war in which Germany became involved would become a two-front war in east and west. In contrast to Bismarck, who always remained essentially an old-style cabinet diplomatist, Caprivi believed that alliances were only worthwhile if they represented a real community of interests; and as he was also convinced that, whatever assurances of monarchical solidarity might come from the Romanov court, the Russian people were inveterately antipathetic to the German Empire, he felt that Bismarck's policy of holding on to Russia by accommodating her was a dangerous illusion that only risked alienating Germany's friends elsewhere. Germany should rather – and here Caprivi was in line with the deterrent theory advocated by Moltke ever since 1871 – build up her military strength and stand by her friends and allies. Herein would lie the best chance of preventing war or, if deterrence should fail, of prevailing in a war. The second Bismarckian alliance system was in Caprivi's view not only impossibly subtle and complicated – and he certainly doubted his own competence to manage it – but positively dangerous. The Reinsurance Treaty was a weapon that Russia could use at any time, simply by revealing its existence, to disrupt Germany's relations with her friends in Vienna, Rome and London. This last argument was one that was strongly pressed in the Wilhelmstrasse, where Holstein was now coming to the fore, and it seems to have been a decisive element in the German decision of March 1890 not to renew the Reinsurance Treaty when it expired in June (even though the Russians, nervous at the prospect of isolation, were willing to renew it without the Bulgarian clauses). It was not so much the failure to renew the Treaty that worried the Russians, however, as the evidence of the new and entirely un-Bismarckian emphasis that Germany was beginning to give to the other aspects of the second Bismarckian alliance system.

If this trend had been discernible in German policy even before the fall of Bismarck, it became clearly dominant in Caprivi's *Neue Kurs*, with its single-minded concentration on Germany's links with her allies and with Great Britain; and as Caprivi had a far less 'compartmentalized' view of policy than Bismarck, the new course soon made itself felt in a number of areas. In the Near East, for example, when the regime in Sofia sought the Sultan's approval for the appointment of more Exarchist bishops in

Macedonia, to promote the Bulgarian cause against Greek and Serbian Patriarchist competition, the German ambassador at Constantinople was instructed to join his Mediterranean Entente colleagues in supporting the request against Russian and French opposition. In the economic field Caprivi, who realistically accepted the connection between commercial policy and diplomacy that Bismarck had always so stubbornly denied, granted a whole series of tariff reductions – to Austria-Hungary, Italy, Romania, Belgium and Switzerland – in an effort to underpin Germany's alliance system and influence in central Europe by economic co-operation. It was not until 1894, however, that a commercial treaty put an end to the virtual tariff war with Russia. After all, even the tariff concessions to the allies had caused problems at home: Caprivi had been hoping to conciliate the masses by lowering the price of food; but his partial success in this direction had been counter-balanced by the appearance on the scene of a vociferous Farmers' League (Bund der Landwirte) to defend the interests of landowners, facing, as it turned out, a fall in grain prices of nearly 50 per cent between 1892 and 1895. Similarly, in the extra-European field, Caprivi had a more integrated view of Germany's objectives than Bismarck: the concessions he made to Great Britain over a number of East African frontier questions in the Heligoland-Zanzibar agreement, concluded quite quickly, after years of haggling, in July 1890, were a realistic – and not unsuccessful – attempt to improve Anglo-German relations generally. Here too, however, his efforts were not always appreciated at home, and the concessions he made provoked the formation of another noisy pressure group, the Pan-German League, dedicated to the promotion of German interests throughout the world. These pressure groups were ultimately to become, when they gained the ear of the emperor and his advisers, a dangerously destabilizing element in German foreign policy. For the present, however, Caprivi pressed on regardless.

The summer of 1891 witnessed the apotheosis of the *Neue Kurs*. In May, the Triple Alliance was renewed without a hitch, the 1887 protocols relating to Africa and the Near East being incorporated into the actual text of the treaty. In June, Lord Salisbury's parliamentary under-secretary alluded in the House of Commons to Great Britain's shared interest with Italy in the Mediterranean *status quo*, and the Italian foreign minister Rudiní, in a flamboyant parliamentary speech not only proclaimed the renewal of the Triple Alliance but went on to boast of Italy's links with Great Britain. July saw the Italian and Austrian monarchs welcoming a British naval squadron at Venice and Trieste, while William II embarked on a ten-day visit to England. In this atmosphere, it was not surprising that rumours of Great Britain's impending adhesion to the Triple Alliance received wide currency in the European press.

The success of the *Neue Kurs* policy was bought at price, however. Although the British had not in fact undertaken any new commitments, both their co-operation with the Triple Alliance powers in day-to-day diplomacy and the revelation by the Italians of the existence of the Mediterranean Entente were regarded in Paris and St Petersburg as evidence of a deeply disturbing shift in the European states system. From Berlin's point of view, all still seemed well: Caprivi's Germany was the lynchpin of a power combination as formidable as any Bismarck had devised, and if anything, more coherent. The emphasis might now be on the central powers' links with Great Britain rather than with Russia, but the peace of Europe still rested, as in Bismarck's day, not on a balance of power but on a preponderance of a group of conservative powers dedicated to upholding the order of 1871. In terms of possible alternative solutions, however, Caprivi's system was to prove far more vulnerable than Bismarck's. In contrast to the early 1880s, when France, deeply estranged from Great Britain over extra-European questions, had been neither willing nor able to join with the other 'excluded' power to form a counterweight to the preponderant bloc, in the early 1890s the other 'excluded' power was Russia. France and Russia had no conflicts of interest. On the contrary, they had a common interest in seeing Great Britain weakened outside Europe; and although their chief preoccupations in Europe – Alsace and the Straits – might not be identical, they had since 1887 been moving towards a working relationship in Egypt and the Near East; and both were encouraging native resistance to Italian ambitions in Abyssinia. No doubt both powers had been disconcerted by the festivities surrounding the renewal of the Triple Alliance in 1891; but there could be no greater incentive to draw them together than signs of a rapprochement between the central powers and Great Britain, their common opponent in world affairs, or, as Giers gloomily put it on 18 July, 'l'accession plus ou moins directe de l'Angleterre à la Triple Alliance'.

Already at the Russian grand manoeuvres in the summer of 1890 General Boisdeffre had been assured by Russian generals that in the event of a German attack France would be able to count on Russia; and in the spring of 1891 the Russian government itself declared that an 'accord intime' between France and Russia was essential for the preservation of 'an equitable balance of power'. Nothing more concrete was achieved, however. The Russians were nervous of provoking Germany and had no wish to tie their hands by a binding commitment to France – all the more so as neither the Tsar nor Giers felt anything but revulsion for 'toutes ces canailles' that constituted the republican establishment. It was only the shock effect of the demonstrations of solidarity by the Triple Alliance and the Mediterranean Entente in the summer of 1891 that moved the Russians to commit themselves further. A sensational visit by a French squadron to Kronstadt was followed on 27 August by an exchange of notes in which the two powers promised to 'concert together on all questions that affect the general peace' and, if threatened by aggression, 'to agree upon what measures they should immediately and simultaneously adopt'. This was still very far from the explicit military commitment the French were seeking: nothing specific at all had been said as to what kind of assistance might be forthcoming; and concerting together to counteract the designs of the Triple Alliance and Great Britain was simply what France and Russia had been doing in practice for the past few years. The exchange of notes of 27 August marked an important turning point in the development of the European states system nevertheless: a formal written entente now existed between the two powers; and after more than twenty years France was at last emerging from isolation.

The Tsar and Giers seemed perfectly satisfied with what had been achieved and for almost a year showed no inclination to commit themselves any further. The French, however, preoccupied with the military threat posed by the Triple Alliance, began to lose patience: 'Alliance ou flirt?', *Figaro* demanded to know in July 1892. Russia's desperate financial situation after the great famine in the winter of 1891–92 now came to their aid, and Alexander III at last made the gesture of permitting the French and Russian general staffs to investigate the possibility of a military agreement. The negotiations that resulted in the Boisdeffre-Obroutchev military convention of 18 August 1892 were not easy. The objectives of the two parties were by no means identical: the French were really only interested in securing Russian assistance in the event of a German attack, whereas the Russians were equally, if not more, interested in easier successes against the Austrians. In the event, France's main concerns were catered for in the August convention, designed with 'no other object than that of providing for the necessities of a defensive war provoked by the forces of the Triple Alliance'. The two powers committed themselves to fight together in the event of an attack on France by Germany, or by Italy supported by Germany, and an attack on Russia by Germany, or by Austria-Hungary supported by Germany. France committed herself to put 1.3 million men into the field against Germany, Russia about half that number. To get this security, however, the French had to make far-reaching concessions in Article II of the convention concerning mobilization: the two powers were not only to to mobilize but to concentrate their armies on the frontier in the event of the mobilization, not of the whole Triple Alliance (as the French suggested) but of any one member of the Triple Alliance. The proposed agreement was limited in duration to the lifetime of the Triple Alliance and although it was to take the form of a secret military convention (because the French government would have had to seek the approval of the chamber for a formal alliance) it was certainly an alliance in all but name.

Even so, a further sixteen months elapsed before the French and Russian governments accepted the arrangements worked out by Boisdeffre and Obroutchev. At first, the French were assailed with doubts about the very general wording of Article II, pointing out that it could apply to a partial mobilization by one member of the Triple Alliance. This was, however, precisely what the Russians had in mind, and when they insisted that the text could not now be altered, the French acquiesced. They thereby accepted an obligation in the event of, say, a partial mobilization by Austria-Hungary against a Balkan state, to mobilize the French army and move it up to the German frontier – no mean risk, especially at a time when General Obroutchev was writing that, the importance of rapid deployment being so critical in modern warfare, 'the undertaking of mobilization can no longer be considered a peaceful act; on the contrary, . . . it represents the most decisive act of war.' Once the French had swallowed their misgivings, however, doubts arose on the Russian side: in December 1892 the Panama scandal confirmed Alexander III's abysmally low view of the French political system, and when the French press implicated the notoriously venal Russian ambassador and the Tsar insisted on a formal apology from the French government, relations between Paris and St Petersburg became decidedly frosty. It was again the Germans who came to the rescue, as in 1891: the introduction into the Reichstag of a new Army Bill in the summer of 1893, and Caprivi's defence of it in terms of the possibility of a two-front war, reminded the Tsar of harsh political realities and the dangers of isolation. It provoked an act of defiance in the form of a spectacular visit by a Russian squadron to Toulon in October – directed as much against the Mediterranean Entente as against the Triple Alliance; and in an exchange of notes of 27 December 1893 and 4 January 1894 the Russian and French governments agreed that the Boisdeffre-Obroutchev convention was henceforth definitively adopted.

Meanwhile, Toulon had struck the members of the hitherto dominant power constellation, whose demonstrations of solidarity had done so much to call the Franco-Russian combination into being, with the force of a physical blow. The British, so long as France and Russia could be counted as separate entities either isolated from or entangled in a German-dominated power system, had been reasonably confident that they could cope with either the French or the Russian navy, especially since the Naval Defence Act of 1889 had introduced the two-power standard. Already by the summer of 1892, however, there was enough evidence of a developing Franco-Russian entente to lead the British Admiralty to declare that Great Britain simply could not attempt to defend Constantinople against the combined fleets of France and Russia (although it should be noted that Salisbury himself expressly rejected this pessimistic conclusion). In the months after Toulon, the Austrians too began to have serious doubts about the effectiveness of the Mediterranean Entente. Their Italian allies were in a terrible state, with their economy facing ruin from the effects of the tariff war with France and Crispi's expenditure on armaments and on adventures in the Horn of Africa, and with large-scale rebellion breaking out in Sicily in December. As for Great Britain, where Gladstone had replaced Salisbury in August 1892, Kálnoky was no longer sure that the new government was prepared to recognize even the limited obligations its predecessor had undertaken in 1887. True, when he approached Lord Rosebery, the Foreign Secretary, in the spring of 1894, he received an assurance that Rosebery personally was prepared to stand by the late government's policy, although he was not prepared to put the Mediterranean Agreements before the Cabinet. The problem was a practical one, however: the balance of forces in the Mediterranean was no longer what it had been in 1887; and while Rosebery was prepared to fight to defend Constantinople against Russia alone, he told the Austrians frankly that he regarded a Franco-Russian combination as too strong for Great Britain. He would only commit himself to resist Russia if Germany would undertake to keep France quiet, whereupon Kálnoky turned to Berlin. Now in the heyday of the *Neue Kurs*, the German response to such an approach would hardly have been in doubt. The reply Kálnoky received in March 1894, however, showed that in Berlin, too, the conclusion of the Franco-Russian alliance had forced a major reappraisal of policy.

Developments in German domestic politics contributed to this. Both the increase in the Socialist vote in the Reichstag elections of 1893 and the growth of vociferous extra-parliamentary pressure groups on the Right seemed to indicate that Caprivi's domestic policies, while they had failed to check the growth of Social Democracy, had alienated important elements of the establishment. Already in 1893 Caprivi's personal position was gravely weakened when he was replaced as minister-president of Prussia by the reactionary Junker Botho Eulenburg: for the first time in the history of the Empire the dominant German state was removed from the Chancellor's control. The shift to the Right continued in 1894 when Caprivi was replaced as Chancellor by the Kaiser's 'uncle Chlodewig', the venerable Bavarian aristocrat Hohenlohe-Schillingsfürst. Hohenlohe's personal circumstances, notably his princely lifestyle and chronic lack of funds, affected both the tone and the direction of German policy in the later 1890s, making him cling to office despite a series of humiliating imperial interventions in policy-making that Caprivi would never have tolerated, which in turn intensified the confusion at the centre. The fact that Hohenlohe's bear-hunting wife possessed large estates in western Russia, gave the new Chancellor an intense personal interest in avoiding war with that country that had been quite lacking in his predecessor. By 1894, however, a great many people in Berlin had reached the conclusion that Caprivi's policy of confronting Russia in association with his allies and Great Britain had been a mistake: far from bringing security, it had provoked the formation of a Franco-Russian alliance that was undermining the domination of the European states system by a German-led combination of conservative powers. The prospect of a life and death struggle against the combined forces of France and Russia – especially for such objects as Constantinople – was no more attractive to most Germans than to Prince and Princess Hohenlohe; and the decision-makers in Berlin were moving towards the conclusion that the best way to undo the damage was to restore the wire to St Petersburg in the hope of drawing Russia away from France. This reversion to Bismarckian objectives necessarily implied a more restrained attitude towards the powers of the Mediterranean Entente.

As regards the British, the Germans were in any case disappointed with the results of Caprivi's attempts to link them firmly to the Triple Alliance. It seemed that rather than take a firm stand against France and Russia in the disputes that were constantly arising over the delimitation of their extra-European spheres of influence, the British were all too prone to seek an accommodation with their rivals. The way in which in June 1893 the British, after an initial show of bellicosity, acquiesced in the proclamation of a French protectorate over Siam (when it proved in the end to be no challenge to their vital interests) seemed to the Kaiser a prime example of British pusillanimity. Worse, to German minds, Rosebery's suggestion to Kálnoky in March 1894 that Germany should undertake to hold France in check in the event of a conflict with Russia over Constantinople, was no more than a manoeuvre to embroil the Triple Alliance powers in a general conflagration while Great Britain retired as *tertius gaudens* behind the security of her island defences. In this atmosphere it was not surprising that the Germans sharply rejected Kálnoky's request for guarantees: the central powers must not commit themselves to Great Britain unless the latter had actually gone to war. Whether the German decision in fact represented a turning point in the European states system and a great chance had been missed to bind Great Britain to the central powers once and for all, it was, in the context of German distrust of the British – in which a paranoid streak certainly cannot be denied – at least explicable.

Less defensible, but a good indication of the lengths to which the Germans were prepared to go in neutralizing the new threat to their geopolitical position by improving their relations with both their potential enemies, was their clumsy attempt to exploit the Congo Treaty affair of May 1894. It is true that when the British concluded this treaty with King Leopold of the Belgians, providing for exchanges of strips of territory in order to bar French access to the upper Nile valley and to create a continuous strip of British-controlled territory from the Cape to Cairo, the Germans had – in theory at least – some grounds for complaint, as the treaty also interposed a wedge of British-controlled territory between German East Africa and the Congo. The German reaction, however – to join with France in a protest that resulted in the humiliating cancellation of the treaty – betrayed a harsh insensitivity towards British susceptibilities that drove Vienna and Rome to despair and provoked a lasting rift between Berlin and Lord Rosebery, the most pro-German prime minister the British were ever to have. (Nor was the fact that the British parliamentary under-secretary at the time was a young and impressionable Sir Edward Grey to be without its baleful consequences for Anglo-German relations.) It is true that the new policy-makers in Berlin, like Caprivi, and unlike Bismarck, were making extra-European policy with an eye to European alignments (albeit in this case – unlike Caprivi – with an eye to conciliating France, not Great Britain). Their policy was, nevertheless, disastrous by any standard: its impact on French attitudes to Germany was minimal, whereas it provoked Rosebery to warn the Austrian ambassador straight out that 'if Germany continues to show herself so hostile to the Cabinet of St James's, I shall feel obliged to take back the assurances I have given about Constantinople.'

These words made an impact in Vienna and Rome, but not in Berlin, the keystone of the Triple Alliance. There, the decision had been taken that a new policy was required. The conclusion of the Franco-Russian alliance had marked the end of the era in which the European states system was dominated by German-led conservative blocs – whether those of the First and Second Bismarckian alliance systems or that of the *Neue Kurs*. In the face of new and unpleasant realities the Germans decided that it would be unwise to continue to drive France and Russia together by opposing them at every turn, let alone by associating too closely with an unreliable Great Britain that might seek to use Germany as a catspaw. The conservative blocs that had dominated the European states system for the past fifteen years were now either unrealistic or positively dangerous. At the same time, however, hostility between the world empires of Great Britain on the one hand and France and Russia on the other was regarded as eternal and axiomatic by decision-makers in the Wilhelmstrasse. This being the case, they decided to seek salvation in a policy of manoeuvring between the great world empires, exploiting their differences for Germany's advantage but without committing themselves irrevocably to either side: the policy of the *Freie Hand*.

CHAPTER 8

Unstable equilibrium, 1895–1911

If in the era of the *Neue Kurs* the division of the European powers into two broad groupings, with the 'conservative' Triple Alliance supported by Great Britain enjoying a preponderance over the 'revisionist' Franco-Russian partnership, had given a certain stability to the European states system, the shift in the mid-1890s to a more complex, tripartite grouping of the powers proved equally compatible with the maintenance of peace. On the one hand, most powers were becoming increasingly preoccupied with extra-European developments that were of less than vital importance to their status as great powers, and this helped to divert tensions away from the centre to the periphery of the international scene. On the other, the risk of a confrontation between the two continental blocs was diminished when the Germans moved over to the policy of the *Freie Hand*, in a determined effort to restore good relations with St Petersburg while distancing themselves from the British. The resultant 'unstable equilibrium', with Germany adopting an intermediate, balancing, position between the British Empire and the Franco-Russian bloc, lent a degree of flexibility to the states system that served to reduce the risk of polarization and conflict in these years.

This is not to say that all friction ceased, or that the dividing lines between the powers were eliminated. Rivalry between Great Britain and France in Africa, and the 'Great Game' in which Great Britain and Russia vied for influence in a broad swathe of territories from Persia to the Far East continued unabated. In some respects, Germany's tactics of evading any clear commitment to either bloc while seeking to extract concessions and favours from both, only earned her general ill will and had a damaging effect on the tone of international relations, most notably those between Germany and Great Britain. Even so, Germany's *Freie Hand* policy led to a marked lessening of tension between Germany and the Franco-Russian bloc in Europe, which was paralleled by a Franco-Italian *détente* and, even more important, an Austro-Russian entente to stabilize the situation in the most dangerously volatile part of Europe, the Near East. All these arrangements, cutting across the formal alliance system, helped to blur the dividing lines between the great powers. In any case, the alliance system had never been designed to manage extra-European affairs: it left Germany, for example, perfectly free to associate with other powers outside Europe. Indeed, as far as day-to-day diplomacy was concerned, the alliance system began to seem something of an irrelevance.

These trends were reflected in the field of armaments. As the armed confrontations of the later 1880s and the *Neue Kurs* years dissolved, and as the focus of activity moved away from Europe in the later 1890s, the continental powers began to devote more resources to naval development at the expense of armies. Admittedly, this brought little relief to the British; but the land forces of the continental powers, after steadily rising between 1887 and 1893, now settled down; and expenditure on the Italian army was actually reduced in the years following its humiliating defeat at Adowa. Domestic factors contributed to this tendency: the reluctance of the Hungarian parliament to spend money on the central institutions of the Dual Monarchy meant that until 1912 recruitment to the Common Army was frozen at its 1888 level; and the French army, after the Dreyfus affair and the Republican counter-attack, languished in a weakened and demoralized state until the First Moroccan crisis rekindled nationalist feelings. Of course, the expenditure on armaments was felt by all the powers as a burden, and in 1899 the impecunious Russian government summoned the Hague Peace Conference to discuss their reduction. Yet although this elicited little more than pieties, the general trend between 1895 and 1905 was, as David Stevenson has shown, one of stagnation; and this made its own contribution to the relief of tension within the European states system in this decade.

The extra-European world and the European equilibrium, 1895–1902

It was a sign of the growing impact of extra-European developments on the European states system that the catalyst for the dissolution of the dualistic grouping of the *Neue Kurs* years, in which the Triple Alliance powers broadly supported by Great Britain had confronted a

Franco-Russian combination, was provided by a non-European power: Japan. Admittedly, Japan's activity was in part a response to the increased interest shown in the Far East by Russia, who had embarked in 1891 on the construction of the Trans-Siberian Railway and planned to link Vladivostok with the rest of the Empire by a branch line cutting across the Chinese dependency of Manchuria. Fears soon arose in Tokyo that Russia would not be content with this, and might attempt to secure for herself a warm-water port too, say in Korea, another dependency of the Celestial Empire and traditionally an object of interest to expansionists in Japan. Indeed, it was partly to anticipate this that in May 1894 Japan took advantage of disturbances in Korea to invade the kingdom; and this provoked a war with the suzerain power that ended with the Treaty of Shimonoseki of April 1895, which obliged the defeated Chinese to give Japan a large indemnity, political control of Korea and a lease on Port Arthur, potentially an important naval base.

Japan's spectacular success was to have a profound impact on the relations between the powers in the European states system. In St Petersburg, for example, it led to a marked shift in Russian foreign policy priorities towards East Asia. Russia's preoccupation with her interests as a world power in the Far East – an area in which no other European power, at least, had interests at stake that were worth a war – acted as a safety valve in the European states system. Confrontations over the Near East, which involved the vital interests of a great power – Austria-Hungary – that had no other outlet available to assert its standing as a great power, were always infinitely more dangerous. Not that Russia abandoned her interests in south-east Europe: throughout these years she made no troop reductions in the west; and she even managed to recover a measure of influence in Serbia in 1895 – when the erratic King Alexander Obrenovic allowed the Austrian alliance to expire – and in Bulgaria in 1896, when Prince Ferdinand dismissed his Austrophile ministers as the only means of securing recognition from Russia and Turkey. Even so, in the Near East the Russians were now above all concerned that nothing should happen to precipitate the actual collapse of the Ottoman Empire at a time when Russia, with her Far Eastern preoccupations, would be unable to assert her interests in the great reordering of south-east Europe that would then become inevitable. When the Austrians eventually recognized this, in 1897, the way was open for an entente between Vienna and St Petersburg that put Balkan affairs 'on ice' and did more to stabilize the European states system itself than any other bilateral agreement of the era.

The diversion of Russia's attention to the Far East suited the Germans on several counts. In the first place, it reduced the likelihood of an Austro-Russian clash over the Near East, which was as unappealing to the exponents of the *Freie Hand* as it had been to Bismarck. It also offered Germany an opportunity to compete with France for Russia's friendship by supporting her in an area sufficiently remote to give no offence at Vienna. May 1895, therefore, saw the appearance of the 'Far Eastern Triplice', when the Germans joined with Russia and France to compel Japan to disgorge many of her recent gains, notably Port Arthur. By the turn of the year, the Germans seemed to be leaning distinctly towards the Franco-Russian bloc. The rebuke they delivered to imperialists in London in the form of the Kruger telegram of 3 January 1896 was coupled with a hint to Paris about the desirability of a continental league. This fell on stony ground: the French would never join any combination that implied their final acceptance of the Treaty of Frankfort; and they hastened to betray the German proposal to London, with results that could be imagined. But if the Germans had temporarily estranged the British, their improved relations with St Petersburg seemed at least to have weakened the grip of the Franco-Russian vice that had threatened them in the era of the *Neue Kurs*.

Not that the vice was broken. The French, confronted with German competition for Russia's goodwill, redoubled their efforts to oblige their allies. French finance was put at the disposal of Russia in the contest to supply loans to China; and for a Franco-Russian consortium to take over the Chinese Imperial Railway. Indeed, the two powers were soon embarked on ambitious railway building schemes of their own, the Russians operating from Manchuria, the French from Indo-China, with the ultimate objective of squeezing out the other powers altogether. The upshot was, however, in terms of day-to-day diplomacy in the Far East, that Great Britain and Germany, both advanced industrial powers with an interest in upholding the Open Door, drew together. Whatever the objectives of the German foreign office might have been in terms of great power alignments in Europe, the two powers found themselves on the same side in resisting the monopolistic pretensions of France and Russia. Just as Bismarck, after the Congo affair of 1884, had found himself aligned at the Berlin Conference with Great Britain, against his intended entente partner, France, so now the Far Eastern Triplice failed to hold together once Japan had retreated. As a result, by the end of the 1890s the parallelogram of economic and political forces in German foreign policy had obliged Berlin to adopt an intermediate position between the British and their Franco-Russian opponents.

Such a position reflected, moreover, the calculations that inspired the German government after its conversion in 1897 to the doctrines of *Weltpolitik*. The adoption of *Weltpolitik* was a deliberate act of policy by the Kaiser and his advisers, notably Bülow at the foreign office and Tirpitz at the navy ministry. It reflected their disillusionment with the policy of the *Neue Kurs*, which had only conjured up abroad the very Franco-Russian combination it had been designed to counteract, while in attempting to reconcile the Left and Centre at home it had failed to check the growth of Social Democracy while it had alienated and weakened the natural supporters of the monarchy on the agrarian and industrial Right. By 1897 the Kaiser was set on a new 'rallying' (*Sammlung*) of the propertied classes behind the government and on winning over the masses in pursuit of a popular national objective: *Weltpolitik*. Germany was to be transformed from a European into a world power, on a par with Great Britain, Russia and the United States. Certainly, the new policy found a ready echo in intellectual circles and amongst vociferous pressure groups such as the Pan-German League, who chafed under the limitations imposed by Bismarck on German power – as Max Weber declared in 1895: 'We must appreciate that the unification of Germany was a youthful prank played by the nation in its old age, which would have been . . . better not attempted if it was to be the conclusion, and not the starting point of a policy of German world power.' 'I am putting the emphasis on foreign policy', Bülow proclaimed in December 1897, when he launched German *Weltpolitik* with the seizure of Kiao-Chow that started the 'scramble' for China: 'only a successful foreign policy can help to reconcile, pacify, unite.'

In terms of the unity of the powers, of course, and even of material gains for Germany, *Weltpolitik* was hardly a success. Indeed, the gains acquired by Germany in the whole period of *Weltpolitik* – the Caroline Islands and Samoa – were pathetically small. Neither Bülow nor his successors ever had any clear view of specific territorial objectives. The policy was essentially one of boosting the government's prestige at home by successfully asserting Germany's right to an equal voice in all matters of world politics, however trivial the question at issue might be. The effect on the international scene of this 'aimless' or *objektlose*, imperialism, and particularly of the aggressively bombastic style adopted by the German Emperor and his advisers in pursuit of it, was to be a decidedly disturbing one. Not that it threatened to bring the European states system crashing down in a general war: that danger only appeared on those occasions after 1905 when Germany's policy in Europe seemed to threaten the independent existence of other great powers. Indeed, it must be admitted that, in terms of the alignments of the European powers the Germans were scrupulously careful to avoid committing themselves to either the Franco-Russian or the British camp (which they assumed – a fateful miscalculation – to be irreconcilable). It seemed to make good sense, therefore, that they should manoeuvre between the two camps, using smiles and, more often, frowns to extract concessions from both sides – even if this meant, in A.J.P. Taylor's words, that Germany seemed at times to assume the undignified position of a tic-tac man. As far as the other powers were concerned, however, the bullying tactics and refusals of commitment that characterized *Weltpolitik* were ultimately to make Germany an object of universal irritation and suspicion – Lord Salisbury, for example, absolutely refused to contemplate an alliance with a power ruled by one so volatile as William II; and they were to contribute in turn to those almost paranoid feelings of isolation in Berlin that were to pose such threats to the stability of the European states system after the turn of the century.

More immediately, the effect of Germany's venture into *Weltpolitik* was simply to confirm the tripartite grouping of the European powers. When in March 1898 Russia responded to the seizure of Kiao-Chow by securing a lease of Port Arthur, this only intensified Anglo-Russian antagonism. The British, who had originally welcomed the diversion of Russia's attention to the Far East, now began to fear that St Petersburg was set on demarcating an actual sphere of influence in China to the exclusion of British trade. Moreover, their efforts to ward off the danger by diplomacy merely revealed their painful isolation from all the other powers. An attempt to reach agreement with Russia direct by recognizing her special interests while maintaining the open door came to nothing: having reached an agreement with the Austrians to put the Near East on ice, the Russians had no room for an agreement with Great Britain limiting their freedom of action in the Far East. Soundings of the United States and Japan were no more productive: the Americans were in an isolationist mood and about to embark on war with Spain; the Japanese had just concluded the Nishi-Rosen agreement recognizing Russia's position at Port Arthur in return for recognition of Japanese economic interests in Korea. In the end, the British could only attempt to counteract Russia's gains on straight balance of power lines. They were assisted by the willingness of the Chinese, sensing the usefulness to a weak power of the principle of 'safety in numbers', to adopt the tactics long practised by the Ottoman Empire of involving many powers to escape the domination of one: in April the French were granted a lease of Kow-Loon, and by July the British acceptance of an earlier Chinese offer of a lease on Wei-hei-wei did something to reduce the strategic value of Port Arthur. Not that any of this disturbed the alignments of the powers in Europe: it confirmed them. For example, the British colonial secretary, Joseph Chamberlain, who had concluded that Great Britain's isolation was not at all splendid, sounded the alarm about Russian activity in China in his 'long spoon' speech of 13 May, and advocated an alliance with Germany to counteract it. In Berlin, the idea was turned down flat: Bülow's map of Asia lay very definitely in Europe, and whatever peripheral benefits *Weltpolitik* might bring, there could never be any question of jeopardizing the security of east Prussia by involving Germany in a quarrel with Russia over east Asia.

In the event, the interests of the powers in the Far East proved perfectly capable of accommodation and fears of an actual partition of China subsided. On the occasion of the Boxer Rising of 1900, as many as ten powers, displaying (except for Japan) that same sense of Christian solidarity that they had formerly displayed towards the Armenian massacres in Constantinople and the Greco-Ottoman war, joined forces in an international expedition under the Kaiser's friend, General Waldersee, to inflict condign punishment on the violators of the legations in Peking. Even Great Britain and Russia had reached agreement, in April 1899, the Russians recognizing Great Britain's special interests in the Yangtse valley, the British Russia's special interests – but no exclusive sphere of influence – in Manchuria, where, for example, British ownership of the North China Railway was safeguarded. A framework for co-existence had been established within which the scramble for loans and concessions could continue, British and German financiers generally co-operating against French and Russian.

Some younger members of the British Cabinet – notably Chamberlain and Balfour – were not satisfied with Great Britain's somewhat ambiguous position between the powers, and hoped to develop Anglo-German co-operation to the point of a diplomatic revolution, in which Great Britain would abandon isolation for a German alliance. They were willing to make colonial concessions to Germany to secure it, and when Salisbury demurred, Chamberlain merely retorted that 'blackmail is sometimes worth paying'. His chance seemed to come with the outbreak of the Boer War in October 1899. Whereas the continental press (apart from in Italy and Hungary where memories of 1849 lived on) was quite rabid in its denunciations of the British, the German government was studiously correct. Berlin had in fact abandoned the Boers in an agreement, concluded with Balfour in August 1898, conceding to the British control of the Boers' only link with the outside world through Portuguese Mozambique and extracting in return British recognition of a eventual German reversionary right to a share of the Portuguese colonial empire. It was in accordance with this – and with the principles of the *Freie Hand* that forbade Germany to join either world power bloc – that Berlin rejected a Franco-Russian proposal for a continental league to restrain the British in South Africa. By the same token, however, in November 1899 Bülow also rejected – resorting, foolishly, to the extremely wounding device of a speech to the fiercely Anglophobe Reichstag – a public appeal from Chamberlain, for German participation in an alliance of Anglo-Saxon powers. More limited agreements could still be made, however: by the 'Yangtse Agreement' of October 1900, for example, the British and Germans recognized their common interest in safeguarding the Open Door in the Celestial Empire against any exclusive pretensions of third parties. Significantly enough, however, this agreement contained no commitment to oppose Russian activities in China's Manchurian dependency: the Germans were still not minded to commit themselves irrevocably to either of the contending world power blocs.

As far as the alignments of the European powers were concerned, the most intractable conflicts of interests were still those between the British Empire and the Franco-Russian alliance. It was partly rumours of the approach of French expeditions, from West Africa, and, encouraged by the Russians, from Abyssinia, towards the headwaters of the Nile – their objective being to establish a belt of French territory across Africa from the Atlantic to the Red Sea – that determined the British (with the bless-ing, in turn, of the Triple Alliance powers) to undertake the reconquest of the Sudan from the Mahdist forces that had held sway there for the past twelve years. No sooner had Kitchener achieved his crushing victory at Omdurman in September 1898 than he was obliged to move south to demand the withdrawal of a token French force that had just established itself at Fashoda. Not that there was ever any question of war over the issue: however much the French press might rage, no one in the govern-ment, the chamber, or even the *Parti Colonial* seriously thought of challenging the British, with their overwhelming military superiority on the spot and with their imposing naval presence in the Mediterranean. (British naval estimates were to increase from £19 million in 1895 to £31 million by 1900.) The new French foreign minister, Théophile Delcassé was realist enough to abandon hope of ever dislodging the British from Egypt, and to accept the newly proclaimed Anglo-Egyptian condominium in the Sudan. The British for their part were as willing to accept a *modus vivendi* with the French in North Africa as they had just accepted one with Russia in the Far East: in April 1899 the French accepted British control of the Nile valley in return for what Salisbury rather gallingly described as 'light soils' in north-west Africa. But for Delcassé, this did not amount to anything like the *entente cordiale* that was later to be associated with his name. On the contrary, he continued to regard both Great Britain and Germany as the inveterate enemies of France. He made no attempt to initiate them into the plans which he was now considering for establishing French control of Morocco, and confined his diplomatic soundings to Italy and Spain.

An even more striking illustration of Delcassé's attitude was the remodelling of the Franco-Russian alliance in 1899–1900. This was partly motivated by the revival of nationalist conflicts in the Habsburg monarchy and French distrust of Germany's intentions in the event of its dissolution (which would, of course, also entail the dissolution of the Triple Alliance). In its revised form of 1899, therefore, the duration of the Franco-Russian Alliance was no longer linked to that of the Triple Alliance; and its purpose was extended to cover the maintenance of the balance of power in Europe (which would obviously be endangered if Germany expanded to absorb the territories of her ally). In 1900 supplementary military agreements were added: in the event of an Anglo-Russian war France would move 100,000 men to the Channel coast; while in the event of an Anglo-French war, Russia would move troops to the Indian frontier (and would in the meantime, aided by French finance, speed up the building of the Orenburg-Tashkent railway). Clearly, in Russian and French eyes, Great Britain was no less an opponent than Germany.

The Austro-Russian Entente

The increasing flexibility within the European states system in the late 1890s – and the correspondingly diminished risk of a general war – owed much to the development of the Eastern Question, which since the later 1880s had divided the powers into two embattled camps. The gradual disintegration of the conservative bloc of the Mediterranean Entente powers backed by Germany, that had done so much to ensure stability in the years of the *Neue Kurs*, was both a cause and a consequence of the Austro-Russian Entente of 1897; and it proceeded hand in hand with the loosening of Great Britain's ties with the Triple Alliance generally. Yet as far as the stability of the states system itself was concerned, if it might be undermined by the weakening of the deterrent power of a conservative bloc, this might be more than made good if the two powers whose conflicting interests in the Near East were most likely to precipitate a general catastrophe could devise a means of containing, or even reconciling, those interests. The fact that the Austrians and Russians managed to achieve this for over ten years constitutes their major contribution to the stability of the European states system in the decade around the turn of the century.

At first, when Count Agenor Goluchowski succeeded Kálnoky at the Ballhausplatz in May 1895, it seemed that the conservative combination of the *Neue Kurs* years was set to continue, albeit, with Germany's retreat into the policy of the *Freie Hand*, in a somewhat truncated form. From late 1894 the Ottoman Empire had appeared to many to be in terminal crisis, shaken by a series of massacres provoked by Armenian nationalists in an attempt to secure the intervention of the powers. The latter were certainly less willing to contemplate a Near Eastern upheaval than they had been in the 1870s, and the Tsar, in particular, had troublesome Armenian subjects of his own; but by the end of 1895 even Salisbury was speaking of the partition of the Empire as a distinct possibility. This prospect Goluchowski regarded with deep apprehension. It was his firm conviction that if the Ottoman Empire should ever disappear, the interests of Russia and Austria-Hungary would prove irreconcilable: whereas Austria-Hungary had no desire herself to absorb the Slavs of the western Balkans, her security would be threatened if Russia gained control of them; and if Russia ever established herself at Constantinople she would exercise such influence over the Orthodox Slavs of Austria and Hungary that the Habsburg Monarchy would become ungovernable. He decided, after the Tsar's visit to Vienna in August 1896, that there was simply no point in trying to discuss such unbridgeable differences with the Russians; and that the Monarchy could only cling to the Mediterranean Agreements. The Germans, of course, set on restoring their wire to St Petersburg, took a different view, and told Goluchowski straight out that as far as they were concerned, Russia could have Constantinople. William II disapproved strongly of Austrian attempts to work with Salisbury to moderate the Sultan's treatment of the Armenians: 'Goluchowski ought to go to school again.'

However, the real obstacle to Goluchowski's hopes of reactivating the Mediterranean Agreements lay, not in Berlin, but in London. Salisbury was becoming increasingly disillusioned with the Turks, as his attempts to help the Armenians made no headway – thanks, in fact, to the obstructiveness of his pretended French and Russian collaborators. When in February 1896 and again in February 1897, Goluchowski pressed him to declare his hand and revise the consultative Mediterranean Agreements of 1887 to include a definite commitment to fight for Constantinople, Salisbury demurred. In 1896, while he was still hopeful of persuading the country to fight, he refused to give any pledge that he could not be sure of honouring: the decision would have to rest with parliament when the occasion arose. By 1897 he regretfully confessed his doubts as to the willingness of the British public to fight for the bloodstained Sultan. Goluchowski was disappointed; but as he was still convinced of the incompatibility of Russian and Austro-Hungarian interests, he decided that there was nothing for it but to cling to the Mediterranean Agreements in their existing form and hope that the public would never get wind of Salisbury's latest reservations.

Goluchowski's decision to abandon the Mediterranean Agreements for an entente with Russia has been criticized: after all, as J.A.S. Grenville has observed, the Mediterranean Agreements, even in their consultative form, offered Austria-Hungary a greater measure of active diplomatic support than the British were to offer France in 1904 or Russia in 1907. On the other hand, it should be noted that Goluchowski's decision was taken, not in response to Salisbury's theoretical speculations in February 1897, but in response to British actions in the Near East in the succeeding months. In short, it was simply that the situation of 1873 and of 1881 recurred: despairing of support from London and Berlin, the Austrians found themselves forced to consider the possibility of an accommodation with St Petersburg.

The catalytic event was the outbreak of war between Greece and Turkey in April 1897. As this was provoked by Greek interference in a rebellion that had been raging in Crete since 1896 and a Greek invasion of Macedonia, most of the powers had scant sympathy for Athens – all the more so as if Greek aggression were seen to be rewarded this would be likely to precipitate an avalanche of compensatory claims from the other Balkan states and the powers might find themselves confronted with the awful task of disposing of the Ottoman Empire in Europe. The British, however, took a markedly less condemnatory line and Salisbury, in response to strong pro-Greek feeling at court, in the Cabinet and in the country at large, even tried to mobilize France and Russia as co-protecting powers to lend Greece diplomatic assistance when she was soundly defeated and in turn invaded by the Turks. Helped by the fact of Turkish victory the powers managed, by and large, to uphold the *status quo*, although their sense of Christian solidarity was sufficiently strong to uphold the principle that Christian territory once freed from Ottoman rule should never be returned; and the Greek aggressors escaped with no significant losses. Even so, Goluchowski had been deeply dismayed by the behaviour of the British, who he now decided could no longer be counted on to uphold the *status quo*. He had been equally pleasantly surprised, however, by the scrupulously correct attitude of the Russians, who had rebuffed Salisbury's feelers and who seemed determined – whether on account of their Far Eastern preoccupations or from a genuine desire to co-operate – to uphold the *status quo*. Equally important, the Turkish victory had transformed the situation in the Near East: the Ottoman Empire was clearly not on the verge of extinction; and if Goluchowski had despaired of reconciling Austro-Hungarian and Russian interests in the event of the Empire's disappearance, an agreement to uphold a *status quo* that was, after all, broadly acceptable to both powers, might indeed be worth pursuing.

On the occasion of Franz Joseph's visit to St Petersburg in May 1897 agreement was in fact reached, and subsequently recorded in an exchange of notes, on four broad principles: the maintenance of the *status quo* in the Near East for as long as possible; strict observance of the principle of non-interference in the internal development of the Balkan states; co-operation between the representatives of the two powers in the Balkans (to impress on the Balkan states that they could no longer hope to play off the two powers against each other); finally, if the maintenance of the *status quo* should prove impossible the two powers, while expressly renouncing all designs of expansion for themselves, would come to a direct agreement as to the future territorial settlement of the Balkans – and would, moreover, impose this agreement on the other powers. Admittedly the new entente was initially not much more than a general agreement in principle, resembling the Three Emperors' League of 1873 rather than the more specific Alliance of 1881. Indeed, on some specific points differences persisted: whereas it was agreed that the future of Constantinople and the Straits could only be decided by Europe as a whole, St Petersburg argued that the same applied to an eventual annexation of Bosnia, which Vienna insisted was a matter for Austria-Hungary alone to decide upon. Nor was much achieved – apart from from an agreement envisaging an independent Albanian state – towards defining the future map of the Balkans. The question of possible changes to the *status quo* was always a delicate one, liable to focus attention on the differences between the entente partners; indeed, their attempt to resolve it was eventually to destroy the entente in 1908. It is also true that from the start the entente did nothing to prevent the creeping advance of Russian influence, and a concomitant diminution of Austrian influence in the capitals of the Slav Balkan states. Indeed, the

Austrians made considerable sacrifices for the sake of the entente, most notably when they refrained from intervention in Serbia to prevent the establishment of a nationalist regime after the overthrow of the Obrenovic dynasty in 1903. On the other hand, the entente had done much to banish the nightmares of an uncontrollable upheaval on the Monarchy's southern borders or a determined Russian bid to dominate the Balkans. So long as the two powers concentrated their efforts on the maintenance of the *status quo*, the entente served the interests of both: the Russians with their Far Eastern preoccupations, and the Austrians, faced with deepening national conflicts that were soon to paralyse the parliament in Vienna.

The entente also contributed to the stability of the European states system as a whole, in that the two powers whose vital interests were most dangerously in conflict had abandoned confrontation for a policy of *détente* that was soon to develop into positive co-operation. At the same time, however, certain traditional safeguards against a Russian advance had been abandoned. Austro-Russian 'dual control' of the Eastern Question as enunciated in the fourth article of the entente effectively spelt the end of Austria-Hungary's ties with Great Britain and Italy through the Mediterranean Agreements. At the end of 1902, for example, the British decided that the passage of Russian destroyers into the Black Sea constituted a violation of the rule of the Straits. Lansdowne sought to enlist Austrian support for a protest at Constantinople, and even offered to revive the Mediterranean Agreements; but for the sake of the entente with Russia, Goluchowski refused to co-operate. The Committee of Imperial Defence in London decided that in these circumstances, and so long as Great Britain held Egypt, keeping the Russians out of Constantinople was no longer of vital importance. Henceforth, the chances of the Austrians' reactivating the link with London should the Russian threat ever revive, were slim. The implications of the entente for the Austro-Italian partnership in the Near East were even more sinister. True, the Austrians and Italians soon reached an agreement (belatedly formalized in 1900) on the desirability, in the event of the collapse of the Ottoman Empire, of creating an independent Albanian state on the Adriatic – if only because neither could contemplate the prospect of the other's establishing control of the area. But the fact that Goluchowski only informed the Italians of the entente in the vaguest terms sat oddly with his obligations under Article VII of the Triple Alliance; and Vienna's steady refusal to admit Rome as a third party to the entente with St Petersburg soon bred a festering resentment in Italy that boded ill for the future of Austro-Italian relations.

Certainly, it posed a more serious threat to the effectiveness of the Triple Alliance within the states system than Italy's efforts to secure her own interests outside the framework of the Alliance. The humiliating defeat of Italy by the Abyssinians at Adowa in 1896 not only precipitated the fall of Crispi, but led to a great revulsion of feeling against his whole policy of imperialist adventures in East Africa. His successors shared the general opinion that he had taken hostility to France too far, and had made Italy unhealthily dependent on Triple Alliance partners who were in any case both unable and unwilling to assist her expansion overseas. (As Bülow had never tired of reminding Rome, the Triple Alliance was an insurance company, not a joint stock enterprise.) Consequently, they embarked on a search for accommodation with France, starting with the tacit recognition of the French position in Tunis in 1898, in return for which Italy was granted a commercial treaty that put an end to the damaging tariff war. It must be emphasized that – whatever accusations of Italian disloyalty were later to be bandied about – the *détente* was heartily welcomed by both Italy's allies, neither of whom had the slightest desire to be dragged into Franco-Italian conflicts that did not concern them.

The same could be said of the agreement concluded between Visconti Venosta and the French ambassador Barrère in 1900, which reconciled Franco-Italian interests in North Africa and offered the Italians the prospect of a colonial future in a less perilous area than Abyssinia. By this agreement Italy recognized France's right to 'maintain order' not only in the areas of Morocco bordering on Algeria, but in the whole Sultanate; France declared her disinterest in the Ottoman province of Tripoli and recognized Italy's right to take action there 'in her own interests', if – an important proviso – France should ever decide to 'modify the *status quo*' in Morocco. Again, there was nothing in this agreement that conflicted with Italy's obligations under the Triple Alliance. Indeed, insofar as that Alliance had hitherto been directed against France in Africa, that was a feature that had been introduced by Italy in the first place, and its removal only accorded with the peaceful purposes of the Alliance, as Vienna readily recognized. Despite its proviso linking Italian action to a French action in Morocco, the agreement gave the Italians all they needed for the moment: they still had to extract similar assurances from the other powers (obtained from Germany in 1891, from Great Britain and Austria-Hungary in 1902, but not from Russia until 1909); and they were not in fact ready to move against Tripoli for over ten years.

It was an egregious blunder, therefore, on the part of Visconti Venosta's successor Prinetti (a former bicycle manufacturer unversed in diplomacy) when, simply for the sake of removing the proviso regarding prior French action in Morocco, he concluded with Barrère the famous agreement of 30 July 1902 relating to Italy's alliance obligations. It is true that, in a strictly technical sense, there was no contradiction between the Prinetti-Barrère agreement and the Triple Alliance. The latter obliged Italy to assist Germany in the event of an unprovoked French attack, and pledged her to benevolent neutrality if France should provoke Germany to go to war. Under the Prinetti-Barrère agreement Italy promised France strict neutrality in the event of an unprovoked German attack, or if Germany should provoke France to go to war – eventualities not mentioned in the Triple Alliance. In practice, of course, the problem would be one of defining 'provocation' – which Prinetti told the French would cover such cases as the Ems telegram or Fashoda. Perhaps even more ominous was the fact that the Italians failed to inform their allies of the contents of the agreement – although in the context of Bismarck's Reinsurance Treaty and the Austro-Russian entente it could be said that such behaviour was only normal within the Triple Alliance. In fact, Italy's relations with Germany continued cordial. Bülow – who might have done well to reflect that he was himself married to an Italian lady who had deserted her husband for him during his youthful years at the Rome embassy – nonchalantly told the Reichstag that 'in any healthy marriage the husband has no objection if his wife has an occasional waltz with another'. The Austro-Italian marriage was decidedly less healthy. Matters were not helped by Austrophobe inclinations of King Victor Emmanuel III (who had succeeded to the throne on the assassination of the conservative King Umberto in 1900) and his Montenegrin wife, and of the anti-clerical and pro-irredentist Zanardelli-Prinetti ministry. Moreover, the end of Franco-Italian hostility, however desirable in itself, had the unfortunate consequence of focusing Italian attention on Article VII and the 'Near Eastern' aspects of the Alliance. Here, Goluchowski's determination to exclude Italy from a voice in Balkan affairs and the Italian public's obsession with the *altera sponda*, so long and so ill-advisedly fostered by official propaganda, threatened seriously to undermine the Alliance as an effective power combination.

Even the centrality of the Austro-German Alliance in the European states system decreased as a result of Germany's adoption of the *Freie Hand* and Austria-Hungary's opting for the Russian entente. On the one hand, German support for Austria-Hungary in the Near East became both unobtainable and unnecessary; on the other, the Austro-Russian entente itself was faintly resented in Berlin, as an Austrian attempt to manage the Eastern Question without even consulting Germany. After all, one important aspect of *Weltpolitik* was the development of German economic interests in Asia Minor, as proclaimed by the Kaiser's proffering the hand of German friendship to 3,000,000 Muslims during his visit to the Holy Land in 1898, and the securing of a contract to build a railway in Asia Minor – the 'Berlin to Baghdad' railway project – in 1899. Henceforth, German policy at Constantinople became one of actively cultivating the Sultan and his camarilla; and when, after the turn of the century the joint activity of Vienna and St Petersburg took on a distinctly anti-Turkish edge, as they sought to assuage the grievances of the Balkan Christians over Ottoman misrule in Macedonia, this was anything but welcome to Berlin. Meanwhile, if Austria-Hungary's quietist policy reflected a deepening domestic crisis – the Czech-German dispute over language laws, accompanied by loud, and not entirely unsuccessful, appeals to Berlin from Pan-German and anti-Catholic movements in the Monarchy – the conflict introduced further elements of irritation and suspicion into Austro-German relations.

When in 1903 the Czech deputy Kramarz described the Triple Alliance as 'a worn-out piano' this merely reflected the fact that the focus of international affairs had moved away from the conflicts that had made the Alliance so central to the states system a decade before. This was in turn reflected in the slackening in the pace of land armaments in all three Triple Alliance countries in these years. If the Austro-Hungarian army stagnated as the Hungarian parliament stubbornly refused (and was to refuse until 1912) to sanction any increase in the size of the Common Army beyond the level fixed in 1888, in Italy the revulsion of feeling against militarism that followed the disaster of Adowa actually saw a reduction in the defence estimates; and in Germany spending on the army slowed down as the focus shifted to *Weltpolitik* and the demands of the navy. These developments all contributed to the relative quiescence of the European states system at the turn of the century.

The end of Anglo-German collaboration

If a chance offered in the spring of 1901 that the tripartite division of the powers in Europe might yet resolve itself into a dual balance, it soon disappeared. Russian troops had remained in occupation of the Chinese dependency of Manchuria ever since the international intervention against the Boxer Rising; and by March 1901 rumours were circulating of an agreement between the Russian commander, Admiral Alexeieff, and the Chinese authorities that seemed to portend the permanent and exclusive control of Manchuria by Russia. At this the Japanese took alarm, and asked both the Germans and the British whether, if Japan went to war with Russia, she could count on their 'benevolent neutrality' to keep France neutral. Lansdowne, although he doubted whether the Anglo-German 'Yangtse Agreement' of 1901 could be stretched to apply to Manchuria, which was not part of China proper, thereupon approached Berlin. He was informed that any German neutrality would be 'strict and correct'; and Bülow followed this up with a speech to the Reichstag on 15 March proclaiming to the world that the fate of Manchuria was 'a matter of complete indifference to Germany'. After this, the crisis faded away, as rumours of the 'Alexeieff-Tseng' agreement proved to be exaggerated, and the Russians withdrew from Manchuria in 1902. It was clear, however – as it had been, in fact, ever since Germany had embarked on the policy of the *Freie Hand* – that Great Britain could not count on Germany for assistance against France and Russia in the Far East; and despite Lansdowne's readiness to admit the technical correctness of the German case, this unpalatable truth left a residue of resentment against Germany in high circles in London.

The Manchurian affair came in the middle of another – the final – round of Anglo-German alliance negotiations. These were essentially the brainchild of Baron Hermann von Eckardstein, a well-connected Counsellor in the German Embassy in London, whose strategy for bringing the two sides together was to put the idea around in London that his government was genuinely anxious for a British alliance, while he assured his superiors in Berlin that it was the British who were seeking an alliance. This was bound to be a recipe for disaster. Nevertheless, and despite the Manchurian affair, Eckardstein and Lansdowne got as far as drafting a treaty by which Great Britain would actually join the Triple Alliance. When the idea was exposed to the light of day, however, it perished. In a devastating memorandum of 29 May 1901 Lord Salisbury argued that Great Britain's success at Fashoda, and the failure of the continental powers to unite against her in the Boer War, showed that there was no need to beg for foreign support; while the price – a commitment to fight for Austria-Hungary and Italy – far outweighed any assistance that Germany could give Great Britain in her worldwide conflicts with France and Russia. The prime minister's memorandum finally killed the project in London. Lansdowne was still willing to offer the Germans a limited entente – for co-operation in the Mediterranean or the Persian Gulf (which was more than he offered the French in 1904). But the idea of ruining for ever their relations with Russia and France for anything less than a British commitment to fight in a continental war was in turn unacceptable to the Germans, who insisted that it must be 'all or nothing'. The negotiations faded away and, with the steady deterioration of Anglo-German relations after 1902, they were never revived.

The Germans have been criticized for missing a great opportunity that might have turned the course of world history. But it should be borne in mind that if the domestic situation in Germany in 1901, when Anglophobia was at its height owing to the Boer War, was unfavourable to an Anglo-German alliance, in international terms, in 1901 as in 1898 and 1899, the risks of an alliance with Great Britain still seemed to Berlin to outweigh any possible benefits. Even the very fact that there were no serious conflicts between the two powers, the settlement of which (as in the case of Great Britain's agreements with France and Russia later) might have drawn them together, was perhaps an obstacle to an agreement. Of course, for the exponents of the *Freie Hand* in the Berlin Foreign office it was an article of faith that Great Britain's differences with France and Russia were insuperable, and that as the British came under increasing pressure from those powers they would be bound to come begging for an alliance on Germany's terms. As even the relatively Anglophile Holstein confidently declared: 'Time is on our side, we can wait.' On the other hand, a doubt must remain as to whether the Germans would ever have found it in their interests to opt for a British alliance on any terms at all; all the more so as *Weltpolitik* had recently acquired a new dimension that suggested that, if Germany ever did decide to take sides between the world powers, it would be the Russian side that she would take, and not the British. This was certainly the implication of *Flottenpolitik*.

Flottenpolitik – the construction of an ocean-going battle fleet – was designed, like *Weltpolitik* itself, with both internal and external objectives in view. Whereas for Bismarck, who had regarded Germany as essentially a continental power, a coastal defence fleet had been perfectly adequate, for the Kaiser and Admiral Tirpitz, set on raising Germany to the ranks of the world powers, an ocean-going fleet and overseas bases were absolutely essential. Tirpitz's First Navy Law, of 1898, had important domestic implications. By fixing in advance the financing and construction arrangements for the new fleet, Tirpitz planned to allow the Reichstag, once it had agreed his initial proposals, even less control over the navy than it had over the army under Bismarck's Septennial Law. That Social Democrats and Liberals might object to this was of no concern to the government: on the contrary, William II declared, 'the people must be induced to revolt against the Reichstag'. At the highest level, *Flottenpolitik*, like *Weltpolitik*, was designed to rally the forces of order behind the government. If the industrialist wing of the Bismarckian Alliance of Steel and Rye would obviously be won over by the economic advantages of a naval construction programme, the disgruntled agrarian wing could be reconciled by presenting the Navy Law as part of a package including the raising of tariffs against foreign grain. When Caprivi's commercial treaties expired in 1902 this part of the bargain was indeed implemented, and the agrarians duly forgot about their threats to vote against 'the hideous fleet'. In the wider political arena, meanwhile, and to an even greater degree than *Weltpolitik* itself, *Flottenpolitik* became the subject of an intensive campaign of pamphlets and lectures throughout Germany, led by intellectuals imbued with the doctrines of the Pan-German League. The resultant wave of popular enthusiasm soon gave birth to yet another extra-parliamentary pressure group, the Navy League, with a membership of over one million – more than ten times the size of the comparable organization in Great Britain. In later years, the Kaiser and his advisers found the Navy League to be something of a Frankenstein monster restricting their freedom of manoeuvre in international affairs. Initially, however, all seemed to be going well for their plans to 'emancipate large sections of the community from the spell of the political parties by rousing their enthusiasm for this one, great, national issue'.

As far as the international scene was concerned, the purpose of *Flottenpolitik* was to secure Germany's acceptance as a world power by forcing the existing world powers, chiefly Great Britain, to make way for her. The Germans recognized that, given the burdens of sustaining the largest military budget on the continent, they had simply not got the resources to 'outbuild' the world's largest naval power. To meet this difficulty, Tirpitz developed his so-called 'Risk Theory': it would be sufficient if Germany could build a fleet of such a size that the British could not risk a conflict with it without leaving the Royal Navy dangerously weakened to face Great Britain's primary opponents, France and Russia. Once this had been achieved, Germany could use the new fleet to extract concessions from Great Britain by blackmail. *Flottenpolitik*, therefore, was fundamentally and in the long term an anti-British device; and the blackmailing tactics inherent in it implied the certainty of a cold war, and the possibility – if the British failed to respond as predicted – of an actual conflict, between Germany and Great Britain. It could not possibly be reconciled with a policy of alliance with Great Britain; and by the same token, it dictated that Germany must avoid alienating Russia, a possible ally against Great Britain in the long term. Not that, in the short term,

Germany was seeking to challenge the British. On the contrary, so long as the new fleet was in its infancy, it would be vulnerable to an attack from the Royal Navy in the style of Nelson's pre-emptive strike at Copenhagen in 1807. As a corollary of the Risk Theory, therefore, Tirpitz developed the 'Danger Zone Theory', according to which, until the new fleet was strong enough to play its predestined role, Germany must seek to maintain good relations with Great Britain, and must avoid any commitment to the Franco-Russian camp. More than ever, therefore, it was essential to continue the policy of the *Freie Hand* between the rival world powers.

In fact, in its early stages the construction of a German battle fleet had remarkably little impact on Anglo-German relations. It was not until the end of 1902 that a British Admiralty memorandum even drew attention to the possible uncomfortable consequences of the German Navy Laws of 1898 and 1900; and British naval construction and the disposition of the Royal Navy continued to be directed against France and Russia. If Anglo-German relations deteriorated steadily in the aftermath of the failure of the alliance negotiations of 1901, this was the result, not of *Flottenpolitik*, but of a series of entirely disconnected incidents, the cumulative effect of which was to build up a store of resentment and distrust between London and Berlin.

For example, In January 1902, Bülow's foolish attempt to curry favour with the Reichstag by casting aspersions on the honour of the British Army in South Africa earned him a crushing public rebuke from Chamberlain which even the Austrians admitted 'friend Bülow richly deserved', and called forth an outburst of anti-German feeling reminiscent of the Kruger Telegram affair. The failure of the two governments, in the face of United States disapproval, to pursue their joint debt-collecting expedition against Venezuela led to a further round of recriminations; and soon even the German government began to have misgivings about the effect of the Anglophobia it had so long fostered in its of pursuit of *Weltpolitik*, on public opinion in Great Britain – where the alarm was also being sounded about Germany as a commercial competitor. It was ominous, for example, that when in 1903 Lansdowne negotiated an agreement with Berlin to safeguard British interests in Persia by internationalizing the proposed Baghdad railway project and reserving to Great Britain the construction of the final section terminating in the Gulf, a violent press campaign in London compelled him to abandon the plan. Even more ominous, the changed atmosphere was reflected in the Foreign Office, where, with the assistance of Edward VII, a generation of younger men was rising to power who took violent objection to Germany's grasping and exploitative methods. For the time being, however, and so long as the imperturbable Lansdowne continued to direct British policy, any deterioration was confined to the tone in which Great Britain and Germany conducted their relations. There was nothing dividing the two powers comparable to the conflict of interests that divided Great Britain from France and Russia – a conflict that was sharpened in January 1902 when Great Britain proceeded to make an alliance with their chief opponent in the Far East, Japan.

The Anglo-Japanese Alliance was a product of the situation in the Far East and had little impact in Europe except to confirm the tripartite grouping of the powers. The reaction of the Japanese to the failure of their soundings in London and Berlin in March 1901 had been to seek agreement with St Petersburg. In Tokyo, Prince Ito and the Russophiles hoped for a renewal of the Nishi-Rosen agreement of 1898 that had recognized Japanese control of Korea in return for Russian control of Manchuria; and Ito was still hopeful of success when he set out on his mission to Paris and St Petersburg in December 1901. It was only after his failure in St Petersburg, when the expansionist party that sought control over both Korea and Manchuria prevailed over Lamsdorff and the foreign ministry, that Ito made his way to London. For the British, it was the naval balance that was the most worrying aspect of the situation in the Far East, where four British battleships faced five Russian (soon expected to become six). France and Germany, with one battleship each in the area, could hardly affect the issue either way. It was Japan, who had six battleships that was the crucial factor; and it was fear of a possible Russo-Japanese combination that made the British Admiralty so keen to make sure of Japan and that persuaded the British Cabinet to accept the rather one-sided terms of the Alliance of 30 January 1902. In this, the Japanese secured their objective – a promise of British assistance if France intervened in a Russo-Japanese war, however it might arise. The British gained security against the (by then rather improbable) nightmare of a Russo-Japanese combination and could hope that the news of the alliance might deter Russia from pushing matters too far. The price they paid was a heavy one, however, in terms of their much cherished freedom of action. They had in effect placed themselves at the mercy of third parties over whose actions they had no control whatever: if Japan should choose to attack Russia – the Anglo-Japanese Alliance was not limited to defensive wars like the alliances between the European Powers – and if France should choose to come to Russia's assistance, the British were committed to fight. Indeed, Salisbury and other exponents of Great Britain's freedom from commitments for unforeseen contingencies, such as Rosebery, were quick to voice their apprehensions on this score. In this respect, at least, the British had abandoned isolation with a vengeance.

As regards Great Britain's position in the European states system, however, nothing had changed. On the contrary, the Alliance had rendered the British position in the Far East more secure than any arrangement with Germany could have done; and Great Britain now stood in less need than ever before of far-reaching commitments to either of the continental blocs. Indeed, the tripartite grouping of the past few years was only confirmed. France and Russia lost no time in replying to the news of the Alliance with a defiant counter-declaration that underlined their differences with Great Britain. Delcassé continued to treat the British in a high-handed manner: in the summer, for example, he brusquely asked them to grant France a free hand in Morocco, but offered nothing at all in return. Needless to say, Lansdowne, conscious not only of the fact that Great Britain had more trade than any other power with Morocco, but of the strategic threat that would arise from the establishment of a strong power on the Moroccan coast opposite Gibraltar, turned him down flat. The Germans, meanwhile, were confirmed in their belief in the consummate wisdom of the *Freie Hand* policy. William II was relieved that the British 'noodles have had a lucid interval' and had ceased to bother Germany with their requests for support; and he was careful to evade an invitation from France and Russia to accede to their counter-declaration. At the same time, however, the Germans welcomed the deepening of the rift between Great Britain and the Franco-Russian alliance and began covertly to incite Russia and Japan against each other, while taking good care, in the best traditions of the *Freie Hand*, to remain in the background themselves.

The end of Anglo-French antagonism

It was only when Delcassé began to encounter problems in his forward policy in Morocco, inaugurated in 1900 with the occupation of a few oases near the Algerian border, that he gradually came round to seeking a settlement of extra-European disputes with Great Britain on something approaching equal terms. Already in the summer of 1902 he had reached agreement with Madrid on the delineation of French and Spanish spheres of influence in Morocco; but he found the Spaniards unwilling to finalize the arrangement without the approval of Great Britain. With the outbreak at the end of 1902 of a serious rebellion against the Sultan of Morocco that might demand French military intervention the situation became decidedly urgent, and Delcassé at last decided to offer the British a substantial *quid pro quo* – in the form of French recognition of their position in Egypt – in return for a free hand in Morocco. From the start, the British authorities in Egypt, in particular, Lord Cromer, who was about to seek the approval of the International Commission in Cairo for a series of reform proposals, urged London to seize the chance to get rid of French obstruction on the Commission once and for all. Progress at governmental level was slow, however. Certainly Edward VII's outstandingly successful state visit to Paris in May 1903 and the return visit of President Loubet and Delcassé to London did much to banish the atmosphere of outright hostility that had prevailed between the two peoples for over twenty years. In the haggling over long-standing disputes, however, from West African frontiers to the provisions of the Treaty of Utrecht relating to the Newfoundland fisheries, Delcassé drove a hard bargain, persisting until the end of the year with a demand for the cession of the Gambia which Lansdowne dismissed out of hand. Insofar as the negotiations might have any broader international implications, these were equally problematic. The British would indeed have welcomed a parallel ironing out of differences with Russia over such areas of friction as Tibet, Afghanistan and Persia; but the Russians, absorbed in an increasingly bitter dispute with Great Britain's Japanese allies, were in no mood to respond, and Lansdowne rejected point blank repeated French requests to exercise a restraining influence on Tokyo. As late as January 1904, Delcassé was telling the British that he had not even informed his colleagues in the government of the state of his negotiations.

Although there is no concrete evidence for a connection between the outbreak of the Russo-Japanese War on 4 February 1904 and the relatively rapid conclusion of the Anglo-French negotiations two months later, the common and avowed desire of both parties to avoid involvement in the Far Eastern conflict, and perhaps even the thought that an improvement in their own relations would make such involvement less likely, may well have counted for something. At any rate, once negotiations resumed, on a horse-trading basis, in March, they resulted by 8 April in a series of agreements. A Convention tidied up existing treaties relating to West Africa and extinguished French rights in the Newfoundland fisheries; a Declaration delineated spheres of influence in Siam, established a condominium in New Hebrides, and recognized the French position in Madagascar. Most important, a second Declaration, accompanied by five secret articles, clarified the policy of the two powers in Egypt and Morocco. In Egypt, the French promised to cease pressing the British to fix a time limit for the occupation and to support Cromer's proposed reforms; in Morocco, the British recognized France's right to 'preserve order' and institute reforms. A secret article made provision, 'if the Sultan's authority should lapse' for the establishment of a Spanish, rather than a French, sphere of influence on the coast opposite Gibraltar. It must be emphasized that the articles that were to give most trouble in future – providing for British support for the French position in Morocco – had not been among Delcassé's original desiderata: they were only added at the last minute when the British, fearing German obstruction at Cairo, asked for positive support from France in Egypt. As it turned out, all the powers including the Germans – after an attempt to haggle was brushed off with great indignation in London – accepted Cromer's reforms readily enough; and as Morocco remained relatively quiet in 1904 the significance of the British commitments to France was not appreciated, even insofar as they were known. For the moment, it seemed that the agreements of 8 April had simply cleared up all outstanding extra-European differences between Great Britain and France (except the position in Abyssinia, which was settled in 1906), and heralded the end of the Egyptian question for many years.

It was widely agreed at the time that the British had got the better of the bargain. Apart from Rosebery, still distrustful of the French, there were few critics of the agreements in Great Britain, whose gains, after all, were effective immediately. In France, by contrast, Delcassé was much criticized for having given away too much – especially in the Newfoundland fisheries – in return for gains that were only hypothetical: they could only possibly be realized if France embarked on forward policy in Morocco, a prospect that was unpopular with the French public anyway. France had made a cash payment in return for a promissory note that might never be presentable. In the event, matters turned out very differently. The cash payment to the British proved to be no more than nominal: for twenty years the British had managed perfectly well without French support in Egypt; and as the other great powers had long since ceased to challenge them there the French were not called on to lend them assistance in the years after 1904. The British promissory note, however, was made out for a much larger sum; and when in 1905 the French chose to make a forward move in Morocco and were challenged by Germany, the British found themselves entangled in the continental alliance system to an unprecedented degree.

True, Germanophobe circles in Great Britain had from the start been very much alive to the possible anti-German implications of the Anglo-French agreement: 'What an effect it will have in Europe and how the

Germans will hate it!' wrote Sir Charles Hardinge, soon to be ambassador at St Petersburg and eventually, under Grey, permanent under-secretary. This was emphatically not the view of Lansdowne, however, who had made the agreement with France, like the alliance with Japan, from motives of imperial security, and who did not intend it to have any anti-German connotations. In June, he was just as sincerely pleased as the Germanophobes were dismayed when Edward VII paid a highly successful visit to his German nephew at Kiel. After all, on the world scene disagreements between Great Britain and Russia remained as intractable as ever. The British had wasted little time in making it clear to St Petersburg that they would oppose by force any attempt to reinforce the Russian fleet in the Far East with warships that were confined by the rule of the Straits to the Black Sea. In this atmosphere British suggestions for a settlement of Anglo-Russian differences in Asia along the lines of the recent agreement with France made no progress, despite the expressed sympathy of the French and the energy of Hardinge in St Petersburg. Besides, if there were Germanophobes in London, there was an equally vociferous Russophobe lobby; and when in October 1904 the Russian Baltic fleet on its progress to the Far East fired on British fishing boats off Dogger Bank (in the delusion that they might be Japanese destroyers) Lansdowne and Balfour came under serious pressure to declare war. In sum, therefore, while the Anglo-French agreements by reducing friction overseas had made a contribution, like the Franco-Italian agreements of 1900–2, to the stability of the European states system, they still left the British uncommitted to either of the two power blocs on the continent and the tripartite grouping of the powers survived.

Meanwhile, the elimination of the Near East as a potential source of conflict between the powers was confirmed by the strengthening of the Austro-Russian Entente. After the turn of the century the two powers were increasingly preoccupied with the problems that had encouraged them to make the 1897 agreement in the first place: Russo-Japanese rivalry intensified steadily to the point of actual war; and the national conflicts that had paralysed the parliamentary system in Vienna were compounded by a conflict between the monarch and Budapest over control of the Common Army that by 1905 compelled the chief of staff to draw up contingency plans for the military occupation of Hungary. In this situation there was no sympathy in either Russia or Austria-Hungary for the attempts of Christian factions in Macedonia to use terrorism to provoke the Turks into committing atrocities – whereupon Europe would intervene to liberate the country from Ottoman rule. Their machinations did indeed provoke international intervention – not, however, by a Turcophile Concert but by Russia and Austria-Hungary; and in the opposite sense from that intended by the nationalists. The Entente powers were more determined than ever to preserve the territorial *status quo*, and decided that this could best be done by pressing the Sultan to make life tolerable for his Macedonian subjects. In January 1903, the Austrians and Russians produced the Vienna Note, prescribing the appointment of a Turkish 'Inspector General', irremovable without their consent, to root out abuses in the administration of Macedonia; and with the support of the other powers forced the Sultan to comply. Needless to say, as the aim of the terrorists was to end, not improve, Ottoman rule, these measures failed completely to prevent a serious Bulgarian uprising in August. This failed, as the Greek and Serbian inhabitants of Macedonia refused to support it; but it moved the Austrians and Russians to devise the Mürzsteg Punctation of October 1903. This was the starting point for a series of reforms in the Macedonian gendarmerie, finances and judiciary, to be implemented by the Ottoman Inspector General, advised by Austrian and Russian officials and assisted by personnel drawn from the other great powers.

It is true that the latter greeted the Mürzsteg programme with limited enthusiasm. The Germans feared that any European intervention, however cautious and well-meant, could only make the problem worse by undermining the Sultan's authority and encouraging the malcontents – although the ostentatious aloofness they displayed towards the reform proposals was also calculated to enhance their influence at Constantinople. At the other extreme, the British and the Italians complained that the reform programme was insufficiently radical; and the Italians, particularly, resented their relegation to a secondary role. Their attempts to substitute control by the concert for the principle of Austro-Russian 'dual control' enshrined in Mürzsteg, came to nothing, however, not least because the French would do nothing that might offend St Petersburg. With the Mürzsteg Punctation, the Austro-Russian Entente had progressed from co-existence to active co-operation. The effect of this was, of course, to cut across and to blur still further the lines of division drawn by the formal alliance system of the previous decade.

The most striking demonstration of this was the Austro-Russian neutrality treaty of 15 October 1904, by which the two powers not only reaffirmed their determination to continue their co-operation in Macedonia but promised to observe 'a loyal and absolute neutrality' if either should find itself at war with a third power. Insofar as it reflected Russian anxieties about a possible British intervention in the war with Japan, this provision was unremarkable enough; but insofar as it was also coupled with a strengthening of Austrian frontier defences in the Tyrol, it was a telling comment on the state of Austro-Italian relations. Moreover, as the treaty was drawn up in such general terms as to commit Austria-Hungary to neutrality even in the event of a Russo-German war, it was, in theory at least, even more difficult to square with the Dual and Triple Alliances than Bismarck's Reinsurance Treaty and the Prinetti-Barrère agreements. In practice, of course, it had no anti-German implications; indeed, its chief architect, and Austro-Hungarian ambassador at St Petersburg, Aehrenthal, hoped to develop it eventually into a Three Emperors' Alliance directed from Vienna. As things stood, however, it was yet a further example of the fluidity that had come to characterize the alignments of the European powers in the years of unstable equilibrium.

In the years around the turn of the century, therefore, with the Near East under control, and with the central and western powers eschewing active participation in the Far Eastern conflict, the stability of the European states system was only enhanced by the fact that day-to-day diplomacy was focused on issues that not only left the vital interests of the great powers untouched, but offered opportunities for compromise and conciliation. Nothing occurred to threaten the security of any of the great powers in Europe. It was perhaps ominous that these years witnessed no attempt at an agreement between France and Germany comparable to the Austro-Russian, Franco-Italian and Anglo-French agreements. Indeed, the news of this last had been received with considerable dismay in Berlin: a fundamental premise of the *Freie Hand* policy – that Anglo-French differences were irreconcilable and that Germany would be able to exploit them for ever – had been shattered, and Holstein concluded gloomily that henceforth 'no overseas policy is feasible in opposition to England and France'. But for the present the Anglo-French agreements had produced nothing tangible that the Germans could object to in either Egypt or Morocco, let alone in Europe. There, their attention was focused on the explosion of anti-German feeling with which the British press reacted to the Dogger Bank crisis, denouncing Germany as a cynical *tertius gaudens* as fiercely as it attacked the Russian aggressors. A spate of irresponsible articles pointing to the danger from the German navy, and hinting at the possibility of a preventive strike against it – as was, indeed, being urged by Admiral Fisher at this time – provoked a panicky German proposal to Russia for a continental league against Great Britain. On this occasion, a French veto killed the idea and the alignments of the powers continued as before. But both the proposal itself, and the alarm of the

British when they eventually got wind of it, indicated that momentous changes might yet be impending. Four months later such changes did indeed occur, when a French move in Morocco provoked a confrontation with Germany that called in question the standing within Europe of several great powers and produced something of a diplomatic revolution within the states system.

The First Moroccan crisis and the solidification of the Anglo-French Entente

Insofar as the St René Taillandier mission, sent by the French to Morocco at the end of 1904, with a programme of reforms that included the supervision of the police by France and Spain, implied a special position for those two powers, it was in clear contravention of the Madrid Convention of 1880 that had declared Morocco to be the concern of all sixteen signatory powers. In terms of international law, therefore, the Germans had a respectable case when on 31 March 1905 the Kaiser interrupted his Mediterranean cruise to land at Tangiers and declare that, as far as Germany was concerned, Morocco was an independent state in which no power had special rights; and when in April the Wilhelmstrasse began to demand a review of the question by the signatories of the Madrid Convention. All this made sense also in terms of German domestic politics, both as a manoeuvre to stir up nationalist feeling for the 1906 Navy Law, and simply out of regard for German trade in Morocco, which ranked third after that of France and Great Britain, and had a vocal pressure group at home, the Marokko Association, to defend it.

The motivations behind German Moroccan policy were, however, altogether wider and more complex. At the most basic level, Berlin not surprisingly saw in Delcassé's proceedings – buying off Italy, Great Britain and even Spain, without a word to Germany – a challenge to Germany's standing as a great power which could not be ignored. Beyond this defensive reaction, however, German policy was decidedly ambitious. The opportunity seemed too good to miss to inflict a salutary humiliation on France: with her Russian allies reeling from the military disasters in the Far East, and her new British friends – so the Germans calculated – likely to shrink from a confrontation, the French would have to yield; and in their disillusionment might throw overboard not only Delcassé, but his whole policy of co-operation with Great Britain. Best of all, this would in turn clear the way for a chastened France to be brought into a combination with the three Eastern Empires that would establish German domination of the European states system.

The Germans set about implementing their plans with a vigour, indeed brutality, that made an unfavourable impression in all other European capitals, and that was to make the First Moroccan crisis a landmark in the deterioration of the international atmosphere in the final decade of peace. Legally, they were no doubt perfectly entitled to reject no fewer than three offers of a bilateral settlement from Delcassé in April, and to insist on the summoning of a conference of the signatories of the Madrid Convention. Their intimation to Paris, however, that Franco-German differences could never be resolved so long as Delcassé remained in office, was a demand of an altogether different order. It touched on the standing of France as an independent great power, and transformed the crisis from an extra-European affair into a crisis of the European states system, the first major confrontation of the powers in Europe for twenty years.

Certainly, it made the very worst impression on the British, who now determined – quite contrary to German expectations – to honour their commitment to lend France diplomatic support in Morocco. True, German calculations about the limits of Anglo-French co-operation were not entirely unfounded. Throughout the summer, London continued to shrug off French appeals for pressure on Japan to end the war in the Far East: in Lansdowne's view, the advantages of the progressive weakening of Russia as a world power more than compensated for any shift in the European balance in favour of Germany. Even in Morocco, the British had an uneasy feeling that the French were 'on thin ice'; and Lansdowne's famous proposal of 17 May to the French ambassador that Great Britain and France should 'concert their policy' generally was intended as a warning against any Franco-German deal behind Great Britain's back. Equally, the reaction of the French government, when Delcassé misinterpreted Lansdowne's suggestion as an offer of an alliance and urged his colleagues to stand up to Germany, showed that Anglo-French solidarity was by no means the cornerstone of French policy either. If the prime minister, Rouvier, like most of his cabinet, had never been enamoured of Delcassé's Moroccan adventures (and let the German ambassador know it) a policy of challenging Germany at a time when neither Russia, staggering to defeat on land and sea, nor Great Britain, essentially a naval power, could lend France any effective military assistance, seemed to Delcassé's colleagues the height of criminal folly. Indeed, when Delcassé, finding himself isolated in the cabinet, resigned on 6 June and when Rouvier – albeit infuriated to find Germany still completely unyielding – agreed to submit the Moroccan question to a conference, it seemed that the Germans had calculated correctly.

Their plans seemed to advance a stage further when on 24 July, in an emotional meeting on the Tsar's yacht in the Gulf of Björkö, William II prevailed on his Russian cousin to sign a treaty of alliance, pledging Germany and Russia to assist each other 'in Europe' in the event of an attack by a third power; and when Nicholas promised to seek the adherence of his French allies to this arrangement. It was against this background that the Germans proved astonishingly yielding in the preliminary negotiations with Paris over the agenda for the forthcoming Moroccan conference, conceding in advance that France was entitled to a special position in Morocco after all. (When the German negotiators tried to haggle they were called to order by the Kaiser himself, by now 'thoroughly fed up' with all the 'disgusting bickering': German interests in Morocco were minuscule in comparison with the great prize of a continental league.) In the autumn, however, the whole diplomatic house of cards collapsed: the Tsar was persuaded by his ministers that the Treaty of Björkö was incompatible with Russia's alliance with France, and Bülow, whose doubts about the value of a treaty that did not oblige Russia to move against Great Britain in Asia were sharpened by pique at being upstaged by his imperial master, also came out against it. By the end of the year the Treaty of Björkö, perhaps the most spectacular example of monarchical diplomacy in the twentieth century, had proved to be a worthless scrap of paper. Meanwhile, the Germans, in pursuit of their grand designs, had gravely weakened their negotiating position in the approaching Moroccan conference, while the French had strengthened theirs, both by enhancing their own military preparedness and embarking on military conversations with the British.

True, the Algeçiras Conference of January to March 1906 was not a total defeat for Germany: Article I of the Final Act expressly recognized the independent status of Morocco 'in the Name of Almighty God'; the open door to trade was guaranteed for thirty years; and over the arrangements for international control of the Moroccan state bank it had been France and Great Britain who had found themselves isolated and obliged to make concessions. On the main point at issue, however, the control of the Moroccan police by France (and in a few instances Spain), with all its political implications, the Germans, supported only by Austria-Hungary and Morocco, suffered a signal defeat. Their expectations of support from Italy (who remained scrupulously loyal to the Prinetti-Barrère agreement) and the United States, proved totally ill-founded; while the French received full backing not only from St Petersburg but from London, whence Grey even overruled the complaints of the British negotiators at Algeçiras that the French were asking too much. When deadlock loomed, the Austrians, desperate, as Franz Joseph put it, 'to bring the Emperor William to see reason', saved the situation by devising a fig leaf of international control in the form of a neutral inspector-general reporting to the diplomatic body in Tangier; but in practice the way was now clear for France to proceed gradually to establish her political predominance throughout the cherifian empire.

It is true that, in strictly military terms, the First Moroccan crisis hardly constituted a significant milestone on the road to war. Despite some ominous signs of heightened military preparedness, at the start of the crisis on the German side, at the end on the French, it had no lasting impact on the continental military balance. At no point had the Kaiser been prepared to contemplate going to war over Morocco: not only did he shrink from condemning his infant fleet to annihilation; he also rejected the cavalier prognostications of his military advisers, declaring in December 1905 that Germany's chances even in a land war were 'especially unfavourable'. In terms of the functioning of the European states system, by contrast, the consequences of the First Moroccan crisis were momentous. Insofar as it convinced the British that Germany was seeking to establish her domination over France, her Russian ally, and the states system as a whole, it transformed the Anglo-French entente from an essentially extra-European arrangement into an anti-German power grouping in Europe; and it marked a decisive step towards the replacement of the flexible, multipolar system that had served since the mid-1890s to blur the edges of international conflicts, by a simpler, but more dangerously confrontational, bipolar system.

It was particularly unfortunate for the Germans that their challenge to France over Morocco happened to coincide with the coming to power of a new government in London, with Sir Edward Grey at the Foreign Office. Grey's view of the tripartite balance of power was already jaundiced as a result of his experiences as parliamentary under-secretary in the Liberal government of 1894–95, when Rosebery's pursuit of an understanding with the Triple Alliance 'did not prevent trouble with either side. . . . Germany was exacting and we were perpetually on the brink of war with France and Russia. The situation was intolerable.' To Grey's mind, the recent entente with France had freed Great Britain from a veritable nightmare; and it did not need the urgings of a ginger group of rising young Germanophobes at the Foreign Office to convince him of the necessity of holding on to it at all costs.

In this respect, his objectives were radically different from those of his predecessors: whereas Salisbury had been wary of restricting Great Britain's freedom of action by agreements with continental powers, and Lansdowne had entered into agreements with them (and with Japan) primarily in order to safeguard Great Britain's imperial interests, for Grey the cultivation of the entente with France became something of an end in itself. Hence, he not only gave the French full support at Algeçiras regardless of the merits of the issues involved, but gave his blessing to military conversations with Paris that envisaged the sending of a British military force to fight alongside France in a war against Germany. It is true that these conversations did not constitute an actual commitment to go to war – indeed, not all members of the Cabinet were even informed of them. They were, however, symptomatic of the new outlook in the Foreign Office. Whereas Lansdowne had felt it prudent in June 1905 to warn the German ambassador that public opinion might force Great Britain to fight if Germany should 'lightheartedly attack' France, by 1906 Grey was talking – to both the French and German ambassadors – in far more general terms, of Great Britain's coming to the aid of France 'if war should break out between France and Germany over Morocco' – a statement that Lansdowne had never made to the French. Under Grey, in fact, Great Britain had begun to abandon the intermediary position she had held in the tripartite balance in favour of participation in a bipolar system.

That London began to focus its attention on Germany as a potential opponent, drawing closer to Paris as a result, totally wrecked the assumptions on which the Germans had based their calculations since the inauguration of the *Freie Hand* policy. If they could no longer count on a permanent hostility between the British Empire and the Franco-Russian alliance to enable them to extract concessions from both sides in furtherance of their *Weltpolitik*, the Anglo-French rapprochement was to have equally disastrous implications for their *Flottenpolitik*. It was not just that, with the French navy ceasing to pose a threat to Great Britain, the basic assumption of Tirpitz's Risk Theory was called in question. The simultaneous annihilation by the Japanese of Russian naval power – hitherto, after all, the chief threat to the Royal Navy – meant that the attention of the British was bound to shift to the potential threat posed by Germany, regardless of how the latter chose to behave on the international stage; and insofar as the recent Moroccan crisis seemed to indicate that Germany was indeed aiming to dominate the continental states system, the British were only confirmed in their determination to counter the German naval threat. After all, whether Germany actually managed to establish her domination of the continent or not, the disparity between British and German military power was so great that if Germany were ever allowed to attain a position of naval strength that could render an invasion of the British isles even a remote possibility, Great Britain's very existence as an independent great power would be in jeopardy. Even radical ministers in London who had been hoping to concentrate government spending on social reform, had to accept this harsh reality.

February 1906 saw the laying down of the first Dreadnought battleship, and although this marked a temporary weakening of Great Britain's naval supremacy (in that it rendered all pre-Dreadnought ships, in which Great Britain had had a comfortable lead, out of date) it gradually became clear in the new, incomparably more costly naval race that now ensued, that Germany would never be able either to outbuild Great Britain (given the demands on the German budget consequent on maintaining the most expensive Army on the continent) or even, given the new diplomatic constellation, to achieve that blackmailing power that underlay the rationale of the *Freie Hand* policy. These setbacks for Tirpitz's naval plans were compounded by ominous developments on the domestic scene: while on the one hand the propaganda so rashly fostered by the regime had created a head of steam that simply compelled the government to press on with a naval programme that could never achieve its aim, the cost of building the new battleships could clearly not be met without recourse to new taxation, which in turn threatened to explode that consensus between landowners and industrialists that was essential to the government's policy of *Sammlung* to reinforce the social and political order at home. In short, on both foreign and domestic fronts the confident assumptions of German policy-makers since the late 1890s were giving way to frustration and disillusionment; and it was perhaps appropriate that Bülow should be overcome by a fainting fit when he attempted, in April 1906, to explain Germany's international situation to the Reichstag.

It must be said that the reaction of the Germans to their discomfiture only made their position worse. For example, Italy's behaviour at Algeçiras had been perfectly predictable, given her commitments to France in Morocco. Like the Austrians, the Italians had been primarily concerned to avert a confrontation between the great powers; and relations between Germany's two allies began to improve as Tittoni, who saw in the Triple Alliance a valuable guarantee against the perils of isolation, began to clamp down on irredentist propaganda at home: 'What clowns! With the '48ers and their idiocies we shall finish up at the Treaty of Berlin and at Adowa!' William II, however, raged against Italy: 'this romance cat's meat betrays us right and left', and even talked wildly of war against her. Similarly, the German wire to St Petersburg was gratuitously cut when the Kaiser, brushing aside pleas from conservatives in Vienna and Berlin to bolster the Tsar's position by responding favourably to Russian feelers for a loan, vetoed German participation, with the result that Russia turned again to France for money, both tightening the links with her ally and strengthening the position of the pro-western liberal lobby in St Petersburg. Even with Austria-Hungary, Germany's relations were less than harmonious in the wake of the Kaiser's tactless 'brilliant second' telegram to Goluchowski, and of Germany's stubborn refusal to participate in a naval demonstration to press the Sultan to implement the Austro-Russian reform programme in Macedonia. To relatively harmless gestures of British diplomacy in 1907 – the conclusion of an agreement between Great Britain, France and Spain to maintain the *status quo* in the Western Mediterranean, and Campbell-Bannerman's efforts to press a profoundly sceptical Foreign Office into initiating a serious discussion of arms limitation at the Hague Peace Conference – the Germans reacted with a nervousness bordering on paranoia; and the notion that Great Britain was working steadily for the 'encirclement' of Germany found new sustenance with the conclusion of the Anglo-Russian Convention of 31 August.

German fears were exaggerated. So long as Russia refused to align herself with the Anglo-French entente against the Central Powers, there could be no question of Germany's being encircled. Certainly, under Lansdowne, Anglo-Russian relations had been decidedly frosty. Although Lansdowne had been alert to the advantages of an agreement demarcating Russian and British interests – in Persia, for example, where the Russians seemed to be set on extending their influence as far as the Gulf – and had in 1904 disavowed the Younghusband mission to Tibet as a needless provocation of Russia, St Petersburg had haughtily rebuffed all British suggestions of a deal. Lansdowne for his part, in the very months when he was lending the French his support over Morocco, remained deaf to all suggestions, from Paris, and from his own officials alarmed at the weakening of Russia as a factor in the continental balance of power, that Great Britain use her good offices to facilitate an end to the Russo-Japanese War; and he had proceeded in August 1905 to renegotiate the Anglo-Japanese Alliance to provide for British assistance to Japan in a future war against Russia alone, in return for a promise of Japanese assistance in the event of Russian moves in the direction of India. The arguments in favour of an accommodation with St Petersburg remained powerful, however: the prospect of having to find 100,000 men for the defence of

India was a daunting one for the British, especially in the context of an inexorably rising naval budget. By 1906, the Russians, too, chastened by their defeat in the Far East and the collapse of the autocracy at home, were prepared for negotiations. The resultant convention of 31 August 1907, like the Anglo-French agreements of 8 April 1904, was essentially designed to remove potential sources of conflict outside Europe: Tibet and Afghanistan were neutralized and spheres of influence agreed in Persia, giving Russia domination in the north, and Great Britain in the southern and eastern provinces bordering on Afghanistan and the Gulf.

It is true that Grey's attitude to Russia's role in the states system was more European-oriented and less narrowly imperial than Lansdowne's. Already in February 1906 Grey was 'impatient to see Russia re-established as a factor in European politics'; and by 1907 he was becoming increasingly alive to the potential advantages of an Anglo-Russian agreement beyond the areas it specifically related to: 'an entente between Russia, France and ourselves would be absolutely secure. If it is necessary to check Germany, it could then be done.' But although this would have made interesting reading in Berlin, there is no evidence that St Petersburg was thinking in such broad terms. On the contrary, Izvolsky assured the Germans, à propos the Mediterranean Agreements of May 1907, that Russia had no intention of joining any combination whatever against Germany; and the British ambassador in St Petersburg warned Grey to 'be exceedingly careful with M. Izvolsky just now, and not alarm him. . . . He fears . . . that we are weaving webs and forming rings round Germany.' Certainly the Austrians, who were continuing to work with Russia in Macedonia, and who saw in German nervousness a welcome enhancement of Austria-Hungary's stock within the Dual Alliance, were content to regard the Convention of 31 August as essentially an Asian affair. Even if the British were moving towards an alignment with France against Germany, and had settled their extra-European differences with Russia, it would have been an exaggeration to describe the states system of 1907 as polarized into two distinct blocs.

The textbook view that the check the Russians suffered at the hands of Japan diverted their attention from the Far East to an attempt to recoup their prestige by a forward policy in the the Balkans, setting them on a path of confrontation with the Central Powers that led directly to 1914, is misleading. It is true that by the summer of 1907 the Russians were ready to wind up both their conflict with Japan and the secular struggle for influence with Great Britain – the 'Great Game' – in Asia. The fundamental determinant of Russia's external policy was, however, the stark fact that the Empire had been so shaken by war and revolution that it could not contemplate a confrontation with any power whatever; and Stolypin's declaration to the council of ministers that Russia would be in no position to consider going to war for twenty years became an axiom of Russian foreign policy – for the next five years at least. If Izvolsky was unwilling to be led by the alliance with France and the rapprochement with Great Britain into a confrontation with Russia's powerful German neighbours, he was equally impervious to hints from Vienna and Berlin that Russia should seek salvation in a restoration of the Three Emperors' Alliance: not only would this accord ill with Russia's new constitutional regime; it would imperil the French alliance, and it was the most anti-British combination conceivable. Izvolsky sought security, therefore, in a policy of balancing between the Central and the Western Powers, to gain time for the government to rebuild Russia's military strength and stamp out the embers of the revolution at home, while he tried to restore Russia's shattered great-power position by concluding agreements with as many powers as possible.

Thus, if the reconciliation with Great Britain was accompanied in July 1907 by a treaty resolving outstanding problems with Japan, it was balanced by an agreement with Germany to safeguard the *status quo* in the Baltic, and, in September, by Izvolsky's visit to the new Austro-Hungarian foreign minister, Aehrenthal, in Vienna. There, the two ministers agreed to continue their joint efforts to implement the Mürzsteg reform programme in Macedonia, while Izvolsky suggested extending the agreement of 1897 to take account of possible changes in the *status quo*, for example, the revision of the rule of the Straits to give Russian warships freedom of passage between the Black Sea and the Mediterranean. As late as September 1907, therefore, all the signs were that, despite the sharpening of differences between the western powers in the past two years, the entente that controlled what was potentially the most explosive area of Europe, the Near East, was set to continue – and to avert the polarization of the states system into two hostile blocs.

The Near Eastern crisis and the end of the Austro-Russian Entente

Even in those years when the problem of instability in Turkey had driven Russia and Austria-Hungary to co-operate, their entente had been undermined by the chronic instability of the Balkan states, where the two powers were committed by the 1897 agreement to observe the principle of non-intervention. True, it was partly out of respect for this principle that Vienna had refrained from action when in June 1903 a *coup* by radical army officers in Belgrade had put a bloody end to the Obrenović dynasty, although it must be said that the Austrians shed no tears for the unreliable King Alexander, and were initially hopeful that his replacement, Petar Karageorgević, would prove more dependable. It soon became clear, however, that the new ruler was merely a puppet in the hands of a fiercely nationalistic clique whose irredentist ambitions in Bosnia, the Herzegovina and other south Slav territories of the Monarchy were openly proclaimed in such radical newspapers as the significantly entitled *Piemont*. When at the end of 1905 the Serbs demonstrated their determination to resist Austro-Hungarian domination by concluding a customs union with Bulgaria and by placing armaments contracts in France, rather than, as usual, in Bohemia, Goluchowski finally lost patience and launched the notorious 'Pig War', essentially an embargo on exports of livestock from Serbia to the Monarchy (which had hitherto accounted for some 90 per cent of Serbian foreign trade). Yet not only did this fail to bring Belgrade to heel, serving rather to fan the flames of hatred of the Monarchy among the mass of the population in Serbia; it also exposed the Monarchy to international humiliation, as the Serbs found alternative markets in western Europe and – especially humiliating – in Germany, who made no bones about moving in on the markets her ally had renounced. Even more serious, however, was the outcry in St Petersburg, where the foreign ministry was confronted by increasingly vocal demands for a policy of solidarity with brother Slavs, and an end to the entente with their oppressors in Vienna and Budapest.

All this was ominously indicative of the new elements that had come to influence Russian foreign policy since the inauguration of the constitutional monarchy in 1905. On the one hand, the establishment of the Duma and the granting of freedom to the press (at least as regards the discussion of foreign affairs) now provided a forum for the propagation of the nationalist ideas so long fashionable among the educated élite of 'unofficial' Russia. On the other hand, the new foreign minister, Izvolsky, was a man of very different stamp from his stolid bureaucratic predecessors, being not only a liberal 'westerner' by training but highly strung, vain, and inordinately sensitive to criticism in the press and Duma. Certainly, even under the conservative Lamsdorff, as the embarrassments that had culminated in the Austro-Russian neutrality treaty of October 1904, the high water mark of the entente, gave way to the total paralysis of defeat and revolution in 1905, the Russians had begun to doubt the wisdom of working solely with Austria-Hungary in the Near East: with Russia so weak, dual control of Macedonia could easily lead to Austro-Hungarian control. From the end of 1905, therefore, the Russians had sought to bring in the other powers: in implementing financial reforms in Macedonia, the representatives of the other powers were put on a basis of equality with those of the Mürzsteg Powers. Aehrenthal, for his part, strove to get the entente back on to its original conservative track. After all, a close relationship with Russia was essential if the Monarchy was to escape the kind of unhealthy dependence on Berlin suggested by the Kaiser's 'brilliant second' telegram. But his attempts to revive the *Dreikaiserbund*, this time led by Austria-Hungary rather than by Germany, were rebuffed in both St Petersburg and Berlin; and by the end of 1907, in the negotiations over the forthcoming judicial reforms in Macedonia, the Russians seemed to the Austrians all too willing to listen to radical suggestions from the British that risked provoking a paralysing confrontation with the Sultan, or possibly even an explosion.

The entente suffered a further blow in January 1908 when Aehrenthal, in an attempt to exploit what remained of Russian goodwill, announced his plans to exercise Austria-Hungary's rights under the Treaty of Berlin to construct a railway linking the Bosnian and Turkish networks through the Sanjak of Novibazar (the strip of Ottoman territory separating Serbia from Montenegro). Indeed, the howls of indignation with which the Russian press greeted the news were eloquent of the danger that attended any attempt whatever to tamper with the *status quo*. Izvolsky naturally questioned Aehrenthal's rather disingenuous claim that his plans were of purely economic significance and declared that they amounted to an alteration of the political *status quo* that contravened the agreement of 1897. Neither Izvolsky nor Stolypin was prepared for a direct confrontation with Austria-Hungary, however, and they decided to content themselves with furthering a rival railway project, for a 'Danube–Adriatic' line that would give Serbia access to the sea through Albanian territory and free the kingdom from dependence on the Austro-Hungarian railway network once and for all.

The crisis intensified in February when, simultaneously with the announcement of Turkey's consent to the Sanjak railway project, the ambassadors of the great powers at Constantinople decided to postpone their long-debated scheme for judicial reforms in Macedonia. Although all had been acting unanimously and in defiance of their instructions, it was soon a virtual article of faith in London and St Petersburg that the

Austrians had, as Grey put it, 'played the mean game' of sacrificing the reforms for the sake of their railway project; and Izvolsky seized the opportunity, as he told the British, 'to get out of the dual action with Austria to rally himself to those . . . Powers who are sincerely desirous of reforms'. Grey responded with alacrity, sending off to St Petersburg a set of proposals that culminated, after Edward VII's meeting with Nicholas II at Reval on 9 June, in Anglo-Russian proposals for a more stringent international control of the Macedonian budget, and for the employment of European officers in action against the terrorists.

The replacement of Austro-Russian control of Macedonian reform by Anglo-Russian leadership of the concert constituted a significant shift in great power alignments. True, the enthusiasm with which the Foreign Office seized on the Sanjak railway affair – 'the struggle between Austria and Russia in the Balkans is evidently now beginning and we shall not be bothered by Russia in Asia' seems, in the light of events that were to be 'bothering' them by 1914, somewhat shortsighted. Equally ill-judged was their conviction that the Austrians were acting as puppets in the hands of a Germany that was now seeking to 'test' the Anglo-Russian entente in the Balkans just as it had 'tested' the Anglo-French entente in Morocco: 'this marks a very important development of the Anglo-French and Anglo-Russian agreement policy. Russia is now asking for our co-operation in the Near East.' By the summer of 1908 the Anglo-Russian 'Asian' entente had clearly come to Europe, and in Germany the Reval meeting precipitated a new wave of hysteria about 'encirclement' and isolation. Meanwhile, in Turkey, the prospect of even more radical international intervention in Macedonia sparked off the Young Turkish revolution of 13 July, in which patriotic army officers forced Abdul Hamid to restore the constitution of 1876. Although, when even the Macedonian terrorists laid down their arms to greet the constitutional era, all the powers were relieved to be rid of reform negotiations that had 'hung like a millstone round our necks for the past five years', the fact that the revolution also replaced the Sultan's pro-German camarilla by a cabinet of liberal politicians, eventually headed by 'English Kiamil', only sharpened the Kaiser's anxieties about Germany's position in the Near East.

The Austrians, by contrast, were decidedly complacent. Not only did they welcome the weakening of Germany's influence at Constantinople, which had been all too often exercised to the detriment of Austro-Hungarian commerce. Aehrenthal also calculated that German nervousness over events at Reval and Constantinople could only increase Austria-Hungary's value as an ally. His confidence was further increased by signs that Izvolsky, even if he had in Macedonia abandoned Mürzsteg for co-operation with the British, was still pursuing a two-track policy and was even talking of developing the more general Austro-Russian entente of 1897. By 2 July, for example, a series of proposals for co-ordinating Austria-Hungary's and Russia's Balkan railway projects had culminated in Izvolsky's famous offer of a bargain, involving a revision of the rule of the Straits to permit the passage of Russian warships and the annexation by Austria-Hungary of not only Bosnia and the Herzegovina but the Sanjak of Novibazar – although Aehrenthal, for his part, at first tended to dismiss the proposal as a clumsy attempt to tie the Monarchy's hands.

By mid-August he was forced to reconsider, in the light of disturbing reports from Constantinople. There, demands were growing for the inclusion of representatives, not only from the semi-independent principality of Bulgaria, but from Bosnia and the Herzegovina, in the forthcoming Ottoman parliament – which would clearly imply a diminution of Franz Joseph's authority over the occupied provinces. Apart from that, should the new regime fail and the Ottoman Empire dissolve in chaos, the Monarchy's garrisons in the Sanjak of Novibazar might draw it directly into the mêlée. On 19 August, therefore, a council of ministers in Vienna resolved to withdraw altogether from the Sanjak and to annex Bosnia and the Herzegovina in full sovereignty. It must be emphasized that, questionable though such a unilateral alteration of the Treaty of Berlin might be in terms of international law, to Austro-Hungarian minds and in real terms, this was not a forward move against the *status quo* so much as an attempt to clarify and stabilize the situation. If it was partly designed to demonstrate to irredentists in Serbia the futility of their aspirations in Bosnia, the withdrawal from the Sanjak finally put paid – as Izvolsky and his advisers indeed noted with satisfaction – to such fabled expansionist plans as an Austro-Hungarian 'march on Salonica'.

The decision once taken, Aehrenthal decided to take up Izvolsky's offer of negotiations after all, and the upshot was the momentous *tête-à-tête* between the two statesmen at Buchlau on 16 September. There, it was secretly confirmed that Russia would adopt a 'benevolent attitude' towards the annexation, planned for early October, while Austria-Hungary would simultaneously withdraw from the Sanjak and support Izvolsky's plans to secure freedom of passage for Russian warships through the Straits. Aehrenthal also concurred in Izvolsky's plans to secure full independence for the principality of Bulgaria; but convinced, like his predecessors in 1859 and 1866 that any recognition of the national principle would pose a threat to the very existence of the Monarchy, he was adamant that there could be no question of territorial compensation to Serbia for the blow the annexation would strike at her hopes of some day acquiring Bosnia. In this, Izvolsky acquiesced, 'ineffably happy' with the results of the meeting. Buchlau seemed to mark a new zenith in the history of the Austro-Russian entente.

Appearances were deceptive. In the first place, the entente was imperilled by Izvolsky's incorrigible fondness for over-subtle diplomatic combinations. As the Russian archives on Buchlau, opened in the 1960s, show conclusively, just as he had manoeuvred in Macedonia between an Austro-Russian and an Anglo-Russian entente, so now he planned, while exploiting the Austro-Russian entente for Russia's strategic purposes, to advance Russian influence in the Near East (and to safeguard his position at home) by engineering a conference in which Austria-Hungary 'would appear, as it were in the position of the accused', while Russia came forward as the upholder of international law and the defender of the interests of Turkey and the Balkan states. In the second place, Izvolsky's assumptions about the general diplomatic situation proved disastrously cavalier. Although – despite his later public denials – he had been aware that the annexation was scheduled for early October, he failed in the course of his leisurely European tour to secure the endorsement of his plans by the other powers. Indeed, he was most disagreeably surprised when, the day before the announcement of the annexation, the Bulgarians – without waiting for Russia and apparently in collusion with Austria-Hungary – declared their independence; and when the British, concerned both for the prestige of the Anglophile regime in Constantinople and for their own interests in the eastern Mediterranean, refused to see the Straits question raised at this juncture. In the third place, Izvolsky found his whole compensations policy disavowed by his ministerial colleagues in St Petersburg, whom he had arrogantly neglected to take into his confidence. As the Russian press raged against the annexation and the very idea of negotiations with Austria-Hungary, Stolypin and the council of ministers protested furiously to the Tsar about the immorality of Russia's seeking to profit from the enslavement of Slav brothers in Bosnia. Thereupon Nicholas II, who had initially greeted Izvolsky's diplomatic achievements with delight, performed a volte-face, leaving Izvolsky to scramble out as best he could – by disavowing the whole Buchlau bargain and posing as the innocent victim of Aehrenthal's duplicity.

The Austro-Russian entente that had contained the Eastern Question for eleven years was dead. It had perished as a result of a combination of factors, contingent and systemic: Izvolsky was certainly over-subtle and incompetent; indeed, both negotiators at Buchlau overestimated their ability to control the dangerously volatile situation in the Near East. The precedents were there to see: in 1854, 1878 and 1886, Austro-Russian ententes had been destroyed by the attempts of one party to modify a mutually beneficial *status quo* to the disadvantage of the other. The fact that in the constitutional Russia of 1908 an excited public opinion counted for more than at any time since the 1870s made the situation all the more dangerous. The charge levelled at Aehrenthal by an Anglophile colleague applies also to Izvolsky: 'too much a minister of the eighteenth century, who believes only in negotiations between cabinets and disregards the great currents of public opinion'. Now, powerful demons had been raised. October 1908 was not to be the last, or the most disastrous occasion on which Nicholas II felt it politic to defer to his ministers' appeals for a show of Slav solidarity. Buchlau was the last attempt before the catastrophe of 1914 to regulate the states system by old-style cabinet diplomacy. Certainly, the forces that prevailed against it were to make the system increasingly difficult to manage in the last six years of peace.

The Russian decision to make difficulties over the annexation of Bosnia precipitated a major crisis in the states system, and a more serious confrontation between the two power blocs than even the First Moroccan crisis. In the next few months, violent demonstrations, accompanied by extensive mobilization measures, in Serbia and Montenegro, led to a militarization of diplomacy that portended the first shots fired in anger in Europe for nearly twenty years. On the one hand, Izvolsky succeeded in enlisting the diplomatic support of both western powers for his refusal to accept the annexation unless it was endorsed by a conference, which was also to provide compensation, even territorial compensation, for Serbia and Montenegro. The British were his most forceful supporters: indignation at Austria-Hungary's unilateral alteration of an international treaty combined with a desire to protect the new regime at Constantinople determined them 'to be the Turk's friend in the contest: 'inclination and policy both point that way, for, . . . with our numbers of Mohammedan subjects, it will never do to quarrel with Musselman patriots in Turkey.' Perhaps more rashly, having been unable to oblige Izvolsky over the Straits, they promised him their diplomatic support over Serbia's claims. The French had other problems on their minds: they were facing a rebellion in Morocco and hoping for Austrian good offices in soothing over an embarrassing dispute with Berlin over the arrest at Casablanca of a number of German deserters from the Foreign Legion. On the main issue, however, they joined readily enough with Izvolsky and Grey to demand an international conference to review the Bosnian question – an ill-judged display of unity by the Triple Entente that really did divide the powers into two blocs. If initially William II had deplored his ally's reckless provocation of Constantinople – 'there goes twenty years' work in Turkey' – the Entente's conference proposal evoked bitter memories of Algeçiras, and Berlin threw its support behind Vienna in resisting a conference to call Austria-Hungary to account. By the end of the year, negotiations for a conference had broken down, and Turkey was refusing to recognize either the annexation or Bulgaria's declaration of independence. The deadlock seemed complete.

In contrast to subsequent crises, in which the military balance was more dangerously even, the outcome of the Bosnian annexation crisis in the early months of 1909 was really a foregone conclusion. The fundamental fact was – as Izvolsky himself admitted to the Austrian ambassador – that Russia was still too weak to consider taking up arms; and in these circumstances, it simply remained for the Triple Entente powers to extricate themselves as best they could from the untenable diplomatic position they had so rashly taken up in the autumn. It is true that although they were militarily at a disadvantage in the successive tests of will through which – rather than through concert diplomacy – the crisis was resolved, the Entente powers could take some comfort from the Austro-Turkish settlement in January, when Aehrenthal at last admitted defeat and paid the Turks additional financial compensation, disguised for prestige purposes as payment for Turkish property in the annexed provinces. Even more gratifying, the contest between the Entente and the Central Powers for the privilege of brokering a Turco-Bulgarian settlement ended in a victory for Izvolsky. Over the most contentious, and most dangerous, issue, however – Serbia's claims for economic, and even territorial, compensation – the Entente suffered a total defeat. From the start Aehrenthal was prepared, albeit reluctantly, to use force to compel Serbia to abandon her attitude of protest and accept the annexation. At the same time Izvolsky was acutely aware that Russia was unable, and her Entente partners unwilling, to fight – in which case the result of an Austro-Hungarian punitive expedition against Serbia could only be to demonstrate Russia's impotence to the world and annihilate her influence throughout the Near East. By mid-March this prospect, together with Aehrenthal's threats to reveal to the public Izvolsky's betrayal of the Serbian cause at Buchlau, combined to produce Izvolsky's desperate appeal to Berlin both to restrain Vienna and find a way out of the crisis. The response of the acting German foreign minister, Kiderlen-Waechter, was brutally clear: St Petersburg could end the crisis by simply recognizing the annexation of Bosnia without further ado. When the Russians complied and the Serbs followed suit – promising in addition to live henceforward as good neighbours of Austria-Hungary – the crisis came to an abrupt end.

The flexibility of the European states system, 1909–11

The Bosnian annexation crisis has been seen as a significant landmark on the road to polarization and war, if not actually a 'dress-rehearsal' for 1914. Bülow himself claimed (admittedly, after the war) to have given the Kaiser the valedictory advice: 'Do not repeat the Bosnian crisis.' Nicholas II vowed that Russia 'will not forget' the German 'ultimatum' of March 1909, and a determination not to tolerate a repetition was certainly a factor in his decision to mobilize in 1914. As for the Central Powers, the exchange of letters between the German and Austro-Hungarian chiefs of staff, in March 1909, in which Moltke gave Conrad a most un-Bismarckian assurance of military support if an Austrian move against Serbia should provoke a Russian attack, has been seen as marking the transformation of the Dual Alliance from a defensive into an offensive instrument, setting the states system on course for the collision that occurred five years later. Moreover, even if there was never any question of a general war between the great powers in 1909, the military measures taken by Serbia and Montenegro against Austria-Hungary, and the threat of coercion by the latter, implied the involvement of a great power in war over a European question for the first time since the great eastern crisis of the 1880s; and precipitated an ominous build-up of armaments by all the Balkan states over the next few years. As for the great powers, the militarization of diplomacy in the Bosnian crisis encouraged the drawing of dangerous conclusions about the efficacy of negotiating from strength that left its mark on the *mentalités* of decision-makers on both sides. If William II congratulated Archduke Franz Ferdinand on a success that had 'demonstrated visibly to the world that when the two empires stand together, Europe just *has to* pay attention to them,' the Entente Powers too admitted, albeit with bad grace, that the 'mailed fist' had prevailed; and the British urged the Russians to look to their armaments in view of 'the close solidarity between Germany and Austria-Hungary and the tendency which was shown to establish an Austro-German hegemony in Europe' – an analysis which Nicholas II endorsed 'with great emphasis'. Perhaps most ominous of all, the Austro-Russian entente, that had served for over a decade to contain the most dangerous problem of all on the European scene had been shattered – beyond repair, as it turned out. Henceforth both Russia and Austria-Hungary handled this explosive question from positions of mutual hostility, each assuming the worst of the other's intentions, until their final confrontation in 1914.

Yet this view of the significance of the Bosnian annexation crisis is perhaps too deterministic. It is true that the formation between 1905 and 1908 of Anglo-French and Anglo-Russian ententes operating within Europe showed the potential for polarization within the states system; and that the annexation crisis indeed divided Europe into two antagonistic blocs and could only be resolved when one side succeeded in imposing its will on the other (albeit, thanks to the uneven military balance, without recourse to war). There was, however, no straight line running from 1909 to 1914. The breakdown of the system in 1914 was the culmination of an unremitting crisis that started in 1911 and that lasted for three years, a crisis partly thrust upon the powers, partly exacerbated by their own responses to it, but one which finally produced a pessimism that amounted almost to desperation in many European capitals. In the two years of relative calm that followed the end of the annexation crisis, by contrast, the states system quite rapidly recovered a degree of flexibility. Feelings of insecurity and fears of isolation which, during the confrontation over Bosnia, had put a premium on maintaining solidarity within power groupings, were dissipated, and separate interests reasserted themselves. The blocs that had seemed to dominate diplomacy in 1908–9 were weakened, as conflicting interests reappeared within them and as common interests gave rise to links between members of theoretically opposing blocs. The polarization of 1908–9 had not proved permanent. The flexibility of the system had indeed been impaired by the growth of Anglo-German antagonism after the First Moroccan crisis, and, even more, by the breakdown of communication between Russia and Austria-Hungary after the Bosnian crisis; but it had not yet been destroyed.

In St Petersburg, for example, indignation over Germany's brutal 'ultimatum' – in any case largely a myth put about by Izvolsky to gain sympathy in London and Paris – soon gave way to a cooler appraisal of Russia's long-term interests. True, Izvolsky's own reputation never recovered from the 'diplomatic Tshushima' of 1909: Stolypin promoted his own brother-in-law, Sazonov, to keep an eye on him in the foreign office, before installing him as foreign minister on Izvolsky's transfer to the Paris embassy in 1910. For Stolypin, and his supporters in the Octobrist and Moderate

Right factions in the Duma, salvation still lay in the middle course they had advocated prior to the Bosnian crisis. While they were determined to hold on to Russia's links with the Western Powers, resisting demands from reactionary elements at court and from the Extreme Right in the Duma for a return to the *Dreikaiserbund*, they were equally deaf to Liberals and Nationalists who were willing to risk a confrontation with the Central Powers. Admittedly, nobody in St Petersburg was interested in attempting to do business with Austria-Hungary: on the contrary, at the diplomatic level, Stolypin and Sazonov continued to pursue Izvolsky's plan for a defensive bloc of Balkan states, possibly even including Turkey, to frustrate what they were convinced were Vienna's expansionist designs. As the Balkan states were more concerned to carve up Turkey than ally with her, and as they were deeply at odds over their respective claims to the Ottoman inheritance, little progress was made towards the realization of this exceedingly dangerous objective, one that threatened to precipitate a fatal clash between the defensive proccupations of Austria-Hungary and Russia – and the Eastern Question subsided into three years of relative calm. It is also true that it was partly in order to pre-empt any future humiliations from Germany that St Petersburg embarked in 1910 on a new military programme designed to improve the effectiveness of Russia's mobilization plans against both Central Powers (as well as to guard against possible dangers in the Far East). As, however, this plan involved the transfer of a sizable number of troops from exposed positions in the Polish fortresses into the interior (where they could be more efficiently concentrated) the new programme was, initially at any rate, received in Berlin with relief. Meanwhile, the resumption of annual meetings between the Kaiser and the Tsar, in the Gulf of Finland in July 1909 and, most importantly, at Potsdam in November 1910, pointed to a possible restoration of the the Bismarckian 'wire' between Berlin and St Petersburg.

For the Germans, this was a most welcome development. In October 1908 panic fears of encirclement had driven them to support an Austrian action of which they had not really approved, and they found Austrian pretensions to leadership of the Dual Alliance exceedingly irksome. Certainly, Berlin's gestures were not to be taken at face value. Moltke's assurances to Conrad, for example, were of no practical significance whatever – given the absolute impossibility of Russian intervention in an Austro-Serbian conflict – nor was Kiderlen's brutal diplomatic intervention at St Petersburg simply a demonstration of alliance solidarity. It was also an attempt, by ending a tiresome crisis that was keeping Germany in thrall to its ally, to recover leadership of the alliance for Germany; and to Austrian ears the visiting Kaiser's famous 'shining armour' speech was as gratuitously patronising as his 'brilliant second' telegram after Algeçiras. Indeed, even if Kiderlen's 'ultimatum' had been a terrible blow to Izvolsky personally, this fitted in only too well with a sophisticated diplomatic design that the Germans were to pursue for the next five years: namely, to 'negotiate' the encircling bloc apart – in this instance by persuading the Russians to abandon a useless western alignment that had brought them only humiliation and return to a *Dreikaiserbund*. When Nicholas II and Sazonov came to Potsdam in November 1910, for example, the Germans were not only assiduous in demonstrating that Russian and German separate interests admitted of accommodation – recognizing Russia's sphere of interest in Persia, in return for Russian acceptance of Germany's plans for the Baghdad Railway. They went on to assure their guests that they would withhold support from any Austrian activities in the Balkans that might even by implication appear to be directed against Russia. It was also significant that the Germans gave this last assurance in exchange for a Russian promise to abstain from any combinations Great Britain might contrive against Germany; and that Kiderlen hoped to get this promise, 'the Alpha and Omega of the agreement', in writing, in order to make use of it in London. In fact, even if the Russians refused in the end to commit themselves to paper, it seemed by the end of 1910 that the Germans were making good progress towards their related objectives: restoring the wire to St Petersburg and cutting loose from dependence on Vienna. Far from providing a blueprint for German policy until 1914, the Conrad-Moltke exchange had been finally buried, and Germany had returned to a Bismarckian stance in the Near East.

All this had serious implications for Austria-Hungary. Although Aehrenthal had boasted to the council of ministers that the annexation had been a 'textbook example' of a diplomatic success, and that Europe had again learned to respect Austria-Hungary as a great power, the reality was somewhat different. True, he had managed to bring Serbia to heel without involving the Monarchy, let alone Europe, in war. In fact, that the militarization of diplomacy had not gone further owed much to Aehrenthal's iron nerve: unlike his successor in 1914 he remained impervious to the bellicosity of his military advisers, coolly refusing to respond to Serbia's military bluster and only stepping up the Monarchy's military preparations to clinch his final diplomatic victory. It soon became clear, however, that even the local Serbian problem had not been resolved: public opinion in Serbia was now irretrievably hostile to the Monarchy, while the government in Belgrade ignored Vienna's offers of a commercial treaty to end the Pig War, and connived at an increasing flow of agitators and propaganda into the south Slav territories of the Monarchy in flagrant violation of the promise of good-neighbourly behaviour by dint of which it had escaped military chastisement in March 1909. From here the road led straight to Sarajevo.

More immediately, Aehrenthal's forceful assertion of the Monarchy's independence in the annexation crisis had damaged its international position generally, exposing it to virtual isolation and rendering it more dependent than ever on Germany – the very opposite of what Aehrenthal had planned. The Austro-Russian entente, on which the Monarchy had relied to achieve a measure of independence of its allies was now lost beyond recall; the French and British were deeply distrustful, especially the latter, who during the Bosnian crisis had been enthusiastic advocates of Russia's plans for a Balkan league to 'spell checkmate to Aehrenthal's policy of obtaining Austrian supremacy in the Balkans'. In Italy, the government had loyally refrained from demanding compensation for the annexation, which did not come within the purview of Article VII of the Triple Alliance; but public opinion was of a very different mind, as a host of irredentist and nationalist demonstrations bore witness; and even such a staunch advocate of the Triple Alliance as Tittoni was piqued at Aehrenthal's cavalier behaviour. At any rate, on the occasion of Nicholas II's visit to King Victor Emmanuel at Racconigi in October 1909, the Russians and Italians agreed to guard against future surprises, to work to maintain the *status quo* in the Balkans, and to refrain from making secret agreements with third parties (i.e. with Austria-Hungary in the manner of Buchlau). Very much in the manner of Buchlau, however, was a secret exchange of assurances regarding Russia's and Italy's interests in the Straits and in Tripoli respectively.

In this situation, the task facing Aehrenthal was clear: if he were ever to attain that independence by which he set such store, he must smooth over the feathers ruffled by the annexation crisis and must avoid being drawn into confrontations, the inevitable consequence of which could only be to increase the Monarchy's dependence on Germany. In the last three years of his life, therefore, he transformed himself into an almost Metternichian advocate of stability and the *status quo*. Not that this cut any ice with the Russians, whose distrust went far deeper than Izvolsky's personal grievances: within months of taking office Sazonov was urging the Greeks to look to their armaments, lest they 'see Austria at Salonica some day'. Nor were the Balkan governments impressed by Aehrenthal's schoolmasterly adjurations to uphold the *status quo* and his lofty dismissal of their dreams of expansion at the expense of the Ottoman Empire. On the contrary, his attempts to promote stability only tended to play into the hands of Russian diplomats who, in their untiring efforts to construct a league of Balkan states, were by no means averse to pandering to their dreams of aggrandizement.

With Italy, by contrast, Aehrenthal was more successful. In December 1909 an Austro-Italian *status quo* agreement did something to draw the teeth of Racconigi, especially when Aehrenthal volunteered to bring the Sanjak within the purview of Article VII – a clear declaration that the Monarchy had no plans to expand further into the Balkans. True, harsh realities dictated that the Triple Alliance retained its ambiguities: as simple geographical facts dictated that neither could concede domination of the Adriatic to the other, the years after the Bosnian crisis saw the two allies engaged in a naval race to build Dreadnoughts, and it was significant that, until the great Balkan crisis of 1912, it was still Italy rather than Russia that loomed largest in the eyes of Austrian military planners. Aehrenthal, however, insisted that higher political considerations demanded that military and naval expenditure be kept within bounds. With the emperor's support he prevailed even against such powerful Italophobes as Archduke Franz Ferdinand and Conrad, the former being excluded from any role in policy-making, the latter – after a major row with Aehrenthal in December 1911 – being dismissed from his post as chief of staff. Altogether, Austro-Italian relations were improving steadily. These two powers were not yet on the road to 1914.

Nor did Anglo-Austrian antagonism remain a permanent feature of the international scene. By the time of his of death in February 1912, Aehrenthal was eulogized even by Grey as 'an element of stability in the councils of Europe' who would be 'much missed'; and Asquith termed him 'not only the doyen, but also the most important of all the foreign ministers'. Their growing appreciation of his efforts to uphold the *status quo* was matched by a distinct coolness towards Russia's activities in the Near East. The close collaboration with St Petersburg that had been such a striking feature of the Bosnian crisis proved a fleeting phenomenon as the British found Izvolsky's constant harping on the need for a barrier against Austria-Hungary's alleged expansionist plans increasingly unconvincing; and they began to view the failure of Sazonov's attempts to construct a Balkan league with complete indifference. In contrast to the Bosnian crisis, in neither the Balkan Wars nor in the July crisis did Balkan issues in themselves count for anything in British decision-making. If, at critical moments in the great crisis of 1912–14, the British aligned themselves with St Petersburg against Vienna it was not on account of such issues, but because they felt that the real issue at stake was the survival of France and Russia, and by extension of Great Britain, as independent great powers.

In the day-to-day diplomacy of calmer times entente solidarity was somewhat less central to British calculations. It was in vain that the British embassy in St Petersburg urged Grey to transform the Anglo-Russian entente into a formal alliance as the best guarantee against the machinations of reactionary advocates of a *Dreikaiserbund*. Although Grey and his advisers were certainly disconcerted by the meetings between the Kaiser and the Tsar (about which they found out very little) they were realists enough to see that an actual alliance with the tsarist state would never be acceptable to the mass of Liberal opinion. Instead, they continued to put their trust in Nicholas II personally while doing what they could to appease the Russians in bilateral questions. For example, they persistently connived at Russia's interventions in Persia well beyond her sphere of influence as defined in 1907 and brushed off vociferous protests from their own left-wing supporters in parliament. Although the shadow of polarization never quite disappeared, the three years of relative calm that followed the Bosnian crisis saw British diplomacy recovering a degree of detachment that made a real contribution to the restoration of flexibility to the states system.

For the British, a slackening of interest in those issues of entente solidarity in the Near East that had dominated the states system during the the Bosnian crisis was matched by an increasing preoccupation with a bilateral problem of their own, which until 1912 did not impinge directly on their relations with their entente partners: naval rivalry with Germany. The years 1908 to 1912 saw Anglo-German hostility reach its height as successive attempts to reach agreement by negotiations *à deux* ended in failure. The British had few illusions: the Kaiser had told them, on the occasion of Edward VII's visit to Kronberg in August 1908, that any attempt to press him to modify his naval construction plans would be tantamount to a declaration of war, and, in the *Daily Telegraph* interview three months later, he lamented his helplessness in the face of the ingrained Anglophobia of the German people. By the spring of 1909 the growing conviction that the Central Powers were set on establishing their hegemony over the continent precipitated a veritable naval scare in Great Britain: 'We want eight, and we won't wait'. True, by this time the Germans were beginning to have second thoughts. The chronic inability of the conservative landowners and National Liberal industrialists in the

Reichstag to agree on the apportionment of the new taxation necessitated by the Dreadnought programme ended with the collapse of Bülow's 'Bloc', whereupon the Kaiser appointed the Prussian bureaucrat Bethmann Hollweg to preside over a government of the Right that lacked any stable majority in the Reichstag. In this situation, and confronted with the results of ten years of propaganda by the Navy League, the new Chancellor could not contemplate driving the Nationalists into opposition by simply abandoning *Flottenpolitik*. On the other hand, he recognized its ultimate futility, and it was partly from a genuine desire to reduce what was ultimately pointless expenditure, that in 1910 he and Kiderlen made a series of proposals to London for the limitation and slowing down of naval construction programmes. Even more important to them than financial considerations, however, was their overriding diplomatic objective: the disruption of the encircling Entente – in this case by means of a highly political naval agreement with Great Britain. All German offers of concessions on the naval question were conditional on Great Britain's giving an absolute promise to remain neutral in a continental war. The British, for their part, would certainly have welcomed an agreement that would reduce their financial burdens, but they were never prepared to pay the political price demanded by the Germans; and the failure of the negotiations testified to the continuing centrality of the ententes in the thinking of British decision-makers, even in these years of relative calm. Equally, however, the fact that the negotiations took place at all, with no attempt by the British to involve their Entente partners or to co-ordinate their naval plans with those of France and Russia, showed that, even in this ultimately hopeless case, elements of flexibility still survived within the system.

Of all the great powers, France offered perhaps the most striking example of this flexibility. Even in the Bosnian crisis – apart from joining Russia and Great Britain in their ill-starred conference proposal – France had hardly behaved as a member of a tripartite group. French priorities lay not in the Balkans but in North Africa. There, it was a question of bolstering up the French-controlled regime in Morocco against internal rebellion and possible external challenges from Germany, guardian of Moroccan independence enshrined in the Act of Algeçiras. To this end, the French were quite prepared to seek an accommodation with Berlin, and by the spring of 1909 had succeeded in persuading the Germans both to resolve the tiresome Casablanca dispute by arbitration and to accept an extension of French political control in Morocco that went well beyond Algeçiras. A Franco-German agreement of 8 February promised fair treatment for German economic activities in Morocco and Germany accepted French political predominance in the sultanate. Partly, the Germans were yielding to the inevitable: already by December 1908 the Kaiser had decided that the preservation of Moroccan independence was simply an unrealistic aim: 'Well then, it becomes French after all.' Their calculations also extended, however – as with Russia at Potsdam and with Great Britain in the naval conversations – to an attempt to break up the Entente. The timing of the February agreement – at the height of the Serbian crisis – and accompanied by an extraordinarily tactless note from Paris to St Petersburg, informing the Russians that Serbia was not among Russia's vital interests, marked the very nadir of Franco-Russian relations in the prewar years.

Nor was a recovery assisted by the confusion that had developed in French policy-making since the fall of Delcassé. As J.F.V. Keiger has shown, a succession of weak foreign ministers had allowed two groups of officials to aspire to a directing role in the formulation of policy. The long-serving 'grands ambassadeurs' in the European capitals – Barrère in Rome, the Cambon brothers in London and Berlin, Crozier in Vienna, but no comparable figure, significantly enough, in the allied capital – were working assiduously to develop special ententes with the governments to which they were accredited. (It was not just the Germans who were obsessed with dissolving opposing power constellations.) Meanwhile, the permanent officials of the Quai d'Orsay, guardians of the traditions of the Parti Colonial, were striving to advance France's position in North Africa against all comers, friend and foe alike. Ultimately, insofar as these people precipitated the Second Moroccan crisis, it was to be in Paris that the chain reaction started that ended in 1914. For the time being, however, France's almost ostentatious lack of enthusiasm for confrontations in Europe was yet another contributory factor to the apparent return to normality.

CHAPTER 9

Polarization and war, 1911–14

The Second Moroccan crisis

The crisis that erupted in the summer of 1911 from Franco-German disagreements over remote regions of Morocco and Central Africa was to prove the start of a truly awesome chain reaction. In the following three years of almost continuous crisis, first the Ottoman possessions in North Africa and then the Ottoman Empire in Europe, were overwhelmed, until finally a direct threat was posed to the vital interests of the great powers in Europe that plunged them into the first general war for over a century. True, for two years the European states system showed enough flexibility to manage the crisis without embroiling the great powers in wars amongst themselves. Morocco and Tripoli were too remote from the vital interests of the powers to produce a relapse into the polarization of 1908; and if there were disturbing signs of both polarization and the militarization of diplomacy during the Balkan Wars of 1912–13, these proved just sufficiently serious to frighten the powers into putting their common interests in the maintenance of peace before their separate concerns, without, however, posing the kind of threat to their vital interests that was in 1914 to plunge them into war.

In the long term, however, the apparent vitality of the Concert of Europe was deceptive. In the first place, three years of continuous crisis inflicted irreparable damage on the states system: the constant strain on the international nerves led to a steady diminution of trust, polarization, and a concentration on an armaments race that had by 1914 produced an extremely dangerous situation, in which both groups of powers were better prepared for war than ever before. The military imbalance that had helped to keep the peace in 1905 and 1909 had disappeared. In the second place, the destruction of the Ottoman Empire in Europe, a buffer state that had performed a vital stabilizing function even after, or especially after, the collapse of the Austro-Russian entente, created by 1913 a power vacuum throughout the Near East. That the fiercely competitive successor states were all too willing – unlike the Turks – to throw in their lot with one side or the other in pursuit of their ambitions, made both Vienna and St Petersburg fearful for their most vital interests; and the implications of this for their allies and entente partners made the developing crisis in the Near East a crisis of the whole states system. It was no coincidence that within less than a year the system dissolved in general war.

The Second Moroccan crisis, like the First in 1905, was precipitated by France. In the spring of 1911 a ginger group of officials in the Quai d'Orsay decided to take advantage of disturbances in Morocco to occupy the capital, Fez. Clearly this implied a threat to the independence of the sultanate enshrined in the Act of Algeçiras. The French, as even their British friends had to admit, were 'on thin ice'; and Jules Cambon in Berlin, working hard to improve Franco-German relations, was horrified at this reckless challenge to a Germany already disgruntled at the meagre results of the Franco-German Moroccan agreement of February 1909: 'We are going to Fashoda by way of Ems.' It was the German reaction, however – again as in 1905 – that transformed the affair into a European crisis.

Of course, issues of international law and the Act of Algeçiras were no more central to the German position in 1911 than the Madrid Convention had been in 1905. In fact, the Germans were prepared to see Moroccan independence, which the Kaiser had written off already in 1909, replaced by a French protectorate. But France must pay them a handsome price for their acquiescence. In contrast to 1905, this price need not be paid in Morocco. It is true that, prior to the dispatch of the *Panther* on 1 July, Kiderlen had launched a press campaign to stir up public interest in Germany's alleged commercial and mining interests in Morocco. This was partly a move in German domestic politics, designed to strengthen the parties of the Right in the forthcoming Reichstag elections – especially as even the Social Democrats were no longer impervious to the attractions of *Weltpolitik* in terms of working-class prosperity. It was, however, a move that was to backfire very badly – in fact, a veritable object lesson in the dangers of whipping up public opinion as a diplomatic device. The public became in fact all too seriously engaged; and once the Kaiser vetoed the idea of war, and the diplomatic focus moved away from Morocco to Kiderlen's real objectives, the government found itself under strong attack for its pusillanimity. Kiderlen's aim – unfortunately rather less well publicized – was to lay the foundations of a German *Mittelafrika* by acquiring nothing less than the whole of the French Congo, in return for handing over Morocco to France. If this aim was from the start unrealistic, the rough methods by which Kiderlen pursued it proved fatal: he was gambling on extracting a bilateral agreement from the French, after first 'bringing them to their senses' by a 'blow on the table' – the demonstrative appearance of the gunboat *Panther* in the internationally closed port of Agadir.

This move was completely counter-productive. It not only roused the French to resist but brought the British on to the scene. As in 1905, and despite – or even because of – the prospect of a Franco-German deal, the British were again seized with the *idée fixe* that Germany was out to disrupt the entente. On 4 July Grey warned the German ambassador that Great Britain must not be ignored in any agreement France and Germany might reach over Morocco; and when after two weeks the Germans failed to reply, Lloyd George made the same statement in public in his famous Mansion House speech. Whether or not A.J.P. Taylor is correct in his claim that the speech, intended rather as a warning to Paris than to Berlin, simply exemplified the tendency of diplomacy by public speeches to hit the wrong target, it certainly caused a furore in Germany. Indeed, by August, the crisis appeared to have become primarily an Anglo-German one, as something of a war scare developed in Great Britain, where the fleet was temporarily alerted and the government considered plans for sending a force of 160,000 to assist the French. By the autumn, however, Franco-German negotiations were under way and although the British at times urged the French to show more consideration for Spain's rights in Morocco, and even for German demands in West Africa, they were never in any doubt about the primary importance of standing by the entente. In the event, the support they gave the French in resisting the more extreme German demands helped to bring Kiderlen to accept a genuine compromise in the Franco-German agreement of 4 November: Germany agreed to recognize a French protectorate over Morocco (duly established in February 1912), and in return received slices of French Congo and Cameroon – but only modest slices: *Mittelafrika* remained a distant dream.

The Second Moroccan crisis was an important landmark in relations between Germany and the two Western Powers. By reawakening British apprehensions about a German threat to the independence of France, it strengthened the Anglo-French entente in a number of ways – not least by converting Churchill and Lloyd George, hitherto leading advocates of restraint in the Anglo-German naval race, into ardent exponents of the need to stand up to Germany. In the autumn of 1911 the full Cabinet was at last initiated into the consultations that had been going on since 1906 between the British and French naval authorities. By the following summer the decisions of the British and French governments, in theory taken independently, to reposition their battle fleets, the French concentrating in the Mediterranean and the British in the North Sea, implied at least a heightened moral commitment on the part of the British to defend the north coast of France; and although the British insisted that the exchange of letters, in November 1912, between Grey and the French ambassador Paul Cambon, providing for consultation in the event of a threat to peace, contained no actual commitment to fight, the French certainly read a good deal more into it.

True, these developments roused some misgivings in London. Throughout the Moroccan crisis a number of cabinet ministers had been alarmed at the extent to which their colleagues seemed to be allowing France to drag the country into an unnecessary conflict with Germany; just as a vocal left-wing faction in the Commons was outraged by Grey's connivance at Russia's attempts to crush the constitutional movement in Persia. It was to appease these critics that in November 1911 Grey promised to keep the Cabinet informed of his dealings with France and Russia in future; and in March 1912, in an ultimate gesture to pacify the advocates of an improvement in relations with Germany, the government allowed the Lord Chancellor, Haldane, to go to Berlin to investigate the possibility of a naval agreement. In the event, however, Grey and his officials persisted in their secretive ways, while the Haldane mission, the last attempt at a naval agreement with Germany, came to nothing. On the one hand, Bethmann Hollweg, under pressure from Tirpitz and from Anglophobe elements stirred up by the Moroccan crisis, had to acquiesce in an actual increase in the German naval programme (the *Novelle* of 1912); on the other, the British, solicitous as ever for their ententes with Paris and St Petersburg, remained impervious to German demands for a political agreement that amounted in effect to a non-aggression pact. Although it is true that, once this dialogue of the deaf was finally abandoned, the tone of Anglo-German relations was to improve steadily over the next two years, this could not offset the tightening of links between Great Britain and France that remained one of the enduring results of the Second Moroccan crisis.

Even so, perhaps the crisis only confirmed the British in a policy they had been pursuing for the past five years. In France, by contrast, it was the catalyst of a decisive and momentous change. That the Franco-German settlement of November 1911 was in fact a genuine compromise was shown by the outrage with which it was greeted by the Right in both countries: in Germany, for example, the crown prince descended in person on the Reichstag to applaud the opposition speakers and the colonial minister was forced to resign. In France, a great wave of anger against German bullying seized the nation, and found expression in the elections of January 1912 that swept the Right to power with the Lorrainer Poincaré, the embodiment of the *réveil national*, as prime minister. The upshot was a marked toughening of French attitudes towards all international issues – including the explosive situation in south-east Europe – that was also reflected in the adoption by the Army in the spring of 1912 of the recklessly offensive strategic Plan XVI. From the start, Poincaré was determined to put an end to the drift and confusion that had afflicted French policy since the fall of Delcassé, and to get a grip on both irresponsible *bureaux* of the Quai d'Orsay and insubordinate *grands ambassadeurs*. The former were henceforth closely supervised by the prime minister himself, while the latter were forbidden to pursue their independent foreign policies: Jules Cambon in Berlin and Barrère in Rome were reined in, and Crozier in Vienna dismissed; while the ailing and ineffective ambassador at St Petersburg was replaced by the forceful and trustworthy Delcassé. Poincaré's view of the purpose of foreign policy was straightforward and simple: to support one's friends and keep one's alliance bloc in good shape; flirtations with the other side, and ententes cutting across the alliance system he rejected as likely to cause confusion and increase the risk of war as a result of misunderstanding or miscalculation. This approach certainly had the virtue of clarity; but like Caprivi's in the early 1890s, it perhaps underestimated the dangers inherent in a polarized states system. If the 'interpenetration of alliances' was not without its drawbacks, a rigidly polarized system that restricted contacts between the blocs could equally easily lead to misconceptions and the escalation of crises. In shrinking from the risks involved in seeking security through *détente* Poincaré was in fact committing France to a gamble – perhaps a disastrous gamble – on the efficacy of deterrence.

The long-term impact of the Second Moroccan crisis on Germany's role in the states system was equally ominous. True, insofar as its disappointing outcome led the German government to question the usefulness of both *Weltpolitik* and *Flottenpolitik*, it served to reduce possible sources of conflict. For example, although Tirpitz tried to exploit the crisis to increase expenditure on the Navy, Bethmann, with the support of the

Army, managed to keep his plans within bounds; and once Great Britain and Germany agreed to differ after the failure of the Haldane mission, naval expenditure assumed a decidedly secondary role in German defence planning. Similarly, once the government had concluded that its forceful pursuit of *Weltpolitik* in Africa had only been counter-productive, it brushed aside the continuing outcry from the Pan-German lobby it had so unwisely aroused and decided to settle for what it could get by conciliation: two years of (eventually successful) negotiations with Great Britain over the future of the Portuguese colonies seemed to show that imperialist activity outside Europe could still be successfully accommodated within the states system.

Ironically enough, however, these more hopeful developments were in part only reflections of distinctly ominous features of the German reaction to the Second Moroccan crisis. For example, declining influence of the naval lobby reflected a growing concentration on the Army. The *réveil national* in France was matched by a nationalist backlash in Germany that gave birth in January 1912 to the *Deutsche Wehrverein* (German Army League), a new pressure group that was soon to put the imperialist and navalist preoccupations of the Pan-German League and the *Flottenverein* in the shade. It was, indeed, a striking consequence of the Second Moroccan crisis that it led to much more open discussion of the possibility of war among the general public; and the widespread disappointment over the resultant settlement fed the belief that Germany would only be able to get her way by means of a general war. Not that these were yet the ideas of the ruling élite: the Army leaders managed to fend off the *Deutsche Wehrverein*'s demands for a massive increase in the size of the army that would have diluted its élitist composition and undermined its usefulness as a bastion of the social order. Even so, a new Army Law of March 1912, which put the emphasis on preparedness, bore witness both to the government's heightened awareness of France as a potential enemy, and to its determination to meet this growing threat. Equally ominous, the lower priority the government henceforth accorded to African questions reflected not the abandonment of *Weltpolitik*, but a shift in its focus, to a greater concentration on Germany's remaining imperialist concerns in infinitely more explosive areas such as Asia Minor – and by extension the Ottoman Empire as a whole and the Balkan states through which ran the line of communications from Berlin to Baghdad.

This was a problem for the future. In 1911 the Ottoman Empire was still functioning as an effective buffer state containing great power rivalry at a tolerable level, and the Second Moroccan crisis had little impact on the relations of Russia and Austria-Hungary with Germany and with each other. Russo-German relations continued in the spirit of Potsdam. The Russians were too conscious of their own military weakness, and too indifferent to west African questions to go beyond platonic expressions of sympathy in Paris; and like the conclusion of the Franco-German agreement on Morocco in February 1909, at the height of the Serbian crisis, Russia's ratification of the Potsdam agreement in August 1911, at the height of the Moroccan crisis, and the express reaffirmation of the Potsdam declarations by the Kaiser, the Tsar and their ministers in a very cordial meeting at Port Baltic in July 1912, showed that the states system was still flexible enough to allow alliance partners to pursue their separate interests.

By the same token, the coolness that had characterized Austro-German relations since the end of the Bosnian crisis was if anything confirmed by the events of 1911. In the first place, Aehrenthal regarded the *Panthersprung* (of which he had received no advance warning) as a needless provocation of the Western Powers, while the Hungarian prime minister declared openly in parliament that Morocco lay outside the scope of the Triple Alliance. In the second place, Vienna and Berlin were increasingly at odds in the Near East. The Austrians were exasperated when the Germans, concerned above all for their influence at Constantinople, refused point blank to give restraining advice to the Young Turk regime, whose brutal centralizing policies had resulted in a bloody conflict with its Albanian subjects. Certainly, Aehrenthal appreciated the advantages of a strong regime at Constantinople – 'the lid on the pot that keeps the stuff inside from boiling over'; at the same time, however, he had no desire to see Italy usurping the Monarchy's three-hundred-year-old role as protector of the Catholic tribes of northern Albania, and he was desperately striving to persuade Constantinople to abandon repression for conciliation – after all, the Albanians might some day prove, for both Turkey and Austria-Hungary, an invaluable barrier against Slav domination of the western Balkans. On this occasion, the Albanian rebellion ended when the Young Turks offered concessions. Meanwhile, Austro-Hungarian and Russian influence in the rest of the Balkans remained in a state of balance. The Russians had the upper hand in Serbia and Bulgaria, although their efforts to bring the two states into a defensive alliance against Austria-Hungary continued to founder on the rock of their rival claims in Macedonia. The Austrians still had the upper hand in Bucharest and even managed to exploit the revival of hostility between the rulers of Serbia and Montenegro (sharpened by the elevation of Prince Nikita of

Montenegro to the rank of king, and by repeated attempts by Montenegrin exiles living in Belgrade to contrive his assassination) to draw Montenegro into the Monarchy's orbit. Even so – and despite the disappearance of the entente of 1897 – so long as Austro-Russian rivalry was contained at this relatively low level of indecisive diplomatic manoeuvres, it could still be accommodated within the states system.

The Tripoli War and the destabilization of the Near East

In terms of the stability of the states system as a whole, the most far-reaching consequence of the Second Moroccan crisis was its impact on Italy and the Ottoman Empire. For over twenty years the Italians had been collecting assurances from the other great powers that in the event of the collapse of the Ottoman Empire they would have no claims to the Ottoman province of Tripoli; and they had of recent years been irritated when Turkey's all too understandable distrust found expression in discriminatory measures against Italian economic enterprises there. It was, however, the impending alteration of the balance of power in the Mediterranean, consequent on the establishment of a French protectorate over Morocco, that actually precipitated the Italian declaration of war on Turkey and the invasion of Tripoli at the end of September 1911. The operation was to prove a difficult one for the Italians, who although they established themselves easily enough in the coastal towns, found progress frustratingly slow inland, against a combination of Ottoman troops and native guerrilla forces (the latter not being finally suppressed until 1926). Meanwhile, deadlock set in on the diplomatic front, when Italy's formal declaration of the annexation of Tripoli in full sovereignty on 5 November destroyed any possibility that the powers might be able to mediate a compromise solution along the lines of the Bosnian settlement of the Treaty of Berlin. In this situation, with the war aims of the belligerent parties too far apart to admit of compromise, but with neither party possessing the military superiority to impose its will on the other, the powers had a foretaste of the nightmare that was to bedevil the European states system for four years after 1914.

It is true that the extra-European activities of the powers had sometimes acted as a safety valve for tensions within the states system, diverting attention away from potential flash points in Europe to the periphery of the continent. The Second Moroccan Crisis, however, and especially the

Tripoli War to which it gave rise, was a devastating demonstration of the destabilizing consequences of European imperialism. It was not simply that Italy's open flouting of legality – in the most flagrant case of aggression by a great power against the Ottoman Empire since the eighteenth century – and the failure of the other powers to find an effective response to it, undermined the moral fabric of the states system. Over the next two years, the resort to violence seemed set to become the normal way of proceeding: already by January 1912 Sir Arthur Nicolson, experienced permanent under-secretary in the Foreign Office, had 'never seen the world in such a disturbed condition'. At a more concrete level, the Tripoli War set in train a fatal chain reaction. Insofar as it undermined the prestige, stability and, ultimately, the very existence of the Ottoman Empire, it confronted the powers with the gravest European crisis since the 1870s.

Equally serious was the patent inability of the Concert of Europe to take control of the situation. Certainly, the Italo-Ottoman dispute had been rendered decidedly intractable by the Italian declaration of annexation. At the same time, however, the impotence of the concert reflected the fact that to function effectively the states system needed a manager, in the style of Castlereagh, Metternich or Bismarck with whom, it must be said, not one of the decision-makers in the European capitals on the eve of the Great War could remotely stand comparison. Perhaps, even more ominously, the inability of the powers to get to grips with the crisis reflected the deepening polarization of the system: Italy and Turkey were the two most precariously balanced powers in the states system, and in the last resort none of the non-belligerents was prepared to apply serious diplomatic pressure in Rome or in Constantinople at the risk of driving an offended party into the opposing camp. Meanwhile, the divisions that developed, even within the alliance groupings, only further confounded the confusion prevailing in the concert.

Certainly, Berlin and Vienna were united in their embarrassment at seeing their ally, Italy, attacking their friend, Turkey; but they were by no means united as to remedies. This partly reflected their long-standing differences over the value of their alliance with Italy, who was offering material help to Germany in a war with France, but only neutrality to Austria-Hungary in a war with Russia. The Germans, mindful of the overriding importance of the alliance, and calculating that the sooner Turkey could be brought to accept defeat, the sooner they could set about mending fences at Constantinople, not only connived at Italy's efforts to end the stalemate in Tripoli by striking at the Dardanelles and the Dodecanese Islands, but pressed their Austrian allies to fall into line.

Aehrenthal, admittedly, had no wish to jettison the alliance with Italy: he saw in the diversion of Italian military power to North Africa a welcome reduction of the potential threat to the Monarchy's south-western frontier; and when Conrad von Hoetzendorf persisted in pressing him to seize the opportunity of Italy's preoccupation with North Africa to strike her a blow that would render her harmless for ever, Aehrenthal secured his dismissal from the post of chief of staff. All the same, the Austrians were distinctly less willing than the Germans to make light of the threat posed by the Tripoli War to the stability of the Ottoman Empire and of the Near East in general. Even Aehrenthal, in the very first weeks of the war, responded sharply to the appearance of the Italian fleet off the Albanian coast, warning Rome that not only territorial changes, but even military operations in the Balkans would constitute an alteration in the *status quo* entitling Austria-Hungary to claim compensation under Article VII of the Triple Alliance – a redefinition that was to cost the Monarchy dear when it came to undertake its own military operations against Serbia in 1914. After February 1912 his successor, Berchtold, was even less inclined to truckle to Italy, and rather more willing to listen to Archduke Franz Ferdinand, for whom, as an ardent clerical and a grandson of the last king of the Two Sicilies, the House of Savoy and its subjects were simply 'our enemies and will always remain so'. But even the heir apparent could not prevail in the face of a stream of warnings from Berlin reiterating Italy's threats to abandon the alliance if Vienna raised objections to her operations in the eastern Mediterranean. By July, with the Monarchy's allies united against it, and with the Austro-Russian entente lost beyond recall, Franz Joseph and Berchtold were appealing in desperation to London for help in restraining Italy; but the British would not contemplate separating themselves from the French and Russians to the extent of participating in a *démarche* with Austria-Hungary. In the summer of 1912, as William II flaunted his cordial relations with Italy and Russia in meetings with King Victor Emmanuel at Venice and with Tsar Nicholas at Port Baltic, the impotent isolation of the power that had the most direct interest in the stability of the Near East boded no good for the effectiveness of the states system.

Nor was effective leadership or co-ordination to be expected from the Triple Entente powers. The British, once the possibility of a compromise settlement mediated by the powers disappeared, confined themselves to safeguarding their interests in Egypt, which they felt would be threatened 'to an unprecedented degree' if a great power, especially a member of the Triple Alliance, ever established itself in the eastern Mediterranean.

Certainly, the Italians were not best pleased, when London informed them that they would not be allowed to retain possession of occupied Dodecanese islands; or when they were unceremoniously ordered out the fortress of Sollum – one of their few conquests in Tripoli – which the British claimed was Egyptian territory. The Russians were more inclined to seek to exploit the war for their own diplomatic advantage, albeit in a somewhat inconsequential and ineffective fashion. In November 1911 Charykov, now Russian ambassador at Constantinople, revived his dreams of 1908 and offered the Turks an alliance and protection of the Dardanelles against Italy if they would join a league of Balkan states and open the Straits to Russian warships. This so-called 'Charykov Kite' was never a very realistic construction, however, as the Balkan states were interested only in partitioning Turkey, not in allying with her; and in the face of Ottoman distrust and a marked lack of enthusiasm in London, it failed to get off the ground. A move towards the opposite pole, involving Russian support for Italy's position was urgently pressed by their ambassadors at Paris, Izvolsky and Tittoni, but came to nothing when the French made clear their disapproval of special relationships with any members of the Triple Alliance. Poincaré, certainly, had no intention of running after Italy. In the spring of 1912 those Mediterranean rivalries that had precipitated the crisis were revived when Italian warships intercepted the French steamers *Carthage* and *Manouba* and removed some Turkish passengers. In the French Chamber there was talk of war, and Poincaré made sure that Barrère delivered his fierce protest at Rome 'without altering a comma'. In short, in terms of Italy's alignments, the Tripoli War witnessed the end of a decade of drift towards the Triple Entente and the start of her return to the bosom of the Triple Alliance. In terms of the effectiveness of the concert it marked a low point in the history of the European states system: the complete inability of the great powers to devise a common line of action to contain the developing crisis allowed the war to drag on until it destabilized the whole Near East and confronted the powers with the most serious crisis of the long nineteenth century.

It is true that the opening up of the explosive Eastern Question was not actively desired by any of the great powers. Indeed, on the outbreak of the Tripoli War, both Russia and Austria-Hungary had expressly adjured the Balkan states to hold their peace. All the same, for the Russians, ever since the breach with Austria-Hungary in 1908, the stability of the Near East had been of secondary importance compared with the need to construct a barrier against the nightmare prospect of Austrian expansion. Once Charykov's project for a Balkan league including Turkey had failed,

St Petersburg, spurred on by evidence of Austrian interest in Montenegro and Albania, settled for a Balkan league without Turkish participation. This was achieved on 13 March 1912, when Serbia and Bulgaria signed an alliance, under Russian auspices, committing them to joint military resistance to any Austrian advance into the Sanjak. Thus, the Russians could assure their western partners that the alliance was a defensive one; and although the British would have preferred to see Sazonov taking the opportunity of the death of Aehrenthal to re-establish a working relationship with Vienna and thought his policy 'quite wrong', they kept their misgivings to themselves – especially as the French were insistent that any restoration of the Austro-Russian entente would end in a *Dreikaiserbund*. Unbeknown to the other powers, however, Russia had had to pay a high price for her defensive alliance, namely the inclusion of secret articles providing for the eventual partition of Macedonia between Serbia and Bulgaria, with a 'disputed zone' to be apportioned between them by the Tsar.

This was an extremely dangerous development and one to which the other powers, belatedly and imperfectly informed, could find no effective response. Although the March treaty gave Russia a veto over any military action against Turkey, Poincaré had no illusions about the practical value of this when he was presented with the text of the alliance during his visit to St Petersburg in August: 'c'est une alliance pour la guerre!' On that occasion, however, his attention was focused, not on Balkan issues but on the need to persuade the Russians to speed up their mobilization plans and build more railways to the German border. The British were if anything even more dismayed to learn of the secret annex; but in the shadow of the Port Baltic meeting where, Sazonov was careful to inform them, the Germans had been extraordinarily insistent about the need to restore the *Dreikaiserbund*, they decided it would never do to upset the Russians by 'appearing to criticize them'. Meanwhile the Germans, naïvely confident since Port Baltic of Russia's good intentions, not only accepted Sazonov's explanation of the Balkan alliance as a conservative device to restrain the Balkan states, but even foisted it on their more sceptical Austrian allies. That not even Russia, let alone the concert, was in a position to restrain the Balkan states became apparent when Bulgaria and Serbia went on to conclude secret agreements, this time without Russian participation and openly offensive, with Greece in June and with the utterly uncontrollable 'firebrand' Montenegro, in August.

Matters came to a head when the failure of the powers to contain the external threats to Turkey from Italy and the Balkan states combined with a fatal weakening of the Empire internally. On 10 July the Young Turkish regime, its popularity eroded by the stalemate in North Africa and the outbreak of another rebellion in Albania, was overthrown by a *coup* organized by senior army officers. By August it was clear, however, that the well-meaning efforts of the new 'Cabinet of All the Talents', dominated by Anglophile liberals and constitutionalists, had only made matters worse. Admittedly, the government had put an end to the Albanian revolt, by conceding a large measure of autonomy to the Albanians of the western provinces and Macedonia; and they set about purging recalcitrant Young Turkish elements from the civil service and the army. However, the unforeseen consequences of these measures were dire: on the one hand, the concessions to the Albanians caused a tremendous effervescence in the Balkan states, who saw their co-nationals in Macedonia consigned to Albanian domination; on the other, the temporary disorganization of the Ottoman army in the wake of the purge suggested to the Balkan governments that the moment was indeed at hand for the final liberation of Macedonia from the Ottoman yoke.

It was only now that the great powers began to turn their attention to the crisis; and as Austria-Hungary was the power that had most to fear from an upheaval in the Balkans, it was Berchtold who attempted to take the lead in activating the concert. On 13 August, he proposed that the powers should unite to urge the Turks to extend the privileges they had recently granted to the Albanians to the other inhabitants of Macedonia. The other powers, however, were not yet sufficiently alarmed to give the Balkan crisis priority over their own particular preoccupations, and their response to Berchtold's decentralization proposal was of a piece with the unco-ordinated and futile diplomacy of the Tripoli War. The French and Russians refused point blank to follow an Austrian lead (although in September Sazonov was to make his own bid for leadership of the concert with a proposal that was hardly distinguishable from Berchtold's). The British, fearful of giving umbrage to either the Anglophile regime in Turkey or their own Muslim subjects in India, dragged their feet over both Austrian and Russian proposals; and even despite complaints from St Petersburg stubbornly refused to allow the concert to speak in Great Britain's name at Constantinople. In Berlin, Bethmann and Kiderlen made a point of responding frostily, being determined to show Berchtold that they were not prepared to allow Germany's Near Eastern policy to be decided in Vienna.

It is true that by this time there was little chance that even a spectacular demonstration of unity by the concert could have restrained the Balkan governments which, as ever, thought only in terms of their own immediate advantage, and not at all of the ultimate consequences of their actions for the states system as a whole. In the event, Russia's theoretical veto counted for nothing: the Bulgarians, for example, were supremely confident that Russian public opinion would prevent Sazonov from exercising it – especially as the Russian minister in Sofia was all the time urging them to ignore 'foolish Sazonov'. Indeed, such tentative efforts as the powers now made to restrain them only spurred the Balkan states on to act quickly, lest the concert devise some effective intervention after all. At any rate, when at last on 8 October Russia and Austria-Hungary, acting as spokesmen of the concert, formally warned the Balkan states that they would not be allowed to profit from any act of aggression, adding that the powers were about to take in hand the question of reform in Turkey, this belated appeal to the ghost of Mürzsteg held no terrors at all for Montenegro, who proceeded at once to declare war on Turkey, followed within days by Bulgaria, Serbia and Greece.

The Balkan Wars

The Balkan states had calculated correctly in defying the united voice of the concert, and it was soon clear that there was nothing the latter could do to arrest their progress. Even the Austrians had to admit – as in the 1870s – that if they came to the assistance of Turkey they would only consolidate the Balkan league and drive the whole of the Christian Balkans into the arms of Russia. Although the Ottoman government hastened to make peace with Italy, formally ceding Tripoli in October, the disorganization of their forces and their foolish decision to adopt an offensive strategy, in preference to the defensive guerrilla operations envisaged by their Young Turkish predecessors, led to a series of striking defeats in set-piece battles. True, the initial successes of the Balkan states were deceptive: foreign observers were confirmed in their illusions about the effectiveness of *Blitzkrieg* methods – until the events of 1914 proved them wrong – and failed to notice that once the Turks managed to dig themselves in at the Tchataldja lines outside Constantinople the spectacular Bulgarian advance ground to a halt in indecisive trench warfare. Even so, by December 1912 the Ottoman Empire in Europe had been effectively reduced to the three fortresses of Adrianople, Scutari and Janina holding out against Bulgarian, Montenegrin and Greek forces respectively.

From the start, the impending disappearance of the Ottoman shock-absorber posed threats to what several powers considered to be their vital interests. Russia was certainly prepared to consider military intervention to prevent the seizure of Constantinople and the Straits by her Bulgarian protégés. Austria-Hungary, with the wholehearted support of Italy, refused point blank to allow Serbia to acquire territory on the Adriatic, their determination to establish an Albanian state that would prevent Slav domination of the western Balkans being sharpened by fears that a Serbian port on the Adriatic might some day become a Russian port. After all, the ethnic character of the territories in question was overwhelmingly and indisputably Albanian. Throughout November, however, the Serbian army defiantly continued its march to the sea, massacring large numbers of Albanians *en route* and meting out rough treatment to Austrian consular officials who got in the way. (In December, rumours of the kidnapping and mutilation of Consul Prochaska in Prisren were orchestrated into a veritable war scare in Vienna.) Sazonov, meanwhile, under equally strong pressure from public opinion, talked at times of backing Serbia's claims to the point of war.

The Austro-Russian confrontation was more serious than that of 1909, when the imbalance of military power on the continent had ruled out the possibility of war, because now, not one but both powers were prepared to threaten military action to back up their diplomatic demands. An adventurous offensive war plan adopted in St Petersburg in the summer of 1912 reflected a truly remarkable growth of confidence in Russia's military capacity; and if the Germans had initially welcomed the military plan of 1910, with its shifting of preparatory mobilization measures away from the western frontier into the interior, they now had to admit that it had enhanced Russia's military effectiveness after all. From the end of September, the Russians embarked on a whole series of military measures to back up their diplomacy: trial mobilizations; the retention with the colours of the service class due for dismissal (effectively increasing the size of the army by one third); troop movements towards the northern borders of Austria-Hungary; and in November, the Tsar and the military were only restrained by Sazonov's diplomatic and Kokovtsov's financial anxieties from implementing a partial mobilization that might well have sparked off a general war. The Austrians, for their part, were unwilling to negotiate at a military disadvantage and strengthened their forces against both Serbia in the south and Russia in Galicia – the crisis marked a definite shift in the focus of Austrian military planning from the Italians to the Slavs. Nor, so long as the diplomatic deadlock over Serbia's claims continued, was either Russia or Austria-Hungary prepared to relax its military preparations. There was no doubting the seriousness of the situation. Indeed,

Franz Joseph, deeply worried by Russian troop movements, declared the Monarchy's position to be worse than in 1866; and early in 1913 sent a personal emissary to St Petersburg to express his fears that if the tension continued war would break out in a matter of weeks.

If, in this instance, the danger was averted, the fact remained – as David Stevenson has most recently demonstrated – that the violent overthrow of the Ottoman Empire in Europe had inaugurated a period of almost permanent tension, in which civilian restraints on the expansion of armed forces were everywhere weakened, and all the great powers attained an unprecedented level of military preparedness that, within two years, was to make its own fatal contribution to the final cataclysm. Within months of the outbreak of the Balkan Wars, the combination of diplomatic impasse and military confrontation was reflected in a general tightening of alignments and deepening polarization within the states system. The French, for example, no longer attempted to restrain St Petersburg as they had done in 1909. On the contrary, Poincaré now promised support if Russia had to take the offensive against Austria-Hungary; while the French military tendered the advice that the moment was actually favourable for Russia to go to war. Although the British were distinctly reserved over Balkan issues, particularly Serbia's claims, it was in these months that they proceeded to tighten Anglo-French naval links and to confirm the entente in the Grey–Cambon letters; and on 4 December they even warned the Germans – via their friend Haldane, for greater emphasis – not to count on British neutrality in the event of a continental war.

On the Triple Alliance side, Rome was in absolute solidarity with Vienna on the issue of a Serbian port; and after a demonstrative visit by Archduke Franz Ferdinand and the Austro-Hungarian chief of staff to Berlin in November, followed on 2 December by Bethmann's announcement in the Reichstag that Germany would fight if her allies should be attacked 'while making good their interests' in the Balkans, Germany's alliances seemed in fact to have acquired the decidedly offensive edge that had only been a theoretical notion at the time of the Conrad–Moltke exchange of 1909. It should be emphasized, however, that the Germans were by no means minded to give Austria-Hungary *carte blanche* in the determination of alliance policy: on the contrary, Kiderlen was using the semi-official German press to qualify Bethmann's assurances and urge restraint on Vienna. Nor, as a famous 'war council' between the Kaiser and his military and naval advisers demonstrated on 8 December, were the Germans in the least anxious for war at this juncture – given the indifference of the public towards Balkan issues; given that since the Balkan upheaval Germany would no longer be able to count on Turkey in a war against Russia, while her Austrian allies might be distracted by a league of Balkan states equivalent to a seventh great power; and given Haldane's latest message, coupled with Tirpitz's predictions of defeat at sea. (Not only was the fleet as yet no match for the Royal Navy; the deepening of the Kiel Canal to accommodate Dreadnoughts would not be completed until the summer of 1914.) The 'war council' accordingly recommended expanding the army to redress the military balance; educating the public to understand the importance of Balkan issues, and cultivating the British in the hope that they might after all be neutral in a continental war. True, the absence of the Chancellor, indeed, of any civilian authority, from the 'war council' hardly supports the view that its recommendations constituted a 'blueprint' that the German government was to follow with timetable precision until the summer of 1914. On the other hand, the fact that its arguments for avoiding war against the Triple Entente in December 1912 were coupled with a programme for winning a war against France and Russia alone at some later date, was ominous enough.

The fact that, in the event, the great powers managed to subordinate the separate interests that had been paralysing the concert for the past fifteen months to the need to recover a degree of control over the situation and avert a general war testified both to the genuine alarm that had seized them as the Austro-Russian conflict intensified, and to a certain residual vitality of the European states system. In December 1912, the powers agreed to suggestions from Great Britain and Germany for an informal 'conference' of their ambassadors in London – a diplomatic device designed to serve as a clearing centre for information, to prevent the powers' drifting from ignorance or misunderstanding into positions from which they might be unable to retreat. At the same time the powers announced that they were reserving for their own decision those aspects of a future peace settlement (such as the future of the Aegean Islands and of the Ottoman lands on the Adriatic) that were too important for their own vital interests to be left to the belligerent states – a notable reversion to the concert idea in its classic nineteenth-century form. It must be admitted that the London conference, both in its origins and in its later methods of operation, itself pointed up some of the more dangerous features of the international situation: the very fact that in proposing it Great Britain and Germany were effectively acting as spokesmen for two armed camps showed that the polarization of the system was now more or less taken for granted; and the powers' rejection of a full-dress conference in the nineteenth-century style in favour of informal meetings over tea in Sir

Edward Grey's room at the Foreign Office reflected their well-founded fear that a formal conference that failed might indeed have catastrophic results. In the last resort, moreover – as so often in concert diplomacy – the realities of power politics prevailed over any desire for consensus, agreement reflecting not so much a unanimity of view as the ability of a stronger group of powers to impose its will on a weaker group or on an isolated power. The long-term – and disastrous – consequence of this, in both Vienna and St Petersburg, was an erosion of confidence in the concert as a means of safeguarding vital interests. For six dangerous months, however, it was nevertheless something of an achievement that the powers managed to maintain a semblance of unity in implementing the most far-reaching changes to the map of Europe since the Congress of Berlin.

The most explosive issue arising from Serbia's triumphant march to the sea was speedily resolved. While Germany stood firmly behind her allies in their absolute refusal to countenance a Serbian presence on the Adriatic, Russia found Great Britain and France distinctly unenthusiastic about Serbia's claims, and had perforce to fall in line when the conference agreed to the inclusion of the whole of the coast from Greece in the south to Montenegro in the north, in an independent Albanian state. As regards the inland frontiers of this new state, by contrast, the Austrians found they could count on only the lukewarm support of Italy in their demand for a boundary line that reflected ethnic realities; whereas Russia, frantic to secure as much territory as possible for her Serbian and Montenegrin protégés, was supported, not only by the French, but by the British, who in their anxiety to cultivate the entente now decided that, Russia and Serbia having given way over the question of the coast, the principle of 'fairness' demanded that their wishes should now prevail regardless of any ethnic considerations. In the weeks of wrangling that now ensued, the attitude of Germany was decisive. With the Kaiser solicitous for the prestige of his Russian cousin and rating the cause of monarchical solidarity more highly than the fate of 'the grazing lands of the goats of Scutari', and with his ministers set on a rapprochement with Great Britain, the Austrians found themselves under unrelenting pressure from Berlin to concede to Serbia and Montenegro a whole series of undoubtedly Albanian market towns. True, as far as the unfortunate Albanians of Macedonia and western Kossovo were concerned, the frontier line agreed by the great powers in April 1913 was to signal the start of horrendously bloody outbreaks of ethnic cleansing, both in the immediate aftermath of the war and again in the last decade of the twentieth century. As far as the great powers were concerned, however, the settlement was satisfactory insofar as it allowed Russia and Austria-Hungary to withdraw from their positions of armed confrontation and start putting their military preparations on the Galician frontier into reverse. It seemed that the concert had successfully resolved the most dangerous aspect of the crisis.

Even so, to agree on a settlement was one thing, to enforce it quite another. The Austrians had only fallen into line with the concert on the express condition that the important market town of Scutari, still under siege from Montenegrin forces, should be included in Albania. Within days, however, both the settlement and the credibility of the concert itself were called in question when the Montenegrins, in defiance of a series of warnings from the powers, persisted in their siege of Scutari; and when it began to appear that the concert that had devised the settlement was not sufficiently united to enforce it. A naval demonstration off the Montenegrin coast, in which France participated only after much havering and Russia not at all, made no impression whatever on King Nikita, although Great Britain's participation alongside the Triple Alliance Powers was greeted with glee by the Kaiser: 'Oh, Triple Entente!!!' Indeed, when more forceful measures were mooted after the surrender of Scutari on 23 April, the disunity of the concert was starkly revealed. At the critical moment Grey, as ever alert to the sensitivities of St Petersburg and Paris, put the unity of the Entente before the effectiveness of the concert and refused to move.

The impasse was resolved by the independent action of Vienna. There, a veritable war party was in process of formation, including not only Conrad and the usual advocates of a punitive expedition as the best means of establishing the Monarchy's authority over troublesome Slavs at home and abroad, but the majority of the Austrian and Hungarian civilian cabinets. When they prevailed on the Emperor and Berchtold to agree to demonstrative military preparations on the Montenegrin frontier, Europe again appeared to be on the brink of war: Austro-Hungarian military operations against Montenegro were virtually bound to lead to clashes with Serbian troops in the area, and Russia had let it be known that she would not tolerate an Austro-Serbian war. On 4 May, at the eleventh hour, Nikita – whether from fright, or simply because he had completed his dubious operations on the Paris stock exchange – suddenly withdrew his forces from Scutari and Europe could breathe again. The crisis was nevertheless to cast a long shadow: although the war party in Vienna had been reined in for the time being, now even pacific elements like the Emperor and Berchtold had drawn the obvious conclusions about the relative efficacy of concert diplomacy and single-handed threats of action as means of safeguarding the Monarchy's interests.

If the Scutari crisis demonstrated the limitations of concert diplomacy in the face of a defiant small power, its effectiveness in regulating the states system was further undermined by the ineradicable tendency of the great powers themselves to pursue their mutually antagonistic aims outside the framework of the concert. Both trends were at work in the escalation of the conflict between Bulgaria on the one hand and Serbia and Greece on the other, that culminated in the Second Balkan War (28 June to 10 August). Even the positive achievements of the concert had added fuel to the flames: the unanimous decision of the powers to exclude Serbia from the Adriatic coast had made it impossible to implement the Serbo-Bulgarian treaty of March 1912. While the Bulgarians insisted that any Russian arbitration must be confined to the 'disputed' zone, the Serbs, who together with the Greeks had proceeded to occupy, not only the whole disputed zone but territories assigned by the treaty to Bulgaria, were demanding a complete revision of the agreement.

The concert could offer no solution. While Sazonov was striving to prevent the disruption of the Balkan League – Tsar Nicholas even staking his personal prestige on an appeal to the kings of Bulgaria and Serbia to await his decision – Tisza proclaimed openly in the Hungarian parliament that the Balkan states were independent entities over which no power could claim a special protectorate. Meanwhile, Berchtold, discerning in Bulgaria a potential tool to readjust the Balkan balance against Serbia, secretly offered King Ferdinand 'sympathy and active aid' in a conflict with Serbia (provided always that he squared Austria-Hungary's ally Romania with territorial concessions beforehand). In the event, the Balkan states were not inclined to listen to any of the great powers. The Bulgarians, for example, refused to cede an inch of territory to purchase Romanian neutrality and, trusting – quite unjustifiably – to St Petersburg to keep Romania quiet, sought to force the Tsar's hand by a sudden attack on Greek and Serbian positions in Macedonia. When Serbia and Greece responded by a declaration of war, and when Romania and Turkey seized the opportunity to make good their own territorial claims against Bulgaria, the calculations of both Russia and Austria-Hungary were completely overthrown.

The Second Balkan War was of unparalleled ferocity, more lives being lost during the first two weeks of fighting than in the whole of the war against Turkey; and the marginalization of the concert was starkly demonstrated when Russia and Austria-Hungary proved unable, and the other great powers unwilling, to influence the outcome of the conflict. If the intervention of Romania was fatal for any plans Berchtold may have cherished of engineering a Bulgarian victory it equally put paid to Sazonov's hopes of presiding over a peace conference in St Petersburg. In the event, Romania, Serbia and Greece imposed their own terms on Bulgaria at Bucharest on 10 August. As for the concert, it had ceased to exercise even the limited degree of control that it had exercised in the first half of the year. In London, Nicolson termed the war 'one of the saddest spectacles' he had ever witnessed, but Grey was firmly determined to stand aloof, and on 11 August finally wound up the London Conference and went on holiday. Nor had the Germans any relish for an international conference: 'every milestone would be disputed by Austria and Russia and the conference would last for years if it did not break up with disastrous results.' In these circumstances a last-minute affirmation by Austria-Hungary and Russia of their right to revise the peace settlement went for nothing: unlike the six-power declaration of the previous December, it lacked the endorsement of the other members of the concert; and it was in the end vitiated by the polarization of the states system. For although both Vienna and St Petersburg were inclined to revise the Treaty in favour of Bulgaria, they were not really united: although both supported Bulgaria's claims against Greece at Kavalla, this was only because each was seeking to enhance its influence at Sofia against the other; and when France and Germany – again, not so much partners as rivals for influence at Athens – came out on the side of Greece, Russia drew back and talk of revision by the great powers faded away. With the Kaiser's congratulatory telegrams to the kings of Romania and Greece, publicly acclaiming the Treaty of Bucharest as 'definitive' – just when Berchtold had been at pains to dismiss it, equally publicly, as 'un arrangement préalable' – Austrian hopes of revision were finally and most humiliatingly demolished.

Even so, if by refraining – willingly or unwillingly – from intervention the great powers had managed to avoid a conflict between themselves, they had allowed the victors of the Second Balkan War to create a situation that was full of danger all the same. On the one hand, although Serbia was to be preoccupied for some time with digesting her newly acquired territories, Pan-Serbian appetites had been whetted rather than satiated. During the Bucharest negotiations, Pasic had spoken openly of the need, now that the 'first round' had been won against Turkey, 'to prepare for the second round against Austria-Hungary'. On the other hand, although Bulgaria was for the time being *hors de combat* she was now openly revisionist; and in Vienna even the pacific emperor fatalistically observed that the Treaty of Bucharest 'cannot last. We are moving towards a new Balkan war.' For the moment, however, the exhaustion of the Balkan states, combined with the helpless isolation of Austria-Hungary, tended to conceal the more baleful consequences of the failure of the great powers to 'manage' the system in the closing months of the reordering of the Near Eastern power constellation.

The last year of peace

In more general terms, the long drawn out Near Eastern crisis had undermined the concert as an instrument for the peaceful containment of crises in future. This was particularly evident in the military field, where the cumulative effect of the accelerated tempo of the armaments of all the great powers was to leave them better armed and prepared for war than they had ever been. As Churchill observed, 'the world is arming as it has never armed before'; and despite the much remarked Anglo-German *détente*, the British naval estimates for 1914–15 were the biggest ever. Even impecunious Austria-Hungary made a belated and not very successful effort to raise the size of the standing army to avoid having recourse to the sensational and expensive emergency mobilizations that had proved so troublesome during the Balkan wars. Germany's new programme, announced in March 1913, was partly a response to the recent sudden replacement of Germany's potential Ottoman ally by a congeries of expansionist states that might some day paralyse her Austro-Hungarian ally; but it also reflected Germany's desperation to counter the steady growth of French and Russian military power. Indeed, even hitherto sacrosanct conservative objections to the dilution of the army by proletarian elements had to yield to the demand for a larger army; and if the imperial government needed new property taxes to finance it, it was prepared to turn to the Social Democrats to secure them. Equally desperate – and distinctly ominous – was the priority accorded to effectiveness and efficiency at the expense of flexibility: in January 1913, on the assumption that French participation in any Russo-German war was inevitable, the German general staff decided to stake everything on perfecting the Schlieffen plan, and to cease wasting time on the alternative plan for a war against Russia alone. The assumption was perhaps not unreasonable; but it was to have fatal consequences for Germany's freedom of action eighteen months later.

Even before this, it became clear that Germany's strenuous efforts had failed to bring her security, and would indeed, in the long run, be more than countered by her opponents in east and west. It was not simply that

MAP 6 *The Balkans in 1914*

the Russians' retreats during the Near Eastern crisis had whetted their appetite for standing up to the Central Powers in future. By 1913 the Russian government, in contrast to the German, was experiencing the luxury of an increase of resources arising from an economic boom, which at last gave the upper hand to the advocates of military expansion as against their traditional opponents in the Ministry of Finance. The Great Programme, announced in December 1913, envisaged an army increase of two million men by 1917 – a figure that was further increased when in June 1914 the Duma agreed to make permanent the recent emergency practice of extending the service of the senior contingent of recruits. All this was accompanied by the adoption of the distinctly offensive operational Plan 20; by plans to construct a Baltic battle fleet (and to seek naval talks with the British); and by the raising of French loans to develop the Russian railway network to the German frontier. Meanwhile, in France the introduction of the Three Year Service Law of 1913 portended a French army equal in size to the German one that was supposed to defeat it in six weeks.

Now it is true that in the short term these French and Russian plans posed no immediate threat to Germany. On the contrary, the implementation of the Three Year Service Law, planned for the late summer of 1914, would mean that, initially, the French army would suffer a period of disorganization; while much of Russia's Great Programme was still at the drawing-board stage. Indeed, there were military men in both Berlin and Vienna who saw in all this a window of opportunity for the central powers, Moltke declaring on 1 January 1914 for example, that 'from a military point of view, the sooner war comes, the better'. Of course, such talk had been heard often enough in the past; and so long as the idea of a preventive strike was still rejected by the civilian authorities who made the decisions for war and peace – as it was until the summer of 1914 – the six-power states system could continue to function. Under the surface, however, a dangerous shift was occurring in the military balance. As the power and preparedness of the two sides approached convergence, such restraining factors as had helped to keep the peace in recent crises – misgivings about Germany's military preparedness in 1905 or the acceptance by Russia of the overwhelming preponderance of the central powers in 1909 – would be less likely to operate in a future crisis that resulted in polarization and confrontation.

Not that a cataclysm was imminent in the immediate aftermath of the Balkan Wars. The most volatile elements of the states system, the expansionist Balkan states, needed time to recover and digest their recent gains.

True, decision-makers in Vienna had been driven by their recent diplomatic defeats to the dangerous conclusion that whenever the concert made a decision, nobody paid attention, whereas if a single power showed that it would not shrink from war, that made an impression. But they were still helplessly isolated in this view, and *détente*, rather than polarization, remained the keynote of relations between the other great powers. The visit of George V and Nicholas II to Berlin for the wedding of the Kaiser's daughter in May 1913, for example, had, according to William II, been characterized by 'complete agreement' between the three cousins. Certainly, with the Bulgarians at the gates of Constantinople, the Tsar had welcomed the Kaiser's plans to modernize the Ottoman army by what was to become the Liman von Sanders mission. Even when, in December, Sazonov raised objections to the extensive powers accorded to the Liman mission, the British were reluctant to compromise their 'present pleasant relations' with Berlin (and their own naval mission in Turkey) by supporting him.

It was an ominous fact, nevertheless, that even an isolated power, if desperate enough, could seriously impede the functioning of the Concert of Europe. In October 1913, for example, after six weeks of diplomatic pressure had failed to move the Serbs to withdraw their troops from territories assigned by the London conference to Albania, the Austrians, after notifying their allies but not the Triple Entente powers, single-handedly brought the Serbs to heel by presenting an ultimatum in Belgrade. William II was effusive in his congratulations – 'I stand beside you and am ready to draw the sabre whenever your action makes it necessary' – although in this instance the danger had passed, and Berchtold, like all his predecessors, was soon to discover the limited value of verbal assurances of one so volatile as William II. More lasting was the reaction of the Triple Entente powers, who accused Berchtold of presenting 'an ultimatum to the concert'; and the French proceeded to what turned out to be a final closure of the Paris stock market to Austro-Hungarian loans. Two weeks later Austria-Hungary and Italy again sprang to the defence of their Albanian protégé with an ultimatum to Athens demanding the withdrawal of Greek forces from territories about which the six-power frontier commission had not even reached a decision; and in March 1914 when Grey was trying to persuade the Greeks to withdraw as part of a package deal conceding their claims to the Aegean islands, the Adriatic powers again affronted the rest of the concert – this time including Germany – with another peremptory ultimatum to Athens. As the exasperated British concluded, 'Austria and Italy do not seem to think that the Concert of Europe is any longer intact.'

Not that the Triple Entente powers had not themselves contributed to the drift towards polarization. Although the Germans in the end restricted the powers of the Liman von Sanders mission out of deference to Sazonov's display of indignation, the fact that the mission existed at all still rankled in St Petersburg. There, a crown council decided in February that Russia must press ahead with her military preparations so as to be in a position to resist by force any German attempt to control the Straits; and Sazonov's complaints to Paris and London were eloquent of the drift of Russian policy: the Liman affair was 'a test case for the Triple Entente'; and as for Turkey's defiance of the concert over the cession of the Aegean islands, the British:

would never . . . allow the Triple entente to take any action in which the Triple Alliance would not join, for fear of causing a division between the powers. There was, however, no use concealing the fact that Europe was divided into two opposing groups and . . . the Triple Entente ought to assert itself. . . . If we were ever to hold our own in the world, we should have one day to convert the Triple Entente into a regular alliance.

Of course Grey, acutely conscious of his Liberal colleagues' dislike of Russia, could never go that far. But his officials were by now arguing that Germany's refusal to join in the coercion of Turkey meant 'the end of the policy of co-operation between England and Germany' of the previous year; and in his anxiety to accommodate Sazonov he proceeded to agree to regular discussions with the French and Russian ambassadors to co-ordinate entente policy on day-to-day issues in the Near East. Thus, British diplomats were instructed to resist Austro-Italian attempts to establish a virtual protectorate over the new Albanian state; and, on the North Albanian frontier delimitation commission, simply to vote with their pro-Slav French and Russian colleagues even when ethnic considerations favoured the Albanians. After Grey's visit to Paris in April 1914, Russia was initiated into the details of Anglo-French naval and military agreements and by the summer Anglo-Russian naval talks were under way. Admittedly, these did not get very far; but when, at the end of June, the Germans got wind of them through a spy in the Russian embassy in London, Grey's rather disingenuous parliamentary *démenti* made a profound impression in Berlin. There, this apparent tightening of the Entente was considered to undermine – at a particularly unfortunate moment – the case for working towards British neutrality by co-operating with London and restraining Vienna.

Yet even more serious than the decline of the Anglo-German *détente* that had served to blunt the edge of polarization in 1913 was the transformation of Russo-German relations in the first half of 1914. If the Liman affair drove the Russians to intensify their preparations to resist German ambitions at Constantinople, the Germans were in turn affronted by Russia's displays of assertiveness – for example, by her stubborn refusal to renew the Russo-German commercial treaty of 1904 on the (for Russia) highly disadvantageous terms that Germany had extracted from her in her hour of defeat; and, most of all, by her recent activities in the field of armaments. By the spring of 1914 these had provoked a veritable press war between St Petersburg and Berlin, with the Russian chief of staff, General Sukhomlinov truculently declaring that if Germany wished to fight, she would find that Russia was ready; and the German press expatiating on the alleged Russian menace in terms bordering on hysteria. In Berlin, moreover, the hysteria permeated the very highest circles: when on 11 March Count Pourtalès reported from the St Petersburg embassy that the German press was being unduly selective and alarmist, William II disagreed:

Dear Pourzel would have done better to have left this dispatch unwritten. . . . We are here in the no man's land between military affairs and politics, a tricky, unclear area, where the diplomat usually fails. I, as a military man do not, in view of all my information, have the slightest doubt that Russia is systematically preparing for war against us; and I make my policy accordingly.

Indeed, already in February he had decided that 'Russo-Prussian relations are dead for ever'.

Even so, the Kaiser's cataclysmic utterances did not mean that either he or his ministers had adopted Moltke's view that an early war was actually desirable. On the contrary, when in these very weeks the Austrians suggested using force if Serbia should attempt to set foot on the Adriatic by engineering a dynastic union with Montenegro, William II would have none of it: 'This union is absolutely not to be prevented; and if Vienna should attempt this it will be committing a great folly and conjuring up the danger of a war with the Slavs that will leave us completely cold.' The Italians were equally unhelpful, warning the Austrians when they talked of seizing compensation on the Montenegrin coast that this would mean the end of the Triple Alliance. With neither of its allies prepared to assist any longer in preventing that very Serbian advance they had so effectively vetoed in December 1912, the Monarchy's diplomatic position had taken

another turn for the worse. Indeed, Vienna found itself at odds with both
its allies over a whole series of Balkan questions. It was not simply the
polarization of the states system, but the chronic disunity of Triple Alliance
powers that frustrated Austrian efforts to counter the remorseless advance
of Franco-Russian diplomacy in these months, and that by June 1914
created a mood of such desperation in Vienna.

For example, ever since the expulsion of the Turks from Europe the
Germans had been ruthless in ignoring Austrian interests in their determination to secure their own causeway of influence to Asia Minor; but
their naïve attempt to build on their dynastic influence in Romania and
Greece and to develop their economic influence in Serbia was both ill-
conceived – given the unassuaged territorial ambitions of those states at
the expense of Austria-Hungary and Albania – and playing directly into
the hands of Russia and France, who were striving to bring about just
such a combination to isolate Austria-Hungary. Equally quixotic was the
Kaiser's personal dislike of Ferdinand of Bulgaria that underlay German
scorn for Berchtold's forlorn efforts to make sure of the only Balkan state
that had no conflict of interests with Austria-Hungary. Most galling of
all to Vienna, however, was Berlin's advice to make economic concessions
to win over Serbia – where German commerce was, indeed, expanding at
a rate that had convinced Conrad that Germany was trying to 'strangle'
the Monarchy's trade thoughout the Near East. While the Austrians
wearily insisted that no amount of economic concessions could staunch
irredentist passions that had by now seized the whole Serbian nation,
the Germans joined France and Russia in frustrating what they saw as
Austrian attempts to 'browbeat' Serbia – for example, Berchtold's attempt
to construct a syndicate with French bankers to control the Ottoman
railway lines recently taken over by Serbia and Greece. They even joined
the entente powers in opposition to both Austria-Hungary and Italy in
insisting on a cumbersome scheme to internationalize the Albanian finances. When, with Albania drifting into bankruptcy and civil war in the
summer of 1914, the partnership between its two self-appointed protectors
at last dissolved in acrimony, Austrian complaints to Berlin elicited not
sympathy, let alone support, but accusations of frivolously endangering the Triple Alliance. In these same weeks, Berchtold's appeals to the
Alliance for support in the scramble to mark out spheres of interest in
Asia Minor – the primary, if not sole, importance of which for the
Ballhausplatz was as an indicator of the Monarchy's prestige in the great
power hierarchy – failed to extract more than insultingly pathetic scraps
from Rome and Berlin.

Given the disunity of the Triple Alliance powers, it was not surprising that the Triple Entente powers registered one diplomatic success after the other in these months. Certainly, in some cases, circumstances were on their side: if by the autumn of 1913 the Austro-Hungarian envoy in Bucharest was reporting despairingly that the Romanian alliance was no longer worth the ink and paper it was written on, this simply reflected harsh realities, such as Romania's shared diplomatic interests with the other victors of the Second Balkan War, Austria-Hungary's opponents; and the fact that Franz Joseph's loyal friend, King Carol, was very old, while the strong-minded wife of his feeble heir was half English and half Russian. True, matters were not helped by the stubborn refusal of the Hungarian government to conciliate their three million Romanian subjects in Transylvania; but the eyes of Romanian irredentists had in any case long been focused on them, rather than on the one million Romanians under Russian rule in Bessarabia. The Austrians were nevertheless shocked when in June 1914 Tsar Nicholas paid a cordial visit to his Romanian relatives at Constantsa, on which occasion Sazonov and Bratianu made a motor car trip to look across the Hungarian border; and rumours circulated of a possible marriage between the crown prince's heir and one of the Tsar's daughters. (Not that the Germans were perturbed even now, trusting naïvely in their own relations with the old king and considering the poor state of Austro-Romanian relations as a bonus insofar as it encouraged the transfer of the alliance's centre of gravity from Vienna to Berlin.)

Meanwhile, French finance was scoring successes at Athens (where a large loan was concluded at the end of 1913) and – with Russian and British diplomatic support – at Sofia, with the declared aim of using a loan to force Ferdinand to dismiss his pro-Austrian ministers. (In the event, the French strung the bow too tight, and in July the Germans belatedly responded to Berchtold's pleas and provided a loan.) But on the whole, industrially advanced Germany was comparatively short of capital for export and ill-equipped to compete in the field of financial diplomacy with relatively primitive France, whose peasantry preferred high-yielding foreign loans to investing at home. Certainly, the Germans were hard pressed to find the money to secure even their own interests, such as the Baghdad railway; and by the summer of 1914, when Talaat Bey visited the Tsar at Livadia and the newspapers talked of a return to the days of Unkiar Skelessi, Bethmann Hollweg was beginning to have doubts about the whole policy of strengthening the Ottoman Empire: 'Why should we sharpen the sword of the Triple Entente?' In short, the Entente seemed to be gaining the upper hand almost everywhere, and if already in February the leading Viennese liberal newspaper had declared that a revived Balkan league would be 'a dagger pointed at the heart of Austria', in June rumours reached the Ballhausplatz that France and Russia were indeed hard at work to persuade Serbia, Romania and Greece to purchase Bulgaria's alliance by territorial concessions, compensating themselves at the expense of Albania and Austria-Hungary.

It was, indeed, just such a 'step-like [*staffelweise*] shifting of frontiers from east to west' that Berchtold singled out as the ultimate objective of France and Russia in the elaborate *tour d'horizon* drafted by his assistant, Baron Matscheko, for the better information of Berlin on 24 June. Even so, it must be emphasized that, even at this stage, the remedy recommended by the Matscheko memorandum was not to resort to war, but to enlist German support for a co-ordinated diplomatic campaign to make sure of Bulgaria and Turkey and to ask Romania to clarify her attitude towards the alliance. (If she refused to do so, the Monarchy could at least start to fortify the Transylvanian frontier.) It was only after the Sarajevo assassinations of 28 June that the text was amended to reflect the Monarchy's decision to 'tear apart with a firm hand the threads that its opponents are seeking to form into a net about its head' – that is, to take military action against Serbia (in view of which the idea of summoning Romania to show her colours was tactfully dropped). On 3 July Count Hoyos took the revised memorandum to Berlin, together with a letter from Franz Joseph to William II stressing the need to 'eliminate Serbia as a political power-factor' and asking for support if Russia should intervene.

Sarajevo was the decisive event. It finally convinced Vienna that the resources of diplomacy were exhausted and that only military action against Serbia could save the situation. To fail to react forcefully to the challenge to the position of the Habsburgs as lords of Bosnia, and, by implication to the Monarchy's very position in the ranks of the great powers, would constitute such an abject confession of weakness as to positively incite its enemies to proceed against it. On the other hand, if a military *coup* succeeded in 'eliminating Serbia as a political power factor', and if – especially if – Russia had to acquiesce in this, all the remaining Balkan states would surely be awed into submission, while Russia's influence would disappear from the Balkans, Berchtold blandly noted, 'for a long time'. This last consideration, of course, implied the risk of an Austro-Russian, indeed, of a continental conflict: as Franz Joseph himself observed *à propos* the ultimatum to Serbia: 'Russia cannot possibly swallow this.' But such considerations counted for nothing when the honour of the dynasty was at stake; for Franz Joseph in July 1914 – as before in 1859 and 1866 – 'if the Monarchy goes to ruin, at least it should do so decently'. In short, the Sarajevo assassins had contrived a situation in which the decision-makers in both Vienna and St Petersburg (and their associates in other capitals who believed their fate was tied to theirs) saw themselves as confronted with the stark choice between action that risked a European conflagration, and inaction that was tantamount to abdication from the ranks of the great powers. However the chancelleries might manoeuvre there was no escaping this.

Yet even honour was not entirely impervious to the dictates of reason and military realities, and given Germany's wayward behaviour in recent months it was not surprising that Berchtold should feel the need to sound Berlin as to the scope of the Dual Alliance. (As Italy had been, if anything, even less co-operative of late and the Triple Alliance was even more clearly strictly defensive, Berchtold made no attempt to invoke it.) As regards Germany, however, he need not have worried: although formally a suppliant, he was in fact in a commanding position. For given the sharp deterioration in Russo-German relations in recent months and the signs that Great Britain was drawing ever closer to her Entente partners, the Germans felt their diplomatic position to be particularly vulnerable in July 1914. To rebuff their chief ally now, at the risk of seeing it cease to function as a great power or, even worse, join the Franco-Russian camp, was simply unthinkable. The situation of 1908 had returned, in which, regardless of the relative strengths of the partners within the Dual Alliance, the position of the stronger partner within the states system as a whole was so exposed that the weaker could in effect take control. In this sense, the famous blank cheque of 5 July, promising support well beyond anything Bismarck had ever envisaged, was a foregone conclusion.

It is worth noting, however, that the Germans did not feel themselves so dependent on Austria-Hungary that they could not try to influence Vienna. War was still not the preferred option in Berlin. Of course, if Russia refused to back down, Germany was prepared to fight a continental war, especially in view of the encouraging short-term and threatening long-term features of the military situation. As the foreign minister, Jagow, declared: 'I do not want a preventive war, but if we are challenged to fight [wenn der Kampf sich bietet] we must not flinch.' In fact, the Germans' notorious advice to Vienna to act quickly against Serbia reflected their calculation that the shock waves from the Sarajevo regicide might still deter the Tsar from coming to the defence of Serbia, and showed that the Germans were gambling on a brilliant diplomatic victory. A localized success would not only restore Austria-Hungary's standing as a great power, strengthen the Alliance, and secure Germany's causeway to the Near East; it might well also produce a diplomatic revolution, with Russia at last abandoning her useless western partners for a new *Dreikaiserbund*. That would indeed establish an unchallengable German hegemony over the European states system.

It was a forlorn gamble, and one that went very badly wrong. Although a few voices were raised in St Petersburg warning of the danger of revolution and urging solidarity with Russia's monarchical neighbours, others warned that, precisely because of the revolutionary threat, the dynasty could ill afford to alienate the whole spectrum of Orthodox and nationalist opinion. In any case, the vast majority of decision-makers from the Emperor downwards felt that for Russia to stand by while Austria-Hungary crushed Serbia would be not only incompatible with her honour (which counted for as much with Nicholas II in 1914 as with Nicholas I in the final crisis of the Vienna system sixty years before) but tantamount to her abdication as an independent great power, resigned for the foreseeable future to the role of a humble satellite of her German neighbours. Such a retreat, 1909 writ large, was simply unthinkable, especially as the military situation had been quite transformed since then. Germany's gamble on deterrence was doomed to fail.

True, the Russians still tried to save the situation by diplomacy; and it was in an effort to strengthen their hand in their discussions with Austria-Hungary, even after she had declared war on Serbia on 28 July, that the fatal mobilization orders were issued. It is also true that from the Tsar's point of view, mobilization was not technically a decision for war; as he assured his German cousin, unless Russia were attacked, not a single Russian soldier would cross the frontier. Nicholas was well aware of the risks, however – hence his agonized heart-searchings about issuing mobilization orders that would send millions of men to their deaths – for the Schlieffen plan dictated that the moment of Russian mobilization would be the moment when the continental war must begin. The German decision of January 1913 to rely solely on the Schlieffen plan had gravely restricted not only their own freedom of action, but that of statesmen all over Europe. Henceforth, the Germans had simply no plans to fight a war against a Russian army that stood mobilized on the frontier, and would have to fall in with whatever diplomatic solution Russia might dictate – which would, in turn, be totally unacceptable to Berlin. In these circumstances, Russia's attempt at deterrence was doomed, not only to fail, but actually to precipitate the conflict – as it did when the Germans reacted by summoning both Russia and France to cease their military preparations forthwith – that is, to abdicate as independent great powers – and, when they refused, by declaring war.

The outbreak, with the British declaration of war on Germany on 4 August, of a world war engulfing the whole European states system, had nothing to do with issues in the Balkans, or, indeed, with the 'balance of power'. As Grey remarked, 'if Austria-Hungary could make war on Serbia and satisfy Russia, well and good: I could take a holiday tomorrow. But if not, the consequences would be incalculable.' The issue was the threat posed by the continental conflict to Great Britain's existence as an independent great power. Since at the latest 1907 fears for the security of the Empire, without which Great Britain must sink to the rank of a third-class power, had made the need to stand well with France, and, above all, with Russia, the categorical imperative of British foreign policy. True, as David Stevenson has pointed out, British decision-makers also saw themselves, like their peers on the continent as 'custodians of a code of honour'. If Grey warned the Commons that non-intervention would 'sacrifice our respect and good name and reputation before the world'; and if Germany's violation of the 1839 guarantee to Belgium counted for something with public opinion (although a Foreign Office memorandum of 1908 had advised against action if it was France who violated Belgian neutrality), Crowe's realist argument that 'the theory that England cannot engage in a big war means her abdication as an independent state' was also echoed by his peers on the continent. The fact was, as Grey put it to the Commons on 3 August, that 'Great Britain stood to suffer little more if she joined the war than if she stood aside'. Clearly, neutrality was not an option, if only because, equally clearly, whichever side won a continental war, the balance of power would be finished: a British Empire that had stayed neutral would be faced with either a German-dominated continent or a world dominated by a betrayed and vengeful France and Russia. That being the case, Great Britain's decision for war in 1914 was simply another manifestation of those imperial concerns that had been central to her policy in all the permutations of the European states system since 1814.

If the polarization of the states system had had a disastrous effect on decision-making in the summer of 1914, subsequent events were to show that it had not significantly enhanced the cohesion of either group of belligerents as a fighting force. Indeed, for a fortnight or so, the 'world war' was technically not one, but a number of separate wars: it was not until 6 August that the Austrians, under German pressure, declared war on Russia; while the need to ferry French troops from North Africa across the Mediterranean (in the shadow of Austria-Hungary's three Dread-noughts) deferred the French and British declarations of war against the Dual Monarchy for yet another week. Even then, Austro-Hungarian suspicions of Germany's hegemonic designs in the Near East led Conrad to concentrate his efforts entirely on conquering Serbia, to the supreme neglect of the Russian front, until Germany, threatening to denounce the alliance, forced him to switch the weight of his forces belatedly – and disastrously – to the north. Success brought its own problems; Austro-German wrangling over the ultimate fate of their conquests in Russia and the Balkans continued unabated until in the Treaty of Spa in July 1918 an exhausted Dual Monarchy surrendered all its claims, and, in effect, its independence as a great power, to its mighty ally. In the Entente camp, meanwhile, conflicting ambitions, particularly in the Near East, portended equally serious postwar conflicts, both before and after the collapse of Russia. As for those secondary powers, who had eked out their existence by exploiting the differences between the real great powers, the belated entry of both Turkey (November 1914) and Italy (May 1915) into the war confirmed that they – like the Balkan states whose approach was similarly calculating – had perhaps always been somewhat peripheral to the real European states system.

Even for this last, however, 1914 constituted a caesura: after a hundred years in which they had managed, by and large, to adjust the pursuit of their individual interests to the good of the whole, and at least sought to contain the consequences of their occasional resorts to violence within what was still, broadly, a consensual system, the principal members of that system were now seeking, from a mixture of greed and fear, to dictate to each other, to impose their will without compromise, even to destroy each other. And destroy each other they did: the War left four great empires in ruins, and the two surviving great powers of Europe so weakened that within a generation their empires too had disappeared. The European states system of the 'long nineteenth century' had ceased to exist.

Chronology

1813	28 Feb.	Treaty of Kalisch
	24 June	Treaty of Reichenbach
	12 Aug.	Austria enters the war
	18 Oct.	French defeated at Leipzig
1814	Feb.	Congress of Châtillon
	9 March	Treaty of Chaumont
	31 March	Allied armies enter Paris
	30 May	First Peace of Paris
	Oct.	Congress of Vienna opens (until 8 June 1815)
1815	3 Jan.	Anglo-Austrian-French Treaty
	1 March	Napoleon lands at Cannes
	18 June	Battle of Waterloo
	26 Sept.	Holy Alliance
	20 Nov.	Quadruple Alliance
	20 Nov.	Second Peace of Paris
1818	Sept.–Nov.	Congress of Aix-la-Chapelle
1819	Aug.	German rulers meet at Karlsbad
	20 Sept.	Diet at Frankfort sanctions Karlsbad 'decrees'
1820	19 Nov.	Protocol of Troppau
1821	Jan.–April	Congress of Laibach
	Feb.–March	Risings in Wallachia, Moldavia and the Morea
	Oct.	Hanover meeting (Castlereagh and Metternich)

1822	Oct.–Dec.	Congress of Verona
1823	April	French invasion of Spain
1826	4 April	St Petersburg Protocol
1827	6 July	Tripartite Treaty of London
	20 Oct.	Battle of Navarino
1828	26 April	Russia declares war on Turkey
1829	14 Sept.	Treaty of Adrianople
1830	March–June	French expedition to Algiers
	July	Revolution in France
	Aug.	Chiffon of Karlsbad
	Aug.–Oct.	Belgian revolt
	Nov.	Polish revolt
	Nov.	London conference on Belgium begins
1831	March	Austrian intervention in Papal States
	15 Nov.	Treaty of London (Belgian independence) Mehemet Ali invades Syria
1832	Feb.	French occupation of Ancona
	21 Dec.	Egyptians defeat Turks at Konieh
1833	8 July	Treaty of Unkiar Skelessi
	18 Sept.	Münchengrätz agreement
	15 Oct.	Convention of Berlin
1834	22 April	Quadruple Alliance
	18 Aug.	Additional articles to Quadruple Alliance
1839	19 April	Treaty of London guarantees Belgian neutrality
	21 April	Sultan attacks Mehemet Ali
	24 June	Turkish army defeated at Nezib

1840	15 July	Four-power Treaty of London
	27 Nov.	Mehemet Ali submits to four powers
1841	13 July	Straits Convention
1844	June	Visit of Nicholas I to England
1847	Sept.–Dec.	Great-power negotiations on Switzerland
1848	Feb.	Revolution in France
	13 March	Metternich resigns
	17 March	King of Prussia appoints liberal ministry
	22 March	Outbreak of war in Northern Italy
	April	Prussian troops enter Schleswig and Holstein
	May	Palmerston offers to mediate between Austria and Sardinia
	24 July	Radetzky defeats Sardinians at Custoza
	2 Dec.	Franz Joseph Emperor of Austria
	20 Dec.	Louis Napoleon President of French Republic
1849	23 March	Sardinians defeated at Novara
	28 March	Frankfort parliament offers crown to King of Prussia
	25 April	French army enters Papal States
	17 June	Russian army enters Hungary
1850	29 Nov.	Punctation of Olmütz
1852	May	French warship to Constantinople (Holy Places dispute)
	8 May	Five-power Treaty of London on Schleswig-Holstein
1853	Jan.–Feb.	Nicholas I's conversations with Seymour
	Feb.–May	Menshikov mission to Constantinople

	2 July	Russians occupy Danubian principalities
	July–Aug.	Vienna conference on Near East
	7 Sept.	Russian 'violent interpretation' of Vienna note
	23 Sept.	British fleet ordered to Constantinople
	4 Oct.	Ottoman Empire declares war on Russia
	30 Nov.	Ottoman fleet destroyed at Simope
1854	3 Jan.	British and French fleets enter the Black Sea
	28 March	Great Britain and France declare war on Russia
	20 April	Austro-Prussian treaty
	8 August	Austria and western powers agree Four Points; Russia evacuates Danubian principalities
	2 Dec.	Triple Alliance: Austria, Great Britain and France
1855	26 Jan.	Sardinia enters the Crimean War
	March–June	Vienna conference
	June–Sept.	Siege of Sebastopol
	28 Dec.	Austrian ultimatum to Russia
1856	Feb.–March	Congress of Paris
	30 March	Treaty of Paris
	15 April	Tripartite Treaty (Great Britain, France, Austria)
1858	20 July	Napoleon III and Cavour meet at Plombières
1859	23 April	Austrian ultimatum to Sardinia
	12 May	France enters the war
	4 June	Battle of Magenta
	14 June	Prussian mobilization begins
	24 June	Battle of Solferino
	11 July	Armistice of Villafranca
	10 Nov.	Treaty of Zurich

1860	24 March	Sardinia annexes central duchies and Romagna; cedes Savoy and Nice to France
	11 May	Garibaldi lands in Sicily
	22 Aug.	Garibaldi crosses Straits of Messina
	Sept.	Sardinian troops occupy Papal States
	Oct.	Warsaw meeting
1861	17 March	Proclamation of kingdom of Italy
1862	22 Sept.	Bismarck minister-president of Prussia
1863	Jan.	Warsaw uprising
	8 Feb.	Alvensleben Convention
	18 Nov.	Christian IX signs new constitution affecting Schleswig-Holstein
1864	16 Jan.	Austro-Prussian alliance
	Feb.	Austria and Prussia occupy Schleswig and Holstein
	April–June	London Conference on Schleswig-Holstein
	July	Austria and Prussia invade Denmark
	Aug.	Schönbrunn meeting (Bismarck and Rechberg)
1865	14 Aug.	Convention of Gastein
	Oct.	Napoleon III and Bismarck meet at Biarritz
1866	8 April	Italian-Prussian alliance
	12 June	Austria agrees to cede Venetia to France if victorious
	14 June	Outbreak of Austro-Prussian war
	3 July	Austrians defeated at Sadowa
	26 July	Preliminary Peace of Nikolsburg
	23 Aug.	Peace of Prague

1867	April	Luxemburg crisis
	May	London Conference on Luxemburg (until 9 Sept.)
1870	June–July	Hohenzollern candidature crisis
	19 July	France declares war on Prussia
	1 Sept.	Italians occupy Rome
	31 Oct.	Gorchakov Circular on Black Sea clauses
1871	17 Jan.	London Protocol
	18 Jan.	German Empire proclaimed at Versailles
	March–May	Paris Commune
	10 May	Treaty of Frankfort
1872	Sept.	Three Emperors' meeting in Berlin
1873	6 June	Austro-Russian Schönbrunn Convention
1875	April–May	'War in Sight' crisis
	July	Risings in the Herzegovina, then Bosnia
	30 Dec.	Andrássy Note
1876	13 May	Berlin Memorandum
	May–Sept.	Insurrection in Bulgaria
	30 June	Serbia declares war on Turkey
	8 July	Reichstadt Agreement
	12 Dec.	Constantinople Conference (to 20 Jan. 1877)
1877	15 Jan.	Budapest Convention (additional convention, 18 March)
	24 April	Russia declares war on Turkey
	10 Dec.	Fall of Plevna
1878	31 Jan.	Preliminary peace of Adrianople
	3 March	Treaty of San Stefano
	13 June	Congress of Berlin (to 13 July)

1879	4 Sept.	Dual control established in Egypt
	7 Oct.	Austro-German (Dual) Alliance
1880	3 July	Madrid Convention on Morocco
1881	12 May	Treaty of Bardo: French protectorate over Tunis
	18 June	Three Emperors' Alliance
	28 June	Austro-Serbian Alliance
	Winter	Rising in Bosnia: Skobelev tours Europe (1881–82)
1882	20 May	Triple Alliance
	13 Sept.	Battle of Tel-el-Kebir: British occupy of Egypt
1883	Feb.–April	Germans established at Angra Pequeña
	30 Oct.	Austro-Romanian alliance (Germany acceding 30 Oct.; Italy, May 1888)
1884	15–17 Sept.	Three Emperors' meeting at Skiernewice
	15 Nov.	Berlin West Africa conference (to 26 February 1885)
1885	26 Jan.	Mahdi takes Khartoum
	April–Sept.	Penjdeh crisis
	25–6 Aug.	Three emperors' meeting at Kremsier
	18 Sept.	Revolution in Eastern Rumelia
	13 Nov.	Serbia declares war on Bulgaria
1886	3 March	Serbo-Bulgarian Treaty of Bucharest
	14 July	General Boulanger minister of war in France
	7 Sept.	Abdication of Alexander of Battenberg in Bulgaria
1887	12 Feb.	First Mediterranean Agreement (Great Britain and Italy) (Austria-Hungary accedes, 24 March; Spain, 4 May)

	20 Feb.	Triple Alliance renewed
	22 May	Drummond-Wolff Convention
	18 June	Reinsurance Treaty
	7 July	Ferdinand of Saxe-Coburg-Koháry elected Prince of Bulgaria
	Nov.	Lombardverbot
	12 Dec.	Second Mediterranean Agreement
1890	18 March	Bismarck dismissed
	1 July	Anglo-German Heligoland-Zanzibar treaty
1891	4 July	William II's state visit to London
	21, 27 Aug.	Franco-Russian diplomatic agreement
1892	1 Aug.	Mission of General Boisdeffre to St Petersburg
1893	July	Anglo-French crisis over Siam
	15 July	German military bill passed by Reichstag
	13 Oct.	Russian squadron visits Toulon
	27 Dec.–4 Jan. 1894	Franco-Russian alliance ratified
1894	12 May	Congo Treaty between British and King Leopold II
	1 Aug.	Sino-Japanese War (Treaty of Shimonoseki, 17 April 1895)
	Aug.–Sept.	Armenian massacres
1895	17 April	Treaty of Shimonoseki
	Oct.	Armenian massacres: Anglo-Russian reform scheme
1896	3 Jan.	Kruger telegram
	1 March	Italians defeated at Adawa
1897	17 April	Greco-Turkish War (to 18 September)
	May	Franz Joseph's visit to St Petersburg: Austro-Russian entente
	14 Nov.	German forces land at Kiao-Chow

1898	27 March	Russians secure lease of Port Arthur
	28 March	First Navy Law passed by Reichstag
	24 April	Spanish-American War (to 10 December)
	2 Sept.	Battle of Omdurman
	Sept.	Fashoda crisis (to March 1899)
	21 Nov.	Franco-Italian commercial agreement
1899	18 May	First Hague Peace Conference (to 29 July)
	9 Oct.	Boer War (Treaty of Vereeniging, 31 May 1902)
	1 Nov.	Anglo-German Samoa agreement
	25 Nov.	German syndicate decures Baghdad Railway concession
1900	13 June	Boxer Rising and siege of legations in Peking (to 14 August)
	16 Oct.	Anglo-German Yangtse Agreement
	14 Dec.	Visconti-Venosta-Barrère agreement
1901	March–April	Crisis over Russian activities in Manchuria
	May	End of Anglo-German alliance negotiations
	Nov.–Dec.	Ito's visit to St Petersburg
1902	30 Jan.	Anglo-Japanese Alliance
	1 Nov.	Prinetti-Barrère agreement
1903	Feb.	Austro-Russian scheme of reforms for Macedonia
	1–4 May	Edward VII's visit to Paris
	2 Oct.	Mürzsteg Punctation
1904	4 Feb.	Russo-Japanese War (Treaty of Portsmouth, 5 Sept. 1905)
	8 April	Anglo-French agreements
	15 Oct.	Austro-Russian neutrality agreement
	Dec.	St René Taillandier mission to Fez

1905	31 March	William II lands at Tangier
	6 June	Fall of Delcassé
	24 July	Treaty of Björkö
1906	10 Jan.	Start of Anglo-French military and naval conversations
	16 Jan.	Algeçiras Conference (to 7 April)
	10 Feb.	First Dreadnought launched
1907	16 May	Anglo-Franco-Spanish Mediterranean agreement
	15 June	Second Hague Peace Conference (to 18 October)
	31 Aug.	Anglo-Russian Convention
1908	27 Jan.	Sanjak railway project announced
	9 June	Edward VII and Nicholas II meet at Reval
	24 July	Constitution of 1876 restored in Turkey
	16 Sept.	Aehrenthal and Izvolsky meet at Buchlau
	5 Oct.	Proclamation of Bulgarian independence
	6 Oct.	Annexation of Bosnia and the Herzegovina
1909	12 Jan.	Austro-Turkish agreement on Bosnia
	8 Feb.	Franco-German agreement on Morocco
	21 March	German 'ultimatum' to Russia
	24 Oct.	Russo-Italian Racconigi agreement
1910	4–5 Nov.	Nicholas II and William II meet at Potsdam
1911	April–May	French advance in Morocco
	1 July	*Panther* arrives at Agadir
	28 Sept.	Italo-Ottoman War (to 18 Oct 1912)
	4 Nov.	Franco-German agreement on Morocco and Congo
1912	12 March	Serbo-Bulgarian Treaty
	29 May	Greek-Bulgarian Treaty

	21 July	Fall of Young Turkish government at Constantinople
	8 Oct.	Outbreak of First Balkan War (Treaty of London, 30 May 1913)
	17 Dec.	First meeting of ambassadors at London
1913	April	Scutari crisis
	29 June	Outbreak of Second Balkan War (Treaty of Bucharest, 10 Aug.)
	18 Oct.	Austro-Hungarian ultimatum to Serbia
	30 Oct.	Austro-Hungarian-Italian *démarche* at Athens
	Nov.	Liman von Sanders crisis (to Jan. 1914)
1914	8 March	Austro-Italian *démarche* at Athens
	14 June	Nicholas II's visit to Romania
	28 June	Sarajevo assassinations
	3 July	Hoyos mission to Berlin
	23 July	Austro-Hungarian note to Belgrade
	28 July	Austria-Hungary declares war on Serbia
	1 Aug.	Germany declares war on Russia (on France, 3 August)
	4 Aug.	Great Britain declares war on Germany
	6 Aug.	Austria-Hungary declares war on Russia
	12 Aug.	Great Britain and France declare war on Austria-Hungary

Bibliography

This bibliography is intended to be a guide to further reading. It is necessarily selective and it concentrates on books in English. Articles in scholarly journals have in general been excluded on the grounds that their inclusion would swell the list beyond reasonable limits. Most of the books listed below contain bibliographies of a more specialist nature which should be consulted for further reading on particular topics. The bibliography is arranged chapter by chapter for ease of reference. Many of the books are of value for chapters other than those under which they are listed.

Chapter 1 (1815–1914)

The most recent treatment of the European states system, from the sixteenth century to the 1990s, is in Peter Krüger and P.W. Schroeder (eds), *The Transformation of European Politics, 1763–1848: Episode or Model in Modern European History?* (Münster 2002). Over the 'long nineteenth century' as a whole, the fundamental issues in great-power politics and contemporary attitudes towards international relations are discussed in a stimulating way in F.H. Hinsley, *Power and the Pursuit of Peace* (Cambridge 1963); and in A.M. Birke and G. Heydemann (eds) *Die Herausforderung des europäischen Staatensystems* (Göttingen 1989). The development of the international system is handled in considerable detail and with great skill in P.W. Schroeder, *The Transformation of European Politics 1763–1848* (Oxford 1994) and A.J.P. Taylor, *The Struggle for Mastery in Europe 1848–1919* (Oxford 1954). Perhaps more manageable for the general reader, but full, clear and comprehensible is Norman Rich, *Great Power Diplomacy 1814–1914* (New York 1992). The best general survey of great-power politics from a French point of view is P. Renouvin, *Histoire des relations internationales*, vols V, 1815–71, and VI, 1871–1914 (Paris 1954). L. Albertini, *The Origins of the War, vol. 1,*

1878–1914 (London 1965), provides a very detailed, but still readable, account, from an Italian point of view. As far as individual powers are concerned, British policy over the century is illuminated in C.H.D. Howard, *Great Britain and the casus belli from Canning to Salisbury* (London 1961). Perhaps the best introduction is C.J. Bartlett, *Defence and Diplomacy, Britain and the Great Powers 1815–1914* (Manchester University Press 1993). Kenneth Bourne, *The Foreign Policy of Victorian England 1830–1902* (Oxford 1970), is an indispensable study that contains valuable documentary material, as do H.W.V. Temperley and Lillian M. Penson, *Foundations of British Foreign Policy 1792–1902* (Cambridge 1938); C.J. Lowe, *The Reluctant Imperialists, British Foreign Policy 1878–1902*, 2 vols (1967); and C.J. Lowe and M.L. Dockrill, *The Mirage of Power, British Foreign Policy 1902–1922* (1972). Russian policy is well covered in Barbara Jelavich, *A Century of Russian Foreign Policy* (New York 1964); *Russia's Balkan Entanglements 1806–1914* (Cambridge 1991); and the Balkan states in Charles and Barbara Jelavich, *The Establishment of the Balkan National states 1804–1920* (Seattle 1977). On the Habsburg Monarchy, F.R. Bridge, *The Habsburg Monarchy among the Great Powers 1815–1918* (New York 1991) is the most comprehensive account; but the foreign policy sections of Alan Sked, *The Decline and Fall of the Habsburg Empire 1815–1918* (2nd edn, London 2001) are also illuminating, and those in A.J.P. Taylor, *The Habsburg Monarchy* (London 1941) still make lively reading. On Germany, Agatha Ramm, *Germany, 1789–1919* (London 1967) is full, judicious and balanced; as are, on Italy, C.J. Lowe and F. Marzari, *Italian Foreign Policy 1870–1940* (1975) and I.H. Nish, *Japanese Foreign Policy 1869–1942* (1977). Near Eastern issues are lucidly explained in M.S. Anderson, *The Eastern Question 1774–1923* (London 1966), and developments east of Suez in D. Gillard, *The Struggle for Asia 1828–1914* (London 1977). Numerous aspects of the diplomacy of imperialism in Africa are illuminated in two volumes of essays edited by P. Gifford and W.R. Louis, *Britain and Germany in Africa* (New Haven, CT 1967), and *France and Britain in Africa* (New Haven, CT 1972). The military and naval policies of the powers can be studied in the following books: Gordon Craig, *The Politics of the Prussian Army* (Princeton 1955); W.C. Fuller, *Strategy and Power in Russia 1600–1914* (New York 1992), Douglas Porch, *Army and Revolution: France 1815–1848* (London 1974); C.J. Bartlett, *Great Britain and Sea Power 1815–1853* (Oxford 1963); and Paul M. Kennedy (ed.), *The War Plans of the Great Powers, 1880–1914* (Boston 1985). Financial and commercial relations are dealt with in D.C.M. Platt,

Finance, Trade and Politics in British Foreign Policy 1815–1914 (Oxford 1968) and in W.O. Henderson, *The Zollverein* (London 1959). All the major treaties of the period are usefully gathered together in Michael Hurst (ed.), *Key Treaties for the Great Powers* (2 vols) (Newton Abbot 1972).

Chapters 2 and 3 (1812–30)

Very full accounts of the Fourth Coalition and of the abortive peace negotiations with Napoleon can be found in C.K. Webster, *British Diplomacy 1813–1815* (London 1921); and in the same author's *The Foreign Policy of Castlereagh 1812–1815* (London 1931). Less daunting is Douglas Dakin, 'The Congress of Vienna 1814–15, and its Antecedents' in A. Sked (ed.) *Europe's Balance of Power 1815–1848* (London 1979) just as F.R. Bridge, 'Allied Diplomacy in Peacetime: The Failure of the Congress "System" 1815–23' in the same volume is easier to cope with than C.K. Webster's very comprehensive record of British diplomacy in the postwar period, *The Foreign Policy of Castlereagh 1815–1822* (London 1925). A somewhat controversial analysis of the peacemaking and of eight years of postwar diplomacy can be found in H.A. Kissinger, *A World Restored* (New York 1964). C.J. Bartlett, *Castlereagh* (London 1966), A.W. Palmer, *Metternich* (London 1972), the same author's *Alexander I* (London 1974), and Janet M. Hartley, *Alexander I* (London 1994) are all readable surveys. More detailed on Russian diplomacy are P.K. Grimsted, *The Foreign Ministers of Alexander I* (Berkeley, California, 1969) and C.M. Woodhouse, *Capodistria* (Oxford 1973). Paul Schroeder, *Metternich's Diplomacy at its Zenith 1820–1823* (Austin, Texas 1962) gives an admirably clear and concise account of a crucial period of Austrian diplomacy. Robert D Billinger, *Metternich and the German Question . . . 1820–33* (Newark 1991) is useful on the Confederation. Anglo-French rivalry in the Iberian peninsula and Anglo-Russian rivalry in the Near East in the 1820s are fully covered in H.W.V. Temperley, *The Foreign Policy of Canning* (London 1926). A shorter account of Canning's foreign policy can be found in *George Canning* (London 1973) by Wendy Hinde. The South American repercussions of the French intervention in Spain can be followed in H.C. Allen, *Great Britain and the United States* (London 1954); D. Perkins, *A History of the Monroe Doctrine* (London 1960); and C.K. Webster, *Britain and the Independence of Latin America*, 2 vols (Oxford 1938). Two books by Douglas Dakin, *The Unification of Greece 1770–1923* (London 1972), and *The Greek Struggle for Independence 1821–1823*

(London 1973), provide excellent accounts of great-power rivalries in the eastern Mediterranean in the 1820s. Derek Beales, *The Risorgimento and the Unification of Italy* (London 1971), contains short but useful surveys of Italian problems in the restoration period, and V.J. Puryear, *France and the Levant* (California 1968), contains an account of French Mediterranean policy during the Bourbon Restoration.

Chapter 4 (1830–56)

British policy towards Europe in the 1830s is covered in great detail in C.K. Webster, *The Foreign Policy of Palmerston 1830–1841*, 2 vols (new impression London 1969). Donald Southgate, *The Most English Minister ... The Policies and Politics of Palmerston* (London 1966), contains a shorter survey of Palmerston's early diplomacy. J.R. Hall, *England and the Orleans Monarchy* (London 1912) is still a useful book. No modern survey has yet been published in English of the foreign policy of the July Monarchy as such, although Roger Bullen, *Palmerston, Guizot and the Collapse of the Entente Cordiale* (London 1974) ranges much more widely than the title suggests. Roger Bullen, 'France and the problem of intervention in Spain 1834–1836', *Historical Journal* 20, 2 (1977), examines Thiers's attempted change of direction in the mid-1830s. The international repercussions of Italian problems in the 1830s can be followed in C. Vidal, *Louis Philippe, Metternich et la crise italienne* (Paris 1938). E. Kossman, *A History of the Low Countries 1789–1945* (Oxford 1978), contains an authoritative account of the Belgian revolution and of the great-power negotiations which followed it. The two Near Eastern crises of the 1830s have both been subjected to close scholarly scrutiny: G.H. Bolsover, 'Nicholas I and the partition of Turkey', *Slavonic and East European Review XXVII* (1948–49) is an important article; as is also F.S. Rodkey, 'Lord Palmerston and the rejuvenation of Turkey', *Journal of Modern History 1* (1929). P.E. Moseley, *Russian Diplomacy and the Opening of the Eastern Question in 1838 and 1839* (Cambridge, Mass. 1934), is an excellent account. The best survey of French policy in 1840 is the article by C.H. Pouthas, 'La Politique de Thiers pendant le crise orientale de 1840', *Revue Historique CLXXXII* (1938). Douglas Johnson, *Guizot ... Aspects of French History 1787–1874* (London 1963), examines the French retreat from the brink of war in 1840 and also provides a valuable account of the principles and methods of Guizot's foreign policy. Mediterranean rivalry in the 1840s is discussed at length in F.R. Flournoy,

British Policy Towards Morocco in the Age of Palmerston 1830–1865 (London 1935). The diplomatic complications raised by Swiss and Italian problems in 1847 can be studied in Roger Bullen, 'Guizot and the *Sonderbund* Crisis', *English Historical Review* LXXXVI (1971); and in A.J.P. Taylor, *The Italian Problem in European Diplomacy 1846–49* (Manchester 1934), which takes the story down to the collapse of the Italian war effort in 1849. The chapter on international relations by J.P.T. Bury in F. Fejtö (ed.) *1848: The Opening of an Era* (New York 1948), is a readable introduction to the main diplomatic problems raised by the revolutions. E. Eyck, *The Frankfurt Parliament* (London 1968), contains useful comments on Austro-Prussian relations, and C.A. Macartney, *The Hapsburg Empire 1790–1918* (London 1969), is very informative on the political and diplomatic problems faced by the Austrian government in the period 1848–51. W.E. Mosse, *The European Powers and the German Question 1848–1871* (Cambridge 1958), contains useful chapters on German problems in the revolutionary period and is an indispensable book for the diplomacy of the 1850s and 1860s. The best short account of French foreign policy under Napoleon III is that in J.P.T. Bury, *Napoleon III and the Second Empire* (London 1964). For a detailed and stimulating discussion of Crimean War diplomacy, see P.W. Schroeder, *Austria, Great Britain and the Crimean War* (London 1972); but N. Rich, *Why the Crimean War?* (New England 1985) is also thought-provoking and David Wetzel, *The Crimean War* (New York 1985) clear and succinct. The diplomatic history of the War and its aftermath is treated thematically in W.E. Mosse, *The Rise and Fall of the Crimean System* (London 1963). Kingsley Martin, *The Triumph of Lord Palmerston* (revised edn London 1963), examines the impact of the press and public opinion on British foreign policy; and L.M. Case, *French Opinion on War and Diplomacy during the Second Empire* (Philadelphia 1954), deals with the same subject from the French point of view. It also provides very useful background to French diplomacy in the late 1850s and in the 1860s.

Chapter 5 (1856–71)

On the European states system in the later 1850s, W. Baumgart, *The Peace of Paris 1856* (Santa Barbara 1981) ranges far more widely than the title suggests. Definitive and immensely detailed is Katharina Weigand, *Oesterreich, die Westmächte und das europäische Staatensystem nach dem Krimkrieg (1856–59)* (Husum 1997). T.W. Riker, *The Making of*

Roumania (Oxford 1931), is still useful on Romanian independence. The best short introductions to the complex political and diplomatic issues raised by the Italian question can be found in Harry Hearder, *Cavour* (London 1994) and D. Mack Smith, *Italy. A Modern History* (Ann Arbor 1959). The latter author's *Cavour and Garibaldi in 1860* (Cambridge 1954) is very important, as is the more recent collection of essays, *Victor Emmanuel, Cavour and the Risorgimento* (Oxford 1971). E.E.Y. Hales, *Pio Nono* (London 1954), has a good account of papal policy. D.E.D. Beales, *England and Italy 1859–1860* (London 1961), succinctly analyses British policy. The diplomatic complications raised by the Venetian and Roman questions in the 1860s are dealt with in R. Blaas (ed.), *Il Problemo Veneto e l'Europa 1859–1866* (Venice 1966), and in Noel Blakiston, *The Roman Question* (London 1962). O. Pflanze, *Bismarck and the Development of Germany 1815–1871* (Princeton 1963), is a very thorough and judicious account of Bismarck's policy in the 1860s. Two shorter studies, A.J.P. Taylor, *Bismarck* (London 1955), and W.N. Medlicott, *Bismarck and Modern Germany* (London 1965), are also very useful. H. Boehme, *The Foundations of the German Empire* (Oxford 1973), is extremely important for the relations of the members of the Bund in the 1860s. H. Friedjung, *The Struggle for Supremacy in Germany* (London 1935), is also valuable. The diplomatic problems raised by the Danish attempts to alter the *status quo* in the duchies are admirably dealt with in L.D. Steefel, *The Schleswig Holstein Question* (Cambridge, MA 1932). An excellent study of the background to the conflict can be found in W. Carr, *Schleswig-Holstein 1815–1864* (London 1963), and an equally authoritative but more succinct account in the same author's *The Origins of the German Wars of Unification* (London 1991). On the War of 1866, Gordon A. Craig, *The Battle of Königgrätz* (Philadelphia 1966) should be supplemented by Geoffrey Wawro, *The Austro-Prussian War of 1866* (Cambridge 1996), which has useful new material. E. Ann Pottinger, *Napoleon III and the German Crisis 1865–66* (Oxford 1968) fully examines French policy. H. Oncken, *Napoleon III and the Rhine* (New York 1928) covers the same ground but takes the story down to 1870. On the origins of the War of 1870, E. Kolb (ed.) *Europa vor dem Krieg von 1870* (Munich 1987) is a more than usually coherent and illuminating collection of conference papers. G. Bonnin (ed.), *Bismarck and the Hohenzollern Candidature for the Spanish Throne* (London 1957), contains important documents. R. Millman, *British Policy and the Coming of the Franco-Prussian War* (Oxford 1965), is useful. Michael Howard, *The Franco-Prussian War* (London 1961), is an invaluable study of the military conflict.

Chapters 6 and 7 (1871–95)

International relations in the Bismarckian era are very fully treated in
W.L. Langer, *European Alliances and Alignments 1871–90* (2nd edn,
New York 1950), which contains extensive bibliographies. There are
numerous shorter studies illuminating the foreign policy of Bismarckian
Germany. The most manageable and most readable is still W.N. Medlicott,
Bismarck and Modern Germany (London 1965); A.J.P. Taylor, *Bismarck*
(London 1955), is provocative; E. Eyck, *Bismarck and the German
Empire* (London 1950), is clear and straightforward; while W. Richter,
Bismarck (London 1964), presents a German view and places more
emphasis on Bismarck's relations with Russia than most English works.
Bismarck's Russian policy in the later 1880s is among several import-
ant aspects of imperial Germany covered in a series of essays edited
by M. Stürmer, *Das Kaiserliche Deutschland, Politik und Gesellschaft
1870–1918* (Düsseldorf 1970). On Austro-Hungarian policy, in addition
to the works mentioned in the bibliography to Chapter 1, I. Diószegi,
Hungarians in the Ballhausplatz (Budapest 1983) contains useful ana-
lytical surveys, while S. Verosta, *Theorie und Realität von Bündnissen*
(Vienna 1971), provides very detailed and thought-provoking analysis of
Austro-German relations between 1879 and 1914. The sections concerned
with foreign policy in C. Seton-Watson, *Italy from Liberalism to Fascism*
(London 1967), contain illuminating insights as does H. Seton-Watson,
The Russian Empire 1801–1917 (Oxford 1967). W.N. Medlicott,
Bismarck, Gladstone, and the Concert of Europe (London 1956), and B.
Waller, *Bismarck at the Crossroads, 1878–80* (London 1974), are likely
to remain the definitive accounts of the tortuous diplomacy of the three
Eastern Powers, 1879–81.

Chapters 8 and 9 (1895–1914)

The most detailed general account of the relations of all the European
powers with each other after the fall of Bismarck is still W.L. Langer, *The
Diplomacy of Imperialism 1891–1902* (2nd edn, New York 1950), which
includes full bibliographies. On German policy, J. Röhl, *Germany without Bismarck* (London 1967), is a seminal work which treats foreign
policy in the context of domestic developments. The mechanics of foreign
policy-making in Great Britain in the early twentieth century are examined in Zara Steiner, *The Foreign Office and Foreign Policy* (Cambridge
1969), and the actual policy in J.A.S. Grenville, *Lord Salisbury and Foreign
Policy* (London 1964); C.H.D. Howard, *Splendid Isolation* (London 1967);

G.W. Monger, *The End of Isolation* (London 1964); and K.M. Wilson, *The Policy of the Entente* (Cambridge 1985). Roderick R. McLean, *Royalty and Diplomacy in Europe 1890–1914* (Cambridge 2001) focuses largely on Great Britain, Russia and Germany. The Eastern Question in the early twentieth century is the subject of F.R. Bridge, 'Izvolsky, Aehrenthal and the end of the Austro-Russian entente', in *Mitteilungen des österreichischen Staatsarchivs*, 1976. Extra-European developments are fully treated in G.N. Sanderson, *England, Europe and the Upper Nile* (Edinburgh 1965); L.K. Young, *British Policy in China 1895–1902* (Oxford 1970); I.H. Nish's *The origins of the Russo-Japanese War* (London 1985) and his monumental studies, *The Anglo-Japanese Alliance* 1902–07 (London 1966), and *Alliance in Decline, 1907–22* (London 1972).

On the European states system in the final years of peace J. Joll, *The Origins of the First World War* (London 1984) provides the best general introduction to the final crisis, aspects of which are examined in more detail in K.M. Wilson (ed.), *Decisions for War, 1914* (London 1995). The essays edited by H.W. Koch, *The Origins of the First World War* (London 1972), tend to emphasize Germany's responsibility – a theme which is fully developed in the light of events after 1911 in F. Fischer, *War of Illusions* (London 1973). Absolutely essential is David Stevenson, *Armaments and the Coming of War* (Oxford 1996); and equally essential and ranging more widely than their titles suggest are V.R. Berghahn, *Germany and the Approach of War in 1914* (London 1973); Zara Steiner, *Britain and the Origins of the First World War* (London 1977); John F.V. Keiger, *France and the Origins of the First World War* (London 1983); D.C.B. Lieven, *Russia and the Origins of the First World War* (London 1983); Samuel R. Williamson, *Austria-Hungary and the Origins of the First World War* (London 1991); and Richard Bosworth, *Italy and the Approach of the First World War* (London 1983). Of seminal importance is John Leslie's *The Antecedents of Austria-Hungary's war aims: Policies and Policy-Makers in Vienna and Budapest before and during 1914* (Wiener Beiträge zur Geschichte der Neuzeit, Band 20, 1993). British policy in these years is illuminated in detail by K.G. Robbins, *Sir Edward Grey* (London 1971); and in the latest volume of the New Cambridge History of British Foreign Policy edited by F.H. Hinsley, *British Foreign Policy under Sir Edward Grey* (Cambridge 1977). P.G. Halpern, *The Mediterranean Naval Situation 1908–14* (Cambridge, MA 1971); B.E. Schmitt, *The Bosnian Crisis* (New York 1937); E.C. Helmreich *The Diplomacy of the Balkan Wars* (Cambridge, MA 1938) and R.J. Crampton, *The Hollow Detente: Anglo-German relations in the Balkans 1911–1914* (London 1979) are likely to remain the standard works in their respective fields.

Index of persons

General Index

Note: Alliances and Ententes, Battles, Congresses and Conferences, Meetings and Visits, Treaties and Agreements, and Wars are grouped chronologically under separate headings.